SOCIAL STAR

*Peer Interaction Skills
(Book 2)*

Nancy Gajewski

Polly Hirn

Patty Mayo

*Thinking Publications
Eau Claire, Wisconsin*

© 1994 **Thinking Publications** ®
A Division of McKinley Companies, Inc.

Thinking Publications grants limited rights to individual professionals to reproduce and distribute pages that indicate duplication is permissible. Pages can be used for student instruction only and must include Thinking Publications' copyright notice. All rights are reserved for pages without the permission-to-reprint notice. No part of these pages may be reproduced in any form, electronic or mechanical, including photocopy, recording, or any information storage and retrieval system without permission in writing from the publisher.

03 02 01 00 99   10 9 8 7 6 5 4 3

Library of Congress Cataloging-in-Publication Data
(Revised for vol. 2)

Gajewski, Nancy.
    Social star.

    Contents: book 1. General interaction skills—book 2. Peer interaction skills.
    1. Social skills—Study and teaching (Elementary). 2. Social interaction—Study and teaching (Elementary). I. Hirn, Polly. II. Mayo, Patty. III. Title.
HQ783.G33 1993   372.83   92-39097
ISBN 0-930599-79-9 (v. 1)
ISBN 0-930599-91-8 (v. 2 : pbk.)

Illustrations by Kris Madsen

Printed in the United States of America

THINKING PUBLICATIONS®
A Division of McKinley Companies, Inc.

424 Galloway Street • Eau Claire, WI 54703
(715) 832-2488 • FAX (715) 832-9082
Email: custserv@ThinkingPublications.com

DEDICATION

To Luke, Anna, Jenny, and Katie

NG

To Tom, Rebecca, and Matthew

PH

To Mike, Emily, and Jessica

PM

Table of Contents

Preface vii

Acknowledgments ix

Chapter 1—Getting Started..1

Chapter 2—*Social Star:* A Closer Look 15

References..37

Cognitive Planning 41

Body Talk Summary 89

Optimism 91

Playing Cooperatively..125

Respecting Differences 167

Being a Friend..195

Giving and Receiving Compliments 231

Building a Positive Reputation..251

Dealing with Teasing...275

Collaborative Skills 309

Getting into a Group..311

Giving Put-ups 327

Participating 345

Staying on Task...363

Disagreeing Politely 385

Appendix A—Lessons X, Y, and Z..403

Appendix B—Social Communication Skills Rating Scale 408

Appendix C—Student Social Skill Summary Form 411

Appendix D—Class Summary Form 412

Appendix E—Socialville Buildings 413

Appendix F—Socialville Characters 422

Appendix G—Parent Letter 431

Appendix H—Self-Management Sheets 432

Appendix I—Checking Myself 438

Appendix J—Social Gram 439

Appendix K—Great Coupon Caper 440

Appendix L—Blank T-Chart 441

Appendix M—Relaxation Scripts 442

Appendix N—Secret Formula Pages 444

Appendix O—Thought Bubble 446

Appendix P—Pairing Activities 447

Appendix Q—Drill and Practice 455

Appendix R—Roadblock Sheet 458

Appendix S—Social Super Star Badges 459

Appendix T—Thinking Skills Web 461

Appendix U—Dominoes 462

Appendix V—Mind Map 464

Appendix W—Venn Diagram 465

Appendix X—Numbered Heads Together Spinner 466

Appendix Y—My Contract 467

Appendix Z—I Know.... 468

Appendix AA—Brainstorming Guide 469

Appendix BB—Tick-Tack-Toe 470

Preface

We are excited to present *Social Star: Peer Interaction Skills (Book 2)*, an elementary curriculum for teaching social communication skills. We developed *Social Star* to fill a need for a comprehensive, experiential curriculum that teaches students appropriate social skills.

We believe that an effective social skills program must provide numerous structured opportunities for students to apply and practice newly acquired skills. Teaching social skills in a traditional teacher-directed format, where students are rarely given an opportunity to interact, would be like teaching students how to use a computer but never allowing them to actually use one. *Social Star* incorporates frequent opportunities for students to interact cooperatively.

We believe that an effective educator asks, "What are my students' social skill strengths and how can those strengths be used to expand their social skill repertoire?" rather than asking, "What are my students' social skill weaknesses and how can I fix them?" In addition, the effective educator encourages students to be unique, to express their feelings, and to make their own choices rather than attempting to stifle expression of feelings to force compliance.

The social skills in *Social Star* reflect the conventions of mainstream America, which have been traditionally accepted and expected in educational and employment settings. It is critical to remember that there are marked cultural differences in social skill conventions. The intent of *Social Star* is not to strip students of their cultural beliefs or to make them feel that their beliefs are bad. Rather, the intent is to provide students with the flexibility to move between their cultures and that of mainstream America.

In a world with ever-increasing violence, it is critical that our students learn how to communicate and solve problems with one another in a non-violent manner. *Social Star* is not just intended for those children with severe social skill deficits. All children can benefit and grow from direct instruction of social skills.

We hope you enjoy using *Social Star*. Remember, you may be planting seeds that will ultimately change your students' destinies!

Acknowledgments

The authors would like to express their appreciation to all those people who have helped in the completion of this curriculum. We thank Jan Burns, Bonnie Goertz, Ann Gorton, Paula Guhlke, Steve Heer, Paul Kennedy, Barbara Koeckley, Christine McFarlane, Lee Murphy, Teresa Prier, Fran Neilitz, Ann Rajek, Linda Parise, Patty Shirer, Candace Sobotta, Suzanne Steege, Judy Wheeler, and Sara Zacarro for generously devoting their time in field-testing units from *Social Star*. A very special thank you to Dr. Lynda Miller and Pattii Waldo for their many hours in reviewing *Social Star* in its entirety. An additional thank you to Pattii Waldo, who shared many creative ideas which were included in *Social Star*. We are grateful to Nancy McKinley and Linda Schreiber for their technical and editorial advice, to Kris Madsen for her artistic contributions, and to the rest of the Thinking Publications staff for making it possible for this curriculum to be shared with you.

As always, we thank our husbands, Luke Gajewski, Tom Hirn, and Mike Mayo, for their encouragement, support, and patience.

CREDITS:

Page 133, "Alone" by Dorothy Aldis reprinted by permission of G.P. Putnam's Sons from *All Together,* © 1925–1928, 1934, 1939, 1952, © renewed 1953–1956, 1962, 1967 by Dorothy Aldis.

Pages 133–134, Categories of Entry Behavior Generated by Children and Collected from Research Studies by Gayle Macklem, 1987, from "No one wants to play with me," *Academic Therapy, 22*(5), © 1987 by PRO-ED. Reprinted with permission.

Page 142, "Sharing" by Julie Peckham reprinted with permission from C. Lynn Fox and Francine Lavin Weaver, *Unlocking Doors to Friendship,* © 1983, B.L. Winch and Assoc./Jalmar Press.

Page 167, "The Inside, The True Person" by Paul Kreul reprinted with permission from C. Lynn Fox and Francine Lavin Weaver, *Unlocking Doors to Friendship,* © 1983, B.L. Winch and Assoc./Jalmar Press.

Chapter 1

Getting Started

Social Star

SOCIAL SKILL INSTRUCTION—A NECESSITY!

Every educator has experienced the frustration of seeing children isolated or teased by other students. "Mandy" sits by herself at recess. No one wants to work with "Jason." "Peter" makes irrelevant comments. "Ashley" asks a question every sixty seconds. These children are in all classrooms.

Research clearly indicates that children who are unaccepted by their peers will have learning and adjustment problems both in and out of school and later in life (Hartup, 1978; Putallaz and Gottman, 1981; Roff and Sells, 1978). Unpopular students often associate with other unpopular students or with younger children. This makes it difficult for them to gain the skills necessary to interact with more socially skilled children (Bullock, 1988). Children's reputations are often established early in elementary grades and become more and more stable each year (Meichenbaum, 1991).

Therefore, it is crucial that elementary educators address social skills. Time is of the essence for some students. Children who are rejected by their peers or who stand out negatively in some social skills, need to have the opportunity to learn acceptable social behavior. Social skills may well be the single most important subject educators teach their students! By teaching appropriate social skills, educators will have a positive impact on the lives of their students.

SOCIAL STAR: A NEW APPROACH

Instruction of social skills has increased rapidly over the past 10 years. While many strides have been made in the area of social skill instruction (e.g., awareness of the need for instruction, development of curriculum, program research), three major areas of concern remain.

One area of concern is that of teaching social competence as isolated skills when, in fact, any given situation requires that social skills be used in combination with each other. In addition to addressing individual social skills, *Social Star* provides numerous opportunities for students to use a combination of social skills in real-life situations through cooperative experiences.

A second concern (Neel, 1988) is over social skill instruction occurring in isolated environments, thus limiting opportunities for students to interact. *Social Star* is a unique program that provides many opportunities for students to use social skills while they are learning. As stated in the Preface, it is critical that students continually be given opportunities to interact in a positive manner with peers. *Social Star* offers numerous activities structured to encourage cooperative interaction among students. The *Social Star* program is an ideal match for a collaborative regular education program.

A third concern (Lovitt, 1987) is that social skills are taught during a specified time period and then tend to be forgotten during the remainder of the day. *Social Star* advocates teaching a social skills class but, in addition, the program provides numerous strategies to encourage incidental teaching and reinforcement of social skills throughout the school day.

SOCIAL STAR: CULTURAL CONSIDERATIONS

Marked differences in social behavior exist among cultures. *Social Star* teaches social skills that reflect the conventions of mainstream America, which have been traditionally accepted and expected in educational and employment settings. These social skills will not match the norms and expectations within some children's home settings. This awareness of diversity is critical to the success of the program, and educators are encouraged in each unit to invite adults from various cultures to speak with children about differences in cultural conventions.

Never should students be stripped of social skills appropriate for their cultures or be made to feel that their beliefs are bad or wrong. Rather, the intent of *Social Star* is to provide children with the flexibility to move between their cultures and that of mainstream America when they choose to do so.

SOCIAL STAR: GENERAL DESCRIPTION

The *Social Star* program is a series of books that emphasizes general interaction skills, peer interaction, problem solving/dealing with conflict, emotions, and classroom work habits. Each book includes basically the same beginning two chapters and appendices; however, the books contain different social skill units.

Social Star is a curriculum intended for use with elementary-age students (approximately grades 2–5). It is appropriate for students in regular education, special education, and at-risk programs. Professionals (e.g., regular educators, special educators, speech-language clinicians, counselors, psychologists, principals) involved with students will find this resource valuable for providing social skill instruction.

Each unit within *Social Star* includes a goal statement, educator information (information unique to the social skill being addressed), a series of lessons for teaching the social skill, a list of related activities, a list of related literature, and suggested ways to integrate social skill instruction throughout the school day. The length of each unit varies depending on the complexity of the specific social skill.

The units incorporate a wide variety of instructional techniques (e.g., guided practice pages, scripts, cooperative teamwork, games, role plays, puppet shows, cartoons, visualizations, drill and practice). Units do not have to be taught in their entirety. Strategies for adapting units when appropriate are given on page 36. Educators are urged to choose units appropriate for specific students' needs. Most units contain lessons titled Lesson A, B, C, etc. and Lessons X, Y, and Z. Lessons X, Y, and Z follow basically the same format in every unit; therefore, a skeleton lesson for each is provided in *Appendix A*. (The collaborative skills units of *Getting into a Group, Giving Put-ups, Participating, Staying on Task*, and *Disagreeing Politely* follow a slightly different format which is described on page 309).

Each unit lesson provides an objective or objectives, a list of materials needed, a preparatory set, and a specific plan for completion of the lesson. Each unit incorporates six components. (See Figure 1.1.) These six components are described in detail in Chapter 2 and are referred to in the lesson plans within each unit.

Figure 1.1

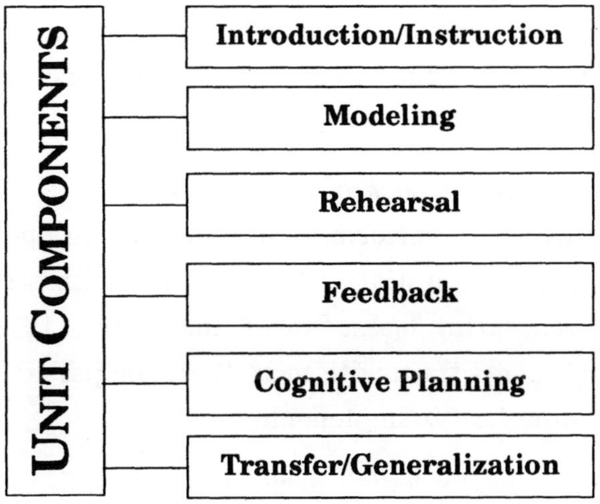

UNIT COMPONENTS
- Introduction/Instruction
- Modeling
- Rehearsal
- Feedback
- Cognitive Planning
- Transfer/Generalization

TYPES OF SOCIAL SKILL DEFICITS

Elliott and Gresham (1991) have conceptualized social skill deficits along five dimensions as summarized in Table 1.1:

Table 1.1 | **Reasons for Social Skill Deficits**
(Elliott and Gresham, 1991)

1. A lack of knowledge
2. A lack of practice or feedback
3. A lack of cues or opportunities
4. A lack of reinforcement
5. The presence of interfering problems

A lack of knowledge indicates that (1) a student has not learned the appropriate goals for social interaction (e.g., "Victor" may believe that the goal of playing a card game is merely to win rather than to get along and have fun with the other players); (2) the student has not learned the specific social skills necessary to reach appropriate social goals (e.g., "Ann" may want to talk more with other kids at school, but doesn't know conversational skills such as listening, asking questions, or staying on topic/switching topics appropriately); or, (3) the student has not learned how to match social skills with appropriate situational contexts. The student may not recognize or understand cues within the environment that prompt use of specific social skills (e.g., when interrupting, "Jolisa" may not recognize reactions indicating that it's the wrong time to do so).

A lack of practice or feedback describes the person who has the knowledge but does not perform the skill. Elliott and Greshman (1991) note that some social skill programs do not provide enough practice for newly learned skills. This can result in the student's appearing awkward or performing the skill in a rote manner (e.g., "Maria" knows how to introduce people, but when she does, her introduction sounds artificial).

A third deficit area involves *a lack of cues or opportunities* (Elliott and Gresham, 1991). Some people can only perform social skills when specific cues are present (e.g., "Victor" may be able to initiate a conversation with someone new only when seeing his mother's reassuring look). Stokes and Baer's (1977) "multiple exemplar strategy" of having students train with more than one person when providing social skills instruction is important to implement.

A lack of reinforcement is the fourth area for social skill deficiencies (Elliott and Gresham, 1991). Some people do not exhibit appropriate social skills because they receive no reinforcement for doing so. For example, "Mike" may not be encouraged by his parents to use self-control. He may even be reinforced for negative behaviors such as fighting (e.g., "What's wrong, aren't you tough enough?").

According to Elliott and Gresham (1991), a final reason for social skill deficiencies is *the presence of interfering problems.* Some behaviors (e.g., word-retrieval problems, hyperactivity, impulsiveness, anxiety) may prevent students from learning or performing social skills.

Social Star includes materials and ideas that will be effective for teaching social skills to students with any type or combination of social skill deficits. In addition, the reader is referred to Elliott and Gresham's (1991) *Social Skills Intervention Guide: Practical Strategies for Social Skill Training* for further information regarding specific strategies to use for each type of deficit.

IDENTIFYING A STUDENT'S SOCIAL SKILL NEEDS

A common concern of educators is determining which social skills are problematic for students. Social competence is a complex and synergistic system. In many respects, social competence and standardized tests are not a natural fit. Few, if any, well-standardized instruments have been developed to assess social competence. A comprehensive system of assessment has yet to be developed. Educators need to be aware of the problems associated with the exclusive use of standardized instruments when assessing social behaviors. The trend appears to be moving away from the use of standardized tests. Close attention should be paid to new research about the assessment of social skills.

Six alternatives for assessing social competence have proven valuable to date (Gresham, 1981; McGinnis and Goldstein, 1990; Schumaker and Hazel, 1984). These alternatives are listed in Table 1.2:

Table 1.2	**Types of Social Skill Assessment**
	1. Naturalistic behavioral observation
	2. Analogue observation
	3. Behavioral rating scales
	4. Behavioral checklists
	5. Sociometric devices
	6. Hypothetical situations

Naturalistic behavioral observation involves observing a person socialize in real-life situations. Information obtained from naturalistic observations can be documented on the Social Communication Skills Rating Scale or the Student Social Skill Summary Form included in *Social Star* (see a description of these forms on pages 6–8; blank forms can be found in *Appendices B* and *C).*

Analogue observation involves observing a person socialize in contrived rather than naturalistic settings. The educator can purposely do something which will result in the student's having to demonstrate use of a specific social skill (e.g., give the student a compliment and observe the response). Information obtained from analogue observations can also be documented on the Social Communication Skills Rating Scale or the Student Social Skill Summary Form.

Behavioral rating scales require an adult to rate on a scale a child's use of various social skills. Again, the Social Communication Skills Rating Scale could be used.

Behavioral checklists require an adult to look at a list of various social skills and check which ones a specific student needs to improve. The Student Social Skill Summary Form could be used for this purpose.

Sociometric devices involve children identifying which of their peers are most accepted and most rejected in their class or group. Reliable (albeit intrusive) data are collected about children's social impact on their peer group, but little information is gained about specific social skills or behaviors. *Social Star* skill assessment forms do not address this type of assessment.

Assessment using *hypothetical situations* involves asking a child to explain what a person should do in various social situations. Each unit in *Social Star* includes hypothetical home, school, and community situations. These situations could be used to assess a child's knowledge of various social skills.

The authors believe that a combination of several approaches will be effective for identifying the social skills to be included for instruction. An educator who has worked with a group of students for a given period of time can usually identify a student's social skill strengths and weaknesses by using observation techniques and checklists.

SOCIAL COMMUNICATION SKILLS RATING SCALE

Social Star provides a Social Communication Skills Rating Scale which can be used for several types of skill assessment as summarized in the last section. The scale could be completed by an educator and/or a parent or another adult who has observed the student's use of social skills in a natural setting. When used as a behavioral rating scale, more than one person might complete the Social Communication Skills Rating Scale because people's perceptions vary. The scale is partially shown in Figure 1.2 and is provided in *Appendix B*.

Figure 1.2

SOCIAL COMMUNICATION SKILL	SELDOM	SOMETIMES	ALMOST ALWAYS
2. PLAYING COOPERATIVELY—Plays in a way that invites everyone to have fun. Comments:	1	2	3
3. RESPECTING DIFFERENCES—Understands that we are all unique and equally important. Comments:	1	2	3
4. BEING A FRIEND—Chooses words and actions that show	1	2	3

The Social Communication Skills Rating Scale asks the adult to rate the student on each of the social skills contained in *Social Star: Peer Interaction Skills (Book 2)* based on past experience with the student. Each social skill is described on the rating scale to make it as explicit as possible. The adult rates the student on a scale of 1–3: 1 if the skill is seldom used correctly, 2 if the skill is sometimes used correctly, or 3 if the skill is almost always used correctly. The educator may view a rating of 1 and possibly 2 as being problematic. The estimated readability for this rating scale is an 8.6 grade level, according to the Flesch-Kincaid Readability Scale (Readability Plus, 1988), and it is evaluated as "easy" reading using the "general purpose" scale for adults.

STUDENT SOCIAL SKILL SUMMARY FORM: DETERMINING INDIVIDUAL NEEDS

When the Social Communication Skills Rating Scale has been completed, the scores may be compiled on the Student Social Skill Summary Form, which is partially shown in Figure 1.3 and is provided in *Appendix C*.

Figure 1.3

STUDENT SOCIAL SKILL SUMMARY FORM					
STUDENT'S NAME:	Identified as a strength	Identified as problematic	Skill has been taught in class		
1. Optimism					
2. Playing Cooperatively					
3. Respecting Differences					
4. Being a Friend					
5. Giving and Receiving Compliments					
6. Building a Positive Reputation					
7. Dealing with Teasing					
8. Getting into a Group					
9. Giving Put-ups					
10. Participating					

The summary form lists all 12 social skills, with a place to mark skills identified as strengths and those identified as weaknesses. It also includes a place to mark the social skills for which the student has received instruction. Two additional blank columns have been provided for the educator to document additional information (e.g., results from naturalistic behavioral observation, analogue observation, or hypothetical situations).

There are several uses for the Student Social Skill Summary Form after its completion. A copy of the summary form may be placed in the student's file and may be attached to a student's report card. For a student in special education, a copy can be included with a specialist's report about the student or in the student's individualized education plan (IEP).

CLASS SUMMARY FORM: DETERMINING WHICH UNITS TO TEACH

The educator may wish to compile each student's data on the Class Summary Form, shown in Figure 1.4, to analyze common needs. The Class Summary Form is provided in *Appendix D*.

Figure 1.4

CLASS SUMMARY FORM

Mark social skills identified as strengths with a "+" and those identified as problematic with a "−".

	STUDENTS' NAMES								
1. Optimism									
2. Playing Cooperatively									
3. Respecting Differences									
4. Being a Friend									
5. Giving and Receiving Compliments									

To complete the form, write the name of each student across the top. For each student, mark the social skills found to be strengths and those found to be problematic areas. Thus, a profile of each student's needs will be established. The Class Summary Form will identify the priority social skills and generate a sequence in which the skills may be taught. If a certain social skill is not problematic for any of the students, instruction may not be necessary for that skill. However, the educator may wish to provide a mini-lesson to promote maintenance of the skill. Suppose, conversely, a social skill is found to be a problem for several students, but not for all. When teaching that social skill, the students who are not deficient in that area can be asked to be "special assistants" (e.g., helping the educator model the social skill).

Although some skills are prerequisites for others (e.g. the *Getting into a Group* unit should be taught before the other collaborative skills units, if *Getting into a Group* is identified as a problem for students), there is no clear-cut hierarchy of skills. Therefore, the educator should teach the skills in the order of need or interest and not necessarily in the order presented in *Social Star*. However, the *Cognitive Planning* unit must be taught before teaching other units, because it introduces students to key strategies used throughout the program. The social skill of *body talk* (an important and more global unit from *Social Star: General Interaction Skills*) must be taught or reviewed with students first because it is incorporated into the skill steps for all social skill units within this book. Refer to the *Body Talk* unit in *Social Star (Book 1)* or refer to the *Body Talk Summary* on page 89 of this book.

SOCIAL STAR CHARACTERS

The *Social Star* program revolves around six main characters, named Mike Olson, Ann Olson, Maria Parra, Victor Parra, Lee Vue, and Jolisa Walker (see Figure 1.5). They are elementary-age children going to McKinley School and living in a community called Socialville. (Major buildings in Socialville are illustrated in *Appendix E* and may be duplicated. Educators are encouraged to build a Socialville community using the building designs provided. Construction of Socialville is further explained in the *Cognitive Planning* unit.)

Figure 1.5

Mike   Ann   Maria   Victor   Lee   Jolisa

These six characters are also incorporated in *Communicate Junior* (Mayo, Hirn, Gajewski, and Kafka, 1991), which is an educational game board activity (see pages 35–36) to reinforce social skills taught with *Social Star*. The children, along with their parents and teachers, are referred to frequently throughout *Social Star*. The

Socialville characters (17 in all and printed in *Appendix F*) provide a common theme and continuity between units. The characters are portrayed as realistic people with social skill strengths and weaknesses. The characters interact in various home, school, and community situations and come from varied ethnic, socioeconomic, and family backgrounds as described in the next sections.

The Jackson (Olson) Family

Mike Olson, Ann Olson, Mary Jackson, and Joe Jackson

Ann and Mike live with their mother and stepfather. Their stepfather (Joe) works in a toy factory (Get Along Toy Factory) and their mother (Mary) works at a restaurant (Good Meals–Good Manners Restaurant).

The Parra Family

Maria Parra, Victor Parra, Juanita Parra, and Ricardo Parra

Maria and Victor live with their mother and father. Their mother (Juanita) is a physician at a clinic (Helping Hands Clinic) and their father (Ricardo) is an executive at the Get Along Toy Factory.

The Vue Family

Lee Vue, Ho Vue, Mika Vue

Lee lives with his father and his grandmother. His father (Ho) is a construction worker for Happy Homes and his grandmother (Mika) is a cook at McKinley School.

The Walker Family

Jolisa Walker, Corin Walker, Jesse Walker

Jolisa lives with her mother and father. Her father (Jesse) works for the Socialville Parks Department and her mother (Corin) is a teacher's aide at McKinley School.

McKinley School Classroom Teachers

Ms. Paula Hess, Mr. Marcus Aaron, and Mrs. Cora Marrero

SOCIAL STAR WALL CHART CONSTRUCTION

Three types of wall charts are utilized during each *Social Star* unit. They include (1) the *Cognitive Planning Formula* chart; (2) classroom posters; and (3) the *Social Super Stars* display. Directions for making these wall charts are provided in the next three sections (or preprinted color wall charts can be purchased through the publisher; see pages 472–473).

Cognitive Planning Formula Chart

During the *Cognitive Planning* unit and in the final lesson (Lesson Z) of each social skill unit, students are taken through the four cognitive planning steps (STOP, PLOT, GO, SO). Cognitive planning, one of the six components to teaching a social skill, is explained in Chapter 2. The educator should construct a large *Cognitive Planning Formula* chart according to the pattern in Figure 1.6. The chart is used to remind students of the four steps of cognitive planning (described in the *Cognitive Planning* unit).

Figure 1.6

COGNITIVE PLANNING FORMULA

STOP....
To Stay Calm

PLOT....
A Plan
- IDENTIFY THE PROBLEM
- BRAINSTORM CHOICES
- CONSIDER THE CONSEQUENCES
- PICK A CHOICE
- THINK ABOUT SOCIAL SKILLS

GO....
Ahead with the Plan

SO....
How Did the Plan Work?

Classroom Posters

Lessons from each unit in the *Social Star* program call for a classroom poster. Each poster includes the skill step(s) for a specific social skill and the symbol for each step. This information is described in Lesson A within each unit and should be reproduced large enough for the whole group of students to see. An example is shown in Figure 1.7. The educator could also construct a second poster that has the Socialville characters saying "catchy" phrases reminding students to use each skill appropriately (e.g., "Be cooperative when you play! You'll have fun every day"). The posters provide an excellent resource for promoting social skills on a schoolwide basis (see page 29).

Social Super Stars Display

Lesson Z (the final lesson in each unit) calls for the use of the *Social Super Stars* display. It is used to display social skill badges that students bring back to school after their parents have signed them (see page 23). The *Social Super Stars* display should be constructed as a large chart with the heading "Social Super Stars." An example is provided in Figure 1.8.

The poster should be laminated for easy removal of the "old" badges when badges from a new unit are brought to school.

Figure 1.7

Figure 1.8

Chapter 2

Social Star: A Closer Look

Social Star provides interesting and creative ways to teach each social skill unit to students, and the variety of activities makes each social skill unit unique. As discussed in Chapter 1, however, all units have six critical components in common:

1. Social Skill Introduction/Instruction
2. Modeling
3. Rehearsal
4. Feedback
5. Cognitive Planning
6. Transfer/Generalization

This chapter describes each of these components in detail.

SOCIAL SKILL INTRODUCTION/INSTRUCTION

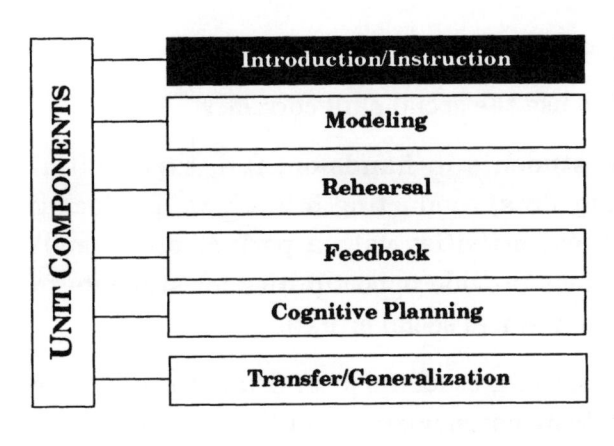

Each unit in *Social Star* includes introductory material that is critical for effective instruction and consists of these sections:

- Unit Goal
- Educator Information
- Related Activities
- Related Literature
- Social Skills All Day Long

The Unit Goal summarizes the overall focus within the chosen social skill area. Most units focus on demonstrating comprehension and use of the social skill.

Educator Information includes background information relevant to each unit that provides data or insights essential for teaching the social skill. This information may influence the way an educator teaches a unit.

Next, Related Activities are suggested that may be completed before, during, or after the lessons in the unit. They may also be used for homework (see page 24).

Similarly, Related Literature may be used at any point in the unit. Related Literature has been included so that children can hear or read stories (or excerpts) that naturally incorporate the social skills being taught. Most units have both picture book and text examples of Related Literature that incorporate the target social skill.

The Related Literature books do not directly teach or discuss the target social skill. Rather, they show characters using a given social skill in context. When text examples are used, the page numbers are included. When the social skill is self-evident on the pages cited, no explanation is provided. When the text example is more subtle, an explanatory comment accompanies the page number(s).

An attempt was made to include award-winning children's literature whenever possible. Consideration was also given to accessibility; books that are commonly found in school and public libraries were chosen over alternative press titles. In general, only stories that depict realistic characters are included (e.g., folk tales were avoided because they tend to have animal or mythical characters).

The Social Skills All Day Long section provides the means for addressing social skills throughout the day. It is the last section in the introductory pages to each unit and is discussed on pages 26–29.

The lesson plans for each unit include a motivating Preparatory Set that can be used at the beginning of each class. After catching students' interest, instruction of the social skill begins. Lesson A within each unit provides students with the following:

1. A definition of the social skill

2. The skill step(s) used to execute the skill

3. A rationale for why it's important to use the social skill correctly

Other lessons within each unit involve students in hands-on, fun, experiential activities (e.g., reading scripts, performing skits, conducting interviews, producing tapes). Students are asked to complete these activities with a partner or in small groups. Partner and small group interactions provide opportunities for students to integrate the skills they are learning within natural social situations.

Printed materials are often included in lessons for students' use. Often, the educator is also instructed to prepare an overhead transparency and read the material along with the student. On the Flesch-Kincaid Readability Scale (Readability Plus, 1988), the student pages range from a 1.7 to 3.5 grade level. Educators should use their discretion when deciding whether to read activity pages to students. The pages are evaluated as "very easy" using the "children's book" scale.

The number of social skill introduction/instruction lessons within each unit varies depending on the complexity of the social skill. The lessons during the introduction and instruction component are labeled A, B, C, etc. depending on the number of lessons. The final three lessons within most units (during which modeling, rehearsal, feedback, and cognitive planning take place) are labeled X, Y, and Z.

The length of each lesson within a unit varies. Educators should allow a minimum of 30 minutes per lesson and plan on spending several time periods for longer lessons. The average lesson length is approximately 45 minutes.

MODELING

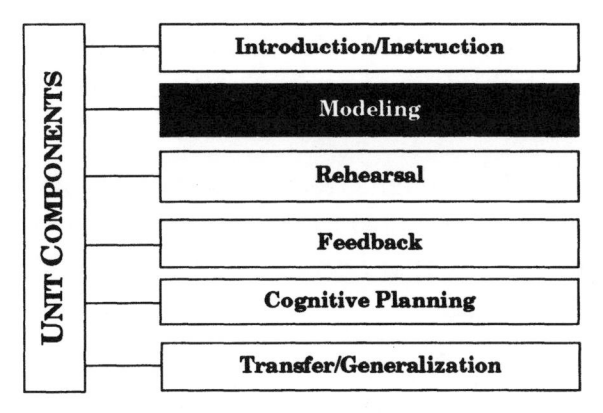

UNIT COMPONENTS
- Introduction/Instruction
- **Modeling**
- Rehearsal
- Feedback
- Cognitive Planning
- Transfer/Generalization

The use of modeling has been documented as an effective strategy for teaching new behaviors (Bandura, 1977; Gresham, 1981). Modeling involves having the educator demonstrate how to use a social skill appropriately. Several opportunities to model correct use of a social skill are built into each unit in *Social Star*.

When modeling, the educator should first demonstrate a social skill while verbalizing thoughts (self-talk) aloud, and then demonstrate the same social skill without verbalizing thoughts aloud. Modeling the use of self-talk for various social skills increases the likelihood that transfer/generalization will occur (Meichenbaum, 1977). Modeling scripts are provided for the educator throughout each unit. Here is an example of modeling with self-talk from the *Being a Friend* unit:

Modeling Example

Model use of the skill step for being a friend while thinking aloud. A scripted example follows:

Introduction

I am going to pretend to be a student your age. I will show you how I can be a friend to others and tell you the thoughts I'm having. When I hold up this Thought Bubble, *you'll know the words that I'm saying are actually what I'm thinking.*

Actual Model

While holding up the Thought Bubble *say, I really like playing with Sam. What can I do to be a friend? I'll ask him to play after school with me. I can say nice things to him and share my toys with him.*

In Lesson X, the educator models the social skill in three different situations (i.e., home, school, and community). Several other tips the educator should keep in mind when modeling social skills are these:

1. Modeling is more effective when a "coping model" (Bandura, 1977) is used. For instance, when modeling the social skill of *dealing with teasing*, the person modeling should look and sound as though he or she isn't bothered by the teasing and then should do or say something to stop the teasing.

2. Careful thinking and planning beforehand of the modeling display is important (McGinnis, Goldstein, Sprafkin, and Gershaw, 1984).

3. At least two examples of the skill should be modeled (McGinnis et al., 1984). For example, situations from the home, school, and/or community should be modeled.

4. Situations modeled should be realistic for the students (McGinnis et al., 1984). The educator may need to alter the role plays included in each unit depending on the age, socioeconomic background, and ethnic heritage of the group of students being taught.

5. Students must pay attention to the modeling display being done. Cuing students that they will be asked to identify or discuss various parts of the social skill when the modeling is completed might increase the students' level of interest while observing the modeling display.

6. Negative modeling involves showing how the social skill should NOT be done (e.g., when modeling the social skill of *receiving a compliment*, one might reject the compliment). Research on the use of negative modeling examples is unclear. McGinnis et al. (1984) advocate that all modeling displays depict positive outcomes. However, Ladd and Mize (1983) state that modeling negative examples may be helpful in making the parameters of the social skill more explicit. Elliott and Gresham (1991) include examples of negative modeling for each social skill in their program.

REHEARSAL

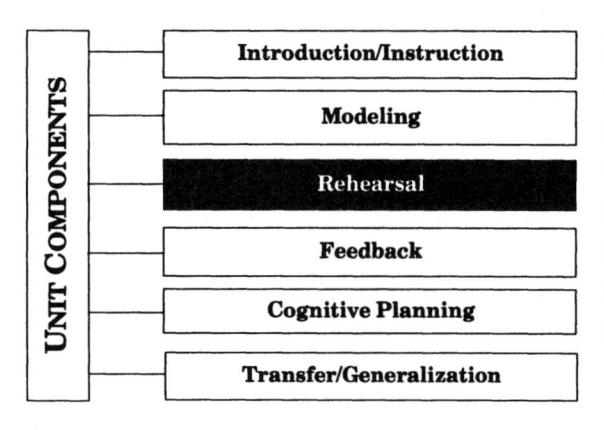

Behavioral rehearsal is an essential component when teaching children social skills. Elliott and Gresham (1991) state that repeated practice of a social skill increases retention of the skill concept and improves performance of the skill. They identify three types of rehearsal:

Covert rehearsal—thinking about and visualizing how to perform a social skill

Verbal rehearsal—reciting the components (skill steps) of a social skill

Overt rehearsal—performing (role playing) a social skill

Covert rehearsal is incorporated in the Preparatory Set of every social skill unit in *Social Star*. A script is provided which the educator reads to guide students through a visualization of the correct use of the social skill.

Social Star emphasizes *verbal rehearsal* by having students work in pairs to tell each other the skill step(s) for the unit several times.

Each *Social Star* unit includes several opportunities for students to engage in role playing, thereby providing *overt rehearsal* of the social skill. Many units also provide opportunities for students to drill and practice individual strategies (e.g., to practice the strategy of joining in during the unit *Playing Cooperatively*). In Lesson X of every unit (after students have watched the educator model correct use of the social skill in a home, school, or community situation), a student volunteer is asked to demonstrate the social skill using the following two-step approach:

1. The student demonstrates the social skill *while* verbalizing thoughts (self-talk) aloud.

2. The student demonstrates the social skill *without* verbalizing thoughts (self-talk) aloud.

In the Lesson Y *Show Time* of units in *Social Star*, each student is provided the opportunity to role play (overtly rehearse) a home, school, and/or community situation. Situations to role play are provided. These examples are from the *Dealing with Teasing* unit:

Home—Pretend your older sister wants you to tease your younger brother in a mean way. Show what you could say to her to let her know you don't like mean teasing.

School—Pretend a boy at school is teasing you at lunch. Show what you could say to yourself to help ignore the teasing.

Community—Pretend that a group of kids always picks on a younger boy while waiting for the bus. Show what you could do or say to help stop the teasing.

Additional role-play situations can be found in other commercially prepared programs such as *Skillstreaming the Elementary School Child* (McGinnis et al., 1984); *Skillstreaming in Early Childhood* (McGinnis and Goldstein, 1990); *Communicate Junior* (Mayo, Hirn, Gajewski, and Kafka, 1991); *Scripting* (Mayo and Waldo, 1987); and *Social Skills Intervention Guide* (Elliott and Gresham, 1991).

The role plays in *Social Star* have been provided to decrease teacher preparation time. However, it is critical that the role-play situations be realistic and relevant for the students. The educator is encouraged to substitute relevant role plays if the ones provided in *Social Star* are not realistic for a specific child or a group of children. The educator may wish to elicit role-play situations from the students themselves.

Other tips the educator should keep in mind when asking students to role play are these:

1. Give students the choice of whether or not they wish to participate in the role play (McGinnis et al., 1984); this will enhance the role play.

2. Determine the role play to be done, then elicit more specific information from the main actor as to the physical setting and events which might precede the role-play situation (McGinnis et al., 1984).

3. Use a multiple exemplar strategy (Stokes and Baer, 1977), which involves students role playing with several different people instead of just one person.

4. Intervene if the student begins to do the role play incorrectly or is not taking role playing seriously (McGinnis et al., 1984).

5. Use role reversal by having students switch roles (Goldstein, Sprafkin, Gershaw, and Klein, 1986).

6. Focus on how the student will use the new role-play behaviors in the future rather than how the behaviors could have been used in past situations (McGinnis et al., 1984).

7. Include a variety of opportunities for the students to drill individual skill steps or strategies for a social skill as opposed to performing the entire social skill only once or twice. Georges (1988) recommends drilling each skill step to the mastery level before moving on to the next skill step.

8. Use the word "pretend" with younger children rather than "role play" when explaining what to do.

9. Provide a box of props that can be used during role playing. Various hats, shirts, and artifacts (e.g., eyeglasses, purses, clipboards and pens, etc.) can be available for students' use.

FEEDBACK

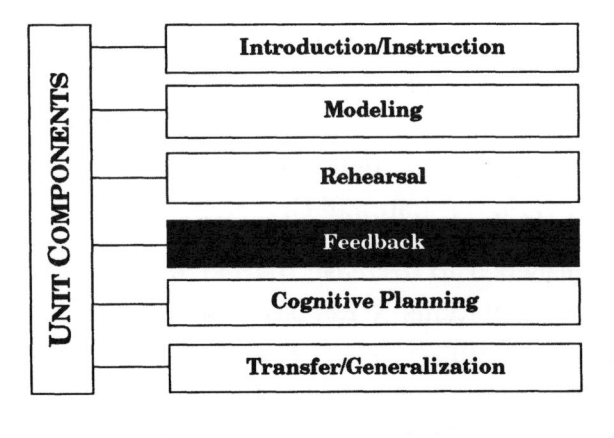

UNIT COMPONENTS:
- Introduction/Instruction
- Modeling
- Rehearsal
- **Feedback**
- Cognitive Planning
- Transfer/Generalization

Master educators recognize the importance of providing feedback to students. Thus, it is important that students receive feedback immediately after they perform a social skill so they can make improvements. The feedback can occur formally (during class while the students are role playing) or informally (throughout the day as appropriate or inappropriate social skill use is observed [see pages 26–29]).

When giving feedback on a student's role play of a particular social skill, be sure to:

1. Give specific feedback on the skill steps of the social skill. Students sometimes forget skill steps or may do them inappropriately. Those students should be asked to redo the role play (possibly with educator assistance) to ensure success.

2. Begin by pointing out the positive aspects of the role play before giving any constructive criticism.

3. Give feedback immediately, particularly to young children. The educator should always provide oral feedback. Additional written feedback is also recommended. For example, the educator could put a smile face next to each of the skill steps the student has successfully performed.

4. Provide feedback to parents on how their children are doing on specific targeted social skills.

COGNITIVE PLANNING

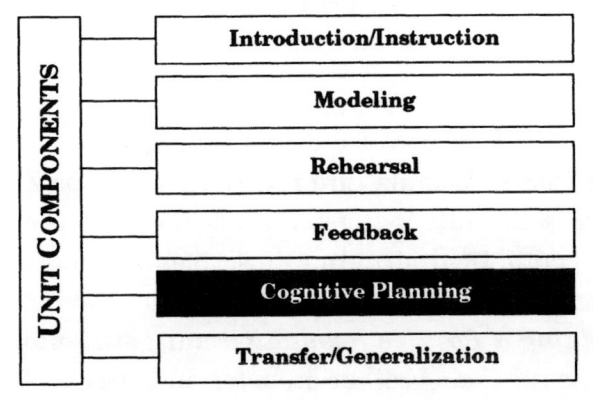

Along with learning comprehension of social skills, students need to learn and use cognitive planning. The phrase "cognitive planning strategies" refers to the independent thinking that students do about social skills.

Students need to be able to do the following:

- Keep themselves calm and in control
- Maintain a positive focus and be open-minded
- Perceive social situations accurately
- Brainstorm social skill options
- Consider consequences for each option
- Choose an option
- Develop a plan
- Carry out their plan
- Evaluate the outcomes
- Reward themselves for their successes and/or decide what to do differently the next time

Social Star has incorporated these cognitive planning strategies into a four-step "secret formula" called STOP, PLOT, GO, SO. Social skill interventions that incorporate cognitive planning strategies are described as being more effective in promoting the acquisition, transfer, and generalization of social skills than programs that do not incorporate these strategies (Hughes, 1988; Kendall and Braswell, 1982).

The first unit in *Social Star* is the *Cognitive Planning* unit. In addition to introducing students to the Socialville characters, this five-lesson unit describes the "secret formula" (the cognitive planning strategies) used by Socialville characters to solve problems and set goals. The secret formula consists of the following steps:

- STOP: Students think "stop" in their minds to stay calm by using self-control strategies.
- PLOT: Students decide what their problem is, brainstorm options, consider possible consequences for each option, and then choose the best option to use in the situation. They also think about the social skills needed to carry out their plan.
- GO: Students implement their plan.
- SO: Students ask themselves, "So, how did my plan work?" They reward themselves for their successes, and/or decide what they may want to do differently next time.

The *Cognitive Planning* unit should be taught first because it is a prerequisite for the remaining units. The four steps of the "secret formula" are reviewed in Lesson Z (Lesson Z Plot Situation) of all other social skill units by having students apply the steps to a hypothetical situation. The hypothetical situation describes a typical problem that a child might encounter and may not be specific to the particular social skill unit. For example, in the *Building a Positive Reputation* unit, students are asked to pretend that they fight often with their brother or sister and they and their parents feel frustrated about the fighting. Students are encouraged to use the "secret formula" to solve the problem.

TRANSFER/GENERALIZATION

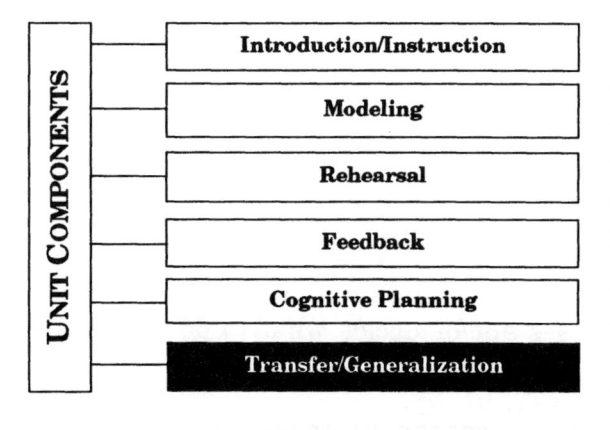

One of the major problems with any social skills training is that the skills often do not transfer/generalize to other settings. Students perform the social skill accurately while in class, yet fail to use the social skill in real-life situations. Each unit of *Social Star* has activities which increase the likelihood that transfer will occur. Some transfer ideas previously discussed are these:

UNIT COMPONENTS:
- Introduction/Instruction
- Modeling
- Rehearsal
- Feedback
- Cognitive Planning
- Transfer/Generalization

- Use of cognitive planning strategies, which includes using self-control statements, developing a plan, evaluating oneself, and rewarding oneself

- Use of self-talk during modeling and role plays
- Use of relevant role-play situations from the home, school, and community
- Use of verbal rehearsal and visualization

In addition, *Social Star* provides and/or encourages use of the transfer and generalization activities described in the remainder of this chapter.

Homework

A homework assignment is included in Lesson Z of every unit. The assignment asks students to take a *Home-A-Gram* and a social skill badge home to their parents or other significant adults. Figure 2.1 below provides an example of a *Home-A-Gram* and a badge.

The *Home-A-Gram* is a note written from a child's perspective. The note should be signed by each child during Lesson Z. The *Home-A-Gram* gives information about the social skill and provides an opportunity for the student to practice the social skill with a parent or other significant adult. The parent is asked to sign the social skill badge verifying that the activity was successfully completed. The student returns the badge to be displayed on the *Social Super Stars* display (see page 13).

Before sending home the first *Home-A-Gram* and social skill badge, supply each student's family with information about the rationale for the activity. A letter is provided in *Appendix G*.

Jackson, Jackson, and Monroe (1983) stress that homework should not be limited due to a lack of skills, time, or interest on the part of parents. Therefore, if a parent is unable or unwilling to complete the *Home-A-Gram*, it should be completed with another predetermined adult.

Figure 2.1

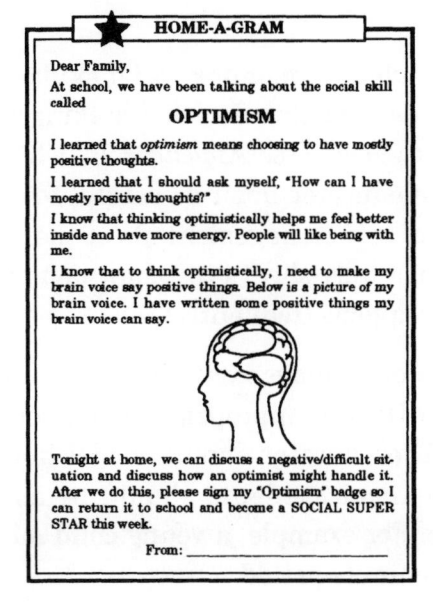

Related Activities

In addition to using the *Home-A-Gram,* the authors advocate that the educator provide motivating homework throughout each unit. The Related Activities listed at the beginning of each unit may also be utilized as homework assignments. These activities help integrate social skills into other content areas and into community settings.

Self-Management Strategies for Social Skills

The use of self-monitoring to learn self-management strategies (e.g., the SO step in the *Cognitive Planning* unit) appears to be a highly promising method for increasing the transfer and generalization of skills (Turkewitz, O'Leary, and Ironsmith, 1975). Dunlap, Dunlap, Koegel, and Koegel (1991) provide a five-step approach for designing and implementing a self-monitoring program. The approach is summarized in Table 2.1 and described in sections 1–5 that follow:

Table 2.1

Self-Monitoring Program
(Dunlap, Dunlap, Koegel, and Koegel, 1991)

1. Define the behavior to be monitored.
2. Develop a method for self-monitoring.
3. Teach the student how to use a self-monitoring device.
4. Allow the student to select reinforcement.
5. Fade the use of a self-monitoring device.

1. Define the behavior to be monitored. Students must understand and accurately assess themselves. For example, if children are to assess the amount of time they are "on task," they will need to understand exactly what "on task" means. In the *Social Star* program, students are asked to self-monitor in Lesson Z of every unit.

2. Develop a method for each student to monitor social skills. It is important that the educator include the student in this decision-making process. *Social Star* includes 10 *Self-Management* sheets (see *Appendix H*) which can be used with various social skill units. The educator must be careful to choose (or encourage students to choose) the type of self-management sheet that would work best for the given social skill (e.g., use a tally-sheet type shown on page 437 with a skill, such as *giving put-ups,* that happens frequently).

3. Teach the student to use the self-management sheets accurately. Students need to understand how to recognize the appropriate behavior and how to record when the behavior occurs. The educator should model how to use the chosen self-management device. Younger students should be asked to self-monitor relatively short, simple tasks. For example, a young child might be asked to self-monitor eye contact for a five-minute period.

4. Allow the student to assist in selecting a predetermined reinforcement for accurately performing the social skill. Students should be rewarded for accurately monitoring themselves in addition to accurately performing the social skill. At first, the educator may provide the reinforcement after the student has completed the self-management sheet. However, students should eventually learn to reward themselves, and extrinsic rewards (e.g., stickers, candy) should be replaced by intrinsic rewards (e.g., self-praise). The educator may wish to ask questions such as "When you learn to use this skill appropriately, what special feelings do you think you'll have? What can you say to praise yourself?" to assist students in moving toward being intrinsically motivated.

5. Fade the use of self-monitoring devices gradually, once the student has demonstrated mastery and generalization of the skill.

Self-Monitoring of Classroom Discussion Skills

In addition to the self-management activity during Lesson Z, students are also asked to self-monitor a classroom discussion skill once within each unit by completing a page called *Checking Myself* (see *Appendix I*). Development of appropriate classroom discussion skills along with social skills will facilitate a positive learning environment.

The educator is provided with a script to model how the *Checking Myself* sheet should be completed. An example follows:

Introduction

I am going to pretend to be one of you completing this sheet during the discussion we will be having. I will tell you the thoughts I'm having while I'm completing the sheet. When I hold up this Thought Bubble, *you'll know the words I'm saying are actually what I'm thinking.*

Actual Model

While holding up the *Thought Bubble* say, OK, *the teacher just called on Bill. I'd better give him eye contact so he knows I'm listening to his answer. I'll circle a T-shirt star because I gave him eye contact.* Put the *Thought Bubble* down and circle a star on the *Checking Myself* transparency.

These classroom discussion skills are emphasized in the *Checking Myself* model scripts:

- Listen to others
- Think about an answer to each question asked
- Use interested body talk
- Use appropriate eye contact

- Use a straight sitting posture
- Raise my hand

Educators may substitute other classroom discussion goals more appropriate for their students. For example, not all educators teach children to raise their hands during class discussion. The purpose of completing the *Checking Myself* activity in each unit is to reinforce the classroom discussion skills relevant to the children being taught. The specific selected content for these skills is up to the individual educator.

If the educator is concerned that a specific student may have difficulty monitoring the selected classroom discussion goal accurately, the educator can monitor the individual and compare the results with those of the student.

Social Skills All Day Long

Social skills should be addressed continually throughout the day. Each unit in *Social Star* provides suggestions in the form of encouraging, sharing a personal example, prompting students, and giving corrective feedback that educators can use to reinforce specific social skills. The authors strongly advocate that social skills be addressed throughout the day in a positive, nonthreatening manner.

Encouraging and giving corrective feedback were inspired by *The Dubuque Management System* (Keystone Area Education Agency, 1990), a highly successful social skill program that focuses on appropriate and inappropriate social skills as they occur throughout the day. The procedures for encouraging and giving corrective feedback are further explained in the next sections.

Encouraging

Educators need to reinforce students as frequently as possible when social skills are correctly used. This reinforcement is called "specific effective encouragement" in *The Dubuque Management System* (Keystone Area Education Agency, 1990). The steps involved in this encouragement are summarized in Table 2.2 and described in the next six points:

Table 2.2

Specific Effective Encouragement
(Keystone Area Education Agency, 1990)

1. Approach the student positively.
2. Describe the appropriate behavior.
3. Provide a rationale for appropriate behavior.
4. Ask for acknowledgment.
5. Tell the consequence.
6. Provide a transition.

1. Approach the student positively—the educator gives an initial positive greeting (e.g., smile at the student).

2. Describe the appropriate behavior—the educator describes the appropriate behavior the student used (e.g., "You offered help to Lee in such a polite way").

3. Provide a rationale for the appropriate behavior—the educator gives the reason for using the appropriate behavior (e.g., "When you offer help in such a nice way, people will want you to help them").

4. Ask for acknowledgment from the student—the educator asks the student to acknowledge (verbally or nonverbally) that there is understanding of what is said (e.g., "Do you understand?").

5. Tell the student the consequence—the educator tells the consequence the student has earned by the appropriate behavior (e.g., "When it's lunch time, you can go a minute early for offering help to Lee").

6. Provide a transition statement—the educator provides a statement that helps the student get back on task (e.g., "Why don't you spend the last five minutes reading quietly?").

Encouraging is also included at the end of each lesson in *Social Star* in the form of positive statements that are made by teachers. Children either listen to the positive statement or read it aloud in unison. The positive statements reinforce appropriate social skills and provide closure for each lesson.

Giving Corrective Feedback

The Dubuque Management System (Keystone Area Education Agency, 1990) uses a 10-step "teaching interaction" similar to that of Northrup, Wood, and Clark (1979), when inappropriate behavior occurs. "Giving corrective feedback" as modeled in *Social Star* encompasses only the first four steps of the 10-step teaching interaction process. The teaching interaction steps are summarized in Table 2.3 and are described in sections 1–10 that follow:

Table 2.3

Teaching Interaction
(Northrup, Wood, and Clark, 1979)

1. Approach student positively.
2. Describe inappropriate behavior.
3. Describe appropriate behavior.
4. Provide a rationale for appropriate behavior.
5. Model appropriate behavior.
6. Have student practice.
7. Give feedback to student.
8. Provide additional practice.
9. Give praise for accomplishments.
10. Give a homework assignment.

1. Approach the student positively—the educator gives an initial positive greeting (e.g., "Hi, Maria").

2. Describe the inappropriate behavior—the educator describes the inappropriate behavior to the student in specific terms (e.g., "Just now you were turned around in your desk making faces at Victor while I was talking").

3. Describe the appropriate behavior—the educator describes the appropriate behavior to be used by the student (e.g., "Maria, you could have been using your listening skills. Your body could have been facing the front and you could have been looking at me").[31]

4. Provide a rationale for the appropriate behavior—the educator gives the reason for using the appropriate behavior (e.g., "When you face the front and look at me, you let me know you are listening. You won't miss the important things I'm saying") and/or the consequences of not behaving appropriately (e.g., "If you are turned around in your chair, not giving eye contact, your teacher or parent may become upset because you are not listening").

5. Model the appropriate behavior—the educator demonstrates the appropriate behavior (e.g., the educator sits in a desk and models body language appropriate for listening).

6. Have the student practice—the educator asks the student to practice the appropriate behavior (e.g., "Maria, show me how to sit so that I'll know you are listening").

7. Give feedback to the student—the educator comments on the student's practice of the appropriate behavior. This feedback may include positive and/or negative feedback (e.g., "You're facing the front with your body. That's great! You still need to look at me when I'm talking, though").

8. Provide additional practice—the educator may request additional practice by the student (e.g., "Try that again, Maria. This time, make sure you are looking at me").

9. Give praise for accomplishments—the educator gives praise to the student for performing and participating.

10. Give a homework assignment—the educator directs the student to practice the appropriate behavior in another setting, or at a later time, or with a different person.

This model provides a positive method for changing inappropriate student behavior. While it may appear to be a time-consuming process, a teaching interaction can often be completed in a few minutes, particularly if the social skill has been previously taught. The use of teaching interactions throughout the day greatly increases the chances for skill transfer and generalization. The authors want to caution that the teaching interaction is but one small component of *The Dubuque Management*

System model. Those wishing further information about this comprehensive program should contact Keystone Area Education Agency, 1473 Central Avenue, Dubuque, Iowa 52001.

Schoolwide Promotion of Social Skills

Transfer and generalization of social skills will occur more readily if the use of appropriate social skills is promoted on a schoolwide basis. The school staff can jointly decide on a social skill to emphasize each week ("Social Skill of the Week"). The skill could be introduced and defined during the morning announcements. A rationale for using the skill can be given.

Educators could prepare a bulletin board which identifies a specific social skill to emphasize schoolwide. This skill could be changed periodically (weekly or monthly). For example, the elementary school cited in Figure 2.2 chose a theme and goal for each month; October's theme was football. The football was moved 10 yards each time a classroom teacher observed 10 incidents of students in his or her class "giving a compliment." The football field board could be cooperative (i.e., once a class reaches the goal, they give their additional yards to the class farthest behind; when all classes arrive at the goal line, there is an all-school reward) or competitive (i.e., the first class to get to the goal line receives a reward).

Figure 2.2

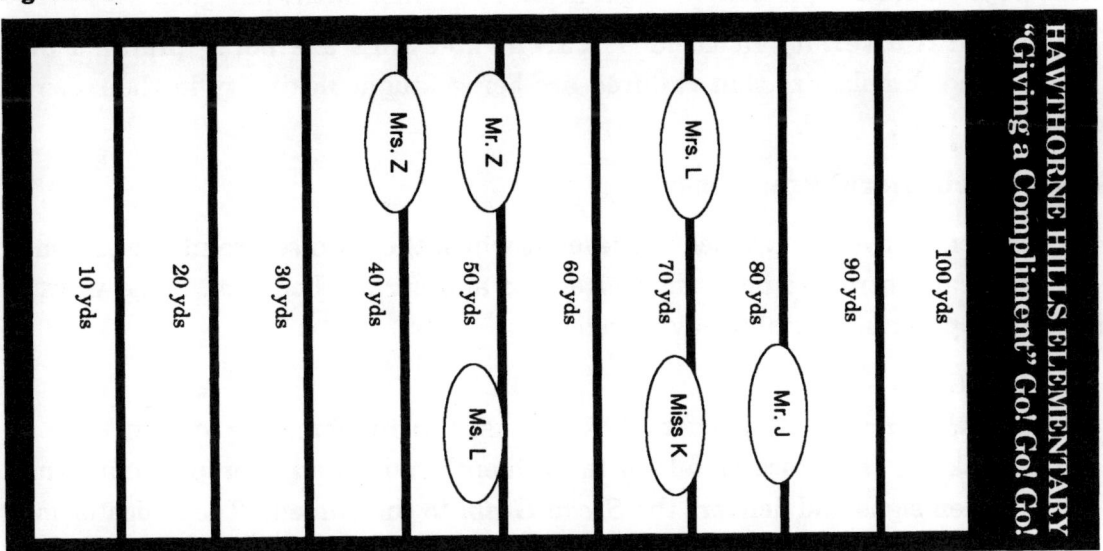

Example of schoolwide promotion of social skills, compliments of Hawthorne Hills Elementary School, Wausau, WI

Individual educators can further teach the skill using materials from *Social Star*. The "Social Skill of the Month" can be described in a school newsletter. Posters (see page 13) explaining social skills can be hung throughout the school. Students displaying appropriate social skills may be awarded coupons (see page 31), which can be turned in for a drawing. Emphasis on social skill excellence should be recognized at award presentations.

Red Flag

McGinnis, Sauerbry, and Nichols (1985) describe a "Red Flag" strategy in which the educator tells students that they will be "set up" later in the day (or the next day). *Being set up* means that the educator will purposely do something which will cause a child to demonstrate use of a particular social skill. For example, a student might be told that sometime later in the day, the educator will give (the student) a compliment. The student is encouraged to demonstrate the proper way to receive a compliment during the set up. After the "Red Flag" situation has taken place, the educator and student should discuss how the social skill situation was handled.

Parental Involvement/Training

In addition to involving parents through the *Home-A-Gram*, training should also be available for parents. Two or three parent meetings would be a start at instructing parents how to identify and praise specific appropriate behaviors in their children. Parents can be taught to view inappropriate behavior as a skill deficit that needs to be taught rather than as "naughty behavior." Parents could learn a shortened version of a teaching interaction (such as steps 1–4) to use with their children.

Often it is difficult to get parents to attend parent-training sessions. One method of getting the message to parents is to ask the PTO/PTA organization to devote one meeting to the topic of "Communitywide Social Skills." Have the PTO/PTA brainstorm ways for their organization to get involved in this worthwhile goal.

Keep cultural diversity in mind as parent meetings are being planned and implemented. Emphasize that children are being taught flexibility in their use of social skills (see page 2).

Reward/Behavioral Programs

Many students have not reached the level at which they can self-reinforce and may need external controls to help themselves use appropriate behavior. Some ways to reinforce appropriate social behavior follow:

1. *Social Gram*

   A *Social Gram* (see *Appendix J*) can be used to reinforce the student's use of social skills. The educator fills in the student's name and appropriate information, then signs and delivers the *Social Gram* to the student. The educator may wish to describe the student's specific behavior in the blank space.

2. *Sunshine Call*

   The *Sunshine Call* is another method for reinforcing social skills. The educator keeps the names/addresses/phone numbers of all students on note cards in a card file box. Each day, the educator takes the first card from the box and either calls or writes a note to that student's family. It is important that the educator discuss only positive behaviors the child has exhibited when writing to or speaking with the family.

3. *The Great Coupon Caper*
   Each member of the class is given one coupon (see *Appendix K*) at the beginning of the day. At random, the name of a specific student is targeted. When other class members observe that student using appropriate social skills (e.g., *playing cooperatively, giving put-ups*), they write down why they are awarding the coupon to the target student, and sign their own name. They then give it to the student. At the end of the day, the student turns the coupons in to the teacher. The next day, a different student is targeted to receive the social coupons. When the class earns a specified number of coupons, the students can earn a reward they cooperatively choose. All students should have an opportunity to be the target student.

4. *Student of the Week Graffiti Poster*
   Display a large paper with the title "Student of the Week" written on it. Choose a class member to be the "Student of the Week" and write that student's name on the graffiti poster. Class members are instructed to write times when the student has used appropriate social skills (e.g., "Lee was participating during reading today. Great job, Lee!"). At the end of the week, send the poster home with the student. Give each student the opportunity to be "Student of the Week."

5. *Bell-Ringer*
   At the beginning of the school day, identify a "Social Skill of the Day" (e.g., *being a friend*). This skill may be chosen by the teacher or the class. When the teacher observes the social skill, the teacher rings a bell in celebration!

6. *We're Hot!*
   Display a large paper thermometer with increments marked. Each time students use appropriate social skills (e.g., *respecting differences*), one increment on the thermometer is colored. When the entire thermometer is filled, the class receives a special reward.

7. *Cooperative Treat*
   The educator may wish to use cooperative reward activities. These include cooperative root beer floats, tacos, cookies and cookie decorating, and pizzas. For example, when making cooperative root beer floats, one person is responsible for glasses, one for the root beer, one for the ice cream, one for the spoons, and one for the straws. The students put the floats together cooperatively. Students are allowed to consume their floats when all of the floats are ready.

Peer Reminders

Students should be encouraged to remind fellow students about using social skills (e.g., "Come on, Ann. Tell yourself to calm down. You can do it"). The educator may need to instruct students on how to give reminders in a positive manner. The *Cognitive Planning* unit uses the analogy of a stoplight to remind students to stay in control of their emotions. Students can use the word "stoplight" to remind each other to stay calm. In addition, students should encourage each other for using appropriate social skills (e.g., "Great job of disagreeing politely").

Student Mediators

"Mediated Dispute Resolution" involves student conflicts being resolved by the students themselves with the help of a trained peer mediator (Koch and Miller, 1987). When a conflict arises, the students are asked if they would like to "get mediated." Students then put the disagreement "on hold" until a peer mediator is found. In a mediation session, the peer mediator first explains the ground rules. Then each student takes turns telling "his side of the story." The students then come up with a list of solutions, decide upon a solution, and sign a written agreement. This strategy, which can be used anytime throughout the school day, teaches students to compromise and negotiate. Transfer of social skills occurs when students learn to solve problems on their own rather than needing adults to intervene. This process may be appropriate for slightly older children, since it requires perspective taking and negotiating skills.

Use of Cooperative Learning

The use of cooperative learning techniques during academic classes reinforces social skills taught to students and promotes transfer and generalization of social skills. A list of Cooperative Learning Resources is provided on page 40.

The major differences between cooperative learning and traditional learning are depicted in Table 2.4.

Table 2.4

Differences in Learning Groups
(Johnson, Johnson, and Johnson Holubec, 1990)

Cooperative Learning Groups	*Traditional Learning Groups*
Positive interdependence	No interdependence
Individual accountability	No individual accountability
Heterogeneous groups	Homogeneous groups
Leadership is shared	One leader is appointed
Responsible for self and to others	Responsible for self
Task and maintenance emphasized	Only task emphasized
Social skills are directly taught	Social skills are assumed or ignored
Educator observes and intervenes	Educator ignores the groups
Group processing	No group processing

Johnson, Johnson, and Johnson Holubec (1990) describe five components necessary for cooperative learning. They are listed in Table 2.5 and elaborated upon in sections 1–5 that follow:

Table 2.5 | **Cooperative Learning Components**
(Johnson et al., 1990)

1. Positive interdependence
2. Individual accountability
3. Face-to-face interaction
4. Social skills
5. Group processing

1. *Positive Interdependence*

   Johnson et al. (1990) state that one necessary component of a cooperative group is that students believe they "sink or swim together." Students have two responsibilities: learn the assigned material, and make sure that all members of their group learn the assigned material. This dual responsibility is "positive interdependence." Positive interdependence occurs when students feel they are linked with group members in a way that they cannot succeed unless their group members succeed. Positive interdependence promotes a situation in which students recognize that their work benefits group members and vice versa. When positive interdependence is clearly understood, students are aware of the following:

   - Each group member's efforts are required and indispensable for group success (i.e., there can be no "free-riders").

   - Each group member has a unique contribution to make to the joint effort because of his or her resources and/or role and task responsibilities.

   Positive interdependence can be structured in a cooperative group in several ways. Group members can work toward a "group goal" (e.g., learn the material, and make sure all group members learn the material). A "group reward" can be offered (e.g., if all group members score 85 percent on the quiz, they will receive 10 bonus points). "Dividing resources" gives each group member a necessary part of the total information to be learned so that the member must teach that part to others. Additionally, the use of "group roles" (e.g., reader, checker, timer, encourager) is yet another way to structure positive interdependence.

2. *Individual Accountability*

   According to Johnson et al. (1990), *individual accountability* means that each student's efforts are assessed and the results are given to all group members. This helps group members understand that they cannot "hitchhike" on the work of others. To structure individual accountability:

- Assess how much effort each group member is contributing to the group's work.
- Provide feedback to groups and individual students.
- Help groups avoid redundant efforts by members.
- Ensure that every member is responsible for the final outcome.

3. *Face-to-Face Interaction*

Cooperative learning requires that face-to-face interaction takes place among students. Johnson et al. (1990) explain that this verbal and nonverbal interaction among group members promotes helping, assisting, supporting, encouraging, and praising. It allows students to pressure unmotivated group members to achieve. Students get to know each other as people.

4. *Social Skills*

Johnson et al. (1990) warn that, oftentimes, simply placing students into a group and telling them to cooperate does not ensure that they will do so. Students need to be taught the social skills needed for positive group interaction (e.g., taking turns listening and talking, giving encouragement, having appropriate body language). These social skills are necessary if the group is to function productively. Social skills are taught by Johnson et al. (1990) through the use of *T-Charts*. *Appendix L* contains a blank *T-Chart* that can be used for any unit in *Social Star*; a completed *T-Chart* is also included in Lesson X of every unit. Use of *T-Charts* is further explained in *Appendix A*.

5. *Group Processing*

Group processing, as described by Johnson et al. (1990), means that students discuss how well they did at achieving their goal and working together. This helps to provide for generalization of the concepts presented. During group processing, students:

- Describe what member actions were helpful and not helpful.
- Make decisions about what actions to continue or change.

The purpose of group processing is to improve each member's effectiveness in achieving the group's goals.

Kagan (1992) describes a cooperative learning structure called "Numbered Heads Together" that is useful in checking for understanding and reviewing key concepts. This structure is incorporated into some of the lessons within *Social Star* and consists of four steps: (1) team members number off; (2) educator announces a question and a time limit; (3) students put their heads together; and (4) educator calls a number.

Step 1. Team members number off.

Each student on the team numbers off. (Teams may not all have the same number of members. For example, some of the teams may have three members and some of the teams may have four members. When this happens, Person 3 from a team of three may answer when either number 3 or number 4 is called.)

Step 2. Educator announces a question and a time limit.

During this step, the educator should pose a question in the form of a directive. Instead of asking, "Why didn't Jolisa give put-ups?" it's better to say, "Make sure everyone on the team can explain why Jolisa didn't give put-ups." To keep the activity moving, the teacher may specify the amount of time teams will be given to put their heads together (e.g., "Why didn't Jolisa use eye contact? You have 45 seconds to make sure everyone on your team knows").

Step 3. Students put their heads together.

Students actually put their heads together to discuss the answer to the proposed question and to make certain everyone knows and can say the answer.

Step 4. Educator calls a number.

The educator calls a number at random and students with that number answer the question. An overhead spinner can be used to truly randomize the numbers being called. The educator then calls on one student to answer the question.

If only one or two students raise their hands (and there are many more than two teams), the educator can say, "Not enough two's have their hands up; I'll give you one more minute to make sure your team's number two knows the answer. Then I want to see all two's hands up." (Or use another system to identify who's ready to answer if raising hands is contrary to your philosophy and/or to the students' cultures.)

If the answer has several parts, then the educator should ask a number one to answer part one, a number two to answer part two, and so on. If a student gives a partially correct response, the educator might ask, "Is there a number three who can add to that response?"

Real-Life Outings

Some students require that social skills be isolated so that direct instruction can be provided. However, in real life, students must identify which social skills to use when and must use a combination of social skills at all times. It is important to provide real-life outings so that students can practice their social skills. Most units in *Social Star* provide a suggestion for a real-life outing in the Related Activities section. The educator should have students develop a list of social skills they feel will be necessary before going on the outing. After the outing, the educator and students should discuss the students' use of social skills.

Communicate Junior

One means of reinforcing social skill concepts previously learned is the use of educational board games, which can be effective, fun, and motivating (Cartledge and

Milburn, 1986). *Communicate Junior* (Mayo et al., 1991) is a game board activity for elementary students that focuses on 12 social skills. Each player earns an invitation to a party by responding appropriately to question or demonstration items. One by one, players earn their invitation, but the party doesn't begin until everyone is invited. Players are encouraged to help each other get to the party so they can have fun together. The original *Communicate* game (Mayo and Waldo, 1986) is appropriate for upper elementary students.

Social Skill Unit Adaptations

Educators may wish to integrate social skill instruction into content area curriculum. For example, an educator may wish to teach the social skill of *respecting differences* as a part of a cooperative learning lesson during social studies by using the page called *Respecting Differences* from Lesson A (the page which provides students with the definition, skill step, and reasons for *respecting differences*).

The units in *Social Star* can also be adapted for use in English-as-a-second-language classrooms. For example, educators may focus on how students can cross between their home cultures and common American cultural norms with regard to social skills when they choose to do so in response to a given situation.

Special attention was given to deleting "should" whenever possible in *Social Star*. Rather than dictating what educators *should* teach children about social skills, the focus is on what *could* be selected. When teaching from *Social Star*, educators are encouraged to honor the "could" terminology rather than lapsing into "shoulds" with children. Likewise, use of "appropriate" is recommended whenever feasible, rather than the more judgmental word "good."

SOCIAL STAR: SUMMARY OF A COMPREHENSIVE RESOURCE

The unit that follows this chapter provides the foundation for other social skills to be taught. *Cognitive Planning* teaches essential thinking strategies and should not be skipped over. The teaching sequence of the remaining 12 social skill units should be determined based upon assessment results.

Each unit contains specific information and materials for teaching a given social skill. Many times, the appendices are cited as containing necessary material to teach the unit. Any materials shared among a number of units are reproduced in an appendix section for easier accessibility.

As units are being taught, respect the diversity among your students. *Social Star* is not intended to produce carbon copies of the teacher's perception of "good" social communicators. Rather, the intent is to teach students the richness and flexibility of social communication rules and their impact on school, home, and community situations.

References

Asher, S., and Gottman, J. (Eds.). (1981). *The development of children's friendships*. Cambridge, MA: Cambridge University Press.

Bandura, A. (1977). *Social learning theory*. Englewood Cliffs, NJ: Prentice-Hall.

Bryant, L., and Budd, K. (1984). Training prosocial behaviors to young children: An analysis of reciprocity with untrained peers. *Journal of Applied Behavior Analysis, 18*(3), 187–199.

Bullock, J. (1988). Encouraging the development of social competence in young children. *Early Child Development and Care, 37*, 47–54.

Cartledge, G., and Milburn, J. (Eds.). (1986). *Teaching social skills to children: Innovative approaches (2nd ed.)*. Elmsford, NY: Pergamon Press.

Charlesworth, R., and Hartup, W. (1967). Positive social reinforcement in the nursery school peer group. *Child Development, 38*, 993–1002.

Cohen, E. (1986). *Designing groupwork: Strategies for the heterogeneous classroom*. New York, NY: Teachers College Press.

Corasaro, W. (1979). We're friends, right?: Children's use of access rituals in a nursery school. *Language in Society, 8*, 315–336.

Curran, L. (1990) *Cooperative learning lessons for little ones: Literature-based language arts and social skills*. San Juan Capistrano, CA: Resources for Teachers.

Dembrowsky, C. (1983). *Affective skill development for adolescents*. Jackson, WY: author.

Derman-Sparks, L. (1989). *Anti-bias curriculum: Tools for empowering young children*. Washington, DC: National Association for the Education of Young Children.

Duck, S. (1983). *Friends for life*. New York, NY: St. Martin's Press.

Dunlap, L., Dunlap, G., Koegel, L., and Koegel, R. (1991). Using self-monitoring to increase independence. *Teaching Exceptional Children, 23*(3), 17–22.

Elliott, S., and Gresham, F. (1991). *Social skills intervention guide: Practical strategies for social skill training*. Circle Pines, MN: American Guidance Service.

Evans, E. (1989). Developing friendship skills: Key to positive mainstreaming. *Journal of Humanistic Education and Development, 27*(4), 138–151.

Faber, A., and Mazlish, E. (1987). *Siblings without rivalry: How to help your children live together so you can live too*. New York, NY: Avon Books.

Freedman, P., Gotti, M., and Holtz, G. (1981, February). In support of direct teaching to counter ethnic stereotypes. *Phi Delta Kappan, 62*(6), p. 456.

Gardner, G. (1983). *Frames of mind: The theory of multiple intelligences*. New York, NY: Basic Books.

Georges, J. (1988, April). Why soft-skill training doesn't take. *Training*, pp. 42–47.

Goldstein, A., Sprafkin, R., Gershaw, N., and Klein, P. (1986). The adolescent: Social skills training through structured learning. In G. Cartledge and J. Milburn (Eds.), *Teaching social skills to children: Innovative approaches (2nd ed.)*. Elmsford, NY: Pergamon Press.

Gottlieb, J., and Leyser, Y. (1981). Friendship between mentally retarded and nonretarded children. In S. Asher and J. Gottman (Eds.), *The development of children's friendships*. Cambridge, MA: Cambridge University Press.

Gresham, F. (1981). Social skills training with handicapped children: A review. *Review of Educational Research, 51,* 139–176.

Hartup, W. (1978). Children and their friends. In H. McGurk (Ed.), *Issues in childhood social development* (pp. 130–170). London: Methuen.

Hirsch, E. (1989). *A first dictionary of cultural literacy: What our children need to know.* Boston, MA: Houghton Mifflin.

Hughes, J. (1988). *Cognitive behavior therapy with children in school.* New York: Pergamon.

Hunter, M. (1992, April). *Increasing your teaching effectiveness.* Workshop presented to educators through the Bureau of Education and Research. Milwaukee, WI.

Jackson, N., Jackson, D., and Monroe, C. (1983). *Getting along with others: Teaching social effectiveness to children.* Champaign, IL: Research Press.

Johnson, D., and Johnson, R. (1985). The internal dynamics of cooperative learning groups. In R. Slavin, S. Sharan, S. Kagan, R. Hertz Lazarowitz, C. Webb, and R. Schmuck (Eds.), *Learning to cooperate: Cooperating to learn.* New York, NY: Plenum Press.

Johnson, D., and Johnson, R. (1989). *Cooperation and competition: Theory and research.* Edina, MN: Interaction Book Company.

Johnson, D. and Johnson, R. (1991). *Teaching children to be peacemakers.* Edina, MN: Interaction Book Company.

Johnson, D., Johnson, R., and Holubec, E. (1988). *Cooperation in the classroom.* Edina, MN: Interaction Book Company.

Johnson, D., Johnson, R., and Johnson Holubec, E. (1990). *Circles of learning (3rd ed.).* Edina, MN: Interaction Book Company.

Kagan, S. (1992). *Cooperative learning.* San Juan Capistrano, CA: Resources for Teachers.

Katz, L. (1993, July 15). Reading, writing, narcissism. *The New York Times,* p. A25.

Kendall, P., and Braswell, L. (1982). Cognitive-behavioral self-control therapy for children: A component analysis. *Journal of Consulting and Clinical Psychology, 50,* 672–689.

Keystone Area Education Agency. (1990). *The Dubuque management system.* Dubuque, IA: Dubuque Community Schools.

Koch, M., and Miller, S. (1987). Resolving student conflicts with student mediators. *Principal, 66,* 59–62.

Ladd, G., and Mize, J. (1983). A cognitive-social learning model of social skill training. *Psychological Review, 10*(2), 127–157.

La Meres, C. (1990). *The winner's circle: Yes, i can!* Newport Beach, CA: LaMeres Lifestyles Unlimited.

Lang, D., and Stinson, B. (1988). *Lazy dogs and sleeping frogs.* LaCrosse, WI: Coulee Press.

Lovitt, C. (1987). Social skills training: Which ones and where to do it? *Journal of Reading, Writing and Learning Disabilities International, 3*(3), 213–221.

Macklem, G. (1987). No one wants to play with me. *Academic Therapy, 22*(5), 447–484.

Mayo, P., Hirn, P., Gajewski, N., and Kafka, J. (1991). *Communicate junior.* Eau Claire, WI: Thinking Publications.

Mayo, P., and Waldo, P. (1986). *Communicate.* Eau Claire, WI: Thinking Publications.

Mayo, P., and Waldo, P. (1987). *Scripting.* Eau Claire, WI: Thinking Publications.

McGinnis, E., and Goldstein, A. (1990). *Skillstreaming in early childhood: Teaching prosocial skills to the preschool and kindergarten child.* Champaign, IL: Research Press.

McGinnis, E., Goldstein, A., Sprafkin, R., and Gershaw, N. (1984). *Skillstreaming the elementary school child: A guide for teaching prosocial skills.* Champaign, IL: Research Press.

References

McGinnis, E., Sauerbry, L., and Nichols, P. (1985). Skill-streaming: Teaching social skills to children with behavioral disorders. *Teaching Exceptional Children, 17*, 160–167.

Meichenbaum, D. (1977). *Cognitive-behavior modification: An integrative approach.* New York: Plenum Press.

Meichenbaum, D. (1991, July). *Cognitive behavior therapy with adults, adolescents, and children. Workshop presented to educators.* Egg Harbor, WI.

Neel, R. (1988). Classroom conversion kit: A teacher's guide to teaching social competency. *Severe Behavior Disorders Monograph, 11*, 25–31.

Northrup, J., Wood, R., and Clark, H. (1979). *Social skill development in children: Application of individual and group training.* Invited workshop, Association for Behavior Analysis, Presented at the Fifth Annual Convention, Dearborn, MI.

Orlick, T. (1978). *The cooperative sports and games book.* Westminster, MD: Pantheon Books.

Orlick, T. (1982). *The second cooperative sports and games book.* Westminster, MD: Pantheon Books.

Pate, G. (1981). Research on prejudice reduction. *Educational Leadership, 38*(4), 288–291.

Perske, R., and Perske, M. (1988). *Circles of friends.* Nashville, TN: Abingdon Press.

Putallaz, M., and Gottman, J. (1981). Social skills and group acceptance. In S. Asher and J. Gottman (Eds.), *The development of children's friendship.* New York: Cambridge University Press.

Readability Plus (1988). Rockville, MD: Scandinavian PC Systems.

Reohr, J. (1984). Friendship: An important part of education. *The Clearing House, 57*, 209–212.

Roff, M., and Sells, S. (1978). Juvenile delinquency in relation to peer acceptance, rejection, and socioeconomic status. *Psychology in the Schools, 3*, 3–18.

Rubin, I. (1967). Increased self-acceptance: A means of reducing prejudice. *Journal of Personality and Social Psychology, 5*, 233–238.

Sapon-Shevin, M. (1983). Teaching young children about differences: Resources for teaching. *Child Development, 38*(2), 24–32.

Schumaker, J., and Hazel, J. (1984). Social skills assessment and training for the learning disabled: Who's on first and what's on second? Part I. *Journal of Learning Disabilities, 17*(7), 422–431.

Secretary's Commission on Achieving Necessary Skills (SCANS) (1992). *Learning a living: A blueprint for America 2000.* U.S. Department of Labor.

Seligman, M. (1990). *Learned optimism.* New York, NY: Pocket Books.

Sherburne, S., Utley, B., McConnell, S., and Gannon, J. (1988). Decreasing violent or aggressive theme play among preschool children with behavior disorders. *Exceptional Children, 55*(2), 166–172.

Stainback, W., and Stainback, S. (1987). Facilitating friendship. *Education and Training in Mental Retardation, 22*(1), 18–25.

Stokes, T., and Baer, D. (1977). An implicit technology of generalization. *Journal of Applied Behavior Analysis, 10*, 349–369.

Tremblay, A., Strain, P., Hendrickson, J., and Shores, R. (1981). Social interaction of normally developing preschool children: Using normative date for subject and target behavior selection. *Behavior Modification, 5*, 237–253.

Turkewitz, H., O'Leary, K., and Ironsmith, M. (1975). Generalization and maintenance of appropriate behavior through self-control. *Journal of Consulting and Clinical Psychology, 43*, 577–583.

Williams, C. (1986). Population trends affect education. *South Carolina School Board's Association Journal,* 20–21.

COOPERATIVE LEARNING RESOURCES

Blueprints for Thinking in the Cooperative Classroom (1990) by J. Bellanca and R. Fogarty. (Skylight Publishing, Inc., 200 E. Wood Street, Palatine, IL 60067; 1-800-922-4474)

Circles of Learning: Cooperation in the Classroom (3rd ed.) (1990) by D. Johnson, R. Johnson., and E. Johnson Holubec. (Interaction Book Company, 7208 Cornelia Drive, Edina, MN 55435; 1-612-831-9500)

Our Cooperative Classroom (1988) by D. Johnson, R. Johnson, L. Johnson, and J. Bartlett. (Interaction Book Company, 7208 Cornelia Drive, Edina, MN 55435; 1-612-831-9500)

Cooperative Learning (1992) by S. Kagan. (Resources for Teachers, 27128 Paseo Espada, Suite 622, San Juan Capistrano, CA 92675; 1-800-933-2667)

Cooperative Learning, Cooperative Lives: A Sourcebook of Learning Activities for Building a Peaceful World (1987) by N. Schniedewind and E. Davidson. (Brown Publishing ROA Media, 2460 Kerper Blvd., Dubuque, IA 52001; 1-800-922-7696)

Cooperative Learning Lessons for Little Ones: Literature-Based Language Arts and Social Skills. (1990) by L. Curran. (Resources for Teachers, 27128 Paseo Espada, Suite 622, San Juan Capistrano, CA 92675; 1-800-933-2667)

The Cooperative Sports and Games Book (1978) by T. Orlick. (Pantheon Books, 400 Hahn Road, Westminster, MD 21157; 1-800-733-3000)

The Cooperative Think Tank: Practical Techniques to Teach Thinking in the Cooperative Classroom (1990) by J. Bellanca. (Skylight Publishing, Inc., 200 E. Wood Street, Palatine, IL 60067; 1-800-922-4474)

The Cooperative Think Tank II: More Graphic Organizers to Teach Thinking in the Cooperative Classroom (1992) by J. Bellanca. (Skylight Publishing, Inc., 200 E. Wood Street, Palatine, IL 60067; 1-800-922-4474)

A Guidebook for Cooperative Learning: A Technique for Creating More Effective Schools (1984) by D. Dishon and P. Wilson-O'Leary. (Learning Publications, Inc., P.O. Box 1338, Holmes Beach, FL 34218; 1-800-222-1525)

Kids Can Cooperate: A Practical Guide to Teaching Problem Solving (1984) by E. Crary. (Parenting Press, Inc., 11065 5th Avenue, N.E. Suite F, Seattle, WA 98125; 1-800-922-6657)

Learning to Cooperate, Cooperating to Learn (1985) by R. Slavin, S. Sharan, S. Kagan, R. Hertz-Lazarowitz, and C. Webb, (Eds.). (Plenum Press, 233 Spring Street, New York, NY 10013; 1-800-221-9369)

The Nurturing Classroom (1989) by M. McCabe and J. Rhoades. (ITA Publications, 1500 W. El Camino, Suite 350, Sacramento, CA 95833; 1-916-922-1615)

Tools for the Cooperative Classroom (1990) by M. Archibald Marcus and P. McDonald. (Skylight Publishing, Inc., 200 East Wood Street, Palatine, IL 60067; 1-800-922-4474)

Tribes: A Process for Social Development and Cooperative Learning (1987) by J. Gibbs. (Center Source Publications, 305 Tesconi Circle, Santa Rosa, CA 954011; 707-577-8233)

Cognitive Planning

UNIT GOAL:

To demonstrate comprehension and use of a cognitive planning strategy called STOP, PLOT, GO, SO (a strategy that enables students to think about their behavior and its consequences before, during, and after initiating it)

EDUCATOR INFORMATION:

Cognitive planning is one of the six components involved in the instruction of social skills (see pages 21–22). These cognitive planning lessons have been provided to assist the educator in teaching the four steps of cognitive planning: STOP, PLOT, GO, SO. Within this unit, the class is instructed to construct the town of Socialville so that the *Social Star* characters might seem more realistic for students.

RELATED ACTIVITIES:

1. Ask students to run for a short time so they can practice one of the self-control strategies from the STOP step while their bodies experience the physical symptoms associated with anger (e.g., increased heart rate, heavy breathing, sweaty skin). Teach students that these are body cues that warn them of angry feelings.

2. Teach students how to do progressive relaxation (see *Appendix M*).

3. Discuss additional strategies for reducing stress (e.g., exercising, eating properly). Explain that having a high stress level can make self-control difficult to maintain.

4. Use the *Secret Formula Pages* (see *Appendix N*) to transfer use of STOP, PLOT, GO, SO to other areas of the students' lives (e.g., at home, with friends). Model the use of these pages. The page with four stars at the top is written in the present tense (e.g., "I can stay calm by..."), while the page with eight stars is written in the past tense (e.g., "I stayed calm by..."). Encourage students to use these pages to think about problems they may be facing or goals they may wish to set.

5. Inform parents of the secret formula strategy. Encourage parents to use the *Secret Formula Pages* with their children at home.

6. Discuss how the STOP, PLOT, GO, SO steps can work for academic subjects (e.g., to solve a math problem). Also, discuss how the STOP, PLOT, GO, SO steps can work for goal setting (e.g., a student could accomplish the goal of earning money to buy something special).

7. Have students work in pairs to write a story about someone using the problem-solving strategy of STOP, PLOT, GO, SO.

Social Star

Lesson A

OBJECTIVE:

To be introduced to the characters in Socialville

MATERIALS:

1. Characters from Socialville (See *Appendix F*; enlarge, color, glue on tagboard, and laminate each character for use within this and other units from *Social Star*.)

2. *Socialville and the Social Star Club* (See pages 59–64; enlarge, color, and laminate, if desired, one copy of the story for educator use; as an alternative, duplicate one copy per student and let each one color the illustrations.)

3. Buildings from Socialville (See *Appendix E*; enlarge one copy of each building.)

4. Markers or crayons for each student

PREPARATORY SET:

Have students sit in a circle. Tell them to close their eyes and put their hands behind their backs. Give each student a Socialville character. (There are 17 characters. Depending on the group size, students may need to have more than one character or students may need to share a character.) Have students open their eyes and look at their Socialville character(s). Tell students they will be showing their character(s) during a story. For older students, the educator may wish to pass out characters and have students tell if the characters remind them of someone they know and/or guess what each character's personality is like.

PLAN:

1. Read *Socialville and the Social Star Club* to students. Stop to interact directly with students when a star appears in the story. As individual characters are introduced, have the student holding that character stand and show the character.

2. After reading the story, discuss the word "social." Webster defines *social* as:

    a. Marked by or passed in pleasant companionship with one's friends or associates b. Relating to human society, the interaction of the individual and the group, or the welfare of human beings as members of society c. Tending to form cooperative and interdependent relationships with one's fellows.

A definition of *social* for students might be "getting along with other people."

Explain that a large amount of our time is spent in social situations.

3. Process this information by asking students the following questions:

- Did any of the families in Socialville remind you of your family?

- Are there any people from Socialville who you want to get to know better?

- What thoughts do you have about their Social Star Club?

4. Tell students that they will be creating a town in which the Socialville characters will live. Distribute the markers or crayons and an enlarged building to each student. (There are nine buildings. Depending on group size, students may need to have more than one building, or students may need to share a building.) Ask students to help construct Socialville by coloring their building(s). After the buildings have been colored, they could be displayed on a bulletin board or propped up in a three-dimensional manner on a table. Roads, trees, etc. can be added as desired. Socialville can be the setting when putting on skits with the characters. Socialville characters can be stored in Socialville and students can be asked to get various characters when needed. The use of Socialville will help make the characters more realistic to students.

Social Star

Lesson B

OBJECTIVE:

To practice the STOP step of the cognitive planning strategy called STOP, PLOT, GO, SO (The STOP step involves staying calm and using self-control.)

MATERIALS:

1. *STOP: Secret Formula Part 1* (See pages 65–71; enlarge, color, and laminate, if desired, one copy of the story for educator use; as an alternative, duplicate one copy per student and let each one color the illustrations.)

2. Bubble solution, a bubble blower, a soup spoon, and a bowl of water (To be used while reading the story during step 2 below.)

3. *Cognitive Planning Formula* chart (See page 12.)

4. Paper and color markers, pencils, or crayons

5. *Thought Bubble* (See *Appendix O;* one cut out for educator use.)

PREPARATORY SET:

Tell students, "I'm going to pretend to be a student in class. The teacher is handing back my corrected spelling test. Watch how I react when I get my test back and find out I got a low grade." During your role play, become upset and respond in an out-of-control manner (e.g., pouting, ripping up the test, saying, "I hate school"). Afterwards, discuss with the class how you looked when you were out of control. Review some of the problems associated with losing control (e.g., you can hurt other people's feelings; you feel embarrassed afterwards).

PLAN:

1. Remind students of the "Social Star Club" to which the Socialville students belong. Tell students you will be reading a story about a secret formula that will help them find a solution to the problem of losing control discussed previously.

2. Read *STOP: Secret Formula Part 1* to the class. Stop to interact directly with students when a star appears in the story. (When the story asks students to practice breathing as if they are blowing bubbles or blowing on a hot spoon of soup, model first for the students using the props listed in the Materials section.)

3. Show the *Cognitive Planning Formula* chart and tell students it will be displayed in the classroom to remind them of the importance of the four steps.

4. Process this information by asking students the following questions:

   - Think about a time recently when you were angry. What did you do?

   - Which "STOP" strategy for calming down do you like best?

   - Have you ever seen your mom, dad, brother, or sister using any of these strategies? Which ones?

   - Why is it important to calm down when you're upset?

5. Point to the first stoplight symbol on the *Cognitive Planning Formula* chart. For younger students, tell them they will hear a story about the stoplight called "Sammy Stoplight." Give them paper and color markers (or pencils or crayons) and tell them to draw a picture of "Sammy Stoplight." Explain how the stoplight on the *Cognitive Planning Formula* chart might be envisioned to grow arms and legs.

   For older students, tell them they will hear a story called "Sam and the Stoplight." Give them paper and color markers (or pencils or crayons) and tell them to draw a picture of Sam, who is a boy their age. They could also include a *Thought Bubble* with a stoplight drawn inside since the story will have Sam thinking about the stoplight.

6. Read one of the stories below, depending on the age of the students.

Sammy Stoplight
(For Younger Children)

Point to the first stoplight symbol on the *Cognitive Planning Formula* chart. Tell students you will be reading a story about Sammy Stoplight. Have them look at their pictures of Sammy Stoplight while you are reading. The story follows:

Sammy Stoplight is going to Traffic School. Sammy really wants to graduate and become a stoplight at one of the intersections in town. One day, Sammy was having trouble learning a few of the traffic rules. Some of the other stoplights teased Sammy about it. Sammy lost control and broke their lights. Afterwards, Sammy felt embarrassed about losing control and sorry about hurting the others. On his way home, Sammy stopped at a very busy intersection to talk with a wise old stoplight named Sir Sidney. After hearing about Sammy's problem, Sir Sidney Stoplight said, "You already have the solution to your problem. You're just not using it." "I do? What is it?" Sammy asked. Sir Sidney said, "At traffic school, you're learning how and when to flash your red light on the outside so traffic knows when to stop. Well, you can also flash your red light on the inside, so only you can see it.

When you have a problem and feel upset, flash your red light on the inside and think 'Stop—stay calm!' You're a smart stoplight, Sammy. If you stay calm, you can think of a good way to solve any problem." Sammy was eager to try the inside red light idea. The next day in school when Sammy was feeling frustrated, Sir Sidney's idea came to mind. Sammy tried it and it worked! Sammy started using the inside red light idea more each day. It helped Sammy use self-control and stay calm. Sammy Stoplight felt very proud!

Tell students that Sammy Stoplight can be either a girl or a boy because both girls and boys need to use self-control. Tell students that whenever they feel upset or frustrated, they can think of Sammy Stoplight. They can picture a stoplight in their minds. This will help them to stop so they can use one or more of the self-control strategies mentioned in the story about the Social Star Club.

Sam and the Stoplight
(For Older Children)

Point to the first stoplight symbol on the Cognitive Planning Formula chart. Tell students that you will be telling them a story about a boy named "Sam." The story follows:

One day when Sam was at school, he was having problems in gym class. He felt really frustrated. Some of the other kids teased Sam. Sam lost control and got into a fight with the kids. Afterwards, Sam felt embarrassed about losing control and sorry about hurting the others. On his way home from school, Sam stopped at his grandfather's house. After hearing about Sam's problem, his grandfather said, "Sam, when I'm driving in my car and I come to a signal with a red light, I know that I'm coming to a dangerous intersection. I need to STOP my car. If I don't stop, bad things could happen." Sam couldn't figure out why his grandpa was talking about driving his car. "Grandpa, what does that have to do with my problem at school?" Sam asked. Sam's grandpa said, "Well, Sam, you can use a stoplight in your head. When the red light flashes, it means, 'Stop, dangerous situation.' When you feel angry, picture a stoplight and say to yourself, 'I need to get calm. If I don't stop, something bad might happen.'" Sam's grandpa continued, "You're a smart kid, Sam. If you stop, you can stay calm and you can think of ways to solve any problem." Sam thanked his grandpa. He was eager to try the stoplight idea. The next day in school when Sam was feeling frustrated, the stoplight idea came to mind. Sam tried it and it worked. Sam started using the stoplight idea more each day. It helped Sam use self-control and stay calm. Sam felt very proud.

Tell students that all people need to use self-control. Tell students that whenever they feel upset or frustrated, they can picture a stoplight in their minds. This will help them to stop so they can use one or more of the self-control strategies mentioned in the story about the Social Star Club.

7. Model use of the cue word "stoplight" while thinking aloud. A scripted example follows:

Introduction

I am going to pretend that someone took my favorite pencil off my desk without asking. I will show you how I stop to stay calm and tell you the thoughts I'm having. When I hold up this Thought Bubble, *you'll know the words I'm saying are actually what I'm thinking.*

Actual Model

Where is my pencil? Oh, no, it's gone. I can't believe this. I am so angry! While holding up the *Thought Bubble* say, *Stoplight! OK, stay calm. Just calm down. I'll take a deep breath. I have to think of a good way to get my pencil back.*

8. Tell students that if they see someone else from their class getting frustrated or angry, they can remind the student to stay calm by quietly saying "Stoplight" to that person. When they see a classmate successfully staying calm in a difficult situation, they can also give a compliment by saying, "Good job using stoplight!"

9. Conclude the lesson by asking students to write a letter to Sammy Stoplight (or to Sam for older children). In the letter, students could say they are proud that Sammy (Sam) is using the inside red light (or stoplight) idea so successfully.

Social Star

Lesson C

OBJECTIVE:

To practice the PLOT step of the cognitive planning strategy called STOP, PLOT, GO, SO (The PLOT step involves deciding what the problem is, brainstorming choices, thinking about consequences, deciding upon the best choice to use, and thinking about social skills to use.)

MATERIALS:

1. *Cognitive Planning Formula* chart (See page 12.)
2. *PLOT: Secret Formula Part 2* (See pages 72–76; enlarge, color, and laminate, if desired, one copy of the story for educator use; as an alternative, duplicate one copy per student and let each one color the illustrations.)

PREPARATORY SET:

Direct students' attention to the STOP step on the *Cognitive Planning Formula* chart and remind them about "Sammy Stoplight" (or "Sam and the Stoplight" for older children) and the inside red light idea. Read one of the following self-control scripts to students. Some students may have a difficult time seeing "pictures" in their heads. It may be helpful to provide them with a picture of the object to be visualized (e.g., a stoplight, the number "10") before they close their eyes so that they can visualize it more easily. (There will be additional opportunities during Lesson Z of each social skill unit to choose from and to use the scripts that follow.)

Self-Control Strategies

Script #1

>*When you have a problem, you need to stay in control so you can solve it. One way to stay calm is by using positive self-talk. That means you actually tell yourself to stay calm. Let's try it now. Pretend that you are being teased on the playground. First, tell yourself "stoplight" and picture a stoplight in your mind. Then tell yourself "Stay in control. Be calm. Think of a good way to solve this problem."*

Script #2

>*When you are angry or upset, you need to be in control so you can think about how to solve your problem. When you are angry, you breathe faster. You need to slow your breathing down to stay calm. It helps to take a deep*

breath. Let's try it now. Pretend you are upset because something that's important to you got broken. First, tell yourself "stoplight" and picture a stoplight in your mind. Then breathe deeply and tell yourself to calm down. When you let the air out, pretend you are blowing bubbles or blowing on a spoon of hot soup.

Script #3

Have you ever been really angry at someone? When you feel yourself getting angry, you need to stay in control so that you don't do or say anything you'll feel bad about later. It might be helpful to put your hand over your mouth to stop yourself from saying something mean. Let's try that now. Pretend you are angry because a friend didn't keep a secret. First, tell yourself "stoplight" and picture a stoplight in your mind. Put your hand over your mouth before you say something mean.

Script #4

When you are frustrated about a problem, you need to help yourself stay in control. One way to give yourself time to stay in control is to count to 10. When you count to 10, you help your body relax so you can think clearly. Let's try that now. Pretend that you are frustrated with a homework assignment. First, tell yourself "stoplight" and picture a stoplight in your mind. Picture the number "10" in your head and count to 10. One, two, three, four, five, six, seven, eight, nine, ten. Take a deep breath.

Script #5

If you are disagreeing with a friend, you might help yourself calm down if you walk away. Let's try it now. First, tell yourself "stoplight" and picture a stoplight in your mind. Picture yourself walking away so you don't say or do something mean. It might be easier to calm down if you are away from the situation. After you have calmed down, you can go back and talk with your friend. Be careful, though. You might get in trouble if you walk away from a parent, teacher, or other adult.

Script #6

When you feel yourself getting upset, stay calm so you can think clearly. First, tell yourself "stoplight" and picture a stoplight in your mind. Now, think of a time when something funny happened to you and you couldn't stop laughing. When you do this, you should immediately feel less angry. This will help you stay calm so that you can solve your problem.

PLAN:

1. Tell students that they will be listening to a story about Mike and how he uses PLOT to solve a problem.

2. Read *PLOT: Secret Formula Part 2* to the class. Stop to interact directly with students when a star appears in the book.

3. After reading the story, direct students' attention to the *Cognitive Planning Formula* chart and review the five steps to PLOT. (PLOT is the most complex component of the cognitive planning strategy because it involves five steps.)

4. Lead students to understand they have more than one choice in most situations. Some students tend to view themselves as having only one choice and, unfortunately, their choice may be a negative one (e.g., when Billy is teased, he may feel that his only choice is to be physically aggressive).

   Ask students to work in pairs to brainstorm at least three choices they could make in each of the following problem situations:

   - You are told to bring a sack lunch for a field trip and you forget to bring one.
   - You spill your milk all over your pants during lunch at school.
   - Your neighbor compliments you on your bike safety and you're not sure what to say or do.
   - You are walking on the sidewalk and an older kid purposely bumps into you.

   Ask each pair to share one of their choices for each situation and record ideas where everyone can see them. Discuss possible consequences for a few of the choices listed.

5. Process the information provided in the story by asking the following questions:

   - Why is it important to know what your problem is?
   - Why is it helpful to brainstorm choices?
   - Why would you want to think ahead about what might happen after each of your choices?
   - How can you tell what your best choice is?
   - Why should you think about social skills when you go ahead and use your best choice?
   - Have you ever had a problem that you had to think about? What strategies did you use to solve your problem?
   - How do you think PLOT could help with a problem you might have?

Cognitive Planning

Lesson D

OBJECTIVE:

To practice the GO step of the cognitive planning strategy called STOP, PLOT, GO, SO (The GO step means putting a plan into action.)

MATERIALS:

1. *Cognitive Planning Formula* chart (See page 12.)

2. *GO: Secret Formula Part 3* (See pages 77–79; enlarge, color, and laminate, if desired, one copy of the story for educator use; as an alternative, duplicate one copy per student and let each one color the illustrations.)

3. *Thought Bubble* (See *Appendix O;* one per pair of students.)

PREPARATORY SET:

Direct students' attention to the *Cognitive Planning Formula* chart and quickly review the STOP and PLOT steps. (Mention "Sammy Stoplight" or "Sam and the Stoplight" and the inside red light idea.) Remind students that they have a variety of choices for any given situation.

PLAN:

1. Tell students that they will be listening to a story about Mike and how he uses the GO step.

2. Read *GO: Secret Formula Part 3* to students.

3. Discuss why it is sometimes difficult to carry out the GO step (e.g., too scared, too embarrassed, it feels strange) even when one has decided on the best choice.

4. Process the information provided in the story by asking students the following questions:

   • Have you ever thought of a good idea, but had a difficult time actually doing it?

   • What are some things you can say to yourself so that you carry out your plan?

5. Read the following situation:

One day after school, Mike saw a student throw a rock and break a school window. Mike thought "stoplight" and pictured a stoplight in his head. He

51

stayed calm and thought about the choices he had. He decided that his best choice was to tell his teacher about what he saw. The next day, Mike got stuck on the GO step from the secret formula. When it was time to carry out his plan, he was having a difficult time actually telling his teacher.

6. Discuss why Mike might have had a difficult time with the GO step (e.g., he's afraid the other student might find out he told; he's afraid people will call him a tattletale).

7. Pair students (see *Appendix P*). Distribute a *Thought Bubble* to each pair. Ask students to work with their partners to write self-talk in their *Thought Bubbles* that Mike could have used to put his plan into action.

Cognitive Planning

Lesson E

OBJECTIVES:

1. To practice the SO step of the cognitive planning strategy called STOP, PLOT, GO, SO (The SO step means asking yourself, "So, how did my plan work?")
2. To review the four steps of cognitive planning during a game activity

MATERIALS:

1. *Cognitive Planning Formula* chart (See page 12.)
2. *SO: Secret Formula Part 4* (See pages 80–87; enlarge, color, and laminate, if desired, one copy of the story for educator use; as an alternative, duplicate one copy per student and let each one color the illustrations.)
3. *Cue Cards* (See page 56; one set cut apart.)
4. *Problem Situations* (See page 57; one set cut apart.)
5. *Score Card* (See page 58; one per student.)

PREPARATORY SET:

Students need to internalize the phrase STOP, PLOT, GO, SO so when they are actually in a problem situation, they can recall the steps. The "Beat the Clock" activities that follow review the phrase. Choose one or more to try. (There will be additional opportunities to use these activities during Lesson Z of each social skill unit.)

Beat the Clock Activities

- Have students stay seated. Go around the room in round robin fashion and have each person say in order one of the words STOP, PLOT, GO, SO. See how many times they can go around the room in one minute.

- Have students say STOP, PLOT, GO, SO quietly to themselves. Each time students finish saying the phrase, they should put a tally mark on a piece of paper. Students could see how many times they can say the words in 30 seconds.

- Have students form small groups and stand in lines facing the front of the room. When the educator says "begin," the first student from each group writes STOP on the chalkboard, runs back, and stands at the back of the line. The next member of the small group then runs up and writes PLOT on the chalkboard, and so on in relay fashion. See how many complete phrases each group can write in two minutes.

Social Star

- Have students form a circle and then pass a ball around the circle. The first person starts out saying STOP and then passes the ball to the next person who says PLOT, etc. The group tries to pass the ball around the entire circle as many times as they can in one minute.

PLAN:

1. Read *SO: Secret Formula Part 4* to students. Stop to interact directly with students when a star appears in the story.

2. After reading the story, process the information provided by asking students the following questions:
    - Do you ever think about things after you do them? Why might it be a good idea to do this?
    - Have you ever heard the saying "Learn from your mistakes"? What does this have to do with the SO step?
    - Why is it important to tell yourself you've done a good job when you do something right?

3. Present students with the following list of reasons a person's plan may not work. Encourage students to add to the list.
    - Didn't stay calm and in control
    - Didn't use an appropriate tone of voice during GO
    - Didn't choose an appropriate time and place for GO
    - Didn't think about the possible consequences of a choice

    The list can be displayed and added to as new reasons come to mind.

4. Model phrases the students can use to praise themselves when things have gone well. Make the model exciting and somewhat exaggerated (e.g., "Hey, way to go. I did an absolutely fantastic job talking with Mr. Bill! Marvelous!").

5. Ask students to participate in several activities at which they can be successful (e.g., jumping rope, skipping around the room, drawing 10 circles). After each activity, invite students to praise themselves. Tell them that for now you'd like them to praise themselves aloud but that normally they would do it quietly inside of their heads.

6. Tell students they will be playing a game of "Problem-Solving Softball" to practice using the STOP, PLOT, GO, SO steps.

7. Ask for six volunteers to fill the following positions: batter, pitcher, first base player, second base player, third base player, and catcher. Have the volunteers stand in an actual softball formation. All volunteers, except for the batter, will be asked to read from *Cue Cards*. You may need to assist with the reading.

- Give the stack of *Problem Situations* to the pitcher.
- Give Cue Card #1 to the first base player.
- Give Cue Card #2 to the second base player.
- Give Cue Card #3 to the third base player.
- Give Cue Card #4 to the catcher.

Explain that to score a run for the class, the batter must correctly follow the secret formula to solve a problem which will be described by the pitcher.

8. Distribute *Score Cards* to the remaining students. Explain that they are the fans.

9. The pitcher draws one of the *Problem Situations* and reads it aloud to the batter. The batter waits to advance to first base.

10. The first base player reads the "STOP means..." statement and any one of the four instructions printed on Cue Card #1 to the batter. If the batter is unable to follow the instruction, other members from the class may offer help or suggestions. The batter must, however, answer in his or her own words or actions after receiving help. After the batter has followed the instruction, the fans write a "1" on the first base of their *Score Cards* (indicating that batter #1 completed that step) while the batter advances to first base.

11. The second base player reads the "PLOT means..." statement and asks the batter all four questions (one at a time) printed on Cue Card #2. After the batter has answered all four questions, the fans write a "1" on the second base of their *Score Cards* while the batter advances to second base.

12. The third base player reads the "GO means..." statement and the instruction printed on Cue Card #3 to the batter. After the batter has followed the instruction, the fans write a "1" on the third base of their *Score Cards* while the batter advances to third base.

13. The catcher reads the "SO means..." statement and asks the batter both questions (one at a time) printed on Cue Card #4. After the batter has answered the questions, the fans write a "1" on the home plate of their *Score Cards* while the batter advances to home base.

14. Depending on class size, participants can be asked to rotate positions, or six new volunteers can take the positions described in step 7. For smaller groups, you can take the role of several positions.

15. The pitcher reads a new problem situation to the second batter, and play proceeds in the same manner as above, only fans write a "2" on their *Score Cards*.

16. Continue the activity until everyone in the group has had a chance to play one or more "parts" in the softball game. You may wish to continue this activity during the next class session. In addition, students may wish to develop their own problem situations for use in the game.

CUE CARDS

Cue Card #1

STOP: Secret Formula Part 1

STOP means stay calm and use self-control.

What can you say to tell yourself to stop and stay calm.

-or-

Show how to take slow deep breaths to stay calm.

-or-

Show how to count to 10 to stay calm.

-or-

Show how to put your hand over your mouth to stay calm.

Go to First Base.

Cue Card #2

PLOT: Secret Formula Part 2

PLOT means you plan how to solve your problem.

What is your problem?

-then-

What are at least two choices you have?

-then-

What might happen after each choice?

-then-

Which choice do you think will work best?

Go to Second Base.

Cue Card #3

GO: Secret Formula Part 3

GO means go ahead and do what you decided to do.

Tell what you can say to get yourself to go ahead and do what you decided to do.

Go to Third Base.

Cue Card #4

SO: Secret Formula Part 4

SO means you ask yourself, "So, how did my plan work?"

Pretend your plan worked well. What can you say to praise yourself?

-then-

Pretend your plan didn't work well. What should you do?

*Good Job! Go to Home Plate.
You scored 1 run.*

PROBLEM SITUATIONS

Problem Situation #1

You are told to bring a sack lunch for a field trip and forget to bring one.

Start the secret formula now.

Problem Situation #2

You spill your milk all over your pants during lunch at school.

Start the secret formula now.

Problem Situation #3

Your neighbor compliments you on your bike safety and you're not sure what to say or do.

Start the secret formula now.

Problem Situation #4

You are walking on the sidewalk and an older kid purposely bumps into you.

Start the secret formula now.

Social Star

Name _____

SCORE CARD

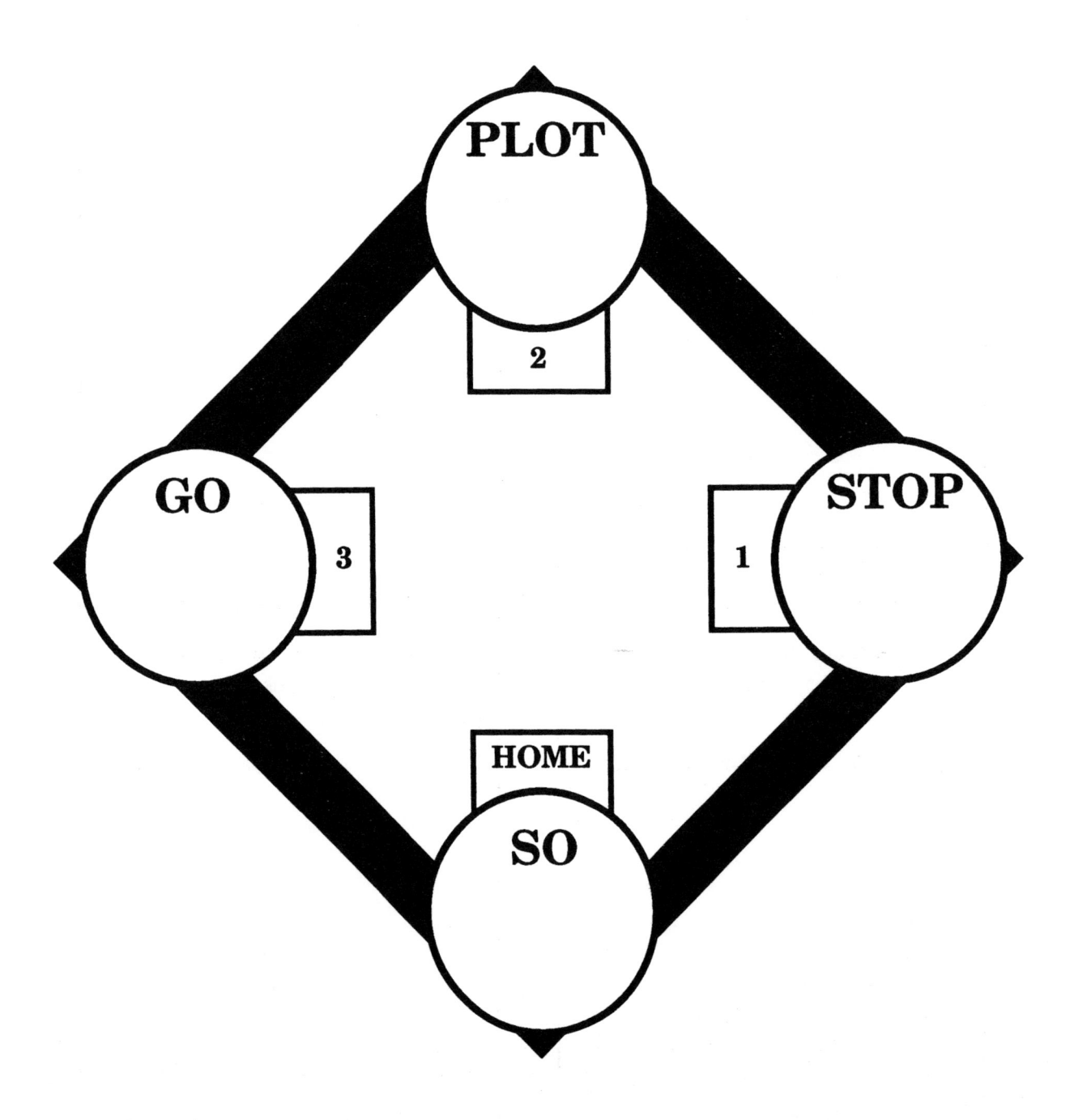

- PLOT — 2
- STOP — 1
- GO — 3
- SO — HOME

© 1994 Thinking Publications — 58 — *Duplication permitted for educational use only.*

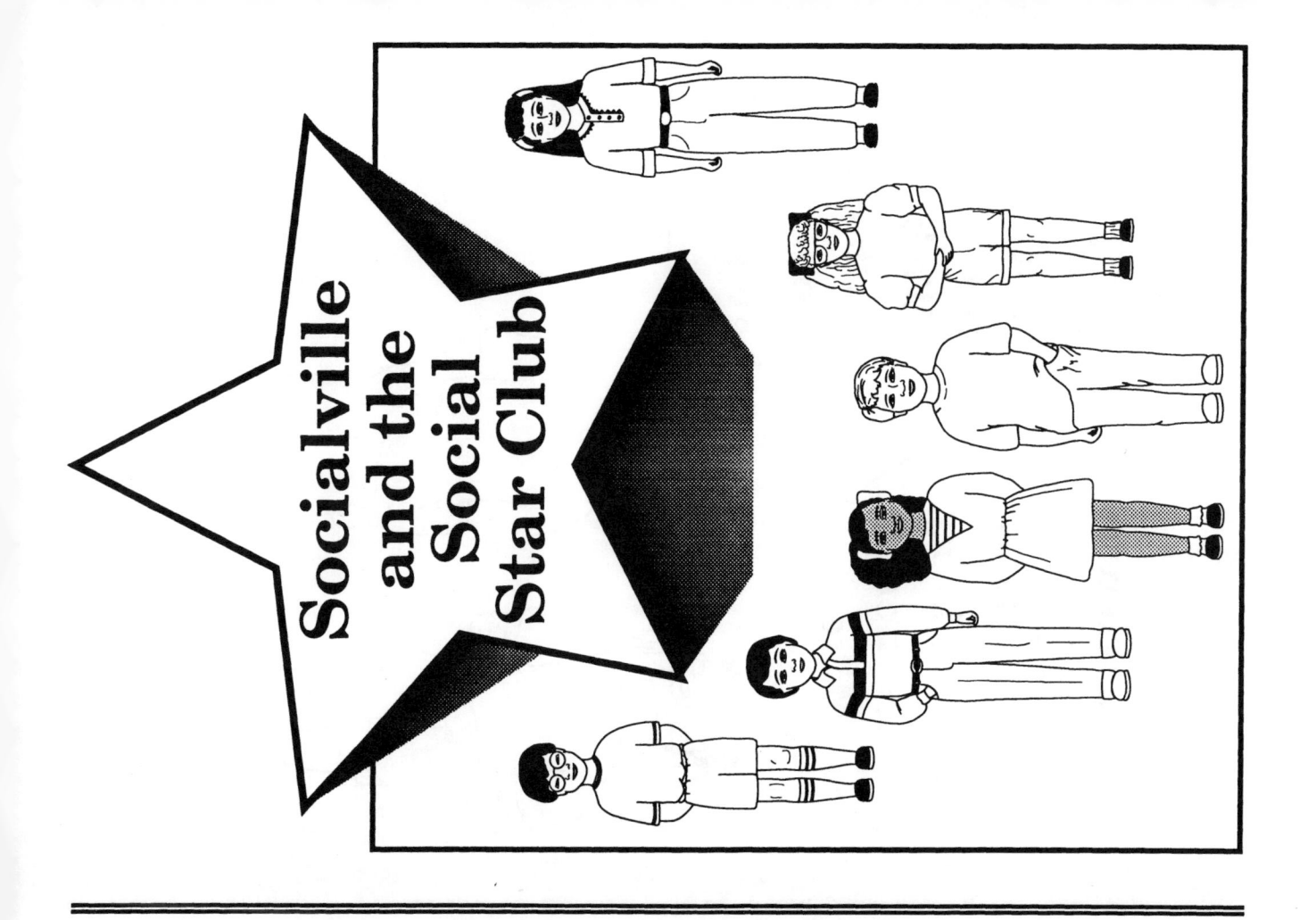

Socialville and the Social Star Club

Hi! Nice to meet you. We live with our mom and stepdad.

Hi! We're friends of Lee. My name is Ann Olson and this is my brother Mike.

Hi! I'm Lee Vue. I live in Socialville and I go to McKinley School. I want you to meet some friends who go to school with me.

Hello!
I'm Mrs.
Jackson.
I'm Mike
and Ann's
mom.
And
I'm Mr.
Jackson.
We're
happy to
meet you!
Our mom works
at the Good Meals—
Good Manners Restaurant.
Our stepdad works at the
Get Along Toy Factory.
He works with Mr. Parra,
Maria and Victor's dad.
You'll meet them next.

Hello! Nice to meet you!
I'm Mr. Parra. This is my wife,
Mrs. Parra, and these are our
children, Victor and Maria. We enjoy
living in Socialville, because
everyone always gets along.

Hi! My name is Jolisa. This is my mom and dad. My dad is the head of the Socialville Parks Department. Sometimes, I visit him at the park. My mom is a tutor at our school, so I really have to be good when she is around! Has Lee introduced you to his family yet?

Well, Mr. Parra's not totally right! We don't *always* get along, but we do our best! Mr. Parra is nice and so is Mrs. Parra! Actually, I call her Dr. Parra, because she's my doctor. She works at the Helping Hands Clinic. Next, I'd like you to meet the Walkers.

I bet you've been wondering about my family! This is my dad. He builds great houses! And this is my grandmother. She lives with my dad and me. She is a cook at our school. The kids at school really like her!

The six of us have joined a club at school called the Social Star Club. Our teachers, Ms. Hess, Mr. Aaron, and Mrs. Marrero, are the club advisors. Can you guess what we talk about in our club? ☆

Wow! It sounds like you already know a lot about getting along with other people! Maybe you could start your own Social Star Club at your school. You'll be hearing more about our club! Well, I've got to go—my grandmother is calling! Bye!

Those were good guesses! In our club, we learn how to get along better with other people so our school, our town, and our whole world can be better! We talk about using appropriate manners and having appropriate behavior. Can you think of some ways to get along with other people? ☆

OUR CLUB

STOP: Secret Formula Part 1

It's called:

SECRET FORMULA

STOP **PLOT**

GO **SO**

Let's all say it:
STOP, PLOT, GO, SO....
STOP, PLOT, GO, SO....
It's kind of catchy!

15

Hi everybody!
Welcome to our
Social Star Club!
We talk about how to get along
with other people. It's a lot of
fun! We have a secret formula
we use to help us
solve problems. It's our
problem-solving
strategy!

14

© 1994 Thinking Publications   66   *Duplication permitted for educational use only.*

STOP

means you STOP to stay calm and use self-control.

Do you know what *self-control* means?☆

Lots of things can happen if you don't STOP to stay calm and use self-control! It's not good to be out of control! It can be embarrassing and it can get you into trouble!

You could say something mean like...

I hate you!

What other things might people do or say if they are out of control?☆

"My parents taught me how to take deep breaths to stay calm. It really works!"

"I breathe in deeply through my nose and I let the air out slowly through my mouth. I pretend I'm blowing bubbles or blowing on a spoon of hot soup. Try it a few times now. ☆ Taking deep breaths helps me relax my whole body so I can stay in control and get along better with people—even my brother, Victor."

19

"To stay calm, the first thing I do is tell myself to STOP and think... Stay calm! That helps me stay in control so I don't do something crazy!"

"Hey! Why don't you try it now? Think, "STOP! Stay calm!" ☆"

18

© 1994 Thinking Publications · 68 · Duplication permitted for educational use only.

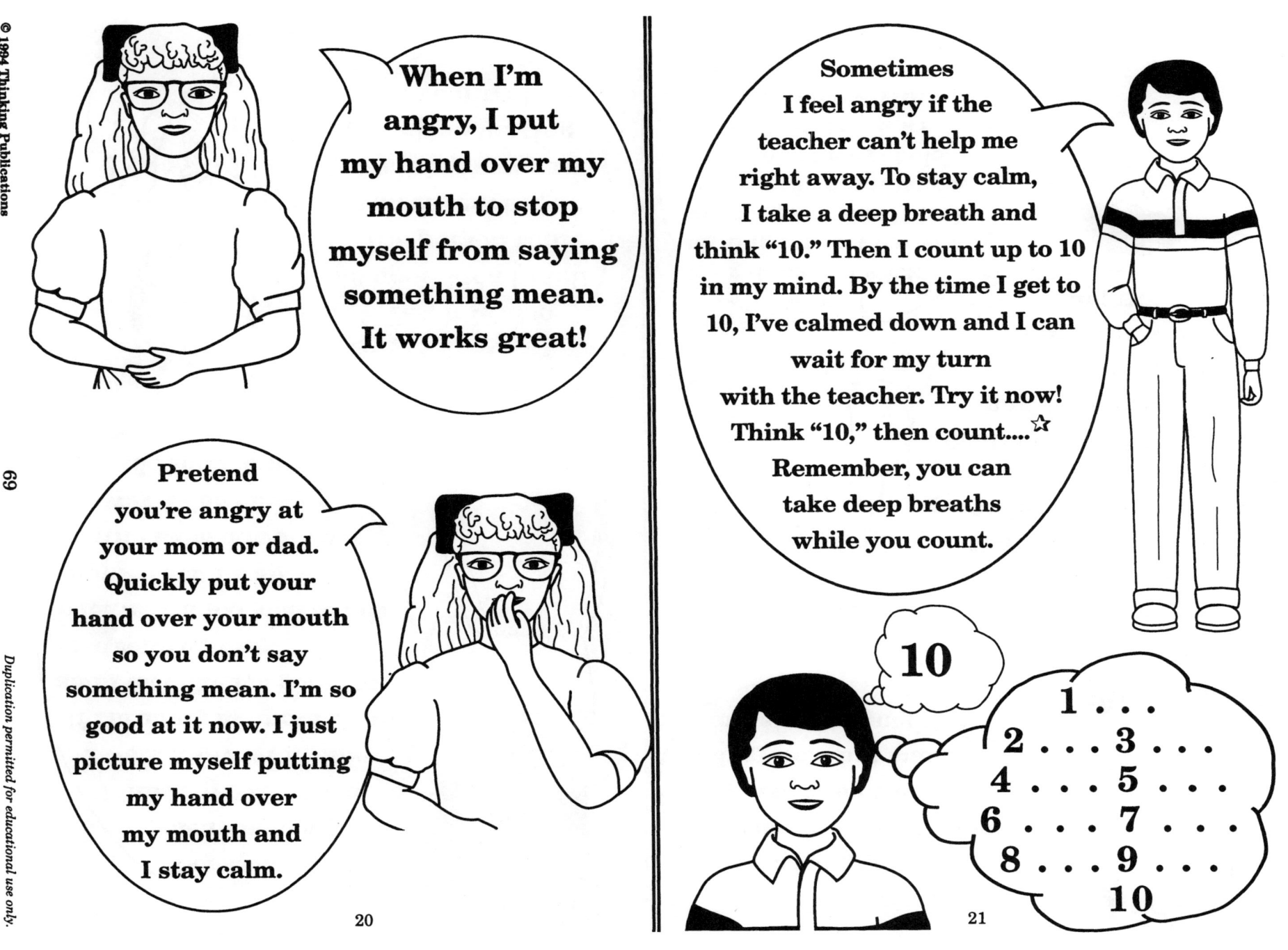

Sometimes I feel angry if the teacher can't help me right away. To stay calm, I take a deep breath and think "10." Then I count up to 10 in my mind. By the time I get to 10, I've calmed down and I can wait for my turn with the teacher. Try it now! Think "10," then count.... Remember, you can take deep breaths while you count.

When I'm angry, I put my hand over my mouth to stop myself from saying something mean. It works great!

Pretend you're angry at your mom or dad. Quickly put your hand over your mouth so you don't say something mean. I'm so good at it now. I just picture myself putting my hand over my mouth and I stay calm.

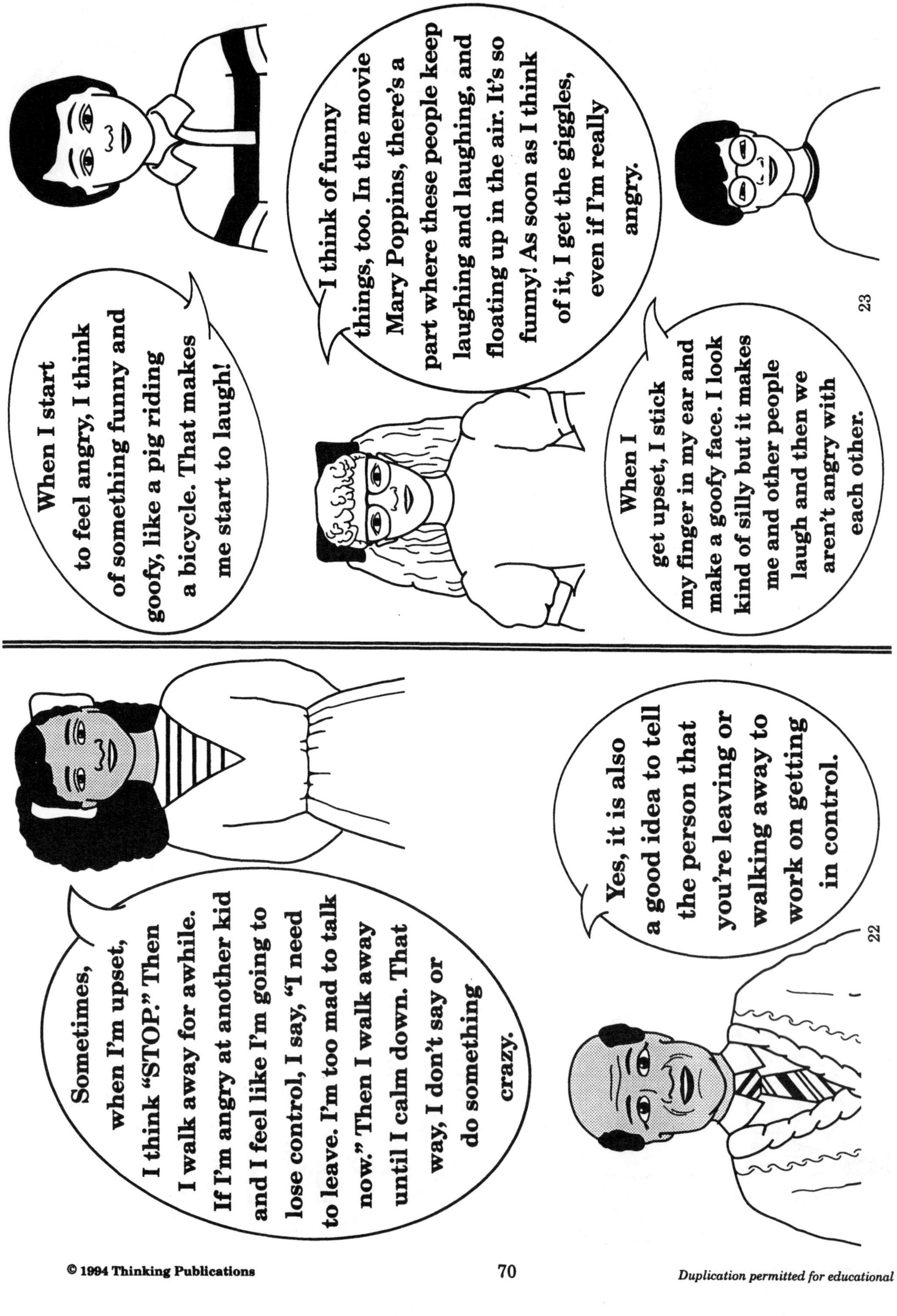

"I think of funny things, too. In the movie Mary Poppins, there's a part where these people keep laughing and laughing, and floating up in the air. It's so funny! As soon as I think of it, I get the giggles, even if I'm really angry."

"When I start to feel angry, I think of something funny and goofy, like a pig riding a bicycle. That makes me start to laugh!"

"When I get upset, I stick my finger in my ear and make a goofy face. I look kind of silly but it makes me and other people laugh and then we aren't angry with each other."

"Yes, it is also a good idea to tell the person that you're leaving or walking away to work on getting in control."

"Sometimes, when I'm upset, I think "STOP." Then I walk away for awhile. If I'm angry at another kid and I feel like I'm going to lose control, I say, "I need to leave. I'm too mad to talk now." Then I walk away until I calm down. That way, I don't say or do something crazy."

© 1994 Thinking Publications

70

Duplication permitted for educational use only.

"Hey, those sound like great ways to stay calm when you're angry. I'm going to use those ideas myself. Let's see . . . you just gave me six ideas. What were some of those ideas again?☆"

To stay in control when you have a problem, you can:

1. Tell yourself to STOP and stay calm.
2. Take a deep breath and relax your body.
3. Put your hand over your mouth.
4. Think "10" and count to 10.
5. Walk away to calm down.
6. Think about something funny.

Can you think of other ways to STOP and stay calm?☆

Keep practicing these ideas and you'll get better at using them.

PLOT: Secret Formula Part 2

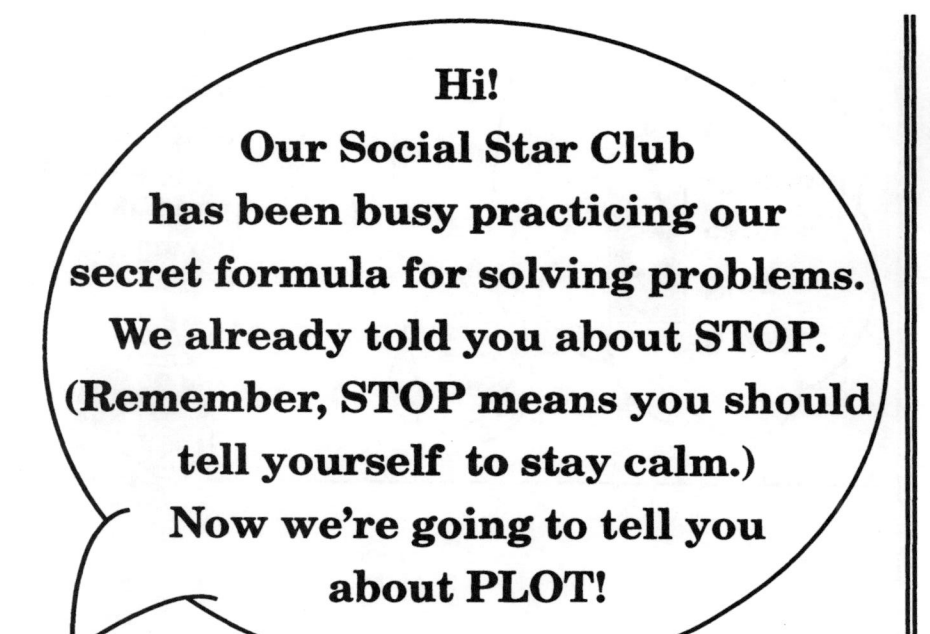

Hi!

Our Social Star Club has been busy practicing our secret formula for solving problems. We already told you about STOP. (Remember, STOP means you should tell yourself to stay calm.) Now we're going to tell you about PLOT!

STOP

PLOT

GO

SO

PLOT means you plot a plan to solve your problem.

When you PLOT you:

1. Decide exactly what your problem is.
2. Brainstorm the choices you have.
3. Think about what might happen after each of these choices (consequences).
4. Pick a choice you think will help solve the problem.
5. Think about the social skills you will need to use.

This is the symbol for PLOT. It reminds me that when I have a problem, I can go in different directions. (I have different choices to solve the problem.)

© 1994 Thinking Publications — Duplication permitted for educational use only.

PLOT

To help you understand PLOT, I'd like to tell you about a problem Mike had.

Mike, you'll need to fix this paper before you can have free time!

STOP... Stay calm... I'll count to 10....

Mike felt angry, but he reminded himself to STOP and stay calm.

Mike knew he should use PLOT in this situation.

I used STOP to calm myself down. Now I have to PLOT.

What is my problem? I don't want to fix this paper, but I'd like to have free time.

First, Mike decided exactly what his problem was.

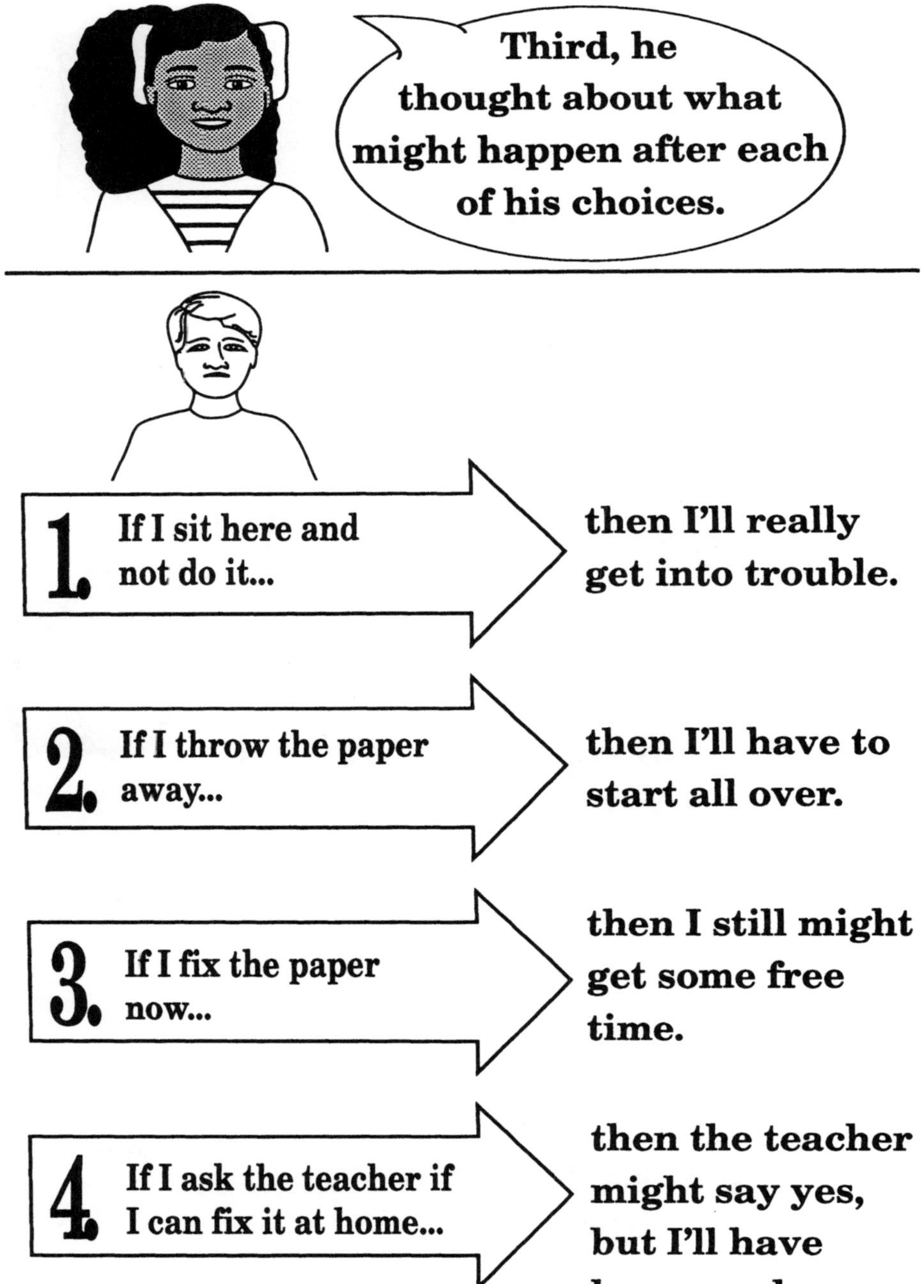

Third, he thought about what might happen after each of his choices.

1. If I sit here and not do it... ⬆ then I'll really get into trouble.

2. If I throw the paper away... ⬆ then I'll have to start all over.

3. If I fix the paper now... ⬆ then I still might get some free time.

4. If I ask the teacher if I can fix it at home... ⬆ then the teacher might say yes, but I'll have homework.

Second, he decided what some of his choices were.

What are my choices?
1. I can sit here and not do it.
2. I can throw the dumb paper away.
3. I can fix it right away.
4. I can ask the teacher if I can fix it tonight at home.

© 1994 Thinking Publications   75   *Duplication permitted for educational use only.*

Fourth, Mike decided which choice was best.

I think I'll fix the paper now. Then I won't have to worry about doing it tonight. Maybe I can still have some free time.

Last, Mike thought about what social skills to use.

I won't pout while I'm working. I'll use an appropriate facial expression.

We all think Mike did a great job using the five parts of PLOT!

Can you remember what they are? ☆ You already know the first half of our secret formula. Before we teach you the second half of the formula, you can start using STOP and PLOT when you are at home, at school, and with your friends. Good luck!

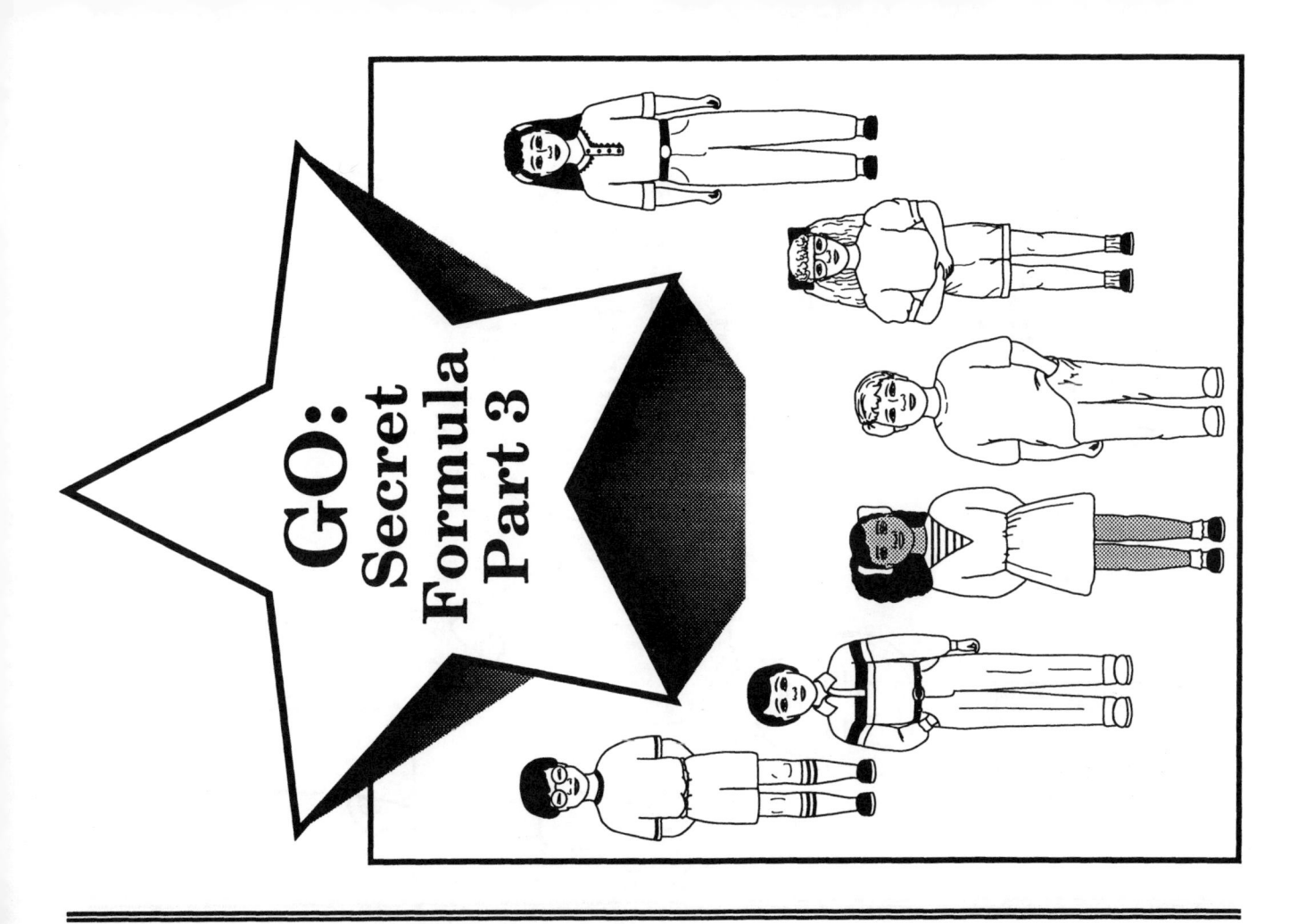

GO: Secret Formula Part 3

77

© 1994 Thinking Publications

Duplication permitted for educational use only.

GO

means you go ahead and do what you decided to do.

> That's so you don't just think about it. You actually do it.

> Can you remember our secret formula? I can! STOP, PLOT, GO, SO; STOP, PLOT, GO, SO; STOP, PLOT, GO! I'm going to tell you about GO! But first, let's review STOP and PLOT. STOP means you stay calm. PLOT means you plan what you will do.

Remember when Ms. Hess asked me to fix my paper before I could have free time at school? I used STOP and told myself to calm down. I used PLOT and decided to fix my paper.

When I followed the GO step of the secret formula, I actually did what I decided to do. Here's a picture of me fixing my paper.

REMEMBER....
GO means that you go ahead and carry out your plan. If you think it is going to be too hard, tell yourself, "I can do it!"

You only have one more part of the secret formula to learn. It's called SO. We'll talk about SO next time.

STOP | PLOT
GO | SO

SO: Secret Formula Part 4

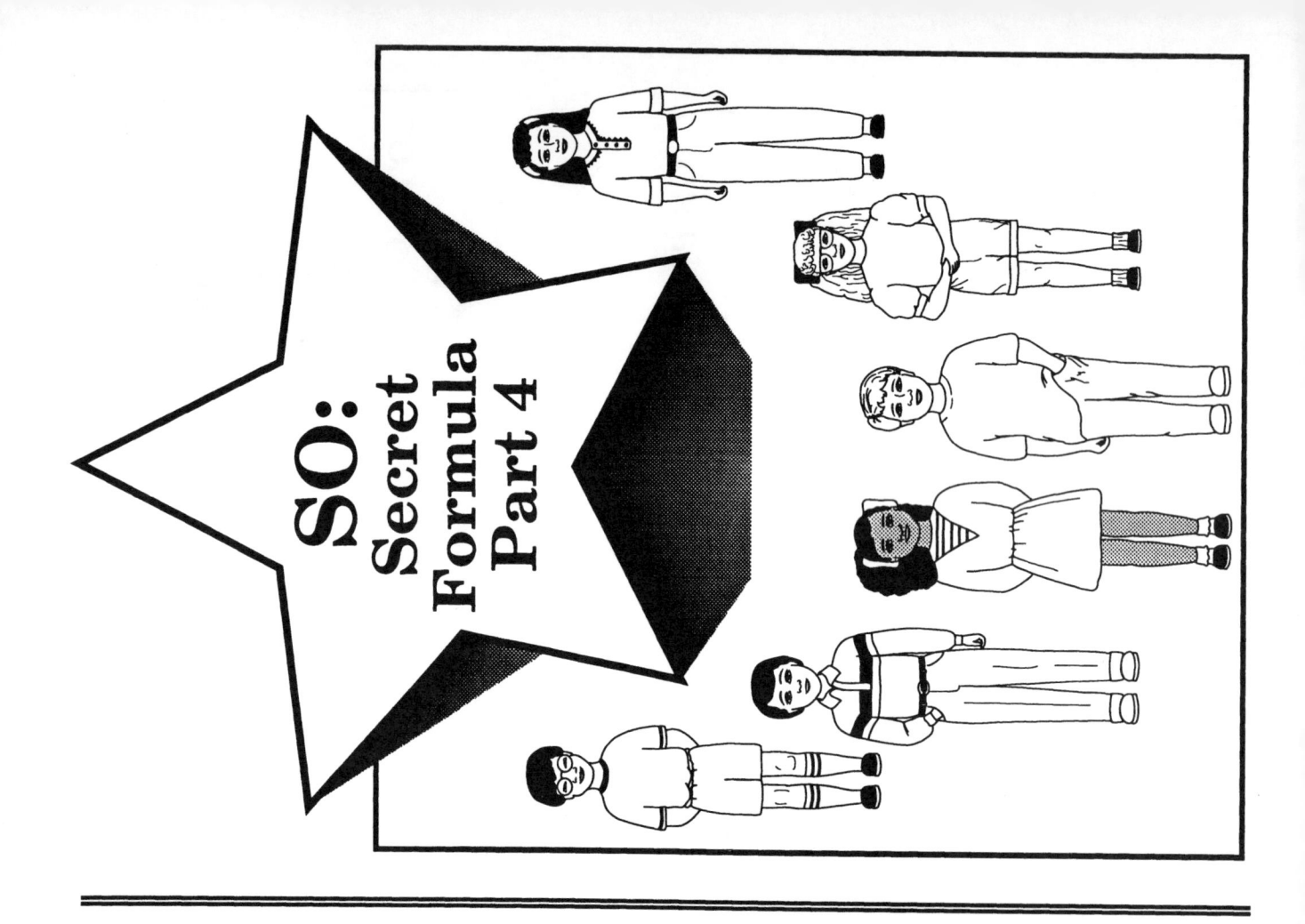

SO means you ask yourself, "So, how did my plan work?"

A question mark is used for this step, because during SO, you ask yourself a question.

What question do you ask yourself? ☆

STOP ✛ **PLOT** ? **GO** SO

Hi! Let's all whisper our secret formula for solving problems five times.... ☆
Can you remember what STOP, PLOT, and GO mean? ☆
Now we're going to tell you about the last step called SO.
Later you can come to an awards ceremony at our Social Star Club.

© 1994 Thinking Publications — Duplication permitted for educational use only.

Praising yourself means telling yourself you did a good job. You could say, "I did great solving my problem." What are some other things you could say to yourself when you make a plan that works well? ☆

47

When you ask yourself, "So, how did my plan work?" you'll either decide that it worked well or that it didn't work well. If you decide your plan worked well, you made a good choice. That's a good time to praise yourself.

SO?

Plan worked well → ← Plan didn't work well

Plan worked well → Praise Yourself

46

STOP, PLOT, GO, SO.

SO is SO, SO, SO important!

It's time for the awards ceremony at our Social Star Club. Mike and Maria are receiving awards today, because they used the secret formula in a real-life situation. You'll find out how they used STOP, PLOT, GO, and SO.

When I first learned about SO, I asked, "Why should I praise myself? Shouldn't I just wait for someone else to praise me for making a good plan?"

I like it when someone else praises me, but I found out I can't always count on other people to notice my good choice or to remember to praise me. I can count on myself though... and besides, it feels good when I say something nice to myself!

"Mike, you told us about using STOP, PLOT, and GO when Ms. Hess asked you to fix your paper before getting free time. Your plan was to fix your paper right away. Please tell us how you used SO in this situation."

"When I asked myself, 'So, how did my plan work?' I decided it worked great! I fixed my paper right away and still had a few minutes left for free time."

"Excellent, Mike! On behalf of the Social Star Club, we'd like to present you with this Social Super Star badge for successfully using the secret formula in your life."

Social Super Star
Mike
Olson

Maria, can you tell us how you used STOP, PLOT, GO, and SO?

Sure! Yesterday, I was leaving to go to Jolisa's house when my mom told me to clean my room first. During STOP, I took three deep breaths. When I PLOTTED, I decided to ask if I could pick up my room right away but wait to dust and vacuum until after I got home.

52

During GO, I went ahead and asked my mom using a nice tone of voice. During SO, I decided my choice worked well because my mom said OK. I told myself, "Great job, Maria!"

Maria, I'm glad you praised yourself during SO. Our Social Star Club would like you to keep this Social Super Star badge as a reminder of how well you used STOP, PLOT, GO, and SO.

53

"One of my plans didn't work very well for me last week. I borrowed Lee's video game and accidentally broke it. I used the secret formula to solve the problem. During PLOT, I decided to keep telling Lee I left it at home. But then Lee said he would come over to my house to get it. My plan didn't work very well. I think I should have picked a different choice. I should have told the truth right away!"

"That concludes our awards ceremony. Do you have anything you want to ask or talk about?"

"During the SO step, what if you decide your plan didn't work very well?"

"Good question, Jolisa! If you decide your plan didn't work very well, you may need to use STOP again so you don't get upset. When your choice doesn't work well, you need to decide what you'll do differently next time."

Plan went well → Praise

SO?

Plan didn't work well → What can I do differently next time?

© 1994 Thinking Publications — 86 — *Duplication permitted for educational use only.*

STOP, PLOT, GO, SO...

Use it when you're in a bind, and hopefully you will find that things are easier every day when you pick the best to do and say!

Let's hear it for the secret formula.

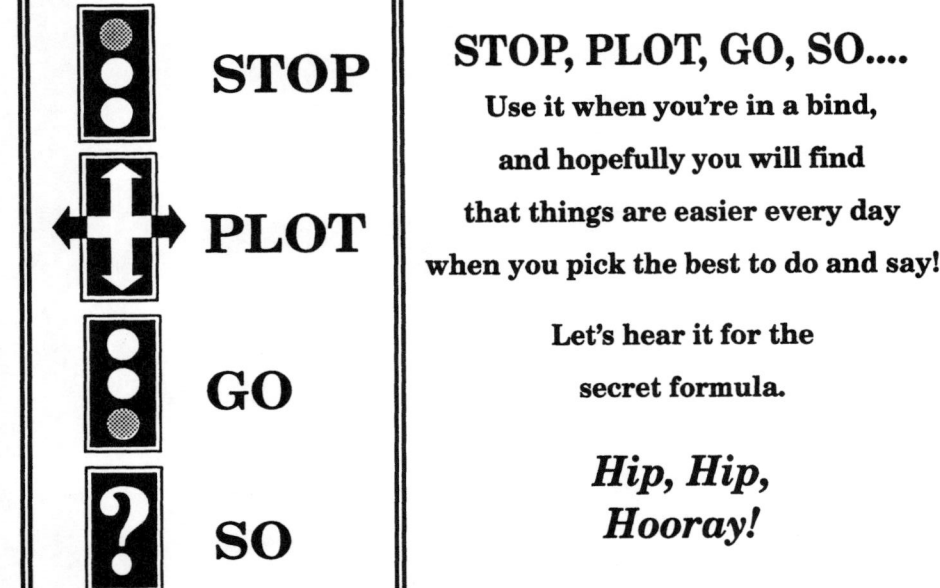

Hip, Hip, Hooray!

SECRET FORMULA
- STOP
- PLOT
- GO
- SO

Mike, you did a great job deciding what you'd do differently next time. You can praise yourself for that.

STOP, PLOT, GO, SO won't always work perfectly, but don't give up using it. When your choice doesn't work well, ask yourself what you would do differently next time.

Body Talk Summary

In each unit of *Social Star,* the symbol for the skill called *body talk* is incorporated in the skill step section. "Body talk" is a term used to describe various components of the human body which can be used in different ways to communicate a variety of messages. The students are reminded that it is important to demonstrate appropriate body talk in conjunction with each individual skill.

Body Talk is addressed in detail as an individual unit in *Social Star: General Interaction Skills (Book 1)*. It emphasizes that students have control over their own bodies and helps students recognize that there are times when they need to demonstrate self-control with their bodies. The unit emphasizes the following body-talk components: eye contact, facial expression, posture, personal space, hygiene, volume, tone of voice, body movements, breathing, and speed of movements. These components (except for body movements, breathing, and speed of movements) are also units in and of themselves within *Social Star (Book 1)*. Though it is not necessary that the *Body Talk* unit be taught in its entirety before teaching the units in *Social Star (Book 2)*, the educator should ensure that students have a basic understanding of the term and its components. The educator is reminded to exert sensitivity and care in generalizing rules about body talk into the children's home cultures.

Optimism

Social Star

UNIT GOAL:

To demonstrate comprehension and use of strategies for developing optimism

EDUCATOR INFORMATION:

1. Optimistic people tend to interact positively with others. Students who are "positive, self-confident, attentive, approving, encouraging, and pleasant are more likely to be accepted" (Stainback and Stainback, 1987, p. 139). A positive relationship exists between the number of positive behaviors demonstrated to peers and the level of positive behaviors received back from peers (Charlesworth and Hartup, 1967). In addition, Evans (1989) reports that positive interactions tend to increase a student's level of self-esteem and self-confidence.

2. The latest research on optimism indicates that the difference between optimistic thinking and pessimistic thinking is more subtle than previously believed (Seligman 1990). Traditionally, optimists have been stereotyped as taking a "look on the bright side" approach even in the gloomiest of situations. Martin Seligman (1990), one of the world's experts on optimism, has identified subtle differences in the way optimists and pessimists explain life events. Seligman asserts that our "explanatory style" is the basis for whether we view the world optimistically or pessimistically. He describes the three crucial dimensions to explanatory style as being permanence, pervasiveness, and personalization. Optimistic thinkers understand that "bad" events are *not* personal, pervasive, or permanent. Examples are provided below.

Permanence

Permanent	*Temporary*
I'll never learn my math facts. (pessimistic)	I'm not doing very good on my facts today. (optimistic)
I always have good behavior during class. (optimistic)	I had good behavior in class today. (pessimistic)

Pervasiveness

Universal	*Specific*
My dad hates me. (pessimistic)	My dad is angry because I wrecked his power drill. (optimistic)
I am so lucky. (optimistic)	I was lucky today when we were playing ball. (pessimistic)

Personalization

Internal	*External*
I can't write very well. (pessimistic)	The assignment the teacher gave us is hard. (optimistic)
I did well on the quiz because I studied. (optimistic)	That was an easy test. (pessimistic)

3. *Learned Optimism* (Seligman, 1990) includes a test to measure children's explanatory style, called the *Children's Attributional Style Questionnaire (CASQ)*. The *CASQ* is appropriate for children ages 8 to 13. (His book includes another questionnaire for people over 13.) Seligman goes beyond merely identifying differences between optimistic and pessimistic thinking. He provides a detailed step-by-step approach (the ABCDE method) for overcoming pessimism and the depression that can accompany negative thoughts. Consider using the *CASQ* with your students.

4. The differences between Seligman's explanatory styles are sometimes subtle on the *CASQ*. Much more obvious examples of his explanatory styles have been built into the unit, but students are never asked to differentiate among the three dimensions of permanence, pervasiveness, and personalization. They are, however, asked to differentiate between optimism and pessimism.

5. This unit teaches students the power of thinking optimistically. The unit uses the metaphor of a brain voice to describe self-talk. Children learn the importance of choosing positive self-talk to think optimistically. The educator should exert sensitivity and care in generalizing rules about optimism into the children's home cultures.

RELATED ACTIVITIES:

1. Adopt a schoolwide philosophy of promoting a positive attitude. A program called *The Power of Positive Students (POPS)* assists all individuals in acquiring positive attitudes, life skills, and feelings of self-worth. The *POPS* program is systematic and involves everyone, not just a select few. The program is built around having a positive *POPS* theme every month. For more information, contact:

   The *Power of Positive Students (POPS)* International Foundation
   Dr. William Mitchell, President
   4325 Dick Pond Road
   Myrtle Beach, SC 29575
   (803) 650-7677

2. Have students keep journals of their thoughts for three days. Have them analyze their journals to determine whether their thoughts are mostly positive or negative. Have students keep journals of the comments other people make to them and then analyze those comments to determine whether they are mostly

positive or negative. Meet individually with students to review the findings in their journals.

3. Have students create a song or rap that deals with optimism and positive thinking.

4. Give students a list of positive quotes or idioms (e.g., "Every cloud has a silver lining"). Discuss what the quotes mean and have students make positive-quote posters to hang around the school.

5. Have students make large suns, stars, rainbows, or smile faces with positive sayings on them and then deliver them to a hospital, nursing home, or mental health facility.

6. Have students choose several television characters and analyze whether they seem to be optimists or pessimists. Ask students to identify their feelings about the various characters.

7. Have students create a puppet show about positive thinking and present it to another class.

8. Research how the brain works and how we are able to send messages to ourselves through our synapses (the points at which nervous impulses pass from one neuron to another).

9. Discuss any recent catastrophes that have occurred throughout the world (e.g., floods, earthquakes, hurricanes). Have students identify the type of thinking or attitude victims might use to help themselves get through these ordeals.

10. Invite adults from different cultures to talk to the students about how their cultures' conventions for optimism compare to the concepts presented in this unit.

It is important for educators to provide opportunities for students to work in groups so they can experience social skills in contexts where social communication is needed. Therefore, educators are encouraged to have students complete the Related Activities in small groups whenever possible. Educators trained in cooperative learning could incorporate the five components (see page 33) into the group activity.

RELATED LITERATURE:

Nick Joins In (1980) by Joe Lasker, Albert Whitman and Co. (Picture book)
　　Even though Nick is in a wheelchair, he is the one who rescues the basketball at school.

Sarah, Plain and Tall (1985) by Patricia MacLachlan, Harper and Row. (Text)
　　Caleb and Anna hope Sarah will stay and be their new mother. (pages 44–50)

SOCIAL SKILLS ALL DAY LONG:

Look for opportunities to teach social skills throughout the day (incidental teaching). Four ways to reinforce appropriate social skills and an example of each follow:

Encouragement

You sure are optimistic. I can tell this assignment is challenging for you and you're sticking with it. I'll bet you're using positive self-talk. What are you telling yourself?

Personal Example

Last night I realized I had made a major error in my checking account. I was upset and I'm still feeling upset. But I've been telling myself that I won't be this upset in a month and probably won't even remember this in a year. I'm usually very good about balancing my checkbook.

Prompting

Well, it looks like the bus isn't here for our field trip. Let's walk back into the classroom while I find out where it is. This is a good time for you to show that you are an optimistic person by imagining that bus pulling up.

Corrective Feedback (must be positive, private, specific, and nonthreatening)

Lee, you keep saying you are stupid. Remember, just because this one assignment is difficult for you, it doesn't mean that you are a stupid person. An optimistic person might think, "This assignment is hard, but I know I'm smart, so I'll get this finished."

Optimism

Lesson A

OBJECTIVES:

1. To state the meaning of *optimism* and tell why it is important
2. To listen to the self-talk associated with appropriate use of the skill
3. To tell what a "brain voice" is

MATERIALS:

1. Two paper sacks
2. *Optimism* (See page 98; one per student and one transparency.)
3. *Thought Bubble* (See *Appendix O*; one for educator use.)
4. *Checking Myself* (See *Appendix I*; one per student and one transparency.)

PREPARATORY SET:

Draw a neutral-looking face on each paper sack (the faces should be identical). Open the paper sacks and set them side by side so students can see the faces. Ask students to imagine that the paper sack faces are real people. Tell them you're going to pretend you can hear the "paper sack people's" brain voices, which means you can hear what they are thinking and saying to themselves. Put your ear by the top of one paper sack and say, "This person's brain voice is saying, 'Nothing ever goes right for me. I'm a dumb person.'" Put your ear by the top of the other paper sack and say, "This person's brain voice is saying, 'Most things work out great for me. I'm a smart person.'" Ask students how they think the two "paper sack people" are different. Accept all responses. Use this activity to introduce the *Optimism* unit.

PLAN:

1. Distribute and display *Optimism*. Discuss the definition. Explain the skill step and the symbol next to it. (While explaining the symbol, be certain to discuss the term "brain voice." The term is used as a metaphor in Lesson C, and the terms "brain voice" and "self-talk" are used interchangeably throughout the unit.) Remind students the symbol is there to help them visualize and remember the skill step. Refer to the body-talk symbol in the left-hand margin. Remind students that appropriate body talk is important in order to develop optimism. Read and explain the reasons for using the skill of *optimism*.

2. Model use of the optimism skill step while thinking aloud. A scripted example follows:

Introduction

I am going to pretend to be someone your age who is going to play in a soccer game. I will tell you the optimistic thoughts I'm having. When I hold up this Thought Bubble, *you'll know the words I'm saying are actually what I'm thinking.*

Actual Model

While holding up the Thought Bubble *say, I'm going to play my best in today's game. I bet we'll win! Even if we lose, it will be fun to play.*

3. Tell students that the opposite of optimism is pessimism. Ask students to create a definition for *pessimism*.

4. Read the story at the bottom of *Optimism*.

5. Distribute and display the discussion guideline sheet called *Checking Myself*. Ask students to complete the thought bubble statement with the words "raise my hand," or use another classroom discussion goal more appropriate for your group (see pages 25–26). Tell students that you will be having a discussion about the story you read to them. Explain that it is important for them to share their answers to have an interesting class discussion. Instruct them to circle a T-shirt star each time they raise their hands to share information (even if they don't get called on).

6. Model use of the *Checking Myself* sheet while thinking aloud. A scripted example follows:

Introduction

I am going to pretend to be one of you completing this sheet during the discussion we will be having. I will tell you the thoughts I am having while I'm completing this sheet. When I hold up this Thought Bubble, *you'll know the words I'm saying are actually what I am thinking.*

Actual Model

While holding up the *Thought Bubble* say, *The teacher just asked a question. I am going to raise my hand to share my ideas. She called on someone else, but I'll still circle a T-shirt star on my sheet because I raised my hand.* Put the *Thought Bubble* down and circle a T-shirt star on the transparency.

During the discussion, periodically remind students to raise their hands to answer questions asked and to mark their discussion guideline sheets.

7. Proceed with the discussion by asking these questions: (The story may need to be reread first.)

    - Who is thinking optimistically—Maria or Lee?
    - What words does Lee say that let you know he is thinking optimistically?
    - How do you think Lee's body talk looks?
    - How do you think Lee's voice sounds?
    - What might happen because Lee is thinking optimistically?
    - What words does Maria say that let you know she is thinking pessimistically?
    - How do you think Maria's body talk looks?
    - How do you think Maria's voice sounds?
    - What might happen because Maria is thinking pessimistically?

    After the discussion, ask students to complete the bottom thought bubble statement on *Checking Myself*.

8. Process use of the sheet by asking the following question or another one more appropriate for your group:

    - Why do you think it's important to raise your hand to share ideas and answers during a group discussion?

    Process further by asking students who raised their hands but did not get called on the following question:

    - What was appropriate about raising your hand even though you didn't get called on?

9. Pair students (see *Appendix P*). Ask student pairs to take turns telling each other the meaning of *optimism* and why it's important to use the skill. Students could be reminded that the information they are to say is printed on *Optimism*.

    As an option to add structure to this activity (see *Appendix Q*), ask partners to come to an agreement about which person will be called "George Washington" and which person will be called "Abraham Lincoln." After students have made their decisions, ask "George" to tell "Abe" the definition of *optimism*. Next, ask "Abe" to tell "George" the definition. Ask the students to use the same procedure to tell each other the reasons for using the skill.

10. Say with excitement to the class: *Liking yourself is very important! When you like who you are, you want to get along with other people by using appropriate social skills.*

Social Star

Name _____

★ Optimism

MEANING OF OPTIMISM: Choosing to have mostly positive thoughts

SKILL STEP:

1. Ask myself: How can I have mostly positive thoughts?

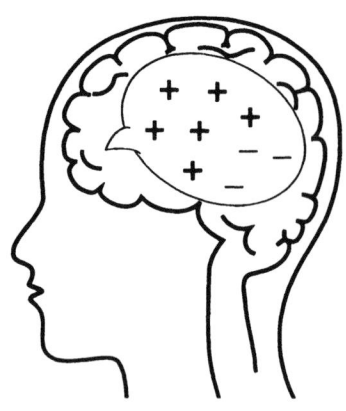

REASONS FOR USING THIS SKILL:

Thinking optimistically helps you feel better inside and have more energy. People will like being with you.

DIRECTIONS: Listen to the story below about Maria and Lee. Decide who is thinking optimistically.

Maria and Lee are working together to do a science experiment with fish. Their fish die before the experiment is finished.

Maria says,

> Oh no! It's all my fault the fish died! Now we can't finish our experiment. Nothing ever works out for me. Everything will probably go wrong today.

Lee says,

> Oh no! It's too bad the fish died, but that happens. Let's get new fish so we can finish our experiment.

© 1994 Thinking Publications — Duplication permitted for educational use only.

Optimism

Lesson B

OBJECTIVES:

1. To distinguish between optimistic thoughts and pessimistic thoughts

2. To develop a positive attitude even in a negative situation

MATERIALS:

1. *Optimism* classroom poster (See page 13.)

2. *Social Star Softball Game* (See page 102; one per pair of students and one transparency.)

3. *Numbered Heads Together Spinner* (See *Appendix X*; one prepared for educator use.)

PREPARATORY SET:

Ask students to close their eyes and think about math. Have them use a finger to "draw" a big picture of the symbol that stands for adding. Next, ask them to draw the symbol that stands for subtracting. While they are drawing, draw a "+" and "–" where everyone can see them. Ask students to open their eyes and compare what they drew to what you drew. Ask, "Does anyone know what else these symbols can stand for?" Lead students to an understanding that a "+" can be used to symbolize something "positive" and a "–" can be used to symbolize something "negative." Discuss the meanings of *positive* and *negative*.

PLAN:

1. Review the definition and skill step for *optimism* by referring the class to the *Optimism* classroom poster.

2. Pair students (see *Appendix P*). Ask student pairs to take turns telling each other the skill step for optimism. Follow the procedure described in step 9 of Lesson A. (As an option, ask students to decide who will be "Sitting Bull" and who will be "Geronimo.") Next, ask students to work with their partners to think of a situation when it's important to think optimistically. Tell students that one or more pairs will be called on to share their situation. Have one or more pairs share their situation.

3. Distribute and display *Social Star Softball Game*. Explain that the picture shows what some of the Social Star Club members are thinking during a softball game they are losing. Read each completed thought bubble and then ask students to work with their partner to put a "+" next to the characters who are thinking optimistically and a "–" next to the characters who are thinking pessimistically. Call on partners to share their answers.

4. Ask students to think about the optimistic thoughts Maria and Jolisa might be having. Have them write the optimistic thoughts in Jolisa and Maria's thought bubbles.

5. Ask students what benefits Jolisa, Ann, Maria, and Lee might experience because they are choosing to think optimistically (e.g., they may have more fun, they may play better).

6. Encourage an understanding that even though it is usually easier to think optimistically in situations when things are going well (e.g., playing well during a game), it is possible to think optimistically in situations when things are not going as well. Following are examples from each of Seligman's (1990) three crucial dimensions to explanatory style:

   Permanence— I'm just not playing well today. I'm sure I'll do better tomorrow.

   Pervasiveness—I'm not a great ball player, but I am great at other things.

   Personalization—I wish that guy was a better pitcher. That would help me get a hit.

   Learning the difference between these three dimensions of style may be too complex for your students. However, you may wish to point out the following about negative situations:

   Permanence—Not all bad situations last forever.

   Pervasiveness—When one situation goes badly, it doesn't mean that other situations will be affected.

   Personalization—When something goes wrong, it doesn't mean that it's all one person's fault and that person is bad.

7. Ask students to pretend they have a bike and it gets stolen. Tell them that if they think pessimistically, their brain voice might say, "I'm sure it'll never show up. It's lost forever. This is all my fault." Tell students that if they are thinking optimistically, their brain voice might say, "Maybe my bike will show up. Even though my bike wasn't locked, it wasn't right for someone to steal it. If it doesn't show up, I'll save my money for a neat new bike." Ask students to brainstorm other relatively negative situations besides losing a softball game and having a bike stolen. Write their ideas where everyone can see them.

8. Using the *Numbered Heads Together* structure (see pages 34–35) with the *Numbered Heads Together Spinner*, ask students to work with their partners to think of something positive in each of the following relatively negative situations: (Two pairs could be asked to work together to form groups of four, if desired.)

    - You are invited to go rollerskating with a friend, but your parents want you to stay home because you're having company.

- You have been saving money to buy a toy or game. When you have enough money and go to buy it, there are none left.

- You get your report card and it isn't as good as you expected.

- You enter a coloring contest and find out that you did not win.

This activity can be continued using some of the negative situations brainstormed during step 6.

9. Ask partners to face each other and stand an arm's length away. Encourage partners to use friendly and confident body talk. Ask partners to shake hands and in unison repeat the following statement after you: *You're a social star! You're a social super star! You can use great social skills every day!*

Social Star

Names _____

Social Star Softball Game

SCOREBOARD

Social Stars 2   Hitters 10

I know we're going to lose. We'll never win a game.

I'll probably get up and strike out or miss a ball. We'll lose and it will be all my fault.

I didn't get a hit last time, but I know I'll whack that ball this time!

OK, I'll tell myself I can do it. I can do it. I can hit the ball!

© 1994 Thinking Publications   102   *Duplication permitted for educational use only.*

Lesson C

OBJECTIVES:

1. To recognize that all people have positive self-talk and negative self-talk, but that optimistic people have a higher ratio of positive self-talk

2. To show how an optimist deals with negative self-talk

MATERIALS:

1. Figures of Mrs. Mary Jackson and Mr. Joe Jackson (See *Appendix F*.)

2. *Brain Voice* (See page 107; one transparency.)

3. One large metal bucket or can and BB's (See step 2 of the Plan.)

4. *Positive/Negative Brain* (See page 108; one transparency.)

5. *Mostly Positive* (See page 109; one transparency.)

6. *Push 'Em Out* (See page 110; one transparency.)

7. *I Can't Draw* (See page 111; one transparency.)

8. *My Brain Talk* (See page 112; one per student and one transparency.)

9. *Super Positive* (See page 113; one per student.)

10. Crayons or markers (An assortment for each student)

11. Scissors (One per student)

12. Hole-puncher (For educator use)

13. Yarn (Enough for each student to have a 24–36" piece)

PREPARATORY SET:

Show the figures of Mrs. Mary Jackson and Mr. Joe Jackson. Tell the class that Mr. and Mrs. Jackson are having a conversation. Ask the class to listen for optimistic or pessimistic comments that each character says. Use the figures and say the following:

Mrs. Jackson: *Mike and Ann didn't pick up their rooms last night. They never pick up their rooms. It's my fault they aren't good at keeping things in order.*

Mr. Jackson: *I saw Ann making her bed this morning. Mike and Ann cleaned up their rooms last Saturday. I think they're usually pretty good about keeping their rooms clean.*

Social Star

Have the class identify and discuss the optimistic or pessimistic comments each character made and the possible consequences of those comments.

PLAN:

1. Display *Brain Voice*. Say, "Each of us has a brain voice inside of our head. Our brain voice is often talking to us. We call this 'brain talk' or 'self-talk.' Whenever I use the *Thought Bubble* in this class, I'm sharing my brain talk with you. Each day we make about 50,000 comments to ourselves. To help you know how many thoughts this is, I'd like you to close your eyes and listen." (Dembrowsky [1983] is the source for "50,000 comments to ourselves.")

2. Drop one BB into the metal bucket. Say, "This represents one brain talk or self-talk message, like thinking, 'Oh, she's a nice person.' Now I will show you how many 50,000 thoughts are." To produce a very dramatic effect, pour a slow, continuous flow of BB's into the bucket. Say, "That's how many thoughts we have in one day." (It is not necessary to have 50,000 BB's to complete this activity. If you pour 1,000 BB's, ask the students to imagine what it would sound like if you poured them 50 times.)

3. Say, "Pause for a moment and listen to your own brain voice. What is your brain talk saying?" (Pause for 30 seconds to a minute.) Have students share some of their brain talk. (Some students will say "I didn't have any brain talk." Explain that their brain voice probably just said, "I don't have any brain talk.")

4. Display *Positive/Negative Brain*. Say, "All people have some positive brain talk and some negative brain talk." Draw a "+" symbol and a "–" symbol inside the brain as in Example 1.

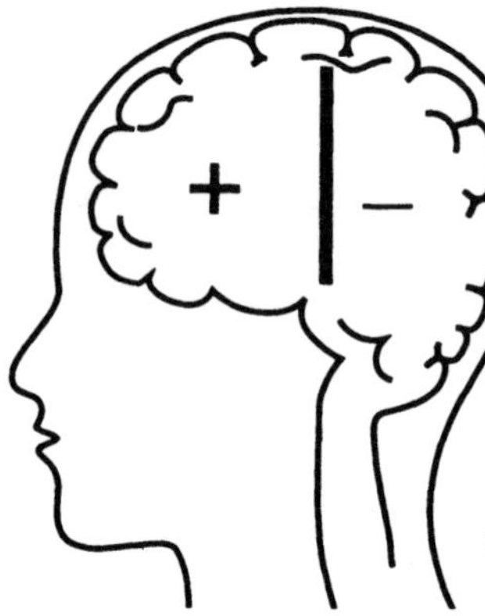

Example 1

Say, "No one has positive thoughts all the time, but optimistic people usually have more positive thoughts than negative thoughts. Most of the time, their brain talk looks like this." Draw more "+" and "–" symbols as in Example 2.

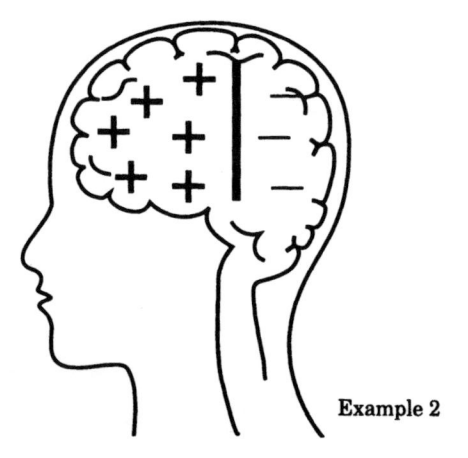

Example 2

104

Say, "Even optimistic people have bad days once in awhile, and then their brain talk might look more like this." Erase the previous transparency and draw "+" and "−" symbols as in Example 3.

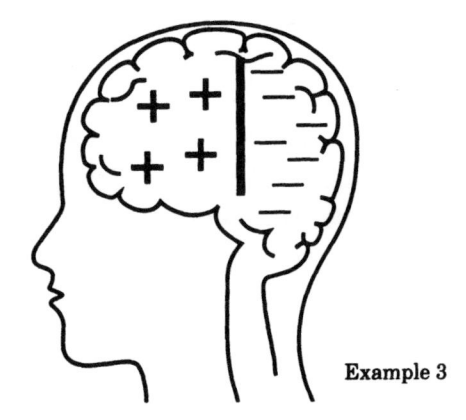

Example 3

Say, "But optimistic people have mostly positive thoughts most days."

5. Display *Mostly Positive*. Say, "This is what some of the brain talk of an optimistic person might look like." Have the students read the brain talk examples.

6. Display *Push 'Em Out*. Say, "It's not easy thinking optimistically. You have to remind yourself often to think positively. This is Super Positive." (Point to the figure with the "+.") "Each of you has a Super Positive inside your brain. Your Super Positive can push back those negative thoughts so they don't take over."

7. Say, "Sometimes negative thoughts sneak into our heads. When this happens, you can say to yourself, 'STOP THAT THOUGHT!' Then give reasons why the negative thought does not make sense, doesn't help, or isn't important."

8. Display *I Can't Draw*. Say, "For example, if you think 'I'm not good at drawing' your Super Positive brain talk could say, 'STOP THAT THOUGHT! Hey, I'm not that bad. I drew a great bird last year. I can draw well when I look at a picture. Besides, there are lots of other things I'm really good at!' It's like your Super Positive is pushing the negative brain talk out of your brain."

9. Display and distribute *My Brain Talk*. Ask students to write a negative thought they might have about themselves (e.g., I'm stupid, I'm ugly) inside the talk bubble of the "−" figure. (Students can write on the back of their paper if the talk bubble is too small.) Complete your own sheet on the transparency with a negative self-talk statement that can be shared with students. Have students tape their *My Brain Talk* sheet somewhere on a wall and stand next to it (do the same with your own sheet).

10. Ask students to pretend they are Super Positive. Demonstrate first, and then ask students to push hard against their sheet on the wall, pushing back the negative thought so it doesn't take over. Tell the students they can't stop themselves from ever having negative thoughts, but they can use their Super Positive brain talk to ask themselves, "How can I think positively in this situation?"

Social Star

11. Have students take *My Brain Talk* back to their desks. Tell students that when they have a negative thought, one thing they can do is think of reasons why their negative thought isn't true, doesn't help, or doesn't matter. Using the negative thought on your sheet as an example, demonstrate what your Super Positive could think to deal positively with the negative thought. Have students write positive self-talk that would "push back" their own negative thought. The students will probably require individual help with this. Collect the sheets and save them for use during the Preparatory Set in Lesson D.

12. Distribute *Super Positive*. Tell the students they will be creating a medallion to help them remember to use their *Super Positive* brain talk. Distribute markers or crayons and scissors. Ask students to color their Super Positive medallion and to cut it out. Punch a hole near the top of the medallion as shown on the finished example. Provide students with a piece of yarn long enough to fit over their heads. Place the yarn through the hole, and tie it to finish the medallion. Have students wear their medallions as a reminder to deal positively with negative thoughts.

13. Say with excitement to the class: *You are very special. There is no one exactly like you in the entire world! Using social skills will help you get along with others so you can discover how they are special too!*

Optimism

BRAIN VOICE

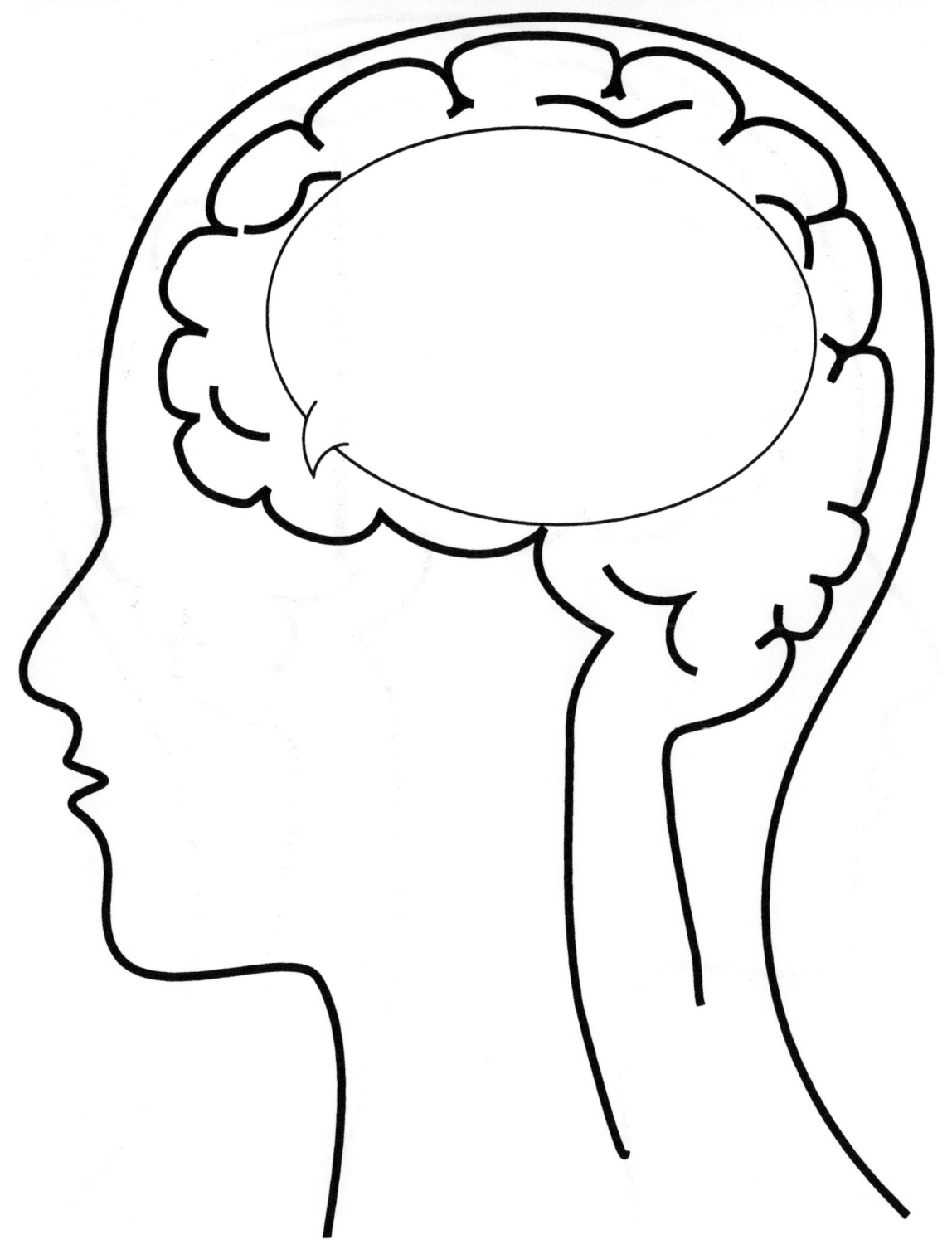

Social Star

POSITIVE/NEGATIVE BRAIN

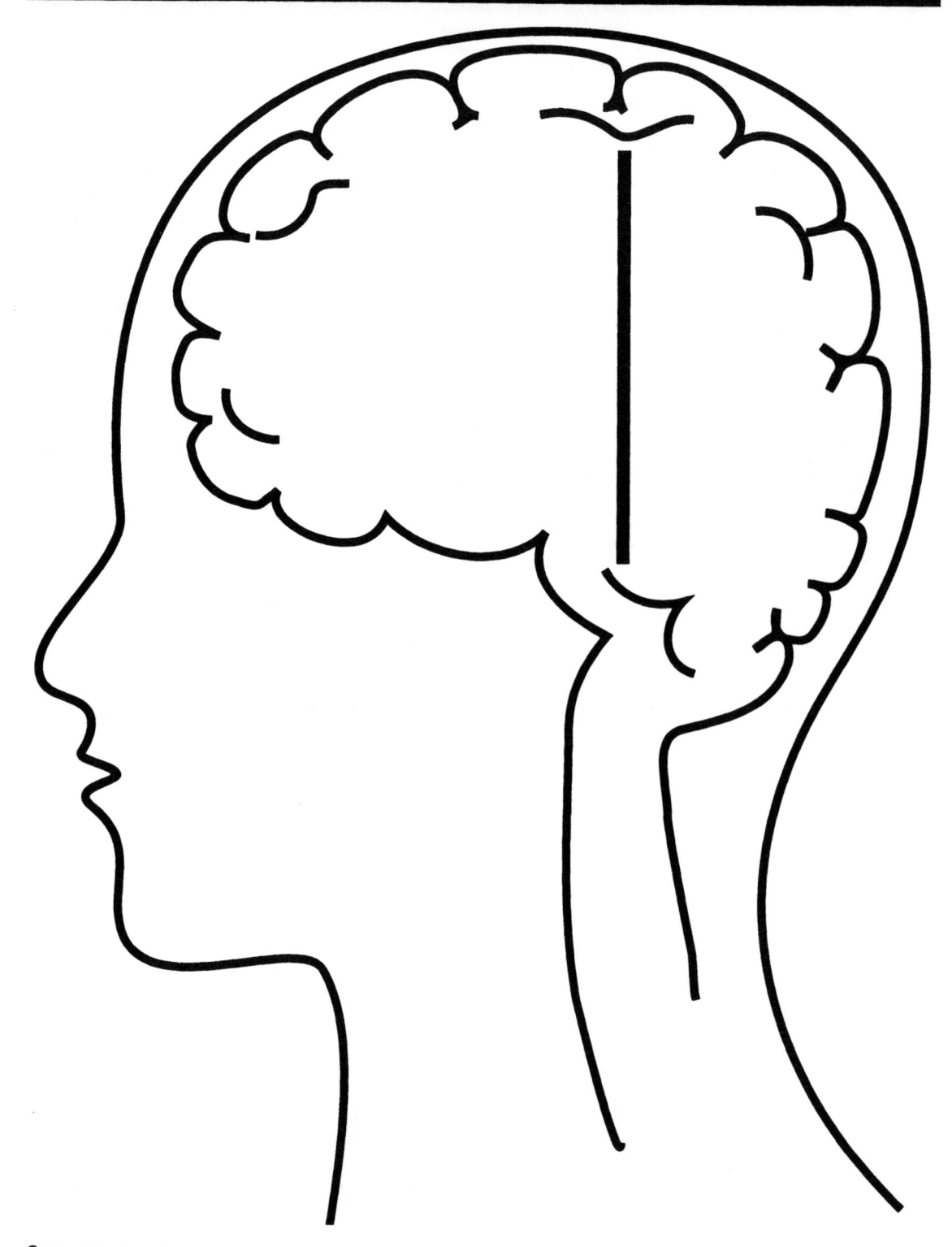

Optimism

MOSTLY POSITIVE

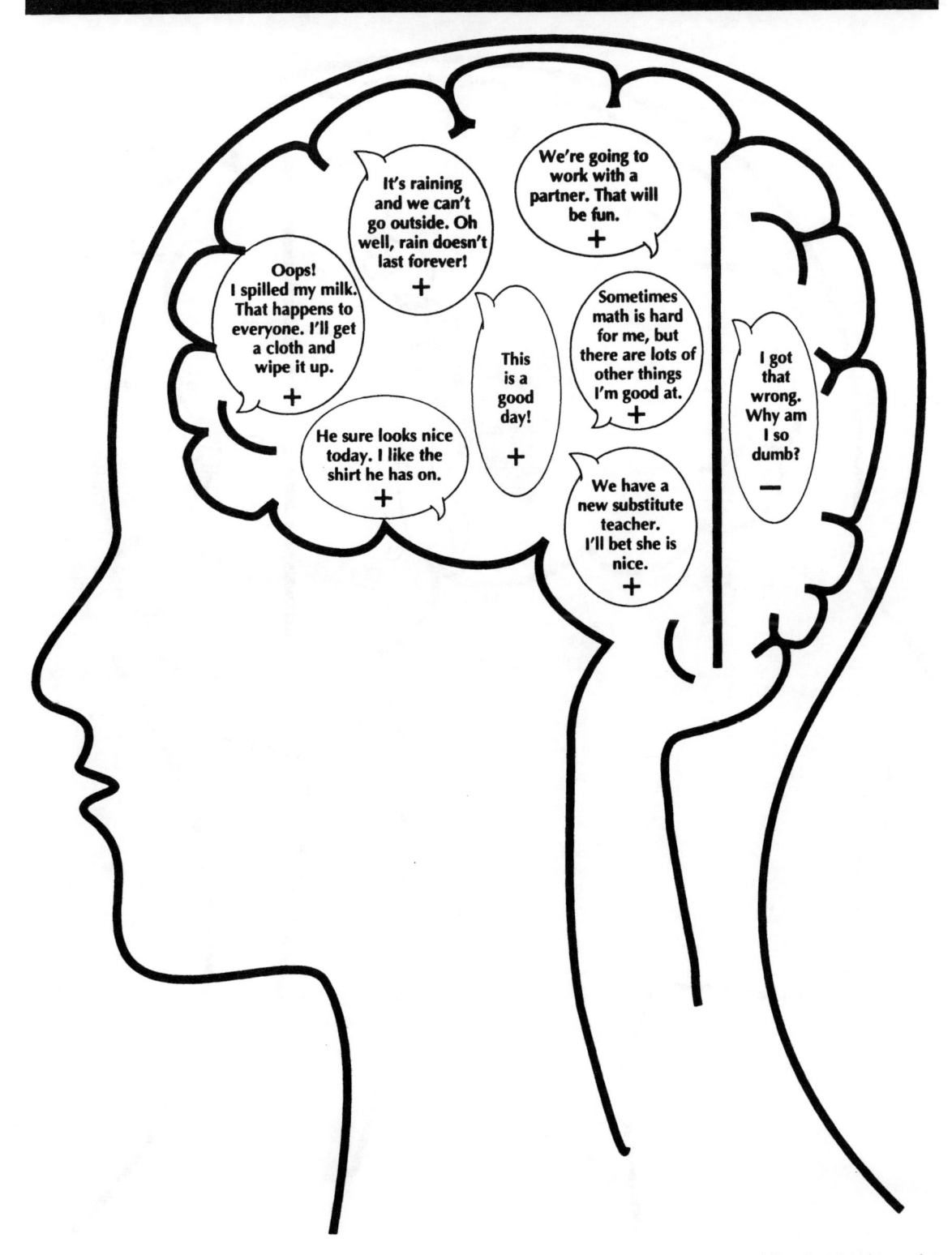

- Oops! I spilled my milk. That happens to everyone. I'll get a cloth and wipe it up. **+**
- It's raining and we can't go outside. Oh well, rain doesn't last forever! **+**
- We're going to work with a partner. That will be fun. **+**
- He sure looks nice today. I like the shirt he has on. **+**
- This is a good day! **+**
- Sometimes math is hard for me, but there are lots of other things I'm good at. **+**
- I got that wrong. Why am I so dumb? **−**
- We have a new substitute teacher. I'll bet she is nice. **+**

© 1994 Thinking Publications 109 Duplication permitted for educational use only.

Social Star

PUSH 'EM OUT

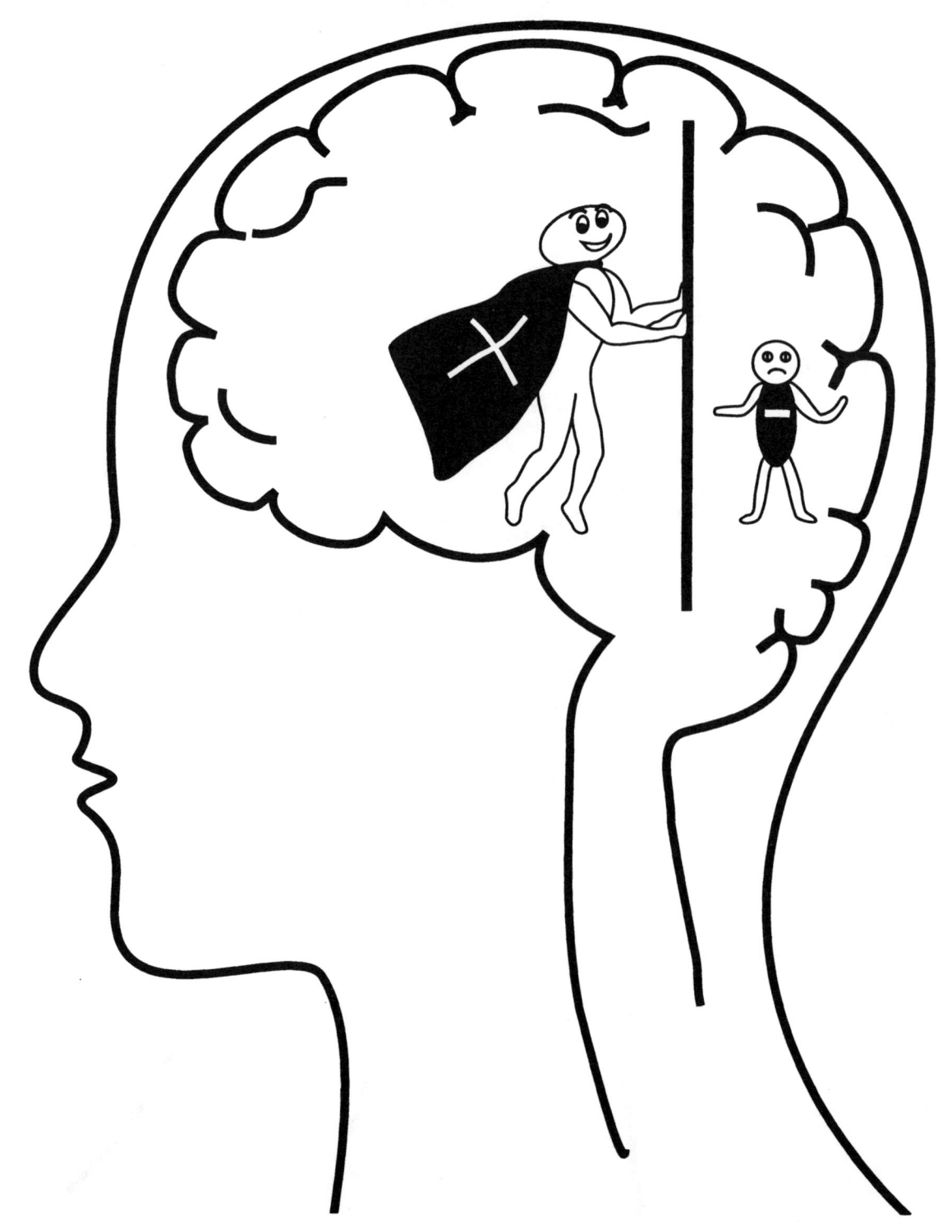

I CAN'T DRAW

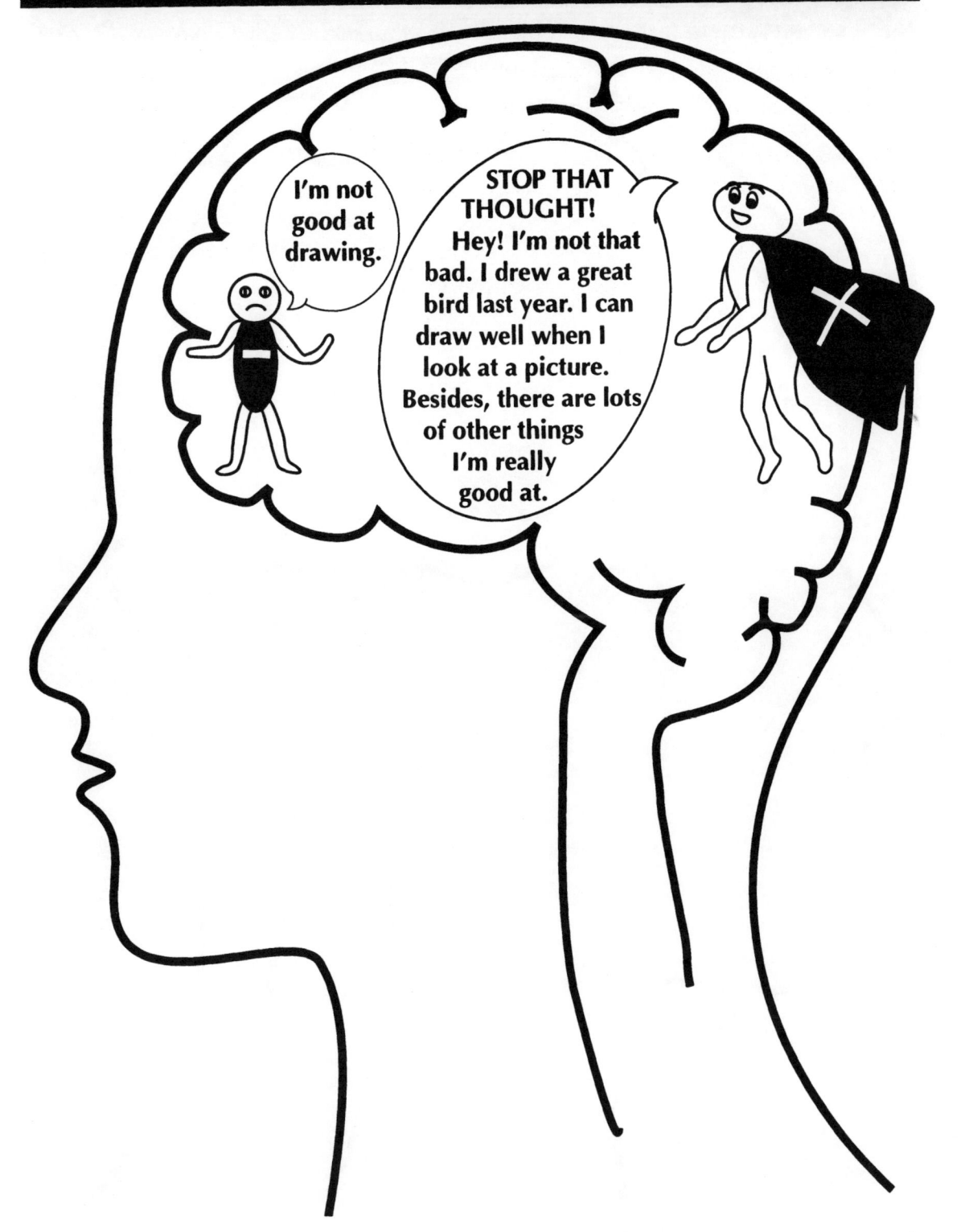

Social Star

Name _____

MY BRAIN TALK

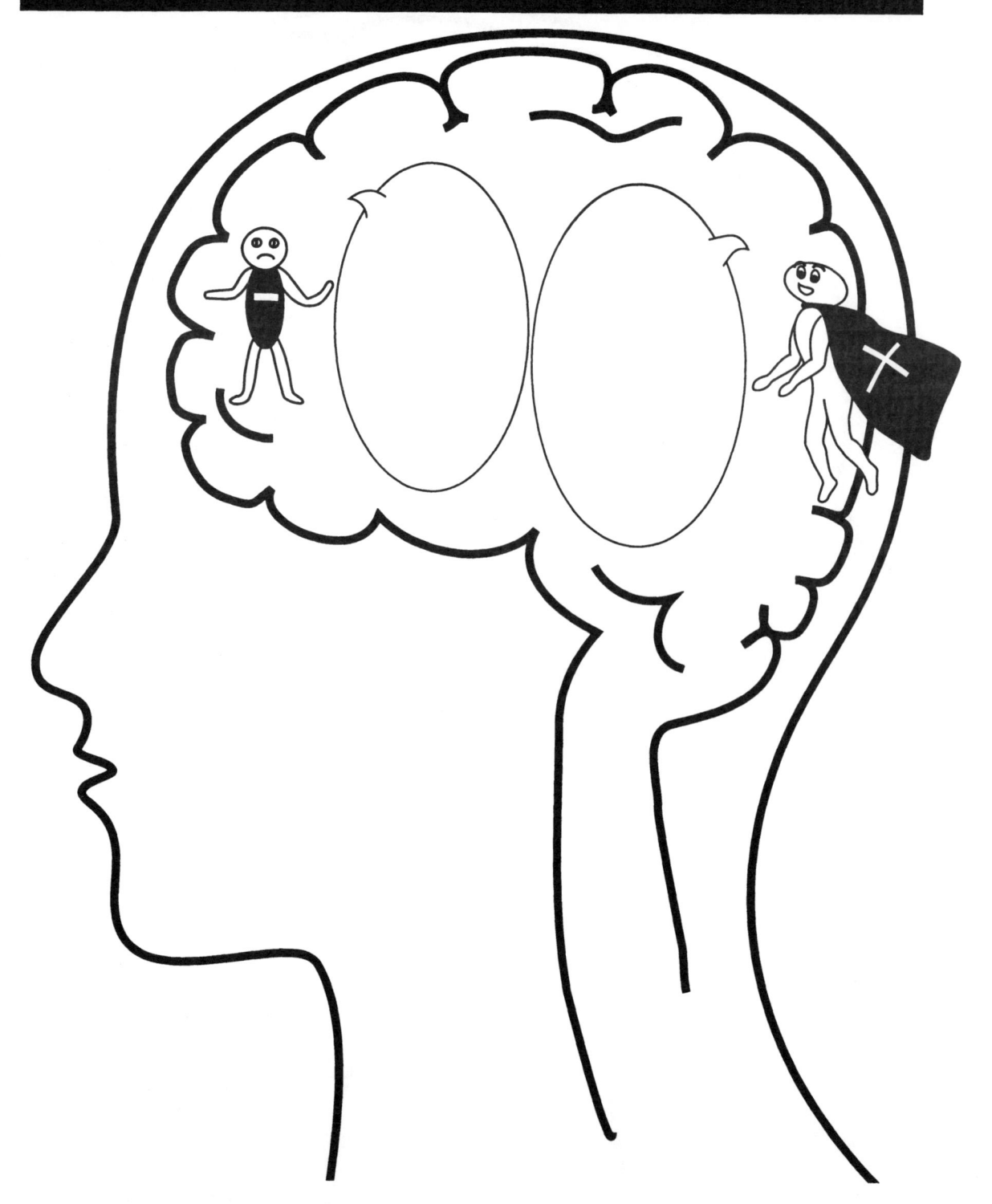

© 1994 Thinking Publications   112   *Duplication permitted for educational use only.*

Optimism

Name _____

SUPER POSITIVE

Picture of finished medallion:

© 1994 Thinking Publications   113   *Duplication permitted for educational use only.*

Social Star

Lesson D

OBJECTIVES:

1. To recognize that people can act negatively or positively with their words as well as their thoughts

2. To tell why it is important to act optimistically with others most of the time

MATERIALS:

1. *My Brain Talk* (Saved from Lesson C; one per student)

2. *Numbered Stones* (See *Appendix P*; one set per pair of students.)

3. *It's a Cookout!* (See pages 116–118; two per pair of students and one transparency.)

4. Figures of Mike Olson, Ann Olson, Mrs. Mary Jackson, Mr. Joe Jackson, Jolisa Walker, Mrs. Corin Walker, and Mr. Jesse Walker (See *Appendix F*; optional for steps 5 and 6 of this Plan.)

PREPARATORY SET:

Distribute each student's copy of *My Brain Talk*. Ask students to look at the negative thought written on their paper. Then ask students to get rid of their negative thought by crumpling up their paper and throwing it away. Have students imagine this negative thought leaving their brain.

PLAN:

1. Pair students using *Numbered Stones* (see *Appendix P*).

2. Ask students if they have ever gone to a cookout. Say, "The Jacksons have been invited to the Walkers' house for a cookout. During today's lesson, we get to decide what their cookout is going to be like."

3. Tell students that each pair will be writing two scripts about the cookout. First, each pair will be writing about the cookout where the characters are acting pessimistically, and then each pair will be rewriting the script to make the characters act optimistically.

   (As an alternative to having students complete the pessimistic script, complete the pessimistic script yourself before class. This would allow more time to emphasize step 6, in which the students write the optimistic script.)

4. Display and distribute one copy of *It's a Cookout!* to each pair. Read the names of the characters and the setting. Read Joe Jackson's first speaking part ("Mike, Ann—Remember, today's the day we're going to the Walkers' for a cookout").

Ask students to think of a pessimistic comment that Ann might say in response and write it on the transparency. Tell students that they will work with their partners to finish the script. Remind student pairs that at this cookout, the characters should act pessimistically.

5. Explain that during the last setting (at the Walkers' house), the students will be writing their own ending to the script. After students have completed the script, ask each pair of students to share their endings. (Students can use the figures of the characters to act out their pessimistic scripts.)

6. Distribute another copy of *It's A Cookout!* to each pair of students. Ask student pairs to work together to write a script in which the characters are optimistic. Remind students that during the last scene, they will be writing their own ending to the script. After students have completed the script, ask each pair of students to share their endings. (Students can use the figures of the characters to act out their optimistic scripts.)

7. Afterwards, discuss how differently the same situation turned out based on how optimistic or pessimistic the people were. Ask students to respond to the following:

   - The families in the pessimistic script used negative words with each other. What thoughts do you think caused them to say negative things? (Students should recognize that negative thinking probably caused the negative comments.)

   - How do you think the families in your pessimistic script felt about their cookout together?

   - The families in the optimistic script used positive words with each other. What thoughts do you think caused them to say positive things? (Students should recognize that positive thinking probably led to positive comments.)

   - How do you think the families in your optimistic script felt about their cookout together?

   - Which cookout would you like to attend? Why?

   - Why is it important to think optimistically with others most of the time? Are there times when you shouldn't act optimistically with people? Can you be assertive (stating your feelings in a firm and confident way without making threats) and optimistic at the same time?

8. Ask partners to face each other and stand an arm's length away. Encourage partners to use friendly and confident body talk. Ask partners to shake hands and in unison repeat the following statement after you: *When I see you use your social skills today, I'll step right up and say, "Great social skills, partner!"*

Social Star

Names _____

It's A Cookout!

Characters: Ann Olson   Mike Olson   Mary Jackson   Joe Jackson
Jesse Walker   Jolisa Walker   Corin Walker

SETTING 1: At the Jackson house before the family leaves for a cookout

Narrator: The Jackson family is getting ready to go to the Walkers' house for a cookout.

Joe Jackson: Mike, Ann—Remember, today's the day we're going to the Walkers' for a cookout.

Ann Olson: _____
_____

Mike Olson: _____
_____

Mary Jackson: Ann, I promised the Walkers we'd bring along some extra lawn chairs. Could you please get them out of the garage?

Ann Olson: _____
_____

Joe Jackson: _____
_____

Ann Olson: _____
_____

Joe Jackson: OK everybody! We need to get going.

Mary Jackson: _____
_____
_____

Mike Olson: _____
_____

© 1994 Thinking Publications — Duplication permitted for educational use only.

Optimism

Names _____

SETTING 2:	Riding in the car

Narrator: The Jackson family is in their car on the way to the cookout.

Mike Olson: What are the Walkers having to eat?

Joe Jackson: _____
_____

Mike Olson: _____
_____

Mary Jackson: I haven't seen Jolisa for awhile.

Ann Olson: _____
_____

Mike Olson: _____
_____

Joe Jackson: We're almost there.

Mike Olson: _____
_____

Ann Olson: _____
_____

Mary Jackson: _____
_____

SETTING 3:	At the Walkers' house

Narrator: The Jacksons arrive at the Walkers' for the cookout.

Corin Walker: Hi. Come in. How are you?

Ann Olson: _____
_____

Jesse Walker: _____
_____

© 1994 Thinking Publications　　　　　　Duplication permitted for educational use only.

Social Star

Names _____

Ann Olson: Where is Jolisa?

Jesse Walker: _____
_____

Mary Jackson: Oh, I forgot the vegetable tray.

Joe Jackson: _____
_____

(_____) _____
_____

(_____) _____
_____

(_____) _____
_____

(_____) _____
_____

(_____) _____
_____

(_____) _____
_____

(_____) _____
_____

(_____) _____
_____

Narrator: The end

Lessons X, Y, and Z

Due to similarities in format, the final three lesson plans for each unit in *Social Star* are provided in *Appendix A*. Substitute the word "optimism" whenever a "____" appears in the lesson plans. Information specific to this unit follows.

LESSON X PREPARATORY SET:

Ask for a physically strong volunteer to come to the front of the room. (These directions are written as if the volunteer were a boy.) Ask the volunteer to hold his strongest arm straight out to his side, at shoulder height. Tell the volunteer you will be pressing down on his arm, and he should use his strength to resist your pressure to make it harder for you to press it down. Complete the activity and comment about how strong the volunteer is. Next, have the volunteer hold out his arm and say aloud several times, "When something goes wrong, it's always my fault!" While the volunteer keeps saying the pessimistic statement, push down on his arm. It should be much easier to press the arm down. Report to the class how much easier it was. Repeat the process, only this time ask the volunteer to keep saying the optimistic statement, "Things usually go right for me, because I am smart!" This time, it should be harder to press the arm down. Report to the class how much harder it was. Ask these follow-up questions:

- What happened to the volunteer's energy and strength when he was pessimistic?
- What happened to the volunteer's energy and strength when he was optimistic?
- Why do you suppose optimistic people tend to get sick less often and pessimistic people tend to get sick more often?
- Why do you suppose optimistic people tend to accomplish more in work and play, and pessimistic people tend to accomplish less?

LESSON Y PREPARATORY SET:

Darken the room, if you prefer, and ask the students to visualize themselves thinking optimistically by reading the following script:

Let's take a few moments to relax.... Make sure you are in a comfortable position.... Close your eyes if you feel like it.... On the count of three, take a very slow, deep breath. Remember to breathe in quietly through your nose. One . . . two . . . three.... Breathe in deeply.... Now breathe out slowly and quietly through your mouth.... Let your entire body relax.... Now imagine that you are with another person who is acting pessimistically and complaining a lot. You say to yourself, "I am still going to think optimistically. I won't let this pessimistic person make my brain talk negatively too!" Think about how proud you are that you chose to think optimistically even though you are with a pessimistic person.

LESSON Z PLOT SITUATION:

Ask students to pretend that an optimistic friend of theirs has been acting like a pessimist lately and they want to help but they aren't sure how.

LESSON Z ROADBLOCK EXAMPLES:

- Being with another person who is pessimistic
- Being an optimist when you don't feel well
- Being an optimist in a really bad or sad situation (e.g., someone dies)

Name _____

Optimism T-Chart

LOOKS LIKE...

using appropriate body talk

- a posture that is confident
- a cheerful facial expression
- energetic body movements

SOUNDS LIKE...

a confident tone of voice

saying

- "Let's see if we can work this out together."
- "This is going to be fun!"
- "I know this is going to get better!"
- "I can be good at whatever I want to be good at."
- "This turned out well because I worked hard."

positive brain talk/self-talk

I know I can do this.

SHOW TIME

HOME

Pretend your mom won't let you have another cookie. (You've already had three.) Tell what you could say to yourself to think optimistically.

SCHOOL

Pretend your teacher has asked you to work in a group. The person you really want to work with isn't in your group. Tell what you could say to yourself to think optimistically.

COMMUNITY

Pretend you're just getting into a swimming pool and the lifeguard blows a whistle for everyone to get out for a 10-minute break. Tell what you could say to yourself to think optimistically.

Optimism

Optimistic People Are POWERFUL!

Social Star

HOME-A-GRAM

Dear Family,

At school, we have been talking about the social skill called

OPTIMISM

I learned that *optimism* means choosing to have mostly positive thoughts.

I learned that I should ask myself, "How can I have mostly positive thoughts?"

I know that thinking optimistically helps me feel better inside and have more energy. People will like being with me.

I know that to think optimistically, I need to make my brain voice say positive things. Below is a picture of my brain voice. I have written some positive things my brain voice can say.

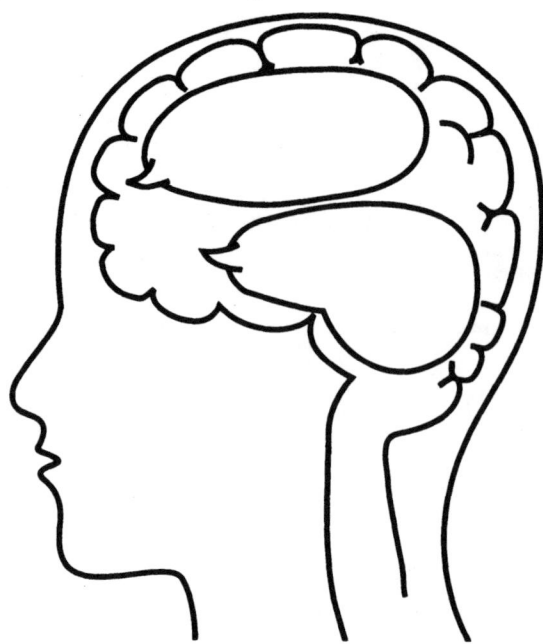

Tonight at home, we can discuss a negative/difficult situation and discuss how an optimist might handle it. After we do this, please sign my "Optimism" badge so I can return it to school and become a SOCIAL SUPER STAR this week.

From: _____

Playing Cooperatively

Social Star

UNIT GOAL:

To demonstrate comprehension and use of strategies for playing cooperatively

EDUCATOR INFORMATION:

This unit teaches strategies for avoiding problems that typically arise when children play together. The strategies include joining in (Lesson B), sharing (Lesson C), following game rules (Lesson D), being a good sport (Lesson E), and playing safely (Lesson F). All too often, children are "turned loose" during recess and play times, with little guidance for those students who have not yet developed appropriate play skills. Some students return from recess emotionally upset and find it difficult to learn, either due to their own difficulty with play or the difficulty they encountered with others' inappropriate play skills. Research and information about specific difficulties with play can be found in the Educator Information sections of Lesson B (joining in), Lesson C (sharing), and Lesson F (playing safely). The educator should exert sensitivity and care in generalizing rules about playing cooperatively into the children's home cultures.

RELATED ACTIVITIES:

1. Use the *We're Hot!* or *The Great Coupon Caper* reward system (see page 31) in which students can earn 10–15 minutes of extra play time for the class. Coupons may be distributed by teachers, the playground supervisor, or peers. (During the reward play time, students will get extra practice at playing cooperatively!)

2. Have students write a letter to a sibling detailing ways in which they can play cooperatively or make their play more fun.

3. Use *My Contract* (see *Appendix Y*) with students who have a difficult time playing cooperatively during recess.

4. Provide a training session for parents (refer to page 30) offering strategies they can use to encourage their children to engage in cooperative play both at home and at school. An excellent resource for parents is the book *Siblings without Rivalry* (Faber and Mazlish, 1987). Consult school social workers or guidance counselors for other resources.

5. Make a weekly bulletin board entitled "Recess Activity of the Week." Each week, describe a cooperative game/activity the children can engage in during recess. Review the directions each day before recess. *The Cooperative Sports and Games Book* (Orlick, 1978) and *The Second Cooperative Sports and Games Book* (Orlick, 1982) provide great resources for this bulletin board.

6. Have students brainstorm play activities for kids playing alone, with a partner, and with a group.

7. Have students observe children playing during recess. Choose a class to observe other than the students' own class. Before observing, discuss with the students what they will be watching for. Ask them to record their observations of the interactions of the children playing.

8. Have students investigate and take part in games that children from various cultures play.

9. Brainstorm cartoons or television shows in which people play aggressively or someone gets hurt. Discuss why real-life play should be different. Ask students to name shows where people get along in play.

10. Invite adults from different cultures to talk to the students about how their cultures' conventions for playing compare with the strategies presented in this unit.

It is important for educators to provide opportunities for students to work in groups so they can experience social skills in contexts where social communication is needed. Therefore, educators are encouraged to have students complete the Related Activities in small groups whenever possible. Educators trained in cooperative learning could incorporate the five components (see page 33) into the group activity.

RELATED LITERATURE:

Dancing the Breeze (1991) by George Shannon, Ill. by Jacqueline Rogers, Bradbury. (Picture book) Papa and his young daughter dance in the garden while the moon rises.

Man Out at First (1993) by Matt Christopher; Ill. by Ellen Beier; Little, Brown, and Co. (Text) (pages 12–13)

SOCIAL SKILLS ALL DAY LONG:

Look for opportunities to teach social skills throughout the day (incidental teaching). Four ways to reinforce appropriate social skills and an example of each follow:

Encouragement

Ann, I saw you share your new headset with the other kids. That's great. Other people will be willing to share with you when you share with them.

Personal Example

Last night, my daughter was using this great bubble-making wand. I tried it out. I was having so much fun making bubbles that I didn't want to give the wand back to my daughter. I reminded myself that it's important to take turns.

Prompting

When you go out for recess today, think about what you can do to make play fun for everyone. Who has some ideas?

*Corrective Feedback (**must be cooperative, private, specific, and nonthreatening**)*

Jolisa, just now when you wanted to play with the kids, you grabbed the ball away from Tom and said, "I'm being the pitcher." You could have said, "Do you mind if I'm the pitcher?" Then Tom and the other kids would be more likely to play with you.

Social Star

Lesson A

EDUCATOR INFORMATION:

During this lesson, students are asked to start a Cooperative Play Paper Chain. During all lessons in this unit, students can earn strips of paper (1" x 6") for demonstrating various aspects of cooperative play. They attach their individual paper strips to the Cooperative Play Paper Chain. The students should attempt to make their chain as long as possible to visually represent how well their class plays together. (Cut a minimum of 10 cooperative play paper strips per student to be used throughout this unit.) The paper chain concept can be continued throughout the school year and can be done on a schoolwide basis with each classroom starting its own paper chain and working to join them together as they grow. Besides the ways described within each lesson, there are other ways students can earn paper strips. A list of ideas follows:

- Informally observe students during recess/free play and reward students for playing cooperatively.

- Before recess, identify a specific cooperative play strategy that you will be looking for (e.g., asking kids to join in). Reward students who demonstrate the strategy.

- Allow a student to earn bonus paper strips for the entire class based on his or her demonstration of cooperative play. Make certain the bonus system is structured so that the targeted child has little chance of failing.

- Give paper strips to the playground supervisor or to students themselves to pass out when they see cooperative play occurring.

- Provide a paper strip daily for students to earn when there are no problems during recess.

Do the following to promote and encourage intrinsic motivation to use cooperative play skills:

- Verbally reinforce students who demonstrate use of cooperative play strategies.

- Ask students to brainstorm positive self-talk they can use to reinforce themselves when they use strategies associated with cooperative play.

OBJECTIVES:

1. To state the meaning of *playing cooperatively* and tell why it is important

2. To listen to the self-talk associated with use of the *playing cooperatively* skill

MATERIALS:

1. *Playing Cooperatively* (See page 132; one per student and one transparency.)
2. *Thought Bubble* (See *Appendix O*; one for educator use.)
3. *Checking Myself* (See *Appendix I*; one per student and one transparency.)
4. Cooperative play paper strips (Cut 1" x 6" strips of paper.)
5. Poster (With the words "Cooperative Play Paper Chain" written large enough so all students can see them)
6. Glue, tape, or stapler

PREPARATORY SET:

List the following words where everyone can see them:

kickball	hangman	cards
tag	Candy Land	kick the can
jump rope	hide and seek	Monopoly

Ask students what the words have in common. After identifying that the words are associated with playing, tell students that in this unit they will be learning about something called "playing cooperatively."

PLAN:

1. Distribute and display *Playing Cooperatively*. Discuss the definition of *playing cooperatively*. Explain the skill step for playing cooperatively and the symbol next to it. Remind students that the symbol is there to help them visualize and remember the skill step. Refer students to the body-talk symbol in the left-hand margin. Remind students that appropriate body talk is important when playing together. Discuss the reasons for playing cooperatively.

2. Model use of the skill step for playing cooperatively while thinking aloud. A scripted example follows:

Introduction

I am going to pretend to be someone your age playing with others. I will show you how I play cooperatively and tell you the thoughts I'm having. When I hold up this Thought Bubble, you'll know the words I'm saying are actually what I'm thinking.

Actual Model

While holding up the *Thought Bubble* say, *OK, when we go out for recess, how can I play cooperatively? I can share and follow game rules. I can use happy body talk and I can ask others to join in.* Put the *Thought Bubble* down and say with excitement, *Who would like to play tag during recess? Who wants to be "it" first?*

Social Star

3. Read the cartoon at the bottom of *Playing Cooperatively*.

4. Distribute and display the discussion guideline sheet called *Checking Myself*. Ask students to complete the goal statement with the words "use interested body talk," or use another classroom discussion goal more appropriate for your group (see pages 25–26). Tell students that you will be having a discussion about the cartoon they just read. Encourage students to demonstrate body talk that shows they are interested in the discussion (e.g., sitting up, leaning slightly forward, nodding, giving eye contact). Tell students that during the discussion, they should ask themselves if their body talk says, "I'm interested in this discussion." Instruct students to circle a T-shirt star each time a new person begins to speak and they are using interested body talk.

5. Model use of the *Checking Myself* sheet while thinking aloud. A scripted example follows:

Introduction

I am going to pretend to be one of you completing this sheet during the discussion we will be having. I will tell you the thoughts I'm having while completing the sheet. When I hold up this Thought Bubble, *you'll know the words I'm saying are actually what I'm thinking.*

Actual Model

While holding up the *Thought Bubble* say, *A different person just started talking. Am I using interested body talk? Yes, I am sitting up straight and giving her eye contact. I'll circle a star on the T-shirt.* Put the *Thought Bubble* down and circle a star on the transparency.

During the discussion, periodically remind students to mark their discussion guideline sheets whenever they find themselves using body talk that shows they are interested.

6. Proceed with the discussion by asking these questions: (The story may need to be reread first.)

   • What are the kids doing and saying to play cooperatively?

   • How do you think these kids might be feeling? Why?

   • Do any of the cooperative play strategies in this cartoon ever happen on our playground?

   • Do you think the kids in the cartoon always play cooperatively?

   • What problems sometimes occur when people play together?

After the discussion, ask students to complete the bottom thought bubble statement on *Checking Myself*.

7. Process use of the sheet by asking the following question or another one more appropriate for your group:

   • Why do you think it is important to use appropriate body talk during a discussion?

   Process further by asking the students who volunteered to speak during the discussion to share their answers to the following questions:

   • You shared one of your answers during the discussion. How could you tell if someone was using interested body talk when you were talking?

   • How did you feel when others used interested body talk while you were speaking?

8. Pair students using the *Inside-Outside Circle* activity (see *Appendix P*). Have each pair think of specific things they can do or say to play cooperatively. Have students share their ideas.

9. Distribute one paper strip to each student. Say, "During this unit, you will be using these paper strips to make a 'Cooperative Play Paper Chain.'" (Show the Cooperative Play Paper Chain poster.) Help students glue, tape, or staple their strips together to form one class paper chain. Suspend the paper chain in a place where students can add to it and see it often. Put the Cooperative Play Paper Chain poster at the beginning of the chain. Say, "I will be watching for examples of cooperative play. You will be able to earn more strips to add to the chain by playing cooperatively. Whenever you see this chain, it should remind you that we are learning about cooperative play." Ask students to guess how long they think the chain might be by the end of the unit. Record "guesses" and save for comparison in Lesson X.

10. Ask student pairs to take turns telling each other the meaning of *playing cooperatively* and why it's important to use the skill. Students could be reminded that the information they are to say is printed on *Playing Cooperatively*.

    As an option to add structure to this activity (see *Appendix Q*), ask partners to come to an agreement about which person will be called "Pocahontas" and which person will be called "Captain John Smith." After students have made their decisions, ask "Pocahontas" to tell "Captain Smith" the definition of *playing cooperatively*. Next, ask "Captain Smith" to tell "Pocahontas" the definition. Ask the students to use the same procedure to tell each other the reasons for playing cooperatively.

11. Say with excitement to the class: *You are all social super, super, super stars! Remember, you have a responsibility to use your social skills and to invite other people to use good social skills too.*

Social Star

Name _____

★ Playing Cooperatively

MEANING OF PLAYING COOPERATIVELY: Playing in a way that invites everyone to have fun

SKILL STEP:

1. Ask myself: How can I play cooperatively?

REASONS FOR USING THIS SKILL:

When you play cooperatively, you make a good impression on others and they may enjoy playing with you. You can have fun playing with others. You feel good inside when you play in a way that invites everyone to have fun.

DIRECTIONS: Listen to what the characters are saying. Look at the pictures of Mike, Ann, Maria, Victor, Lee, and Jolisa while you listen.

"Hey, Lee and Jolisa. When the game is over, could I play jacks too?"

"Ann, is that comic book good? Do you mind if I look at it with you?"

"You're doing great! I think you'll win."

© 1994 Thinking Publications   132   Duplication permitted for educational use only.

Playing Cooperatively

Lesson B

> **ALONE**
>
> I was alone the other day
> And stopped to watch some children play
> Beneath a tree.
>
> They ran and ran and ran around
> And then fell flat upon the ground.
> It looked like fun to me.
>
> I only stood and watched them play.
> I didn't know their names. And they
> Did not know me.
>
> "Alone" by Dorothy Aldis reprinted by permission of G.P. Putnam's Sons from *All Together*, © 1925–1928, 1934, 1939, 1952, © renewed 1953–1956, 1962, 1967 by Dorothy Aldis.

EDUCATOR INFORMATION:

1. This lesson is designed to assist students in entering into play situations. The lesson is modeled after a short-term training program designed to teach "entry" behavior described by Gayle Macklem (1987).

2. Students are taught that initial attempts to enter play situations are frequently rejected (67.5 percent of the time) (Corasaro, 1979), and this rejection should not be taken personally. Putallaz and Gottman (1981) state that even popular children stand a 30 percent chance of being rejected.

3. The following chart shows how various types of entry behavior are received by other students:

CATEGORIES OF ENTRY BEHAVIOR GENERATED BY CHILDREN AND COLLECTED FROM RESEARCH STUDIES

Behaviors likely to provoke rejection:

1. Push, hit, or shove someone.
2. Disrupt the activity.
3. Disagree with the group.
4. Make demands of the group.
5. Help one side cheat.
6. Brag about how great you are.
7. Threaten to cause trouble.
8. Take the ball.

Behaviors more likely to be ignored, but which might occasionally provoke rejection:

1. Stare at one of the players.
2. Walk around the playground.
3. Talk about yourself.
4. Tell how you feel.
5. Give your opinion.
6. Give information to the group.
7. Ask provoking questions.
8. Say something about the game.
9. Change the topic.
10. Watch and hope someone will ask you to join.
11. Say, "The ball belongs to the school."
12. Offer a toy or candy.

Continued

CATEGORIES OF ENTRY BEHAVIOR GENERATED BY CHILDREN AND COLLECTED FROM RESEARCH STUDIES—*Continued*	
13. Claim a play area.	17. Look sad and lonely.
14. Beg or tease the leader.	18. Cry.
15. Clown and be funny.	19. Show toys.
16. Threaten to tell.	20. Ask, "What are you playing?"

Behaviors more likely to result in acceptance, but which might at times be ignored:

1. Ask positive questions.	11. Just start to play.
2. Offer useful suggestions.	12. Ask, "Can I play?" or "Is there room for one more?"
3. Say, "Good try," "Good for you."	13. Start your own game.
4. Imitate the actions of the children playing.	14. Ask the teacher to help.
5. Agree with the group.	15. Suggest a role for yourself.
6. Ask relevant questions.	16. Ask, "What are you playing?"
7. Ask others about themselves.	17. Join in quietly.
8. Say, "Hi! How are you?"	18. Say something nice.
9. Suggest a new activity or game.	19. Ask one child ahead of time so you will be sure to play.
10. Wait until the game ends and then ask to join the next game.	

From "No one wants to play with me" by G.L. Macklem, 1987, *Academic Therapy, 22*(5), 477–484. © 1987 by PRO-ED. Reprinted with permission.

OBJECTIVES:

1. To tell the difference between open and closed play groups

2. To tell appropriate ways to enter into a play group

3. To demonstrate the cooperative play strategy of joining in

MATERIALS:

1. *Thought Bubble* (See *Appendix O*; one per student.)

2. *Playing Cooperatively* classroom poster (See page 13.)

3. *Not This Way!* (See page 138; one per pair of students.)

4. *Try This Way* (See pages 139–140; one per pair of students.)

5. *Mike Wants to Join in* (See page 141; one per pair of students.)

6. Small balls (One for each group in step 11 of this Plan)

7. Cooperative play paper strips

8. Glue, tape, or stapler

PREPARATORY SET:

Distribute a *Thought Bubble* to each student. Tell students to pretend they are out on the playground and they see a group of students with whom they would like to play. Ask students to write down (inside the *Thought Bubble*) what their thoughts would be about joining in to play. As students are writing, draw two large thought bubbles where all students can see them. Inside one thought bubble, write positive self-talk about joining in (e.g., "That looks fun! I'll go over and join in"). Inside the other thought bubble, write negative self-talk about joining in (e.g., "That looks fun! They probably won't let me join in"). When students are finished writing, read your examples and discuss the concept that some children have a difficult time joining in to play in groups, while others find it easy to do. Explain that today's lesson is about how to join in to play with others.

PLAN:

(Due to the length of this lesson, it could be divided into two parts—steps 1–9 could be taught in one session and steps 10–16 in another. Students may need to repeat steps 10–16 more than once to practice the strategy of joining in.)

1. Review the definition and skill step for *playing cooperatively* by referring the class to the *Playing Cooperatively* classroom poster.

2. Ask for a few volunteers to stand outside the room. Close the door and ask the volunteers to attempt getting into the room while the door is kept closed. After it becomes obvious that they can't get in, open the door and ask the volunteers to come into the room. Ask students why it was easier to enter the room when the door was open.

3. Tell students that a play group is similar to a door because a play group can be open or closed. A *closed play group* is one in which there are already enough children to play the game. Two children sitting down with a checkerboard would be a closed group since this is the exact number needed to play. Sometimes a play group may be closed because the game has already started and it is difficult to let people join in the middle of the game (e.g., playing a board game activity or doing an activity that is timed). Emphasize to students that sometimes when their request to play is turned down, it may simply be because the group was closed and not necessarily because the group members didn't want to play with them. Tell them that everyone (even popular children) are turned down at times. Don't overemphasize closed groups, thus causing children to increase the times they turn others away because their group is closed. Have students brainstorm creative ways to change specific closed game situations into open situations.

4. Provide students with some examples of open groups (e.g., a group of kids playing jump rope, kids playing on playground equipment, three kids standing

on Four Square spaces, three desks together with two kids sitting at them, a group of children playing house). Tell students it is easier to join an open group. Explain that sometimes a closed group changes into an open group, and when that happens, it is a good time to enter in.

5. Pair students (see *Appendix P*).

6. Distribute *Not This Way!* to each pair. Have student pairs take turns reading to each other the strategies that do not work when trying to join a group. When student pairs have finished, ask students to brainstorm examples of each strategy and then discuss why the strategies usually don't work. Ask students to work with their partners to identify other strategies to add to *Not This Way!* (The list of behaviors more likely to be ignored but which might occasionally provoke rejection [see #3 of the Educator Information section] includes other strategies that could be added.) Call on student pairs to share their ideas.

7. Distribute *Try This Way* to each pair. Explain that the keys stand for "unlocking the door to joining a group." Have student pairs take turns reading to each other the strategies that may work. When student pairs have finished, emphasize that these strategies will not work all the time but that students will have a better chance of joining in when using these strategies. Ask students to brainstorm examples of each strategy and then discuss why the strategies usually do work. Ask student pairs to work together to identify other strategies to add to *Try This Way*.

8. Distribute *Mike Wants to Join in* to each pair. Read the following story while students look at the picture:

Mike grabbed his jacket and headed out the door for recess. He heard kids talking about what they were going to play, but Mike wasn't sure what he wanted to do. Two kids ran to the slide and four kids ran to the Four Square boxes. One group started to play jump rope and another group started to play kickball. Two kids started bouncing a ball against the school building and some other kids sat in a circle on the grass. Mike looked around to see where he would like to join in.

After reading the story, ask student pairs to work together to identify three activities Mike could join in and explain why. Call on pairs to share their answers. Next, ask student pairs to work together to identify three strategies Mike could use to join in. (They can refer to *Try This Way* for ideas.) Call on pairs to share their strategies and explain why they may work.

9. Explain that students should expect to be told no when attempting to join in, because everyone is turned down at different times. Encourage students not to take a no personally. It probably means that the group is closed or maybe the right strategy wasn't used. Encourage them to try more than once to get into a

play group. Ask students to brainstorm positive self-talk they could use if told no when they try to join in (post these for future student reference).

10. Tell students they will practice hearing no when joining in. Have one-fourth of the students stand in the hallway. Tell them that when you call them in, they should attempt to join in with a play group. Tell them to use one of the strategies from *Try This Way*. Tell them that they will hear no, but they should try a different strategy to get into the same group or try to get into another group. They should keep trying until they are told yes when joining in.

11. Divide the rest of the students into small groups (make some groups of two, three, and four). Pass out a small ball for each group to play with. (Tell groups they must play with their ball within their small area and model how that can be done.) Tell groups that when the students in the hall come back in, they will be asking to join into their play groups. They should say no the first two times someone asks (it could be two different people asking or the same person asking twice) and yes the third time that someone asks. That person should then be allowed to join in their play situation. They should then start the same procedure again saying no the first two times and yes the third time. (Model the activity with one group while the others watch.)

12. As this activity is taking place, randomly reinforce students while they make attempts to join in (even if they are told no) by handing them a strip for the paper chain.

13. After all students have been accepted into groups, switch groups so that other students have a chance to build up their resistance to hearing no. Afterward, discuss how students felt when they heard no and the importance of using positive self-talk and persistence.

14. Have students glue, tape, or staple their paper strips to the paper chain.

15. Ask student pairs to take turns telling each other the skill step for playing cooperatively. Follow the procedure described in step 10 of Lesson A. (As an option, ask students to decide who will be "John Henry" and who will be "Casey Jones.") Next, ask students to work with their partners to think of a situation when it would be important to play cooperatively. Tell students that one or more pairs will be called on to share their situation. Have one or more pairs share their situation.

16. Say with excitement to the class: *You are very special. There is no one exactly like you in the entire world! Using social skills will help you get along with others so you can discover how they are special too!*

Social Star

Names _____

🖐 Not This Way!

These strategies DO NOT work for joining in.

- Hit or push someone.
- Demand that the group do what you want.
- Take the ball away.
- Brag about how great you are.
- Argue with the group.
- Disrupt the game or activity.
- Help one side cheat.
- Threaten to cause trouble.

© 1994 Thinking Publications — Duplication permitted for educational use only.

Playing Cooperatively

Names _____

Try This Way

These strategies are "keys for joining a group." These strategies might work for joining in.

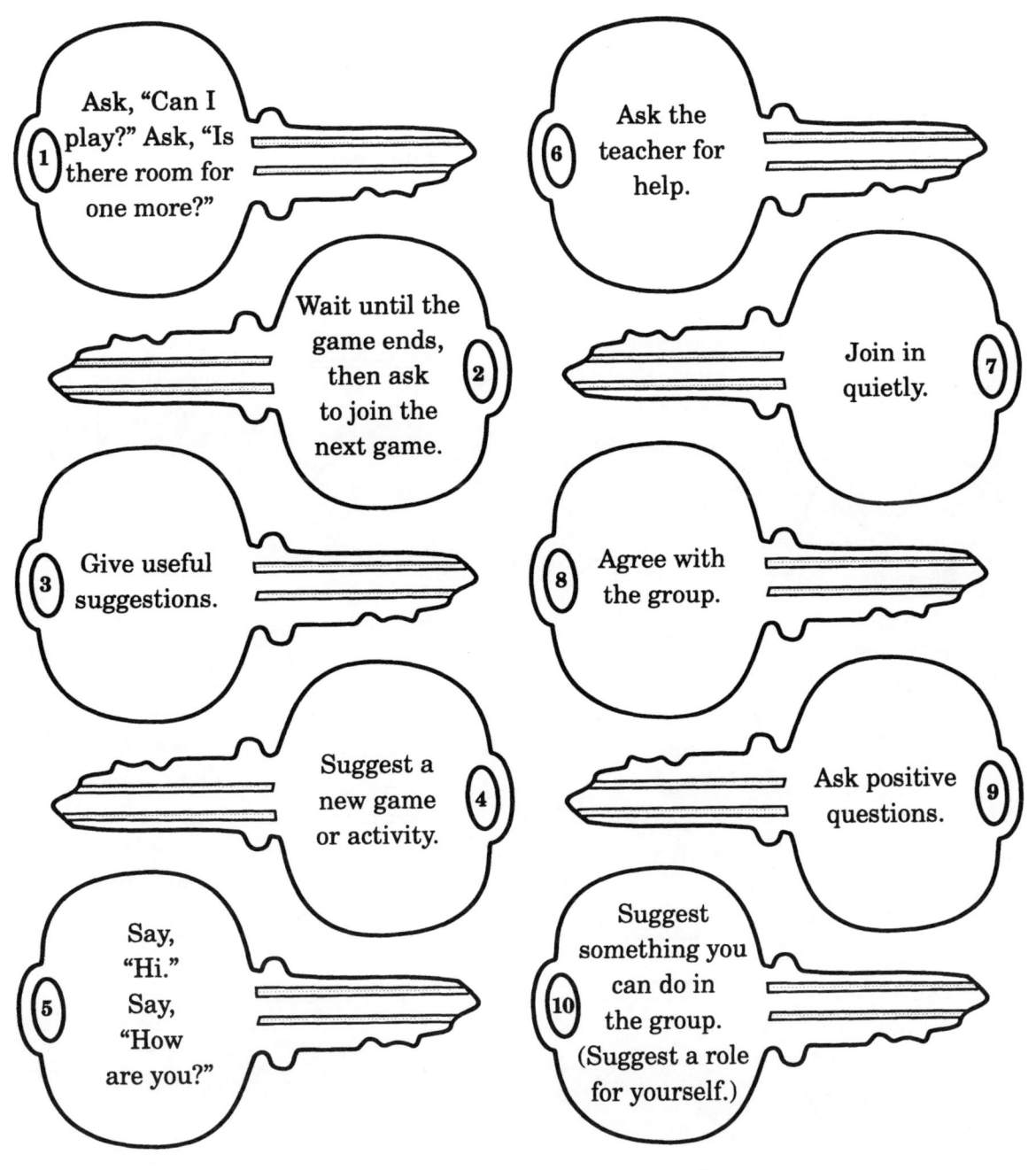

1. Ask, "Can I play?" Ask, "Is there room for one more?"
2. Wait until the game ends, then ask to join the next game.
3. Give useful suggestions.
4. Suggest a new game or activity.
5. Say, "Hi." Say, "How are you?"
6. Ask the teacher for help.
7. Join in quietly.
8. Agree with the group.
9. Ask positive questions.
10. Suggest something you can do in the group. (Suggest a role for yourself.)

© 1994 Thinking Publications — Duplication permitted for educational use only.

Social Star

Names _____

Try This Way
Continued

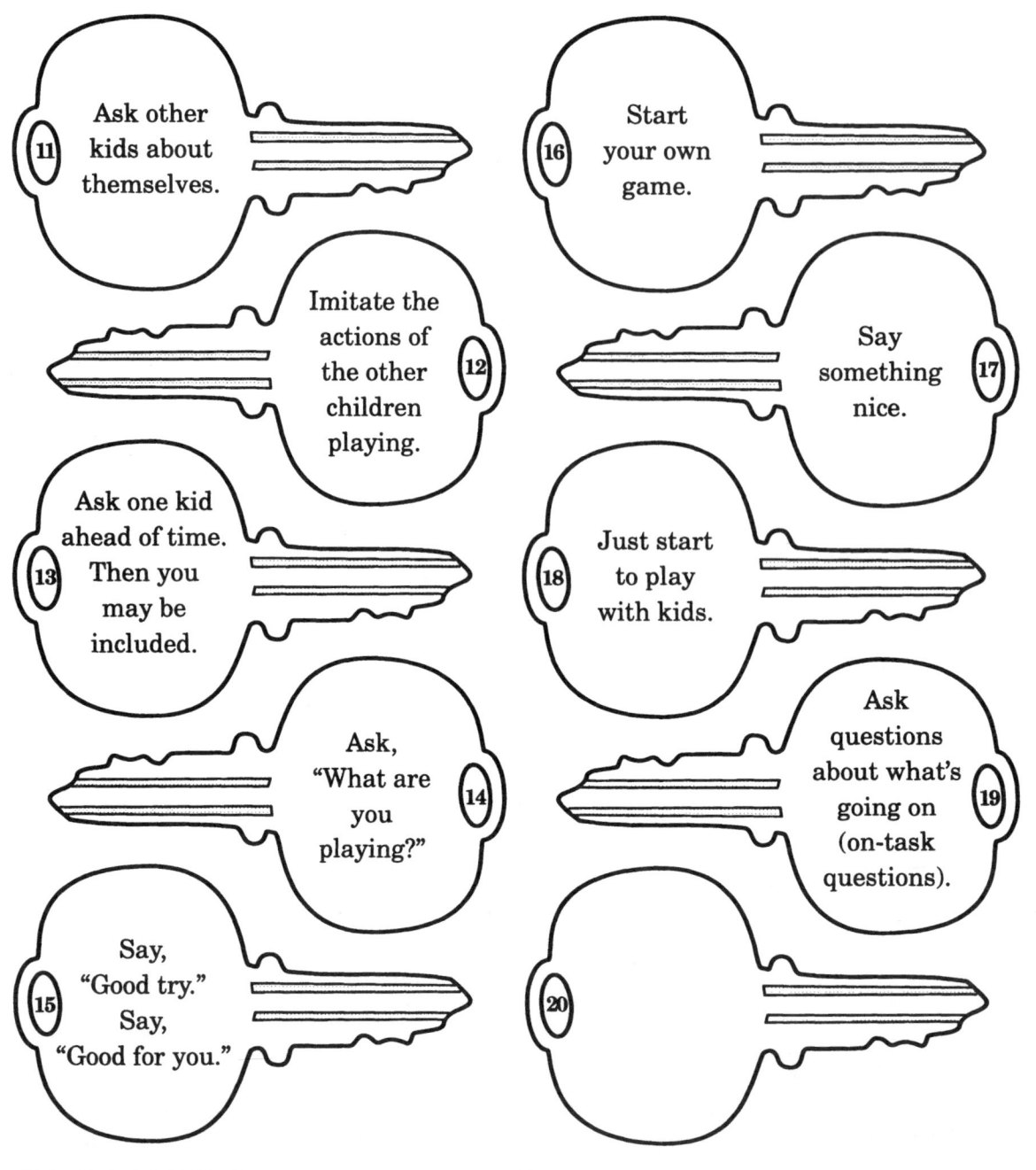

11. Ask other kids about themselves.

12. Imitate the actions of the other children playing.

13. Ask one kid ahead of time. Then you may be included.

14. Ask, "What are you playing?"

15. Say, "Good try." Say, "Good for you."

16. Start your own game.

17. Say something nice.

18. Just start to play with kids.

19. Ask questions about what's going on (on-task questions).

20.

© 1994 Thinking Publications — 140 — Duplication permitted for educational use only.

Playing Cooperatively

Names _____

MIKE WANTS TO JOIN IN

© 1994 Thinking Publications   141   Duplication permitted for educational use only.

Social Star

Lesson C

EDUCATOR INFORMATION:

This lesson targets playing cooperatively by sharing. Tremblay, Strain, Hendrickson, and Shores (1981) show that "normal" preschool children share naturally during play and that sharing results in reciprocal positive social responses by peers. On the other hand, children who do not share "close the door" to opportunities for positive social responses by others (Bryant and Budd, 1984).

OBJECTIVES:

1. To state why it is important to share with others
2. To demonstrate the cooperative play strategy of sharing

By Julie Peckham
San Diego, CA

Reprinted with permission from C. Lynn Fox and Francine Lavin Weaver, *Unlocking Doors to Friendship*, © 1983, B.L. Winch and Assoc./ Jalmar Press.

MATERIALS:

1. Cooperative play paper strips
2. *Trouble on the Playground* (See page 145; one transparency and one per student.)
3. Figures of Lee Vue, Ann Olson, Victor Parra, and Jolisa Walker (See *Appendix F*; one set per group. These figures are optional to use in step 2 of this Plan.)
4. *What Do You Think?* (See page 146; one transparency.)
5. Sharing station materials (Refer to step 6 of this Plan; select sharing stations before teaching this lesson.)
6. *How We Shared* (See page 147; one per group.)
7. Glue, tape, or stapler

PREPARATORY SET:

Present a paper strip to several students whom you observed playing cooperatively in some way during the past day or two. Describe each cooperative behavior observed as you distribute the paper strips. Tell students they can add their paper strips to the Cooperative Play Paper Chain at the end of the lesson.

PLAN:

1. Tell students that in today's lesson, they will learn about the cooperative play strategy of sharing. Ask students what *sharing* means (e.g., dividing something up with others and/or taking turns with others).

2. Divide students into groups of four. Display and distribute *Trouble on the Playground* to each student. Ask students in each group to decide who will read the part of each character. (As an option, distribute a set of character figures to each group.) Ask students to work with their group members to read the script aloud. Announce that you will be asking questions about the script.

3. Display *What Do You Think?* Cover all but question 1. Read question 1 aloud to the students. Explain that groups will be given a specified amount of time to discuss an answer and to make sure everyone can say the answer. Explain that you will call on one member from each group to share the group's answer, but do not tell who the students will be.

4. When the specified amount of time has passed, ask each group member who read Victor's parts in the script to stand. Call on one of the "Victors" to answer question 1. (The person called on may confer with group members.)

5. Follow the same procedure for questions 2–5. (Call on an "Ann" to answer question 2, a "Jolisa" to answer question 3, a "Lee" to answer question 4, and your choice for question 5.)

6. Before class, set up several "sharing stations" (enough so there can be a group of three or four students at each station). Each station should present a sharing dilemma that the group needs to solve (e.g., deciding how to play cooperatively by sharing a game typically played by only one or two people, or sharing when there is a limited amount of something). Following is a list of possible sharing stations. Choose from the list or develop sharing dilemmas more appropriate for your group of students.

   A. Video game station
      Materials: One hand-held video game

   B. Play dough station
      Materials: A small amount of play dough and three or four cookie cutters

   C. Ants-on-a-log station
      Materials: One piece of celery and a few raisins for each group member; one knife and one jar of peanut butter for the group

   D. Game station
      Materials: A two-person game (e.g., checkers, chess, tick-tack-toe)

   E. Gum station
      Materials: Pieces of gum (one less than the number of students in the group)

   F. Cookie station
      Materials: One cookie

   G. Art station
      Materials: One piece of paper for each student and one set of markers

Social Star

    H. Music station
       Materials: One cassette player with headphones and a music tape

    I. Puzzle station
       Materials: One puzzle

    J. Drinking fountain station
       Materials: A drinking fountain

    K. Lego station
       Materials: A supply of Legos

7. Explain that students will be getting into groups of three or four and that each group will work together to solve several sharing dilemmas and practice the cooperative play strategy of sharing. Set out the materials for each chosen sharing station and mark each station with a label. As you do so, explain what each sharing dilemma is. For the video game station you could say, "This sharing station is called the video game station. If your group comes to this station, the dilemma will be that there are three or four of you, but only one video game. Your job is to work together as a group to decide how to play cooperatively by sharing. Once your group decides, you may still have time to actually carry out your plan." After all the stations have been set up and explained, group students and have each group go to a different station.

8. Before beginning the station activity, distribute *How We Shared* to each group. Explain that the groups should write the name of their station and how they shared at that station before moving to another station. Explain how much time will be given, and then ask the groups to begin the activity. Rotate groups through as many sharing stations as time allows.

9. When groups have finished at their last sharing station, ask groups to explain and compare how they solved the sharing dilemma at each station.

10. Discuss situations when students may not want to share something (e.g., when someone asks to share a comb or a drinking glass; when someone forces you to give them something; when you have something very special that could be broken if shared). Ask students what they would do if they were asked to share something that is very special to them, like a new toy.

11. Give each student one strip of paper for the Cooperative Play Paper Chain and congratulate them for participating in solving the sharing dilemmas they encountered. Have students glue, tape, or staple their paper strips to the paper chain.

12. Ask students to face a partner and stand an arm's length away. Encourage partners to use friendly and confident body talk. Ask partners to shake hands and in unison repeat the following statement after you: *Learning social skills is mighty fine. I can use my social skills all the time!*

Playing Cooperatively

Name _____

Trouble on the Playground

Characters: Lee Vue
Ann Olson
Victor Parra
Jolisa Walker

Setting: Lee, Ann, Victor, and Jolisa are on the school playground at recess time. The school has a new set of plastic horseshoes. They all want to play with them. Lee has them in his hands. They are walking out the door. Victor grabs the horseshoes from Lee and runs.

Victor: Hey Ann, c'mon! I have the new horseshoes. This is really going to be fun!

Lee: Hey! I had those first! Give them back.

Ann: We have them now. Too bad! Victor, let's set them up over here. I'll be red.

Victor: No! Give me the red ones. I'm in charge.

Ann: I'm not going to play if I can't be red.

Lee: *(in an angry voice)* I wanted to use those new horseshoes!

Jolisa: *(walking over)* I thought Lee had the horseshoes.

Victor: Too bad. Ann and I are using them now.

Lee: I'm going to tell Mr. Aaron! *(the bell rings)*

Jolisa: Wow! Now recess is over and no one got to play. I wonder how we could have played together more cooperatively?

Social Star

What Do You Think?

★ 1 What was the "trouble" on the playground?

★ 2 The kids were arguing about who would use the horseshoes. What could they have done instead?

★ 3 When would you need to share?

★ 4 You are playing with others. Why is it important to share?

★ 5 You are with a group that is having a difficult time sharing. What could you say?

Names _____
       _____

How We Shared

Station: _____

We shared by: _____

_____

_____

_____

_____

—————————————— ★ ——————————————

Station: _____

We shared by: _____

_____

_____

_____

_____

—————————————— ★ ——————————————

Station: _____

We shared by: _____

_____

_____

_____

_____

Social Star

Lesson D

OBJECTIVES:

1. To tell the importance of following game rules
2. To demonstrate the cooperative play strategy of following game rules

MATERIALS:

1. *What Are the Rules?* (See page 150; one per student and one transparency.)
2. Figures of Dr. Juanita Parra, Victor Parra, Maria Parra (See *Appendix F*; one set per group. These figures are optional to use in step 1 of this Plan.)
3. *Think about This* (See page 151; one transparency.)
4. Playground ball
5. Cooperative play paper strips
6. Glue, tape, or stapler

PREPARATORY SET:

Ask students to tell you names of games they play with others. List the games where all students can see them. Choose a game from the list that is familiar to most students. Ask students to tell rules that are important to follow during the chosen game. Tell the class that in this lesson, they will learn about the cooperative play strategy of following game rules.

PLAN:

1. Divide students into groups of three. Display and distribute *What Are the Rules?* to each student. Ask students in each group to decide who will read the part of each character. (As an option, distribute a set of character figures to each group.) Ask students to work with their group members to read the script aloud. Announce that you will be asking questions about the script.

2. Display *Think about This*. Cover all but question 1. Read question 1 aloud to the students. Explain that groups will be given a specified amount of time to discuss an answer and to make sure everyone can say the answer. Explain that you will call on one member from each group to share the group's answer, but do not tell who the students will be.

3. When the specified amount of time has passed, ask each group member who read Dr. Parra's parts in the script to stand. Call on one of the "Dr. Parras" to answer question 1. (The person called on may confer with group members.)

4. Follow the same procedure for questions 2–7. (Call on a "Maria" to answer question 2, a "Victor" to answer question 3, etc.)

The answer to question 7 is that the game title is "no rules" spelled backwards.

5. Ask students to return to their seats. Hold up the playground ball. Ask students to work as a class to invent a new game by deciding the purpose and rules for the game. List the rules where everyone can read them. Discuss with students the importance of setting rules *before* playing a game.

6. Tell students that self-talk is a strategy they can use to remind themselves to play cooperatively. Ask students to name examples of self-talk they could use to remind themselves to play cooperatively. List the examples where everyone can see them.

7. Next, ask students to play the game they invented. (Moving to a large open area may be necessary.)

Note: This activity is purposefully open-ended. Decide the degree of structure and the amount of time you want to give students for inventing the game. Students may find it necessary to modify or make exceptions to rules after playing the game.

8. After playing the game, give each student one strip of paper for the Cooperative Play Paper Chain and congratulate them for practicing the strategy of following game rules. Have students glue, tape, or staple their paper strips to the paper chain.

9. Say with excitement to the class: *Liking yourself is very important! When you like who you are, you want to get along with other people by using appropriate social skills.*

Social Star

Name _____

What Are the Rules?

Characters: Dr. Juanita Parra
Maria Parra
Victor Parra

Setting: Victor is telling his mom and sister about a dream he had last night. They are eating breakfast.

Victor: I really had a goofy dream last night.

Dr. Parra: What was it about?

Victor: Maria and I were in a different place. Some people asked us to play a game called Seluron.

Maria: I've never heard of that game. What was it like?

Victor: You and I hated it. We were supposed to hit a ball through hoops. But they kept changing the rules. First they said to stand in one place. Then they said to stand in another place. They said *we* got *two* points for getting the ball through a hoop. Then they said *they* got *ten* points. It was really confusing.

Maria: That would drive me crazy. The rules changed all the time.

Dr. Parra: So what did you and Maria do in your dream?

Victor: I'll never know! I woke up before the dream was over. But I don't think I want to play Seluron again!

Playing Cooperatively

Think about This

⭐ **1** What was the "problem" in Victor's dream?

⭐ **2** The rules for Seluron kept being changed. What could Victor and Maria have done?

⭐ **3** Tell about other problems that happen with game rules.

⭐ **4** You don't know or understand the rules of a game. What can you say or do?

⭐ **5** You are playing games with others. Tell why it is important to follow rules.

⭐ **6** You are playing with someone who is choosing not to follow game rules. What can you do or say?

⭐ **7** (Just for fun!) Why do you think the game in Victor's dream was called "Seluron"?

Social Star

Lesson E

OBJECTIVES:

1. To tell the importance of being a good sport
2. To demonstrate the cooperative play strategy of being a good sport

MATERIALS:

1. Cooperative play paper strips
2. Glue, tape, or stapler
3. *The Good Sport Award* (See page 154; one per student and one transparency.)
4. Figures of Ann Olson, Mr. Aaron, and Victor Parra (See *Appendix F*; one set per group. These figures are optional to use in step 2 of this Plan.)
5. *Time to Talk* (See page 155; one transparency.)
6. Coins (One per pair of students)
7. Sheets of paper (One per pair of students)

PREPARATORY SET:

Present a paper strip to several students whom you observed playing cooperatively in some way during the past day or two. Specifically describe each positive behavior observed as you distribute the paper strips. Tell students they can add their paper strips to the Cooperative Play Paper Chain.

PLAN:

1. Tell students that in today's lesson, they will learn about the cooperative play strategy of being a good sport. Ask students what *being a good sport* means (e.g., being a gracious winner and loser, encouraging other people, not laughing when other players make mistakes).

2. Divide students into groups of three. Display and distribute *The Good Sport Award* to each student. Ask students in each group to decide who will read the part of each character. (As an option, distribute a set of character figures to each group.) Ask students to work with their group members to read the script aloud. Tell students that you will be asking questions about the script.

3. Display *Time to Talk*. Cover all but question 1. Read question 1 aloud to the students. Explain that groups will be given a specified amount of time to discuss an answer and to make sure everyone can say the answer. Explain that you will call on one member from each group to share the group's answer, but do not tell who the students will be.

4. After the specified amount of time has passed, ask each group member who read Ann's parts in the script to stand. Call on one of the "Anns" to answer question 1. (The person called on may confer with group members.)

5. Follow the same procedure for questions 2–6. (Call on a "Mr. Aaron" to answer question 2, a "Victor" to answer question 3, etc.).

6. Tell students that you will be asking them to practice sportsmanship.

7. Pair students (see *Appendix P*). Explain that students will work with their partners to practice the cooperative play strategy of being a good sport.

8. Distribute one coin and a sheet of paper to each pair of students. Tell students that they will be trying to beat their partners at flipping coins. Ask students to decide who will be "heads" and who will be "tails." Ask students to create a tally sheet by writing "heads" and "tails" at the top of their papers.

9. Ask partners to take turns flipping their coin and placing a tally in the corresponding column on their tally sheet. Demonstrate how to play the game while students watch.

10. Remind students that this is a competitive game, so one person from each pair will win and one person from each pair will lose. Ask them to brainstorm ways of being a good sport while playing the game.

11. Ask student pairs to begin the game. Give them several minutes to flip before saying "stop." After they stop flipping the coins, ask the pairs to count the tallies to see who is the winner.

12. Ask students to tell how they noticed their partners being good sports during this activity. Ask students if they think it is easier to be a good sport when they are winning or when they are losing.

13. Give each student a strip of paper for the Cooperative Play Paper Chain and congratulate them for practicing the strategy of being a good sport. Ask students to write one thing they learned about being a good sport on their paper strips. Ask students to share what they wrote with their partners and then glue, tape, or staple their strips to the paper chain.

14. Say with excitement to the class: *It is very exciting to watch you practice your social skills! I would like to invite you to use your social skills outside of this room wherever you go.*

Social Star

The Good Sport AWARD

Name _____

☆ ☆ ☆ ☆ ☆

Characters: Ann Olson   Mr. Marcus Aaron   Victor Parra

Setting: Mr. Aaron is the coach of the ball team. He is planning an awards program for his team. He needs help choosing who should receive one of the awards.

Mr. Aaron: Ann and Victor, you're the team captains. I need your help. One of the awards given each year is called "The Good Sport Award." Who do you think should get this special award?

Victor: Does this award go to the person who gets the most points?

Mr. Aaron: No, it goes to a person who is a gracious winner and loser.

Ann: What does that mean?

Mr. Aaron: A gracious winner is someone who doesn't tease or laugh at the person or team that loses. A gracious loser doesn't get angry or pout. A gracious loser knows it was fun just being able to play.

Victor: Oh, I see. This award goes to someone who isn't a sore loser or a braggy winner. I've heard people talk about that.

Ann: What else should you be like to get "The Good Sport Award"?

Mr. Aaron: Good sports don't cheat. They cheer their team on. They keep playing, even if they're losing. They don't give up if a mistake is made. They say and do nice things to the other team. They shake their hands or give them the "high-five." The person who gets the award may or may not be the best at the game, but he or she makes the game fun.

Ann: I know just the person who deserves "The Good Sport Award." I think Lee Vue is a great sport!

Victor: I agree. He makes our games fun and doesn't get upset if we lose.

Mr. Aaron: Thanks for your help. This is one of my favorite awards to give. I'll see you at the awards program!

Playing Cooperatively

Time to Talk

1. What were the characters in the script trying to decide?

2. Mr. Aaron wanted Ann and Victor to help him decide who should get "The Good Sport Award." Why?

3. You are playing with someone who isn't a good sport (e.g., someone who gets angry about losing and laughs at you for making mistakes). How does that make you feel?

4. You are playing with someone who is a good sport. How does that make you feel?

5. It is important to be a good sport. Name other times besides a ball game.

6. What can you say or do to help others be good sports?

Social Star

Lesson F

EDUCATOR INFORMATION:

1. Educators are becoming more concerned with the type of play that occurs during recess. There is evidence that children's rate of verbal and physical aggression may be increased by watching violent acts, by playing with toys that are aggressive in nature, or by playing games that have violent or aggressive themes (Sherburne, Utley, McConnell, and Gannon, 1988).

2. Educators may wish to establish a small area on the playground where children go when they have a violent or aggressive theme to their play (e.g., pretending to shoot guns, making bomb noises). Sherburne, Utley, McConnell, and Gannon (1988) found that restricting children to a small area when their play has an aggressive or violent theme decreases the amount of this type of play. The children were told beforehand that if they played guns or other dangerous games, they would be asked to move to the specified area. Children were free to leave the specific area at any time to engage in other play behaviors.

3. It is helpful to encourage cooperative games/activities as opposed to competitive activities that may lead to verbal or physical aggression. *The Cooperative Sports and Games Book* (Orlick, 1978) and *The Second Cooperative Sports and Games Book* (Orlick, 1982) are excellent resources for educators (see page 40).

OBJECTIVES:

1. To state why it is important to play safely with others
2. To demonstrate the cooperative play strategy of playing safely

MATERIALS:

1. A bag containing a variety of items children sometimes play with (e.g., jump rope, squirt gun, stick, football)
2. *Ouch! That Hurt!* (See page 159; one per student and one transparency.)
3. Figures of Mike Olson, Ms. Paula Hess, and Lee Vue (See *Appendix F*; one set per group. These figures are optional to use in step 2 of this Plan.)
4. *Heads Together* (See page 160; one transparency.)
5. Cooperative play materials (Refer to step 8 of this Plan; select and prepare for cooperative games before teaching this lesson.)
6. Cooperative play paper strips
7. Glue, tape, or stapler

PREPARATORY SET:

Have all of the play items in a bag before class. Give clues to students to help them identify the items. As each item is guessed, take it out of the bag and then ask students if they think it would be possible to get hurt in any way while playing with the item. Ask, "How many of you have ever gotten hurt while you were playing? Was it because you or someone you were playing with wasn't careful? Was it because someone got 'too rough'?" Allow time for appropriate discussion to occur.

PLAN:

1. Tell students that in today's lesson, they will learn about the cooperative play strategy of playing safely. Ask students what they think *playing safely* means (e.g., playing in a way that reduces the chances of getting hurt).

2. Divide students into groups of three. Display and distribute *Ouch! That Hurt!* to each student. Ask students in each group to decide who will read the part of each character. (As an option, distribute a set of character figures to each group.) Ask students to work with their group members to read the script aloud. Announce that you will be asking questions about the script.

3. Display *Heads Together*. Cover all but question 1. Read question 1 aloud to the students. Explain that groups will be given a specified amount of time to discuss an answer and to make sure everyone can say the answer. Explain that you will call on one member from each group to share the group's answer, but do not tell who the students will be.

4. When the specified amount of time has passed, ask each group member who read Mike's parts in the script to stand. Call on one of the "Mikes" to answer question 1. (The person called on may confer with group members.) After the answer is shared, give a paper strip for the Cooperative Play Paper Chain to all of the "Mikes." Tell them they can add their paper strips to the chain later.

5. Follow the same procedure, including handing out the paper strips, for questions 2–6. (Call on a "Lee" to answer question 2, a "Ms. Hess" to answer question 3, etc.)

6. Ask students to glue, tape, or staple their strips to the paper chain.

7. Tell students they will practice the cooperative play strategy of playing safely. Take students to a large open area (e.g., gymnasium, playground). Tell students that they will have physical contact with others in these activities. Explain that you want them to have fun, but that they need to be careful that the fun does not get so rough that someone gets hurt. Tell students that they can use self-talk to remind themselves to play safely with others. Ask them to tell the words they might use while reminding themselves to play safely. Write the self-talk where all can see it.

8. Have students participate in one or more of the following activities. Emphasize the need for playing in a safe manner. Remind students that they should tell their partner if the play situation is becoming "too rough."

   Hop-along (Orlick, 1978)
   Pair students and have partners stand and face each other. Both students in a partnership should raise their right legs straight out in front and then grasp each other's ankle. Partners should balance each other in this position. They can try a variety of maneuvers (e.g., lowering themselves, hopping along, rotating in a circle). This activity requires trust of one's partner and the ability to participate in a safe manner.

   Square Ball (Orlick, 1978)
   This game is played by having four children work together to keep a rope taut and in the shape of a square while at the same time moving a ball with their feet. Children should alternately move the ball from a designated area in the center of the room to a corner spot and then back to the center.

   Collective Blanketball (Orlick, 1978)
   Split students into two teams. Each team's members grab onto the edges of a blanket. A large ball is placed in the center of one blanket. Teams pass the ball back and forth by having all members from one team toss the ball in unison to the other team's blanket.

9. Ask partners to face each other and stand an arm's length away. Encourage partners to use friendly and confident body talk. Ask partners to shake hands and in unison repeat the following statement after you: *When I see you use your social skills today, I'll step right up and say, "Great social skills, partner!"*

Playing Cooperatively

Name _____

OUCH! That Hurt!

Characters: Mike Olson
Lee Vue
Ms. Paula Hess

Setting: Mike and Lee are roughhousing on the playground. It gets out of hand. Mike becomes upset with Lee. He gives Lee a shove. Lee runs over to Ms. Hess.

Lee: (*angrily*) Ms. Hess, Mike shoved me!

Ms. Hess: I saw the two of you playing.

Mike: (*walking up*) I didn't do anything! He twisted my arm first!

Lee: Oh, I didn't do it hard. I was just joking around.

Mike: You twisted it hard. That hurt a lot!

Lee: You're such a baby!

Ms. Hess: Boys, let's talk about this without any name-calling. When you first started playing, it looked like you were both having fun.

Mike: Well, we were. But then it changed.

Social Star

HEADS TOGETHER

★ 1 What caused Mike and Lee to have problems?

★ 2 Why does roughhousing sometimes cause arguments?

★ 3 What can Mike and Lee do to solve their disagreement?

★ 4 Do you think students should be allowed to roughhouse during recess? Why or why not?

★ 5 Another person may not want to play rough anymore or may be getting hurt. How can you tell?

★ 6 Someone wants you to play in an unsafe way. What can you do?

Lessons X, Y, and Z

Due to similarities in format, the final three lesson plans for each unit in *Social Star* are provided in *Appendix A*. Substitute the words "playing cooperatively" whenever a "____" appears in the lesson plans. Information specific to this unit follows.

LESSON X PREPARATORY SET:

Ask students to estimate the length of the Cooperative Play Paper Chain. Compare to students' guesses from Lesson A. Measure the chain to see who estimated the closest. Encourage students to be good sports by displaying a positive attitude toward the winner.

LESSON Y PREPARATORY SET:

Darken the room, if you prefer, and ask students to visualize themselves correctly using this social skill by reading the following script:

> *Let's take a few moments to relax.... Make sure you are sitting in a comfortable position.... Close your eyes if you feel like it.... On the count of three, take a very slow, deep breath. Remember to breathe in quietly through your nose. One . . . two . . . three.... Now breathe out slowly and quietly through your mouth. Let your entire body relax.... Imagine yourself playing cooperatively on a team with others.... Your team just lost the game. You are disappointed, but you smile and tell kids from the other team, "Good job!" Think about how proud you feel because you remembered to be a good sport.*

LESSON Z PLOT SITUATION:

Ask students to pretend they have tried three times to join in to play with a group of kids, but the kids keep saying no.

LESSON Z ROADBLOCK EXAMPLES:

- Playing cooperatively when others are not
- Being a good sport when you are losing or when a game is difficult
- Following game rules when you don't know or understand them
- Sharing something that is very special
- Trying to join in when you are worried that the group might tell you there's not room for you
- Playing with someone who is too rough

Social Star

Name _____

Playing Cooperatively T-Chart

LOOKS LIKE...

using appropriate body talk

- looking at the people you are playing with
- smiling

playing safely

sharing

taking turns

following rules

being a good sport after winning and losing

joining in and letting others join in

SOUNDS LIKE...

a friendly tone of voice

an appropriate volume

saying

- "This is getting too rough! Let's play something else."
- "Can I play too?"
- "When you're finished with this game, can I join in?"
- "What would you like to play?"
- "I'll share with you."
- "It's your turn."
- "Would you like a turn?"
- "Congratulations for winning!"

© 1994 Thinking Publications · 162 · *Duplication permitted for educational use only.*

Playing Cooperatively

SHOW TIME

HOME

Pretend you just got a new remote control vehicle. Your sister really wants to try it. Show how you can share the vehicle with your sister.

SCHOOL

Pretend you want to join a group of kids playing a game on the playground. Show what you could do or say to join the group.

COMMUNITY

Pretend you are playing on a jungle gym at the park. Some kids you do not know are playing very rough right next to you. Show what you could say or do to play safely.

Social Star

Have fun playing every day...

Have fun playing every day...

Have fun playing every day...

Have fun playing every day...

Playing Cooperatively

© 1994 Thinking Publications — Duplication permitted for educational use only.

HOME-A-GRAM

Dear Family,

At school, we have been talking about the social skill called

PLAYING COOPERATIVELY

I learned that *playing cooperatively* means playing in a way that invites everyone to have fun.

I learned that there are things I can do to play cooperatively with others. I can share, join in with others, follow game rules, be a "good sport," and play safely.

When I play cooperatively, I make a good impression on others and they will enjoy playing with me more. I feel good inside when I play in a way that invites everyone to have fun.

Below I have listed some games I enjoy playing with my family:

_____

_____

_____

_____

Let's choose one of the games I've listed to play together tonight. After I show how I can play cooperatively, please sign my "Playing Cooperatively" badge so I can return it to school and become a SOCIAL SUPER STAR this week.

From: _____

© 1994 Thinking Publications — Duplication permitted for educational use only.

Respecting Differences

Social Star

UNIT GOAL:

To demonstrate comprehension and use of respecting differences

EDUCATOR INFORMATION:

1. This unit encourages students to adopt an anti-bias attitude when dealing with people who may be different from themselves. Some types of differences include race, religion, class, physical appearance, gender, intelligence level, and learning styles. The unit asserts that all human beings are important and have special unique strengths. Human beings should be treated with dignity and respect. The unit promotes the idea that people who feel good about themselves (have high self-esteem) tend to have fewer prejudices against others (Rubin, 1967). The educator should exert sensitivity and care in generalizing rules about respecting differences into the children's home cultures.

2. An excellent resource for educators at any grade level is the *Anti-Bias Curriculum* by Louise Derman-Sparks (1989) and the A.B.C. Task Force. This resource includes a wealth of information for educators about individual differences and includes activities to use with children. One of the most helpful parts of the book is the "Caution" section, which provides specific cautions to those who think they are promoting an anti-bias attitude when in fact they may be hindering it. The book can be ordered from:

    National Association for the Education of Young Children
    1834 Connecticut Avenue, N.W.
    Washington, DC 20009
    202-232-8777 • 800-424-2460

The Inside, The True Person
By Paul Kreul
San Diego, CA

Reprinted with permission from C. Lynn Fox and Francine Lavin Weaver, *Unlocking Doors to Friendship*, © 1983, B.L. Winch and Assoc./Jalmar Press.

3. There are many factors to consider when addressing the issue of respecting differences. A list of related information follows:

- It is not enough to simply give factual information about another group or culture when attempting to reduce prejudice (Pate, 1981). The feelings of students must also be addressed.

- Films and other media with an integrated cast have been known to improve students' attitudes about prejudice (Pate, 1981).

- One third of the people in the United States will be nonwhite by the year 2000 (Williams, 1986).

- Direct teaching of respecting individual differences is the most effective means for bringing about attitudinal changes (Freedman, Gotti, and Holtz, 1981; Sapon-Shevin, 1983).

- "Bicultural, bicognitive education is defined as having students: (1) learn the beliefs, values, rules, and language of their own culture in the learning or teaching style appropriate to their culture, and (2) learn the beliefs, values, rules, language, and learning style of the dominant culture" (Derman-Sparks, 1989, p. 6).

- It is best if social interaction between children of different races is structured in a positive manner (Pate, 1981). Students should be able to get to know each other as individuals and should have common interests and characteristics. Interaction should occur in a cooperative atmosphere as opposed to a competitive atmosphere.

- It is important to be open about differences and not tell a child that a boy in a wheelchair is "just like you" (Derman-Sparks, 1989). The educator's response could discuss how the children are different and how they are the same.

- Some multicultural curricula use a "tourist" approach (Derman-Sparks, 1989) in that only extreme differences are looked at (e.g., differences in holidays, food, costume) and the everyday life of the group is forgotten, the result being that a well-meaning educator may inadvertently perpetuate the stereotypes associated with various cultures. An excellent listing of common stereotypes in the areas of gender and disabilities, and stereotypes of various cultures is found in the *Anti-Bias Curriculum* by Louise Derman-Sparks (1989). Educators are encouraged to assess their own use of stereotypes by referring to this list.

RELATED ACTIVITIES:

1. Have students pretend they are traveling into the past in a time machine. The time machine can visit periods when discrimination was occurring. Have students

study some of the less commonly known examples of prejudice (e.g., children viewed as slaves who worked in factories, people with overt physical conditions such as deafness and cerebral palsy regarded as idiots, Japanese viewed as "Japs," Italians viewed as "Wops," Catholics viewed as being unfit for public office, divorced women seen as "fallen," poor people seen as beneath the lower class, left-handed people seen as "sinister"). Next have students visit the present to see what types of discrimination are occurring today. Then students should create their dreams for a future without prejudice.

2. Have students research and plan a lesson about a specific cultural group and why the group came to America (e.g., the Hmong came to this country from a mountainous region in Laos after the Vietnam War to escape persecution and death). Make sure that students have an opportunity to interview people from the culture they are studying. Students can then present their lesson to classmates.

3. Discuss terminology used to describe various groups (e.g., Native American vs. Indian; African-American vs. black, colored, Negroes; women vs. broads). Discuss how these terms have evolved.

4. Have students become "tape-recorder pen pals" with students in a different city (preferably students from a different ethnic background).

5. Have students listen to music, watch dances, and listen to stories from various cultures.

6. Have students establish a classroom picture file of people. This can be used to make a bulletin board for the school about respecting differences or in day-to-day learning activities. It is important that the pictures not be exclusively of typical "white, middle-class American" people.

7. Explain Gardner's (1983) theory of multiple intelligence to students. Explain that there are seven types of intelligence and that all people have strengths in at least some of these areas.

8. Visit a local business person to discuss equal employment laws.

9. Invite adults from other cultures to talk to the students about how their cultures' conventions for respecting differences compare with American common culture norms.

It is important for educators to provide opportunities for students to work in groups so they can experience social skills in contexts where social communication is needed. Therefore, educators are encouraged to have students complete the Related Activities in small groups whenever possible. Educators trained in cooperative learning could incorporate the five components (see page 33) into the group activity.

RELATED LITERATURE:

Josie Smith at School (1991) by Magdalen Nabb, Ill. by Pirkko Vainio, Macmillan. (Text) Josie befriends a new girl at school while other classmates make fun of her. (pages 38–50)

How My Parents Learned to Eat (1984) by Ina R. Friedman, Ill. by Allen Say, Houghton Mifflin. (Picture book/text)

All in a Day (1986) by Mitsumasa Anno, Philomel. (Picture book)
Brief text and illustrations by ten famous artists show a day in the lives of children in eight different countries.

SOCIAL SKILLS ALL DAY LONG:

Look for opportunities to teach social skills throughout the day (incidental teaching). Four ways to reinforce appropriate social skills and an example of each follow:

Encouragement

Mike, you have been so pleasant to Tio since he's arrived at our school. It seems like you have a lot in common and are having fun discovering differences in each of your cultures. I can see you are really concerned about what people are like on the inside.

Personal Example

Yesterday I saw a man who was extremely large. I reminded myself that we are all different and that's OK. I told myself that I'm not better than him because I weigh less.

Prompting

If you go out this weekend and you see someone who's different from you in some way, remind yourself that we are all different and it's important to respect individual differences.

Corrective Feedback (must be positive, private, specific, and nonthreatening)

Jolisa, just now you said, "That kid dresses like a poor boy." Remember, we are all different and that is OK. Remember, that it's better to focus on what people are like inside. You could have asked yourself how you could show that you respect him as a person.

Respecting Differences

Lesson A

OBJECTIVES:

1. To state the meaning of *respecting differences* and tell why it is important

2. To listen to the self-talk associated with correct use of the skill

MATERIALS:

1. Pine cones (One per student)

2. *Respecting Differences* (See page 174; one per student and one transparency.)

3. *Thought Bubble* (See *Appendix O*; one for educator use.)

4. *Checking Myself* (See *Appendix I*; one per student and one transparency.)

5. *Dominoes* (See *Appendix U*; one set cut apart per pair of students, and one set of transparency dominoes.)

PREPARATORY SET:

Have students sit in a circle. Distribute one pine cone to each student. Ask students to get to know their pine cone by looking it over carefully and noticing anything that might make their pine cone different from the other pine cones. Give students a minute to examine their pine cones. Collect the pine cones and then redistribute them. Tell students to start passing the pine cones around the circle in a clockwise direction and to hold onto their own pine cone when it comes around. Afterward, ask students how they were able to find their own pine cones. Discuss the concept that pine cones are like people because they are very similar but there are certain things that make each one different and unique. Use this activity to introduce this unit about respecting differences.

PLAN:

1. Distribute and display *Respecting Differences*. Discuss the definition of *respecting differences*. Explain the skill steps for respecting differences and the symbols next to them. Remind students that the symbols are there to help them visualize and remember the skill steps. Refer students to the body-talk symbol in the left-hand margin. Remind students that appropriate body talk is important when respecting differences. Discuss the reasons for respecting differences.

2. Model use of the skill steps for respecting differences while thinking aloud. A scripted example follows:

Introduction

I am going to pretend to be someone your age who is with another student. I will show you how I can respect someone who is different from me and tell you the thoughts I'm having. When I hold up this Thought Bubble, *you'll know the words I'm saying are actually what I'm thinking.*

Actual Model

While holding up the *Thought Bubble* say, *Phil is different from me because he has a hard time with math and I'm good at it. That's OK. I respect Phil. I'll think about the person Phil is on the inside. I won't tease him about math.*

3. Distribute and display the discussion guideline sheet called *Checking Myself*. Ask students to complete the goal statement with the words "think about an answer to each question asked," or use another classroom discussion goal more appropriate for your group (see pages 25–26). Tell students that you will be asking questions about the symbol for skill step 1. Explain that after you ask each question, it's important for them to be thinking about an answer, even if they are not called on. Instruct them to circle a T-shirt star each time they think about an answer to a question. Provide enough "wait time" before calling on a student to orally answer each question.

4. Model use of the *Checking Myself* sheet while thinking aloud. A scripted example follows:

Introduction

I am going to pretend to be one of you completing this sheet during the discussion we will be having. I will tell you the thoughts I'm having while I'm completing the sheet. When I hold up this Thought Bubble, *you'll know the words I'm saying are actually what I'm thinking.*

Actual Model

While holding up the *Thought Bubble* say, *OK, the teacher just asked, "How are the kids from Socialville different from each other on the outside?" I need to think of an answer. Some wear glasses and some do not. I'll circle a star on my sheet because I just thought about an answer to that question.* Put the *Thought Bubble* down and circle a star on the transparency.

5. Proceed with the actual discussion by asking the following questions. During the discussion, periodically remind students to be thinking of answers to the questions and to mark their discussion guideline sheets.

Respecting Differences

- What differences do you notice about the Socialville kids on the outside? Answers should include information about visible differences (e.g., gender, race, height, length of hair).

- What differences might they have on the inside? Answers could include strengths, weaknesses, thoughts, or feelings.

- What would it be like if they were all the same?

- How might they show respect for each other's differences?

- How could respecting each other's differences help them get along?

- What are other reasons for respecting each other's differences?

- Why don't differences make one person better than another?

After the discussion, have students complete the bottom of *Checking Myself*.

6. Process use of the sheet by asking the following questions or others more appropriate for your group:

    - Why is it important to stay on task by thinking of answers to questions during a discussion?

    - Why is it sometimes hard to stay on task and think of answers?

7. Pair students (see *Appendix P*). Tell students they will be playing a game called dominoes with their partners.

8. Model specifically how to play dominoes using the transparency dominoes.

9. Distribute a set of *Dominoes* to each pair. Each time students match dominoes, have them tell their partners one way that people are alike (e.g., all people have feelings, thoughts, body parts, need food, need love, need water, etc.) and one way they can be different.

10. Ask student pairs to take turns telling each other the meaning of *respecting differences* and why it's important to use the skill. Students could be reminded that the information they are to say is printed on *Respecting Differences*.

    As an option to add structure to this activity (see *Appendix Q*), ask partners to come to an agreement about which person will be called "Babe Ruth" and which person will be called "Jackie Robinson." After students have made their decisions, ask "Babe" to tell "Jackie" the definition of *respecting differences*. Next, ask "Jackie" to tell "Babe" the definition. Ask students to use the same procedure to tell each other the reasons for respecting differences.

11. Ask partners to face each other and stand an arm's length away. Encourage partners to use friendly and confident body talk. Ask partners to shake hands and in unison repeat the following statement after you: *I enjoy learning new social skills. Social skills make the world a happier place!*

Social Star

Name _____

⭐ Respecting Differences

MEANING OF RESPECTING DIFFERENCES: Understanding that we are all unique and equally important

SKILL STEPS:

1. Remind myself: We are all different and that's OK

2. Tell myself: Think about each person on the inside

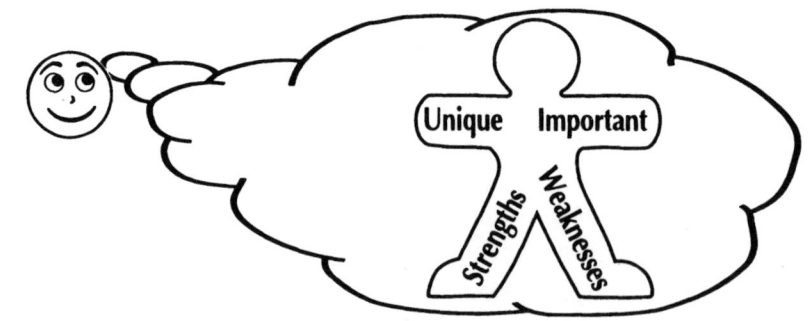

   Unique   Important   Strengths   Weaknesses

3. Ask myself: How can I show respect to everyone?

REASONS FOR USING THIS SKILL:

If you recognize and respect that everyone is unique and equally important, you will invite others to feel good about themselves and about you. Respecting differences helps make your home, your school, your community, and the world more peaceful for everyone.

© 1994 Thinking Publications — 174 — Duplication permitted for educational use only.

Respecting Differences

Lesson B

OBJECTIVES:

1. To identify the differences that exist among individuals
2. To identify the feelings a person may have when being discriminated against

MATERIALS:

1. *Ann's Tale of Two Cities* (See pages 178–183; duplicate pages back to back, cut and assemble one storybook per student.)
2. One variety of candy (One piece per student)
3. *Respecting Differences* classroom poster (See page 13.)

PREPARATORY SET:

Pair students (see *Appendix P*). Tell students there are physical differences people are born with that make them different from one another. Explain that eye color is one of those differences. Ask students to check the eye color of their partners. Next, explain that another trait that some people have and others do not is the ability to roll their tongues. Ask student pairs to work with each other to determine whether they can roll their tongues (curl up both sides of their tongue to make a trough). Ask students the following questions:

- Were you able to choose the color of your eyes?
- Were you able to choose whether or not you can roll your tongue?
- What are some other differences that people are born with and are unable to choose?

PLAN:

1. Distribute *Ann's Tale of Two Cities*. Explain to students that this is a story about Ann, who moves away from Socialville.
2. Read the story aloud as the students follow along in their books.
3. Tell students that you will be asking them some questions about the story they just heard. Explain that as each question is asked, they should talk with their partners and come up with an answer. Explain that one or more pairs will be called on to share their answers. Proceed by asking the following questions:
   - How did people with brown eyes treat people without brown eyes in Color Counts?
   - Would you like to live in Color Counts? Why or why not?

Social Star

- How might the people without brown eyes feel?
- How do you think the people with brown eyes feel?
- Do you know of any time in history (including the present) when people were treated like the people without brown eyes?
- What powerful self-talk could the people without brown eyes use to help themselves when they are being teased in a mean way?
- In Tongue Town, how did the people who could roll their tongues treat the people who could not?
- Would you like to live in Tongue Town? Why or why not?
- How do you think the people who can't roll their tongues feel?
- Do you think the mean tongue rollers have good self-esteem (feel good about themselves)?
- What powerful self-talk could the people who cannot roll their tongues use to help themselves when they are treated poorly?
- Why do you think people would treat other people poorly because they are different?
- Does anything like this ever happen in our school, in our city, or in our world?

4. Tell students they are going to pretend they live in Color Counts. Caution students that what they are about to do is just an experiment, and ask them to remember it is a pretend situation. Tell students with brown eyes to walk around the room and tease students whose eyes are not brown for a short while. Next, ask students without brown eyes to walk around and say and do things to tease students with brown eyes.

5. Tell students they are going to pretend they live in Tongue Town. Hold up the candy. Tell students that you have lollipops (or whatever you have chosen) only for the students who can roll their tongues. Ask those who can roll their tongues to raise their hands and distribute the candy to them.

6. Say the following:

Now we are finished with our experiment. We are no longer going to pretend we are in Color Counts or Tongue Town. Our class will now be back to normal where we aren't mean to each other. How did you feel when you were being teased about your eye color? How did you feel when you didn't get candy because of your tongue? Why do you think we did this experiment? What did you learn from this experiment? Since our class doesn't discriminate, whoever didn't receive a piece of candy can have one now.

7. Review the definition and skill steps for *respecting differences* by referring the class to the *Respecting Differences* classroom poster.

8. Ask student pairs to take turns telling each other the skill steps for respecting differences. Follow the procedure described in step 10 of Lesson A. (As an option, ask students to decide who will be "Rembrandt" and who will be "Pablo Picasso.") Next, ask students to work with their partners to think of a situation in which it would be important to respect differences. Tell students that one or more pairs will be asked to share their situation. Have one or more pairs share their situation.

9. Say with excitement to the class: *I am different from you and you are different from me. That makes us each special. I like you because you're different and special!*

Social Star

Ann's Tale of Two Cities

1

---- ✂ ---

Miss Brunella told Ann to sit in the back of the room with all the other blithering blue-eyed students. Ann didn't know what was happening. She was so scared. During the rest of the morning, Miss Brunella never looked at the blue-eyed kids in the back of the room. She didn't call on them to answer any questions. Once she even said, "Oh, you smart brown-eyed children always understand things right away," and then she looked at the blue-eyed kids with a mean facial expression.

3

© 1994 Thinking Publications   178   *Duplication permitted for educational use only.*

Respecting Differences

1 COLOR COUNTS

It was a dark, rainy Monday when Ann moved to her new school, Brown Elementary, in the town of Color Counts. Her teacher's name was Miss Brunella Browny. The first thing the teacher did was to shine a light in Ann's eyes and say in a nasty tone, "Oh dear, you've got blue eyes. That's not good, not good at all."

2

Things got even worse when they went to recess. Some of the brown-eyed kids came over and started to call her names. They yelled, "Hey you, blue eyes, go back where you came from!" They all started screaming, "Down with blue eyes! Down with blue eyes!" Ann wished that she could go back to McKinley School in Socialville.

4

© 1994 Thinking Publications   179   *Duplication permitted for educational use only.*

Social Star

As she was getting ready to go in after recess, Ann's mom pulled up in the car and told Ann to get in. She hopped in the car quickly. Her mother said they had changed their minds and were moving to a different town. Ann gave a big sigh of relief.

5

Ann decided to walk to the park across the street. On her way, she saw a man walking proudly with his tongue sticking out. Ann was even more surprised when she got to the park and saw that there were more people sticking their tongues out in a strange way. Even a small baby was sticking his tongue out.

7

Respecting Differences

2 TONGUE TOWN

Ann had just finished helping her parents move into their new house in Tongue Town. She was so glad to be away from Color Counts and those mean people. Ann was looking forward to her new school in Tongue Town (even though the name of the town sounded a little strange).

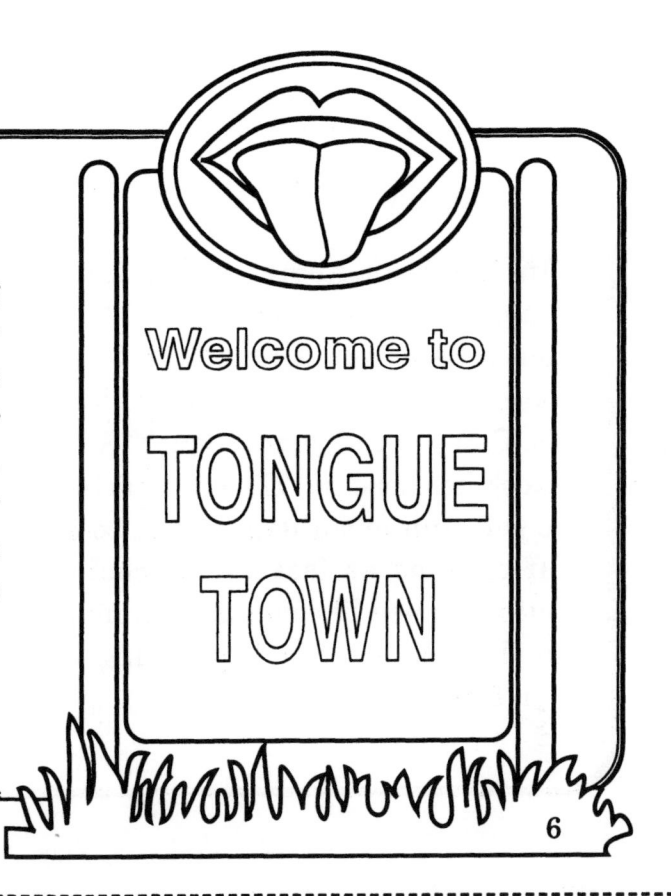

Welcome to TONGUE TOWN

6

Ann noticed one sad looking girl who wasn't sticking her tongue out. Ann walked over to her and said, "Hi." She asked the girl why everyone was sticking their tongues out. The girl said, "You must be new in town. Stick your tongue out. Can you roll your tongue?" Ann looked puzzled and tried to do a tongue roll. She couldn't do it. The girl said, "I can't roll my tongue either. If you can't roll your tongue in this town, you're nothing. People tease you, or worse yet, they don't talk to you at all. You're not allowed to go to certain places like the movie theater or the video arcade." Ann felt just like she was back in Color Counts. She said goodbye to the girl and started to run home.

8

© 1994 Thinking Publications   181   *Duplication permitted for educational use only.*

On her way home, three kids stopped her and told her to stick her tongue out. One of the kids said, "Let's see if you're special like us. Can you roll your tongue?" Ann shook her head no. The kids started to call Ann mean names. She took off running as fast as she could, but it seemed like she was running in slow motion. She kept trying to run faster.

SOCIALVILLE

All of a sudden, Ann woke up. She looked around and saw that she was in her very own bedroom in the wonderful, wonderful town of Socialville. Ann smiled a great big smile and said, "There's no place like home. There's no place like home."

10

Social Star

Lesson C

EDUCATOR INFORMATION:

It is important that an anti-bias curriculum use a developmental approach (Derman-Sparks, 1989). Lessons should respond to children's interest and specific concerns. It is critical to know what the children really want to discuss or what their questions really mean (e.g., a child may ask, "Why does he look like that?" and a parent or educator may give a lengthy discussion of skin color when all the child wanted to know was why the person had a different hair style). Children's perspectives must be taken into account. The educator is encouraged to adapt the situations in this lesson to meet the developmental or interest levels of the students.

OBJECTIVE:

To tell and practice the self-talk one could use to respect the differences of others

MATERIALS:

1. Any version of the Grimm fairy tale *The Beauty and the Beast*

2. *Animal Cards* (See *Appendix P*.)

3. *Thought Bubble* (See *Appendix O*; one or more per pair of students and one transparency— see step 4 of this Plan.)

PREPARATORY SET:

Read the chosen version of the fairy tale *The Beauty and the Beast*. Discuss with the students how the Beauty's initial reaction to the Beast's "different" appearance changed as she got to know the Beast. Discuss the impact that her kindness toward him ultimately had in changing how he felt about himself.

PLAN:

1. Explain to students that when people encounter others who are different from them, they sometimes react by not respecting that difference. They may be unkind to those people by ignoring, teasing, or leaving them out. They may think unkind thoughts about them. They may want to respect another person's difference but may not know how, so they stay away from the person.

2. Explain that it may be difficult to know how to respect another's individual differences. Tell students that one strategy they could use to help themselves respect another's differences is to use self-talk to remind themselves to think about the person on the inside.

3. Pair students using the *Animal Cards*.

4. Distribute *Thought Bubbles* to each pair. Explain that you will be telling about people who have differences. Tell students that after they hear about each person, they should work with their partners to write the self-talk they could use to remind themselves to think about that person on the inside. (After completing steps 5 and 6, read all or some of the situations in step 7 and have the pairs respond to each one. The student pairs will need one *Thought Bubble* for each situation to which they are asked to respond. Call on **pairs to share their self-talk statements.**)

5. Display the *Thought Bubble* transparency. Read the following situation:

    - You are at a pool. A boy who is your age, but is a different size than you is coming out of the locker room. Some of the other kids laugh and call him names.

6. Model use of the *Thought Bubble* while thinking aloud. A scripted example follows:

    While holding up the *Thought Bubble* say: *I need to think of the self-talk I could use to remind myself to think of that person on the inside. Let's see. That kid must feel really bad when the other kids call him names. He is probably a very nice kid. I'm going to write those thoughts down on the* Thought Bubble. Write the thoughts on the transparency.

7. Proceed using the following situations:

    - You are in a supermarket. There is a person whose face looks very different.

    - You are standing in line at the movie. The person in front of you smells different.

    - You are sitting next to a student whose voice sounds odd when he reads. Some of the other kids mimic the way he reads.

    - You are in the restroom at the mall. A person in a wheelchair comes in. You wonder how that person will use the restroom.

    - You are walking home from school. An elderly man is standing on a corner talking to himself.

    - You are at a movie theater. A person who has a different skin color than yours sits down near your family.

    - You are working in a group with a student who is from a special class in your school. This student has difficulty reading.

    - A new student in your class wears the same clothes to school almost every day. The clothes are old and not very nice.

    - At the park, you see a person with no hair.

    - A boy in the neighborhood wears thick glasses. The kids in the neighborhood tease him about his glasses.

    - You are on team that is all boys (girls). A girl (boy) wants to join the team.

- Some people in the neighborhood celebrate holidays that you've never heard of. The other neighbors say they eat and do odd things to celebrate.

- In the store, you see a family talking in a language that you do not understand. Their language sounds very different from yours.

8. Ask students to identify positive self-talk they could use if someone doesn't show respect to them because of a way that they are different.

9. Remind students of the importance of using positive self-talk, no matter what social skill they are choosing to use (not just for respecting differences).

10. Ask partners to face each other and stand an arm's length away. Encourage partners to use friendly and confident body talk. Ask partners to shake hands and in unison repeat the following statement after you: *I can choose what I say to others. I can choose what I say to myself. My choices will affect how I get along with others.*

Respecting Differences

Lesson D

OBJECTIVES:

1. To understand that people who do not respect differences may not feel good about themselves or may be afraid

2. To understand that people are more alike than they are different

3. To develop a plan to spread the concept of respecting individual differences

4. Scissors (One per student)

MATERIALS:

1. Clay or play dough (A small amount for each student)

2. A paper doll chain

3. *Paper Doll Outline* (See page 189; one per student and one transparency.)

4. Scissors (One per student)

PREPARATORY SET:

Remind students of the pine cone activity in Lesson A. The pine cones were very similar, yet each one had individual characteristics that made it special. Tell students that they are going to help spread the word to others about the importance of respecting differences. Have students pretend they are famous artists who will create a symbol (from clay or play dough) that represents people respecting others' differences. Pass out a ball of clay or play dough to each student. Allow time for students to mold their symbols.

PLAN:

1. Ask student volunteers to explain their symbols.

2. Ask students the following question:

   - Why do many people respect individual differences, while a few do not?

   Answers could include that people who respect others' differences probably feel good about themselves (they have high self-esteem), while people who do not accept differences may not feel very good about themselves (they have low self-esteem).

3. Explain that some people think they can make themselves feel better by putting other people down. This will probably not make them feel better. It may make them feel even worse about themselves.

4. Discuss that sometimes people don't respect differences because they don't understand differences and don't like themselves for not understanding, or they

Social Star

are afraid of anything that is different. Their discomfort and fear may cause them to treat people in a disrespectful manner.

5. Tell students, "You can make a difference in the world by doing your part to pass along the idea of respecting differences."

6. Ask students to get into groups of three or four. Ask each group to develop a plan they could use to help other students accept individual differences. Some ideas include:

   - Writing a message for the daily announcements about individual differences

   - Writing a song or poem about individual differences to share with other students

   - Writing an article about individual differences to be sent to the school newspaper

   - Planning a class or school fair in which individual differences are celebrated

7. Allow time during the next few days for students to carry out their plan.

8. Hold up your paper doll chain and say: "All of us in the world are very much alike, but we're not totally the same. We need to work together to help everyone in the world understand that we can accept and respect our differences." Tell students that during the next few days, you will be asking them to color and label paper dolls to represent themselves.

9. Distribute and display *Paper Doll Outline*. Say:

   It's most important to remember that how we look on the outside is not very important. How we are on the inside (write some positive characteristics on the inside of the paper doll outline) *and how we treat other people is what really matters. After you have finished coloring your paper doll, write your name and some of your personal qualities on the inside of the doll. Then cut out your paper doll.*

10. When students have completed their paper dolls, connect them to form a chain, and display the chain in the classroom with a poster that says, "We Can Respect Our Differences!" At the end of the school year, give each student the paper doll of a classmate and encourage calling or writing to the classmate to remind him or her about respecting differences.

11. Say with excitement to the class: *You are all social super, super, super stars! Remember, you have a responsibility to use your social skills and to invite other people to use good social skills too.*

Respecting Differences

Paper Doll Outline

© 1994 Thinking Publications 189 *Duplication permitted for educational use only.*

Social Star

Lessons X, Y, and Z

Due to similarities in format, the final three lesson plans of each unit in *Social Star* are provided in *Appendix A*. Substitute the words "respecting differences" whenever a "____" appears in the lesson plans. Information specific to this unit follows.

LESSON X PREPARATORY SET:

Ask students to think of a code word or phrase they could agree on as a class to say to one another as a reminder to respect each other's differences (e.g., "RED"—Respect Everyone's Differences).

LESSON Y PREPARATORY SET:

Darken the room, if you prefer, and ask students to visualize themselves correctly using this social skill by reading the following script:

> *Let's take a few minutes to relax.... Make sure you are sitting in a comfortable position.... Close your eyes if you feel like it.... On the count of three, take a very slow, deep breath. Remember to breathe in quietly through your nose. One . . . two . . . three . . . Now breathe out slowly and quietly through your mouth.... Let your entire body relax.... Now imagine yourself noticing someone who is very different and that's OK. Picture yourself thinking about how you can show respect to that person. Think about how you feel because you understand that we are all unique and equally important.*

LESSON Z PLOT SITUATION:

Ask students to pretend that someone is teasing them in a mean way because they are different in some way.

LESSON Z ROADBLOCK EXAMPLES:

- Accepting the differences of others who are unkind to you
- Accepting differences when others around you do not
- Accepting differences when you are afraid or unsure about another person

Name _____

Respecting Differences T-Chart

LOOKS LIKE...

using appropriate body talk

- smiling at people

- playing with people no matter what their outsides look like

- giving eye contact to someone who is different from you, but not staring

- not backing away from someone who is different from you

SOUNDS LIKE...

a friendly tone of voice

words that are kind

- "Hi! How are you?"

SHOW TIME

HOME

Pretend a relative makes a mean comment about your neighbors because of their skin color. Tell what you can say to yourself to remember to respect differences.

SCHOOL

Pretend the girl who sits behind you can't read well. Tell what you could say to yourself to remember to respect differences.

COMMUNITY

Pretend you are being introduced to a person with a physical handicap. Show what you could do and say to show respect to the person.

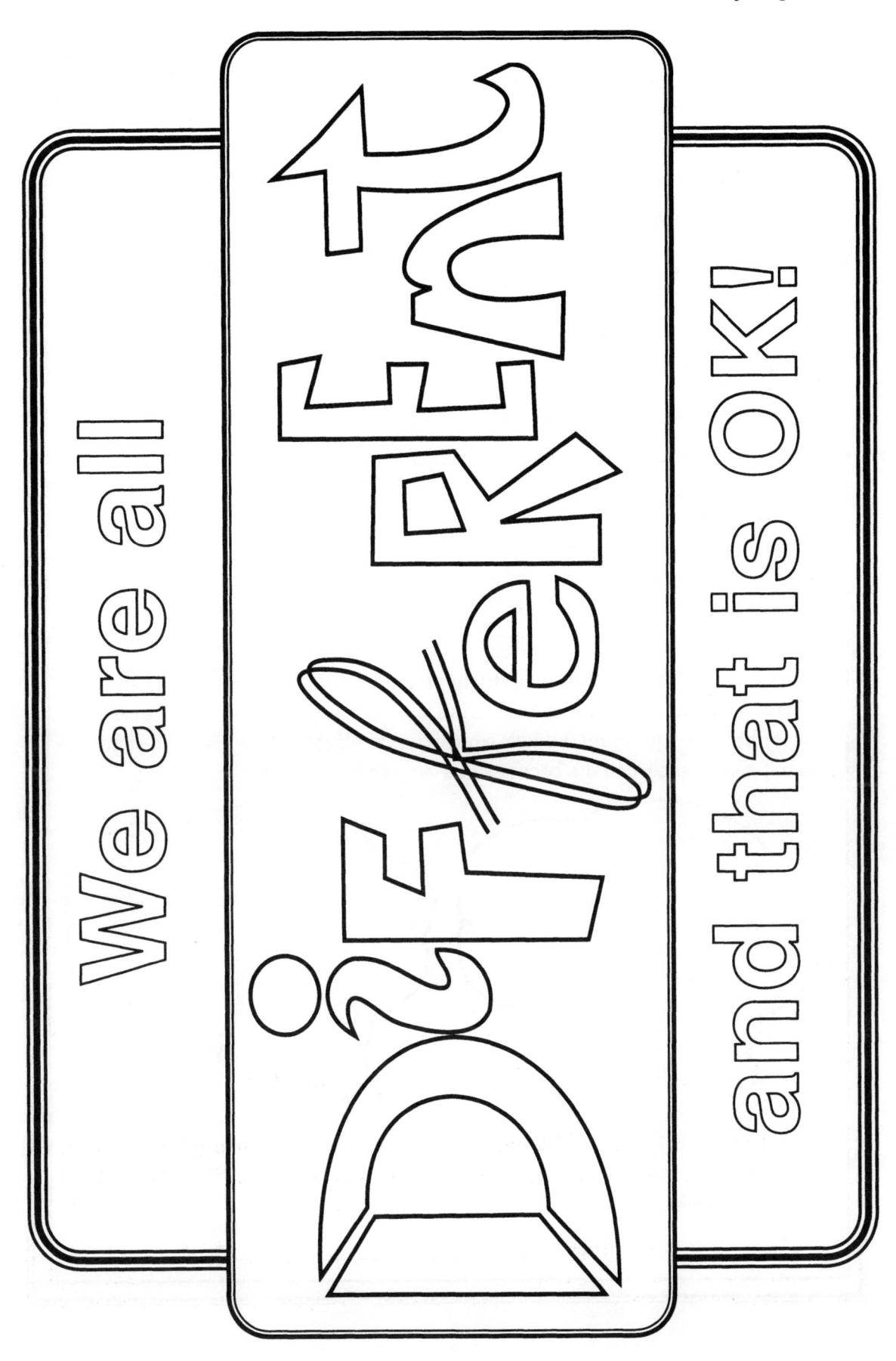

Respecting Differences

We are all Different and that is OK!

Social Star

HOME-A-GRAM

Dear Family,

At school, we have been talking about the social skill called

RESPECTING DIFFERENCES

I learned that *respecting differences* means understanding that we are all unique and equally important.

I know I can remind myself that we are all different and that's OK.

I can think about each person on the inside.

I learned that I can ask myself how I can show respect for everyone.

If I recognize and respect that everyone is unique and equally important, I can invite others to feel good about themselves and about me. Respecting differences helps make my home, school, and community more peaceful for everyone.

Below I have filled in two thought bubbles. The bubble on the left shows a positive thought I can have to remind myself to show respect to everyone. The bubble on the right shows a positive thought I can have if someone doesn't show respect to me because of a way that I am different.

After I explain the thought bubbles to you, please sign my "Respecting Differences" badge so I can return it to school and become a SOCIAL SUPER STAR this week.

From: _____

© 1994 Thinking Publications — Duplication permitted for educational use only.

Being a Friend

Social Star

UNIT GOAL:

To demonstrate comprehension and use of strategies for being a friend

EDUCATOR INFORMATION:

1. Educators are encouraged to concern themselves with interaction that goes on among their students. Little attention has been given to providing opportunities for students to learn skills necessary for friendship development (Gottlieb and Leyser, 1981; Stainback and Stainback, 1987).

2. Duck (1983) reports that socially inappropriate behaviors may result in nonacceptance, acceptance by a deviant group, or withdrawal. The good news, according to Duck, is that "Friendship is something that can be improved, coached, and practiced like any other skill, trained like any other skill and made more fluent" (p. 10).

3. Research indicates that a child's self-esteem and achievement correlate positively with acceptance by peers. When attempting to determine if emotional problems will develop later in life, having friends and being accepted by peers are more significant factors than achievement levels (Reohr, 1984). Yet Asher and Gottman (1981) report sociometric techniques showing that 5 to 10 percent of elementary school children are not named as a friend by anyone in their class.

4. This unit provides tips on how to make friends and how to be a friend. Numerous issues are addressed within the unit (e.g., being able to get along in a group of three and not just in a pair, deciding what to do when your friend wants you to do something that might get you into trouble, being respectful to all students and not just those who are your friends). The educator should exert sensitivity and care in generalizing rules about friendships into the children's home cultures.

5. *Circle of Friends* (Perske and Perske, 1988) is a successful program that helps children with disabilities develop friendships with peers. Students make a commitment to build a friendship with the targeted child. A structured plan is developed initially to ensure that the friendships get off to a good start.

6. The educator is strongly encouraged to teach other related units (e.g., *Playing Cooperatively, Dealing with Teasing*) that promote the development of friendships.

RELATED ACTIVITIES:

1. Have a "Be a Friend Week" at your school. Each day, students can do something "nice" for a friend. (Have students identify what "being nice" looks like and sounds like.) Students may only do things that do not cost money.

2. Encourage students to get a pen pal friend from another city, state, or country. To obtain international information, contact the International Friendship League, Inc., 55 Mount Vernon, Boston, MA 02109, (617) 523-4273 (ages 7–18).

3. Have students collect poems on the topic of friendship. A few sources include:

   - *A Week in the Life of Best Friends: And Other Poems of Friendship* (1986), by Beatrice Schenk de Regniers, Ill. by Nancy Doyle, New York: Macmillan Publishing.

   - *Best Friends* (1986), Poems selected by Lee Bennett Hopkins, Ill. by James Watts, New York: Harper Collins.

   - *Rolling Harvey Down the Hill* (1980), by Jack Prelutsky, Ill. by Victoria Chess, New York: Greenwillow Books.

   Have students make a collage with the poems inside large letters of the word "FRIEND."

4. Americans tend to view friendships only as those which are chosen voluntarily. However, Reohr (1984) states that anthropological studies of other cultures indicate that when people are assigned friends, they have an appreciation for and develop a strong bond with their assigned friend.

   Discuss this practice with the students. Assign students to be "field trip friends." Ask students to plan an outing and include what they will say and do with their "field trip friend" during the planned activity.

5. Ask students to write a friendship poem following the Haiku format (five syllables in the first line, seven syllables in the second line, and five syllables in the third line). An example follows:

   Friendship is caring

   Friends are there when you need them

   Friends are nice to have

6. Friendships are promoted when people get to share information about themselves. Have students conduct a "people search." Have them complete sentences such as "Find someone who (likes the same pizza as you do; has as many brothers as you do, etc.)."

7. Invite adults from other cultures to talk to the students about how their cultures' conventions for being a friend compare with the concepts presented in this unit.

It is important for educators to provide opportunities for students to work in groups so they can experience social skills in contexts where social communication is needed. Therefore, educators are encouraged to have students complete the Related Activities in small groups whenever possible. Educators trained in cooperative learning could incorporate the five components (see page 33) into the group activity.

RELATED LITERATURE:

Aldo Applesauce (1979) by Johanna Hurwitz, Ill. by John Wallner, William Morrow. (Text) Aldo and his family move to the suburbs. Finding new friends is hard for Aldo.

Charlotte's Web (1952) by E.B. White, Ill. by Garth Williams, Harper. (Text) (pages 25–31, 163–164)

SOCIAL SKILLS ALL DAY LONG:

Look for opportunities to teach social skills throughout the day (incidental teaching). Four ways to reinforce appropriate social skills and an example of each follow:

Encouragement

Earlier today I saw Jolisa be very polite and kind to Ann. I know that they are not best friends, but Jolisa treats everyone respectfully.

Personal Example

My friend was feeling sad last weekend, so I sent her a cheerful note in the mail.

Prompting

Mike, when we go out for recess today, ask Lee and Victor if you can play with them. Say, "Can I play ball with you guys?"

Corrective Feedback (must be positive, private, specific, and nonthreatening)

Maria, just now when you were with Ann and Jolisa, I heard you give Ann a put-down and saw you look at Jolisa and laugh. I could tell Ann was really upset. I know the three of you are friends. Remember that three people can get along as friends. What you could have done was make positive comments to both Ann and Jolisa.

Social Star

Lesson A

OBJECTIVES:

1. To state the meaning of *being a friend* and tell why it is important
2. To listen to the self-talk associated with correct use of the skill

MATERIALS:

1. *I Know....* (See *Appendix Z*; one per pair of students and one transparency.)
2. *Being a Friend* (See page 201; one per student and one transparency.)
3. *Thought Bubble* (See *Appendix O;* one for educator use.)
4. *Checking Myself* (See *Appendix I*; one per student and one transparency.)

PREPARATORY SET:

Play charades by asking student volunteers to act out an activity they like doing with a friend. Have the rest of the class guess the activity being acted out. List each activity as it is revealed so students can see the variety of activities friends engage in. Use this experience to introduce the topic of being a friend to the class.

PLAN:

1. Pair students using the *Shoe Match* activity (see *Appendix P*).
2. Distribute and display *I Know....* to each student pair. Tell students you want to find out what they already know about being a friend. Instruct students to write "Being a Friend" on the line above "I Know...." Have students work as pairs to write everything they know about being a friend in the first column. Model this by saying, "I know that if I am being a friend, I don't say mean things to him, so I might write, 'saying nice things.'" Allow students time to think of things they already know about being a friend. They should leave the second column of *I Know....* (i.e., "I Learned....") blank. Ask student pairs to share orally some of the things they listed. Write their ideas on the transparency. Collect the sheets to be completed during Lesson E.
3. Distribute and display *Being a Friend*. Discuss the definition for *being a friend*. Explain the skill step and the symbol next to it. Remind students that the symbol is there to help them visualize and remember the skill step. Refer to the body-talk symbol in the left-hand margin. Remind students that appropriate body talk is important when being a friend. Discuss the reasons for being a friend.

4. Model use of the skill step for being a friend while thinking aloud. A scripted example follows:

Introduction

I am going to pretend to be a student your age. I will show you how I can be a friend to others and tell you the thoughts I'm having. When I hold up this Thought Bubble, *you'll know the words that I'm saying are actually what I'm thinking.*

Actual Model

While holding up the Thought Bubble *say, I really like playing with Sam. What can I do to be a friend? I'll ask him to play after school with me. I can say nice things to him and share my toys with him.*

5. Read the story at the bottom of *Being a Friend.*

6. Distribute and display the discussion guideline sheet called *Checking Myself.* Ask students to complete the goal statement with the words, "listen to others," or use another classroom discussion goal more appropriate for your group (see pages 25–26). Tell students that you will be having a discussion about the story they just heard. When a student is answering a question or making a comment during the discussion, it's important for everyone to show respect by listening to that student. Tell students they can show they are listening by giving eye contact, nodding their heads, asking relevant questions, or making relevant comments. Instruct them to circle a T-shirt star each time someone new talks and they are listening.

7. Model use of the *Checking Myself* sheet while thinking aloud. A scripted example follows:

Introduction

I am going to pretend to be one of you completing this sheet during the discussion we will be having. I will tell you the thoughts I'm having while completing the sheet. When I hold up this Thought Bubble, *you'll know the words I'm saying are actually what I'm thinking.*

Actual Model

While holding up the *Thought Bubble* say, *Eric is telling one of his answers. I'll be polite by looking at him when he's talking and smile at him so he knows I'm listening. I'll circle a star on my sheet because I listened to Eric.* Put the *Thought Bubble* down and circle a T-shirt star on the transparency.

8. Proceed with the discussion by asking students the following questions:

Social Star

- Why did Ann choose Victor to invite along to the beach?
- Why does Ann like having Victor for a friend?
- Ann called Victor her "best friend." What do you think that means?
- Even though Victor is her "best friend," do you think Ann has other friends?
- Do you think Victor has other friends?
- What could happen when a person does things only with a best friend?
- How is a "best friend" different from other friends?
- How is a "best friend" like other friends?
- How should you treat people who are not your best friend? Answers should include specific examples (e.g., treating everyone kindly, not excluding others, sharing your good friends with others, etc.).
- Ann's best friend is a boy. Is it OK for boys and girls to be best friends?

9. After the discussion, have students complete the bottom of *Checking Myself*.

10. Process use of the sheet by asking the following question or another one more appropriate for your group:

    - Why do you think it's important to listen to others while they are talking? Do you like it when your friends listen to you? Do you listen to your friends?

    Process further by asking the students who volunteered to speak during the discussion to share their answers to the following questions:

    - You shared one of your answers during the discussion. How could you tell which people were listening to you? How did it feel to know that others were listening?

11. Ask student pairs to take turns telling each other the meaning of being a friend and why it's important to use the skill. Students could be reminded that the information they are to say is printed on *Being a Friend*.

    As an option to add structure to this activity (see *Appendix Q*), ask partners to come to an agreement about which person will be called "Tom Sawyer" and which person will be called "Huckleberry Finn." After students have made their decisions, ask "Tom" to tell "Huckleberry" the definition of *being a friend*. Next, ask "Huckleberry" to tell "Tom" the definition. Ask students to use the same procedure to tell each other the reasons for being a friend.

12. Ask students to stand and face each other, standing an arm's length away. Ask partners to use friendly and confident body talk. Ask partners to shake hands and in unison repeat the following statement after you: *It was nice working with you today! There are many social skills you know how to use.*

Name _____

★ Being a Friend

MEANING OF BEING A FRIEND: Choosing words and actions that show someone you care

SKILL STEP:

1. Ask myself: What can I do to be a friend?

REASONS FOR USING THIS SKILL:

You can feel proud inside when you show others that you care. When you are a friend to others, you invite them to feel positive about themselves and about you.

DIRECTIONS: Listen to the story below. Look at the pictures of Mr. Jackson and his stepdaughter Ann while you listen.

Ann, would you like to invite one of your friends along when we go to the beach this weekend?

Great idea! Could I invite Victor?

Sure! You two are getting to be great friends!

Victor is my best friend. He's fun to be around. He shares his things with me. He listens when I talk to him.

© 1994 Thinking Publications

Social Star

Lesson B

OBJECTIVE:

To assess one's friendship skills

MATERIALS:

1. *BAF's Letter* (See page 204; one transparency.)

2. *BAF's Friendship Survey* (See pages 205–206; one per student and one transparency.)

3. *BAF's Friendship Hunt* (See page 207; one per student.)

4. *Being a Friend* classroom poster (See page 13.)

PREPARATORY SET:

Tell the class that you have received a very strange letter in the mail. Show *BAF's Letter*. (Before class, put the letter in an envelope to make it appear more realistic.) Display and read *BAF's Letter* to the class. (The creature's name, "DNEIRF," is pronounced də-nərf´.)

PLAN:

1. Tell the class that BAF has asked them to fill out a survey about friendships. Display and distribute *BAF's Friendship Survey*. Read the questions aloud and ask students to complete each answer. Be sure to tell the students that this information will only be read by the teacher and BAF. It will not be shared with other students in the class. Remind them that there are no right or wrong answers. After the surveys are completed, collect them. Put the surveys in a large envelope and pretend to mail them to BAF if you wish.

   (The main purpose of the survey is to provide further insight into the friendships that exist or do not exist within the classroom. Use the information to deal with friendship issues specific to the group of students involved. There may be students who have a difficult time dealing with this survey. Execute sensitivity in dealing with this possibility. The survey may be used later in the year to reassess students' attitudes about their friendship skills.)

2. Tell students that BAF also sent along an assignment for them to complete. Distribute *BAF's Friendship Hunt* and read the directions for its completion with the students. Be sure to discuss the example provided. Have the students complete this assignment before the next lesson. Tell students that during the next lesson, they will be sharing the examples they found.

3. Review the definition and skill step for *being a friend,* by referring the class to the *Being a Friend* classroom poster.

4. Pair students (see *Appendix P*). Ask student pairs to take turns telling each other the skill step for being a friend. Follow the procedure described in Step 11 of Lesson A. (As an option, ask students to identify two outer space or alien names.) Next, ask students to work with their partners to think of a situation when being a friend would be appropriate. Tell students that one or more pairs will be asked to share their situations. Have one or more pairs share their situation.

5. Say with excitement to the class: *Liking yourself is very important! When you like who you are, you want to get along with other people by using appropriate social skills.*

Social Star

BAF'S LETTER

1234 Asteroid Ave.
Kindness, Friendship O*J3♥

Dear _____,

My name is BAF. On my planet they call me the Friendship Wizard. I come from the planet Kindness in the Galaxy of Friendship. I have journeyed to your great planet Earth to get important information on friendships. On our planet, friendships go smoothly most of the time. Occasionally, an evil creature called the DNEIRF comes around to destroy friendships. The people of my planet want to get rid of the DNEIRF forever. They have sent me on a journey across the universe to find out about great friendships so that we can use that information to make our planet a better place. Last week I visited another city on Earth called Socialville. I got some great ideas about friendships from a club in Socialville called the Social Star Club. I am hoping to get some information from your class on friendships. I hope you will help me by completing some things your teacher will explain to you. I've got to go now. I'll be in touch.

Friendliest wishes,

BAF

P.S. Here is my picture, so you'll know what I look like.

© 1994 Thinking Publications · Duplication permitted for educational use only.

Name _____   Date _____

BAF'S Friendship Survey

Please help me by filling out this survey.

1. I have some friends.   YES   NO

2. It is easy for me to make friends.   YES   NO

3. I wish I had more friends.   YES   NO

4. I have a best friend.   YES   NO

5. I have friends in this class.   YES   NO

6. I have friends who live near my house.   YES   NO

7. It is hard for me to make friends.   YES   NO

8. I know how to make friends.   YES   NO

9. Having a friend is important to me because _____
   _____

10. The thing I like to do most with a friend is _____
    _____

Social Star

11. I like it when a friend _____
_____

12. I don't like it when a friend _____
_____

13. One way that I can make a new friend is to _____
_____

14. I have a friend named _____

15. One person in this class that I would like to be better friends with is
_____
_____

16. Draw a picture of you and a friend doing something fun below.

Being a Friend

Name _____

BAF'S FRIENDSHIP HUNT

DIRECTIONS: Be on the lookout for people being a friend. When you notice someone being a friend, mark the information on the chart below. Look at the example.

WHO	WAS A FRIEND BY:
★ 1 Steve	asking Ann to play kickball
★ 2	
★ 3	
★ 4	

Social Star

Lesson C

OBJECTIVE:

To differentiate between a friend and a "DNEIRF" (someone who is not acting as a true friend)

MATERIALS:

1. *BAF's Friendship Hunt* (Completed during Lesson B)

2. Props to simulate a game show (e.g., upbeat music, a bell, a decorated contestants' table with four chairs, an emcee costume, a microphone)

3. *Detect the DNEIRF Game Show Questions* (See pages 210–211; one for educator use.)

4. *Friendship Badges* (See page 212; one per student.)

PREPARATORY SET:

Ask students to share examples of people being a friend that they observed and recorded on *BAF's Friendship Hunt*, as assigned in Lesson B. After the examples have been shared, thank the students and say, "I'm sure BAF the Friendship Wizard will appreciate all this information you are providing to him."

PLAN:

1. Ask students if anyone can guess why the friendship wizard's name is BAF. (BAF stands for "being a friend.")

2. Tell students that BAF wants them to know more about the DNEIRF who causes problems with friendships on his planet. Explain that a DNEIRF is someone who is not a good friend. A DNEIRF may pretend to be your friend, but doesn't like you for who you are. Ask students if they think a DNEIRF can be detected just by the way he or she looks (make the point that a DNEIRF can look like anyone).

3. What are some things a DNEIRF might do to cause problems in a friendship? (Student responses might include: hitting a friend, telling a lie to a friend, not sticking up for a friend, not sharing with a friend.)

4. Ask students where they think the name DNEIRF came from. (DNEIRF is FRIEND spelled backwards.)

5. Ask students if they have ever seen a TV game show and ask for examples. Tell students that today they will be contestants on a game show called "Detect the DNIERF." Explain that you learned about this game from BAF. They play this

game on the planet Kindness. Before the game begins, place students into groups of three or four. Ask students to number off from 1 to 3 (or 1 to 4) within their groups. Check to be certain everyone remembers his or her number by saying something like, "All the one's raise your hands," etc.

6. Explain the purpose of the game by saying, "During the game, I will be describing a person to you. Your job is to decide if the person is acting as a friend or a DNEIRF. You may be asked to explain your answer."

7. Put on the emcee costume, hold the microphone, turn on the music, and say in a theatrical voice, "Welcome to the game show called 'Detect the DNEIRF,' the game show filled with fun and excitement! Without further ado, would all the three's please raise your hands? Congratulations and COME ON DOWN, three's! You're our first contestants on 'Detect the DNEIRF.' Take a seat at our contestants' table."

8. While the three's are being seated, write a number between 1 and 50 on a piece of paper so no one can see it. Ask each three to quickly pick a number between 1 and 50. Say to whoever comes closest to your number, "_____, congratulations! You get to answer the first question on 'Detect the DNEIRF.'"

9. Read the first question from the *Detect the DNEIRF Game Show Questions*. Allow a comfortable period of time for the student to answer. The student can consult with the other three's before answering. You might ring a bell after the answer is completed to signal a transition.

10. Ask all the three's to go back to their seats, and then ask all the two's (or one's or four's) to COME ON DOWN! Continue playing using the same procedure as described above as long as time allows. A scoring system may be implemented (i.e., when the total score reaches a predetermined number, the entire class receives a Friendship Badge).

11. Ask students to find a partner, face each other, and stand an arm's length away. Encourage partners to use friendly and confident body talk. Ask partners to shake hands and in unison repeat the following statement after you: *I can choose what I say. I can choose how I act. My choices will affect how I get along with others.*

Social Star

Detect the DNEIRF Game Show Questions

1. Jolisa only wants to play with you when you have a candy bar. Is Jolisa acting as a friend or a DNEIRF to you? Explain your answer.

2. Victor likes to invite you over to his house to play. Is Victor acting as a friend or a DNEIRF to you? Explain your answer.

3. Mike likes to share his baseball and bat with you and invites you to play ball with him. Is Mike acting as a friend or a DNEIRF to you? Explain your answer.

4. Lee wanted you to call your other friend a mean name. Is Lee acting as a friend or a DNEIRF to you? Explain your answer.

5. You overheard your friend Ann saying something mean about you to Jolisa. Was Ann acting as a friend or a DNEIRF to you? Explain your answer.

6. Jolisa is always truthful with you. Is Jolisa acting as a friend or a DNEIRF to you? Explain your answer.

7. Victor stuck up for you when an older kid was picking on you. Was Victor acting as a friend or a DNEIRF to you? Explain your answer.

8. Mike is usually mean to your younger sister when he comes over to your house. Is Mike acting as a friend or a DNEIRF to you? Explain your answer.

9. Maria treats you nicely. She is also nice to other people. Is Maria acting as a friend or a DNEIRF to you? Explain your answer.

10. Ann likes to "wait up" for you when you go out for recess. Is Ann acting as a friend or a DNEIRF to you? Explain your answer.

11. Victor thinks he can use any of your materials whenever he feels like it, and doesn't ask you if it's OK. Is Victor acting as a friend or a DNEIRF? Explain your answer.

12. Lee helped you go to the nurse when you got hurt on the playground. Was Lee acting as a friend or a DNEIRF to you? Explain your answer.

13. Maria gives you put-downs about your clothes and brags about her expensive "designer name" clothes. Is Maria acting as a friend or a DNEIRF to you? Explain your answer.

© 1994 Thinking Publications   *Duplication permitted for educational use only.*

14. You have a really fun time when you do things with Jolisa. She makes you laugh. Is Jolisa acting as a friend or a DNEIRF to you? Explain your answer.

15. Mike wants you to steal something from a store for him. Is Mike acting as a friend or a DNEIRF to you? Explain your answer.

16. Victor likes to shove you around, especially in front of other kids. Is Victor acting as a friend or a DNEIRF to you? Explain your answer.

17. Ann is really nice to your sister, who has a disability. She enjoys it when your sister does things with the two of you. Is Ann acting as a friend or a DNEIRF to you? Explain your answer.

18. Lee only likes to do things with you when your mom gives you money. Is Lee acting as a friend or a DNEIRF to you? Explain your answer.

19. You and Maria do a lot of things together (e.g., go swimming, go to the movies, play softball), but when she sees you doing something with someone else, she gets angry. Is Maria acting as a friend or a DNEIRF to you? Explain your answer.

20. Jolisa said she will be your friend only if you invite her to your birthday party. Was Jolisa acting as a friend or a DNEIRF to you? Explain your answer.

21. Victor lies and blames you for things so that he doesn't get into trouble. Is Victor acting as a friend or a DNEIRF to you? Explain your answer.

22. Ann is a good listener when you are talking. Is Ann acting as a friend or a DNEIRF to you? Explain your answer.

23. Lee always decides which TV program the two of you will watch. He thinks he should always get his way. Is Lee acting as a friend or a DNEIRF to you? Explain your answer.

24. Maria doesn't laugh at you when you make a mistake. Does Maria act as a friend or a DNEIRF to you? Explain your answer.

25. Mike never chooses you to be on his team during recess. Is Mike acting as a friend or a DNEIRF to you? Explain your answer.

Social Star

FRIENDSHIP BADGES

- Best Friend
- BE A FRIEND
- BE A FRIEND
- FRIENDSHIP
- I KNOW HOW TO BE A FRIEND
- FRIENDSHIP

© 1994 Thinking Publications — 212 — *Duplication permitted for educational use only.*

Being a Friend

Lesson D

OBJECTIVES:

1. To answer questions about the social skill of *being a friend*

2. To be a friend while preparing the game "Blastoff to Friendship Galaxy"

MATERIALS:

1. *Blastoff to Friendship Galaxy Cards* (See pages 216–217; one for educator use and one set per student.)

2. *Blastoff to Friendship Galaxy Questions* (See pages 218–219; one for educator use.)

3. *Blastoff to Friendship Galaxy Game Board* (See page 220; one per student.)

4. Light-colored markers or crayons (An assortment for each pair of students)

5. Scissors and paper clips (One of each per student)

6. *Blastoff to Friendship Galaxy Game Pieces* (See page 221; one per student.)

7. Business-size or larger envelopes (One per student)

PREPARATORY SET:

Remind students that BAF is the Friendship Wizard from the planet Kindness in the Galaxy of Friendship. Ask students what they imagine BAF's planet to be like. Tell students that they are going to be making a game called "Blastoff to Friendship Galaxy" to play with a partner at school and to take home to play with their families.

PLAN:

1. Pair students (see *Appendix P*). Tell students you will be reading through the *Blastoff to Friendship Galaxy Cards* with them so that when they play the game during the next lesson, they will already have some experience with the cards. Read the first statement (card A) from the *Blastoff to Friendship Galaxy Cards*, omitting the consequence statement at the end (i.e., "Flip the coin again"). Have students put their thumbs up if the statement shows an example of "being a friend" and their thumbs down if the statement shows an example of "being a DNEIRF." Ask the corresponding question from the *Blastoff to Friendship Galaxy Questions* and ask students to discuss an answer with their partners. Call on one pair of students to share their answer.

Social Star

2. Follow the same procedure for cards B, C, and D.

3. Tell students, "Let's take a break from these game cards, so you can make the game board for 'Blastoff to Friendship Galaxy.' I will be giving each of you a copy of the game board and markers to color it. Be sure to write your name on your game board. I will be watching for people being a friend to others while you are coloring. What are some examples of things you might say or do to be a friend while you are working?" Encourage the students to share examples.

4. Distribute markers and the *Blastoff to Friendship Galaxy Game Board*. Allow five minutes for students to complete their coloring task.

5. Follow the same procedure described in step 1 of this Plan for cards E, F, G, and H.

6. Tell students, "Let's take another break from these game cards so you can continue preparing your game. I will be giving each of you a copy of the game cards, a pair of scissors to cut them apart, and a paper clip to clip the cards together. I will be watching for people being a friend to others while you are cutting."

7. Distribute scissors, paper clips, and the *Blastoff to Friendship Galaxy Cards*. Allow five minutes for students to complete their cutting task.

8. Follow the same procedure as described in step 1 of this Plan for cards I, J, K, and L.

9. Tell students, "Let's take another break from these game cards so you can continue preparing your game. I will be giving you each a copy of the game pieces to color and cut apart. When you are finished cutting them apart, fold the playing pieces in half on the dotted lines so they form tents. I'll be watching for people being a friend to others."

10. Distribute the *Blastoff to Friendship Galaxy Game Pieces*. Allow five minutes for students to cut them apart and fold them.

11. Follow the same procedure as described in step 1 of this Plan for cards M, N, O, and P.

12. Tell students, "Now we are finished going through all of the game cards. I will be giving each of you an envelope. Please write your name on it. Next, put your game cards that are paper clipped together and your folded playing pieces inside the envelope."

13. Distribute one envelope to each student. Collect the envelopes and the game boards after students have finished.

14. Discuss examples of being a friend that have been observed during this lesson. Ask students to share their observations also.

15. Say with excitement to the class: *You are all social super, super, super stars! Remember, you have a responsibility to use your social skills and to invite other people to use good social skills too.*

Social Star

BLASTOFF TO FRIENDSHIP GALAXY CARDS

A

You saw someone standing alone on the playground. You asked her to play with your group.

Flip the coin again.

B

There is a boy in your neighborhood who you play with only when no one else can play.

Stay on your space.

C

When a friend tells you a secret, you tell the secret to others.

Lose 1 turn.

D

You are kind to kids you are not good friends with.

Move ahead 1 space.

E

When you and a friend are unkind to each other, you never apologize.

Lose 1 turn.

F

When your friends are feeling sad, you do things to cheer them up.

Move ahead 2 spaces.

G

You are truthful with your friends.

Move ahead 2 spaces.

H

When you invite friends over, you won't let them play with your things.

Lose 1 turn.

© 1994 Thinking Publications — *Duplication permitted for educational use only.*

BLASTOFF TO FRIENDSHIP GALAXY CARDS
(CONTINUED)

I

When you saw others teasing your friend, you laughed.

Stay on your space.

J

You do things to be a friend to someone who is new in your neighborhood.

Move ahead 3 spaces.

K

When you are with your friends, you take turns deciding what you'll play.

Flip the coin again.

L

You get angry when your best friend plays with someone else.

Lose 1 turn.

M

When you have a treat to share, you make sure that everyone gets some.

Flip the coin again.

N

When your friend is not around, you say mean things about your friend.

Stay on your space.

O

You laugh and tease your friends when they make mistakes.

Stay on your space.

P

When you need to work with someone who is not a good friend, you don't complain.

Move ahead 2 spaces.

© 1994 Thinking Publications — Duplication permitted for educational use only.

Social Star

BLASTOFF TO FRIENDSHIP GALAXY QUESTIONS

A. How might the person you invited to play feel about your invitation?

   What words could you say to invite someone to play with your group?

B. How might the boy feel during the times that you play with others but don't include him?

   What might you say to someone who plays with you only when no one else is around?

C. Why is it important not to tell a friend's secret to others?

   When is a time that you would need to tell your friend's secret to an adult?

D. Why is it important to be kind to people who may not be your friends?

   What things can you do to be kind to kids you are not good friends with?

E. Why is it important to apologize when you and a friend have been unkind to each other?

   What could you say or do to apologize to your friend?

F. Why is it important to take time to "cheer up" your friends when they are sad?

   Tell things you could do or say to "cheer up" a friend.

G. Why is it important to be truthful with your friends?

   Name some times when it might be difficult to tell a friend the truth.

H. How might your friends feel if you don't share?

   Tell other things you can do to be a friend when someone is visiting your home.

I. How might your friend feel if you laughed?

   What words could you say to support a friend who is being teased?

J. How might the new kid feel about you?

   What things could you say or do to be a friend to someone new?

K. Why is it important to take turns deciding what to play?

What could you say to a friend who will never do what you want to do?

L. Why might someone feel bad if a friend plays with someone else?

What self-talk could you use to tell yourself that you need to share your best friend with others?

M. Why is it important to make sure that no one is left out when you have a treat to share?

What could you say or do if someone passes a treat to everyone except you?

N. What might happen if your friend finds out that you are saying mean things when he or she is not around?

What self-talk could you use to tell yourself that you need to be kind to your friends, even when they are not around?

O. How might your friends feel if you laugh at them and tease them when they make mistakes?

How could you respond positively when a friend makes a mistake?

P. Why shouldn't you complain when you need to work with someone who is not your friend?

What self-talk could you use to tell yourself not to complain when you need to work with someone who is not your friend?

Social Star

Name _____

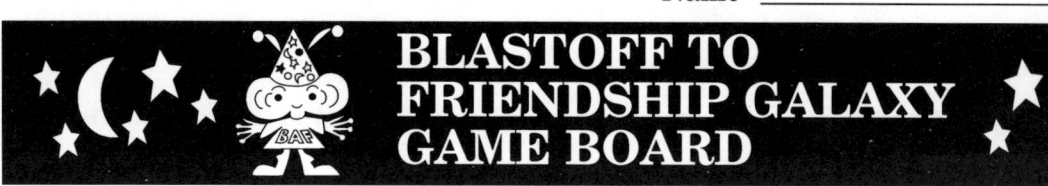

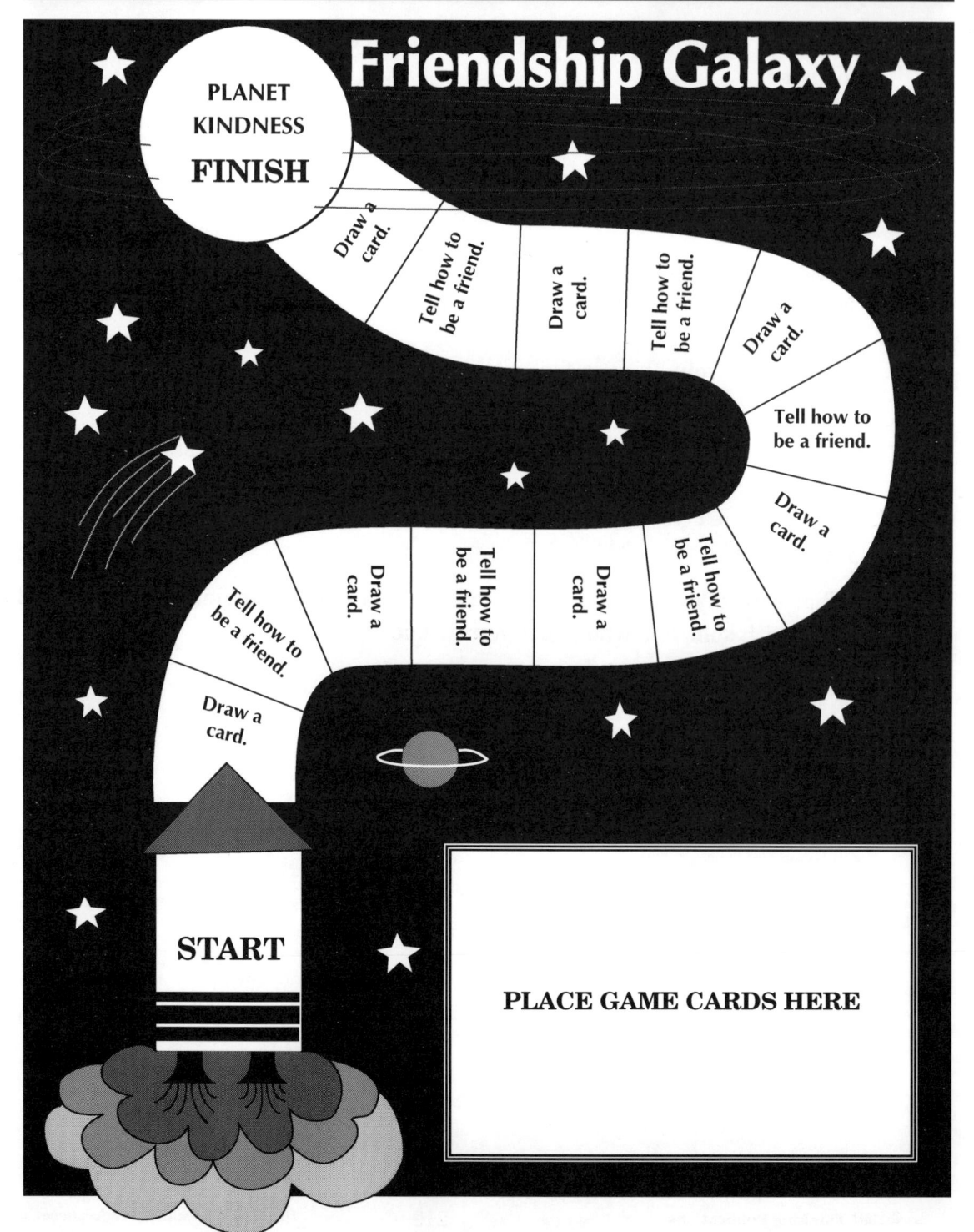

BLASTOFF TO FRIENDSHIP GALAXY GAME BOARD

Friendship Galaxy

PLANET KINDNESS — FINISH

Draw a card.
Tell how to be a friend.
Draw a card.
Tell how to be a friend.
Draw a card.
Tell how to be a friend.
Draw a card.
Tell how to be a friend.
Draw a card.
Draw a card.
Tell how to be a friend.
Draw a card.
Tell how to be a friend.
Draw a card.

START

PLACE GAME CARDS HERE

© 1994 Thinking Publications

Duplication permitted for educational use only.

Being a Friend

BLASTOFF TO FRIENDSHIP GALAXY GAME PIECES

© 1994 Thinking Publications 221 *Duplication permitted for educational use only.*

Social Star

Lesson E

OBJECTIVE:

To play a game about being a friend with a partner

MATERIALS:

1. *Blastoff to Friendship Galaxy Game Boards* (From the previous lesson)
2. Envelopes from previous lesson, filled with game cards and game pieces
3. *Game Rules* (See page 224; one per student.)
4. *I Know....* (Use half-completed pages from Lesson A.)

PREPARATORY SET:

Spread out the *Blastoff to Friendship Galaxy Game Boards* and the envelopes on a counter or table. In an excited manner, tell students that they will be playing "Blastoff to Friendship Galaxy" today and to find their game boards and envelopes.

PLAN:

1. Distribute *Game Rules*. As a class, read and discuss the rules for "Blastoff to Friendship Galaxy." After reading over the rules, ask students to tell things they can do to be a friend while playing the game with a partner (e.g., taking turns, following the game rules, showing appropriate reactions to winning and losing, making positive comments to each other).

2. Pair students (see *Appendix P*). Students should each have their game board and playing pieces.

3. Ask partners to use their friendship skills to determine which person's game board and game pieces will be used to play the game. (There may be time for the game to be played twice, and in that case both games could be used.)

4. Have students play the game as directed with their partners, and when they finish, have them fold their game boards and place them, as well as the game pieces and game cards, in their envelopes.

5. Collect the students' games and save them to be redistributed to students to take home with the *Home-A-Gram* during Lesson Z.

6. Hand out *I Know....*, which was half completed and collected during Lesson A. Using the same student pairs, have them complete the "I Learned...." column together. This provides an opportunity to review all key ideas in this unit. Have students share what they learned.

7. Ask partners to face each other and stand an arm's length away. Encourage partners to use friendly and confident body talk. Ask partners to shake hands and in unison repeat the following statement after you: *Learning social skills is mighty fine. I use my social skills all the time.*

Social Star

Name _____

GAME RULES

1. Place the game cards on the space indicated on the game board. Choose one of the Socialville characters as your game piece and place it on the start space.

2. Get a coin and place it near the game board.

3. The player who is the youngest goes first.

4. Player #1 flips the coin. *Heads* means move 1 space on the game board, and *tails* means move 2 spaces. If "Tell how to be a friend" is written on the space landed on, the player tells any example of being a friend. Then, play advances to the next player. If the player lands on a "Draw a card" space, the player reads the top game card aloud and follows the direction given on the card (e.g., "Move ahead 1 space," "Lose 1 turn," etc.). Reshuffle the game cards, if needed.

5. To enter Friendship Galaxy, a player must flip the exact number needed (e.g., if a player has 1 space to go, a *heads* must be flipped on the coin).

6. The first player to get to Friendship Galaxy is the winner.

Lessons X, Y, and Z

Due to similarities in format, the final three lesson plans for each unit in *Social Star* are provided in *Appendix A*. Substitute the words "being a friend" whenever a "____" appears in the lesson plans. Information specific to this unit follows.

LESSON X PREPARATORY SET:

Direct a class cheer in which students **repeat the word "friendship"** in unison, while gradually increasing volume from very quiet to very loud.

LESSON Y PREPARATORY SET:

Darken the room, if you prefer, and ask the students to visualize themselves correctly using this social skill by reading the following script:

Let's take a few moments to relax.... Make sure you are in a comfortable position.... Close your eyes if you feel like it.... On the count of three, take a very slow, deep breath. Remember to breathe in quietly through your nose. One . . . two . . . three.... Breathe in deeply.... Now breathe out slowly.... Remember to breathe out quietly through your mouth. Let your entire body relax.... Now imagine yourself at your house with a good friend.... You say nice things to your friend and you share your things.... The two of you have a lot of fun together. Think how proud you feel about being a good friend.

LESSON Z PLOT SITUATION:

You are in the restroom at the movie theatre. Your friend pressures you to write something on the bathroom wall.

LESSON Z ROADBLOCK EXAMPLES:

- Being friends with someone who is often mean to you

- Being friends with someone who wants you to get into trouble

- Feeling worried that you can't be nice to kids outside your group of friends because then your group won't like you

- Not knowing how to go up to new kids and start a conversation so that you can make new friends

Social Star

Name _____

Being a Friend T-Chart

LOOKS LIKE... | SOUNDS LIKE...

LOOKS LIKE...

using appropriate body talk
- looking at your friend
- smiling
- sitting close to your friend

not being jealous when your friend does something with someone else
- going to a movie with someone else

giving support when your friend feels bad
- when his lizard dies

SOUNDS LIKE...

saying positive things to your friend

asking, "Would you like some of my _____?"

asking, "What would you like to do?"

saying no if your friend asks you to do something you don't feel is right for you

an appropriate volume

a friendly voice tone

laughing together

© 1994 Thinking Publications   Duplication permitted for educational use only.

SHOW TIME

HOME
Pretend you have a friend staying over at your house. Your friend keeps saying mean things about another friend of yours. Show what you could say to let your friend know that you don't like saying mean things about your other friend.

SCHOOL
Pretend that your friends are being mean to you because your parents won't let you watch certain videos. Show what you could say to your friends to let them know that friends shouldn't treat one another that way.

COMMUNITY
Pretend that you and two other friends go to the swimming pool. One friend starts giving the other friend put-downs. Show what you could say to let that person know that friends shouldn't give one another put-downs.

Be A Friend

HOME-A-GRAM

Social Star

Dear Family,

At school, we have been talking about the social skill called

BEING A FRIEND

I learned that *being a friend* means choosing words and actions that show someone I care.

I learned that *being a DNEIRF* means choosing actions and words that are not respectful. (The word DNEIRF is the word "friend" spelled backwards!)

I can feel proud when I am a good friend, because it invites others to feel positive about themselves.

Below is a picture of my new friend "BAF." Ask me what his initials stand for.

B = _____
A = _____
F = _____

I am bringing home a game about being a friend for us to play. If I do or say something to be a friend while playing the game, please sign my "Being a Friend" badge so I can return it to school and become a SOCIAL SUPER STAR this week.

From: _____

© 1994 Thinking Publications — 229 — *Duplication permitted for educational use only.*

Giving and Receiving Compliments

Social Star

UNIT GOAL:

To demonstrate comprehension and use of giving and receiving compliments

EDUCATOR INFORMATION:

1. This unit combines the two social skills of *giving compliments* and *receiving compliments*. Distinctions have been made between the two skills within the unit. However, it may be necessary for the educator to emphasize one skill more than the other depending on students' needs. This unit teaches students that when they give compliments, they can feel proud because they are inviting others to feel good about themselves. Students are taught that the best way to receive a compliment is to say "Thank you," because it shows they are polite and confident. Students are taught the difference between inside compliments (e.g., "You are a fun person") and outside compliments (e.g., "Nice shirt"). The educator is reminded to exert sensitivity and care in generalizing rules about giving and receiving compliments into the children's home cultures.

2. Educators should model giving sincere compliments to students. Katz (1993) states that the recent emphasis on self-esteem in the schools may be the reason for educators "lavishing praise for the mildest accomplishments." She states that "constant reminders about how wonderful one is may raise doubts about the credibility of the message and the messenger." Educators are encouraged to read the Katz article for specific recommendations.

3. The adjective "sincere" is occasionally included when referring to compliments in this unit. The authors' opinions are that children typically give sincere compliments. Therefore, the term "sincere" was purposely not discussed in detail.

RELATED ACTIVITIES:

1. Have each student pick a school staff member (other than yourself). They should write a compliment on a card for that person (e.g., complimenting the custodian for keeping the school so clean). Distribute the cards to the staff members during a schoolwide staff appreciation week.

2. Have students visit a classroom of younger children. Ask each student to listen to a younger child read and compliment the child on his or her reading skills.

3. As a homework assignment, have students compliment each of their family members. Have them report back how each compliment was accepted and how it felt to give the compliments.

4. Discuss compliments before Valentine's Day. Use the phrase "a gift from the heart" and discuss the importance of giving sincere compliments. Encourage students to write compliments on their valentines instead of just signing their names. Discuss compliments before any day that is associated with giving a card or a gift (e.g., Mother's Day, Grandparent's Day). Encourage students to give a special gift of a compliment.

5. Invite adults from different cultures to talk about how their cultures' conventions for giving and receiving compliments compare with American common culture norms.

It is important for educators to provide opportunities for students to work in groups so they can experience social skills in contexts where social communication is needed. Therefore, educators are encouraged to have students complete the Related Activities in small groups whenever possible. Educators trained in cooperative learning could incorporate the five components (see page 33) into the group activity.

RELATED LITERATURE:

Felicia the Critic (1973) by Ellen Conford; Ill. by Arvis Steward; Little, Brown and Co. (Text) Felicia plans a way to rearrange her mother's broom closet and surprises her family. (pages 25–27)

Hey There, Owlface (1991) by Betty Bates, Drawings by Leslie Morrill, Holiday House. (Text) Brad finds it hard to accept Holly's praise when he shows her an owl family in the hickory tree outside his bedroom window. (pages 64–70)

A Case for Jenny Archer (1988) by Ellen Conford; Ill. by Diane Palmisciano; Little, Brown and Co. (Text) Jenny receives praise for preventing robbers from stealing the neighbor's possessions. (pages 53–61)

SOCIAL SKILLS ALL DAY LONG:

Look for opportunities to teach social skills throughout the day (incidental teaching). Four ways to reinforce appropriate social skills and an example of each follow:

Encouragement

I just heard you say, "Great job in math" to Jolisa. You can feel proud because you invited her to feel good inside!

Personal Example

Today when I got to school, the principal said to me, "I think you are doing a great job in the classroom!" I gave the principal eye contact and said, "Thank you."

Prompting

During recess today, let's give each other "inside" compliments. Remember, an inside compliment tells something nice about a quality or skill a person has on the inside. You might say, "Thanks for being a fun friend."

Corrective Feedback (must be positive, private, specific, and nonthreatening)

Maria, just now when I said, "You did a super job on your spelling test," you put your head down and didn't say anything. You could have looked at me, smiled, and said, "Thank you" to show politeness and confidence.

Social Star

Lesson A

OBJECTIVES:

1. To state the meaning of *giving compliments* and tell why it is important

2. To listen to the self-talk associated with correct use of the skill

MATERIALS:

1. Index cards (Write an individual compliment to each student in class, one compliment per card.)

2. A box (Decorated to look like a gift box)

3. *Giving and Receiving Compliments* (See page 237; one per student and one transparency.)

4. *Thought Bubble* (See *Appendix O*; one for educator use.)

5. *Checking Myself* (See *Appendix I*; one per student and one transparency.)

PREPARATORY SET:

Place the completed compliment index cards inside the decorated box. Tell the class that you have a special gift for them. Explain that you have written a compliment to each one of them. One by one, take the compliments out of the box and hand them to the students. Use this activity to introduce the unit *Giving and Receiving Compliments*. Afterward, discuss the similarities between giving someone a compliment and giving that person a gift.

PLAN:

1. Distribute and display *Giving and Receiving Compliments*. Discuss the definition for *giving a compliment*. (Receiving a compliment will be discussed in Lesson C.) Explain the skill step for giving a compliment and the symbol next to it. Remind students that the symbol is there to help them visualize and remember the skill step. Refer to the body-talk symbol in the left-hand margin. Remind students that appropriate body talk is important when giving compliments. Discuss the reasons for giving compliments.

2. Model use of the giving compliments skill step while thinking aloud. A scripted example follows:

Introduction

I am going to pretend to give a compliment to my sister. I will show you how I appropriately give a compliment and tell you the thoughts I'm having. When I hold up this Thought Bubble, *you'll know the words I'm saying are actually what I'm thinking.*

Actual Model

While holding up the *Thought Bubble* say, *My sister did really well in the school play. Let's see. What compliment can I give to her? Oh, I know!* Put the *Thought Bubble* down and say, *You were great in the play!*

3. Complete the bottom half of *Giving and Receiving Compliments* by reading the story to the students.

4. Distribute and display the discussion guideline sheet called *Checking Myself.* Ask students to complete the thought bubble statement with the words "use eye contact," or use another classroom discussion goal more appropriate for your group (see pages 25–26). Tell students that you will be having a discussion about the story you read to them. When a student is answering a question or making a comment during the discussion, it's important for everyone to give that student eye contact. Instruct them to circle a T-shirt star each time they give eye contact to a student who is called on.

5. Model use of the *Checking Myself* sheet while thinking aloud. A scripted example follows:

Introduction

I am going to pretend to be one of you completing this sheet during the discussion we will be having. I will tell you the thoughts I'm having while I'm completing the sheet. When I hold up this Thought Bubble, *you'll know the words I'm saying are actually what I'm thinking.*

Actual Model

While holding up the *Thought Bubble* say, *The teacher just called on Mike. I need to look at him so he knows I'm listening. I'll circle a star on the T-shirt because I looked at Mike.* Put the *Thought Bubble* down and circle a star on the transparency.

During the discussion, periodically remind students to give eye contact to the student who is answering or commenting and to mark their discussion guideline sheets.

6. Proceed with the discussion by asking these questions: (The story may need to be reread first.)

   - What compliment did Jolisa give to Ann?

   - How do you think Ann felt about Jolisa's compliment? How do you know?

   - What compliment did Mr. Aaron give to Jolisa?

   - How do you think Jolisa felt about Mr. Aaron's compliment? How do you know?

   After the discussion, have students complete the bottom thought bubble statement on *Checking Myself*.

7. Process use of the sheet by asking the following question or another one more appropriate for your group:

   - Why do you think it's important to give eye contact to the person who is speaking during a discussion?

   Process further by asking the students who volunteered to speak during the discussion to share their answers to the following question:

   - You answered one of the questions during our discussion. How did you feel when the other students gave you eye contact while you were talking?

8. Pair students (see *Appendix P*). Ask student pairs to take turns telling each other the meaning of *giving compliments* and why it's important to use the skill. Encourage students to use appropriate body talk while completing this task. Students could be reminded that the information they are to say is printed on *Giving and Receiving Compliments*.

   As an option to add structure to this activity (see *Appendix Q*), ask partners to come to an agreement about which person will be called "John F. Kennedy" and which person will be called "Martin Luther King, Jr." After students have made their decisions, ask "Martin" to tell "John" the definition of *giving compliments*. Next, ask "John" to tell "Martin" the definition. Ask the students to use the same procedure to tell each other the reasons for giving compliments.

9. Say with excitement to the class: *Each of you is truly becoming a social super star!*

Name _____

⭐ Giving and Receiving Compliments

MEANING OF GIVING A COMPLIMENT: When you say something sincerely nice about another person

SKILL STEP:

1. Ask myself:
   What compliment can I give?

REASONS FOR USING THIS SKILL:
You can feel proud inside when you give compliments. When you give compliments you are inviting others to feel good about themselves.

MEANING OF RECEIVING A COMPLIMENT:
When someone says something sincerely nice about you

SKILL STEPS:

1. Ask myself:
   Am I receiving a compliment?

   IF YES,

2. Say, "Thank you!"

REASONS FOR USING THIS SKILL:
You can feel proud inside when you receive a compliment. When you say, "Thank you," you are polite and confident.

DIRECTIONS: Listen to the story below. Look at the picture of Jolisa while you are listening.

On the way to school, Jolisa sat next to Ann on the bus. Jolisa noticed Ann's new folders and said, "Ann, I like your folders. They are really cool!" Ann smiled and said, "Thank you." When Jolisa got to school, Mr. Aaron said, "Jolisa, I enjoyed reading the story you wrote yesterday. The part about the race was really funny!" Jolisa smiled at Mr. Aaron and said, "Thank you."

© 1994 Thinking Publications   *Duplication permitted for educational use only.*

Social Star

Lesson B

OBJECTIVES:

1. To brainstorm examples of outside and inside compliments
2. To give outside and inside compliments

MATERIALS:

1. *Opposites Match—A and B* (See *Appendix P*; one matching set per pair of students.)
2. *Giving and Receiving Compliments* classroom poster (See page 13.)
3. *Brainstorming Guide* (See *Appendix AA*; two per pair of students and two transparencies.)
4. Containers (e.g., milk carton, butter tub, disposable cup; one per student)
5. *Inside/Outside Compliment Cards* (See page 240; one per student.)
6. Paper (To gift-wrap the containers)
7. Scissors and rolls of tape (One of each per pair of students)

PREPARATORY SET:

Pair students using the *Opposites Match* cards (see *Appendix P*). As students are forming pairs, compliment them on their use of social skills (e.g., "You are doing a nice job of quickly finding your partner").

PLAN:

1. Review the definition and skill step for *giving compliments* by referring the class to the *Giving and Receiving Compliments* classroom poster.

2. Ask student pairs to take turns telling each other the skill step for giving a compliment. Follow the procedure described in step 8 of Lesson A. (As an option, ask students to decide who will be "P.T. Barnum" and who will be "Walt Disney.") Next, ask students to work with a partner to think of a situation when it would be important to give a compliment. Tell students that one or more pairs will be asked to share their situation. Have one or more pairs share their situation.

3. Distribute and display the *Brainstorming Guide*. Write "outside compliments" on the blank line inside the brainstorming cloud. Explain that outside compliments tell something nice about things on the outside of a person (e.g., a

Giving and Receiving Compliments

haircut, clothes, toys). Ask students to brainstorm outside compliments. Write their ideas on the transparency. Choose one student to come to the front of the room. Give an outside compliment to the student (e.g., "Lee, I think that is a neat sweatshirt you have on"). Ask student pairs to take turns giving each other an outside compliment. Remind students to use sincere body talk (e.g., give eye contact, have a sincere facial expression).

4. Distribute and display a second *Brainstorming Guide*. Write "inside compliments" on the blank line inside the brainstorming cloud. Explain that inside compliments tell something nice about a quality or skill a person has on the inside (e.g., being honest, being fun, being polite, being kind, being intelligent). Ask students to brainstorm inside compliments. Write their ideas on the transparency. Choose one student to come to the front of the room. Give an inside compliment to the student (e.g., "Jolisa, you are a very helpful person. You are always willing to lend a hand"). Ask student pairs to take turns giving each other an inside compliment. Remind students to use sincere body talk. (Later, transfer compliments from both *Brainstorming Guide* activities onto individual index cards for use during Lesson C.)

5. Distribute the containers, *Inside/Outside Compliment Cards*, paper, tape, and scissors. Explain that each student will make a "compliment container" for a family member. Ask students to choose someone at home to whom they would like to give the container. Ask students to cut out their inside and outside compliment cards. Instruct them to think of an outside compliment they could give to the person chosen (e.g., "Dad, you have some neat sweatshirts"). Instruct students to write the compliment on their outside compliment card, have their partners check to be certain it is an outside compliment, and then tape it to the outside of their container. Next, ask students to think of an "inside" compliment they could give to the person chosen (e.g., "Dad, you are really a nice guy"). Instruct students to write the compliment on their inside compliment card, have their partners check to be certain it is an inside compliment, and then tape it to the inside of the container. Instruct students to wrap their compliment containers. Tell students to take their compliment containers home and explain it to the family member for whom they prepared it.

6. Ask students, "Why do you think you were asked to tape the outside compliment to the outside of the container and the inside compliment to the inside of the container?"

7. Write the following where everyone can see it: I ENJOY LEARNING NEW SOCIAL SKILLS. SOCIAL SKILLS MAKE THE WORLD A HAPPIER PLACE. Have the students say this aloud, in unison, with enthusiasm.

Social Star

Inside Compliment

_____

_____

_____

_____

An inside compliment tells something nice about a quality or skill a person has on the inside (e.g., friendly, kind, good at swimming).

Outside Compliment

_____

_____

_____

_____

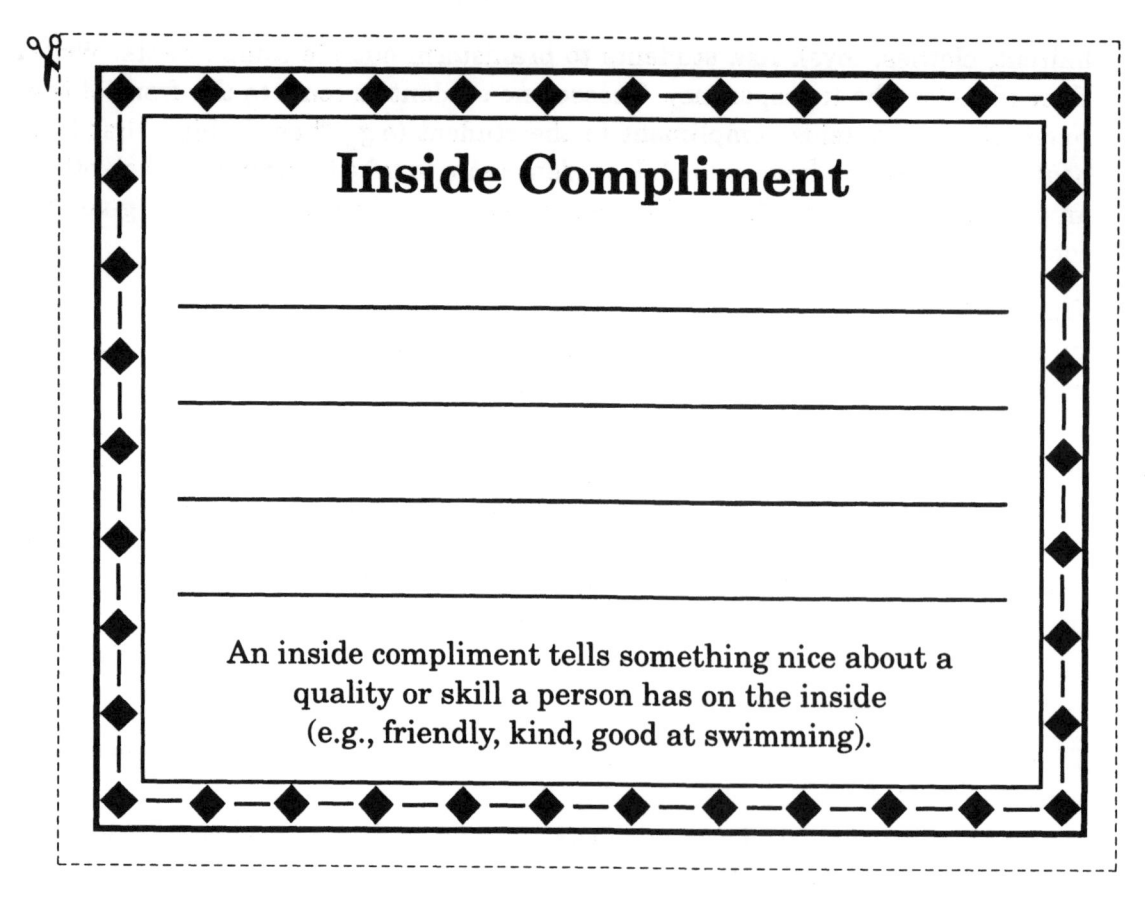

An outside compliment tells something nice about things on the outside of a person (e.g., hair, clothes).

© 1994 Thinking Publications — Duplication permitted for educational use only.

Giving and Receiving Compliments

Lesson C — Social Star

OBJECTIVES:

1. To state the meaning of *receiving a compliment* and tell why it is important
2. To tell the self-talk associated with correct use of the skill
3. To practice giving and receiving compliments

MATERIALS:

1. A camcorder and a videotape (For use during the Preparatory Set)
2. *Giving and Receiving Compliments* (See page 237; one per student and one transparency.)
3. *Thought Bubble* (See *Appendix O*; one for educator use.)
4. Index cards with compliments written on them (See step 4 of Lesson B.)
5. *What's Missing?* (See page 243; one per pair of students.)

PREPARATORY SET:

Tell the students that you are going to walk around the room and videotape each of them. Explain that when the camera is pointed at them, they should smile and say, "Thank you." Walk around the room and videotape each student. Explain that they will watch the videotape of themselves at the beginning of the next lesson.

PLAN:

1. Distribute and display *Giving and Receiving Compliments*. Discuss the definition of *receiving a compliment* (located in the middle of the page). Explain the skill steps for receiving a compliment and the symbols next to them. Remind students that the symbols are there to help them visualize and remember the skill steps. Discuss the reasons for appropriately receiving compliments. Refer to the body-talk symbol in the left-hand margin. Remind students that appropriate body talk is important when receiving compliments.

2. Model use of the skill steps for receiving a compliment while thinking aloud. A scripted example follows:

    Introduction

    I am going to pretend to be a student your age. My grandma just complimented me by saying I am a sweet girl. I will tell you the thoughts I'm having while I'm accepting her compliment. When I hold up this Thought Bubble, *you'll know the words that I'm saying are actually what I am thinking.*

Actual Model

While holding up the *Thought Bubble* say, *Did Grandma just compliment me? Yes, she did. I need to say thank you to her.* Put down the *Thought Bubble* and say, *Thank you.*

3. Tell students they will be practicing giving and receiving compliments. Pair students using the *Line Up–Fold Up* activity (see *Appendix P*). Have students line up in alphabetical order using their first names. After the students have "folded up" and formed two lines, distribute a compliment index card to each student in Line 1. Each student with a card (Person A) in Line 1 should read the compliment to the person standing opposite them (Person B) in Line 2. Person B should say, "Thank you." Then the students in Line 2 should "slide" by stepping to the right until they are facing a new student in Line 1. (The student on the end of Line 2 will need to walk around to the opposite end of the line.) Each student with a card (Person A) in Line 1 should read the compliment to the person standing opposite them (Person B) in Line 2. Person B should say, "Thank you." Continue this procedure until students in Line 2 are back to their original positions. Collect the compliment cards and distribute them to the students in Line 2. This time through the activity, students in Line 2 should read their compliment to students in Line 1, and students in Line 1 should say, "Thank you" and then "slide." When the activity has ended, ask students to find a spot to sit with their partners to complete the remainder of the lesson.

4. Distribute *What's Missing?* to each pair of students. Ask them to read each cartoon and fill in the blank talk bubbles. Tell students that one or more pairs will be called on to share their answers. Have one or more pairs share their answers.

5. Display *Giving and Receiving Compliments*. Ask student pairs to take turns telling each other the meaning of and skills steps for *receiving a compliment*. Remind students that the information they are to say is printed on *Giving and Receiving Compliments*. Follow the procedure described in step 8 of Lesson A. (As an option, ask students to decide who will be "Hans Christian Andersen" and who will be "Captain Hook".)

6. Say with excitement to the class: *I am different from you and you are different from me. That makes us each special. I like you because you're different and special.*

Giving and Receiving Compliments

Names _____

What's Missing?

DIRECTIONS: Read each cartoon. Fill in the blank talk bubbles with words the characters could use to receive the compliments appropriately.

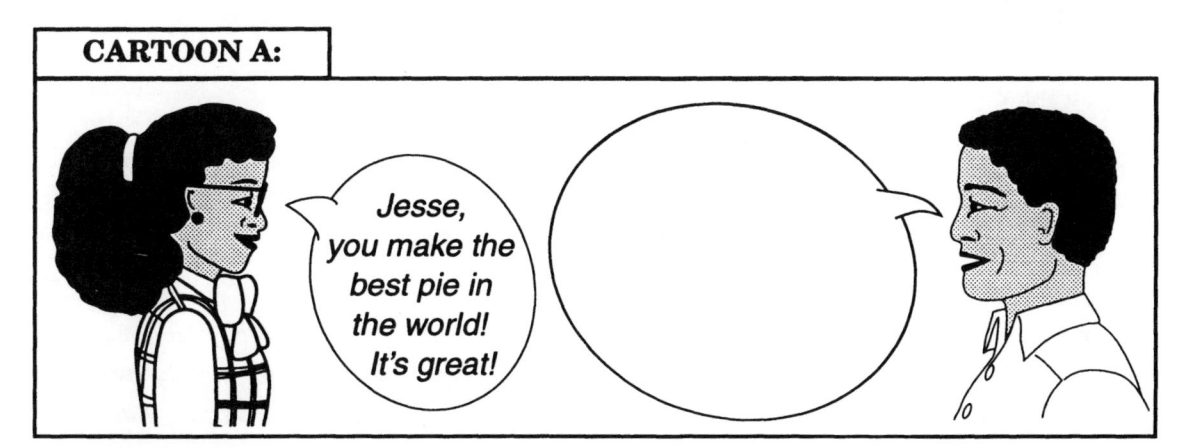

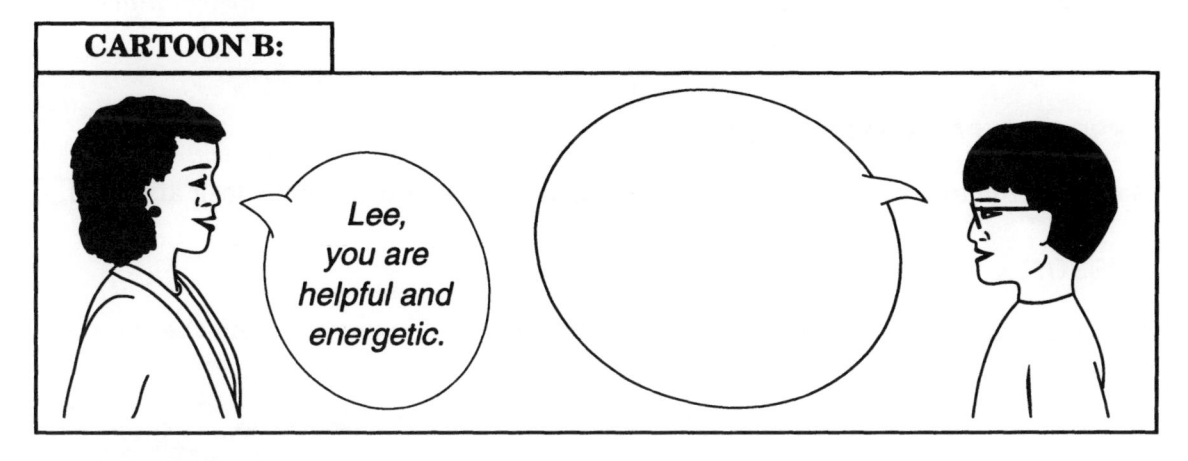

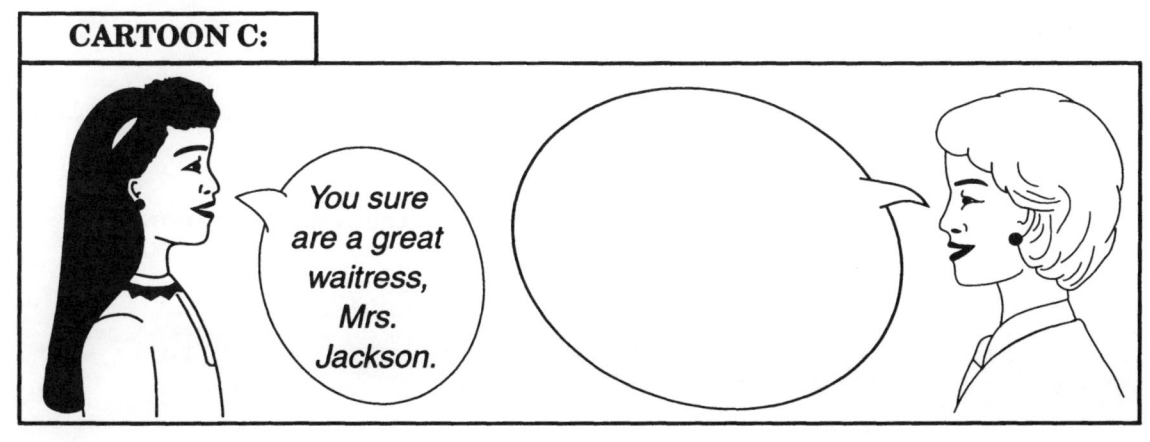

CARTOON A:

Jesse, you make the best pie in the world! It's great!

CARTOON B:

Lee, you are helpful and energetic.

CARTOON C:

You sure are a great waitress, Mrs. Jackson.

© 1994 Thinking Publications   *Duplication permitted for educational use only.*

Social Star

Lessons X, Y, and Z

Due to similarities in format, the final three lesson plans for each unit in *Social Star* are provided in *Appendix A*. Substitute the words "giving and receiving compliments" whenever a "____" appears in the lesson plans. Information specific to this unit follows.

LESSON X PREPARATORY SET:

Ask students to watch the videotape produced during the Preparatory Set of Lesson C.

LESSON Y PREPARATORY SET:

Darken the room, if you prefer, and ask students to visualize themselves correctly using this social skill by reading the following script:

> *Let's take a few moments to relax.... Make sure you are sitting in a comfortable position.... Close your eyes if you feel like it.... On the count of three, take a very slow, deep breath. Remember to breathe in quietly through your nose. One . . . two . . . three.... Breathe in deeply.... Now breathe out slowly and quietly through your mouth. Let your entire body relax.... Now imagine yourself giving an inside compliment. You say to your friend "You are so much fun!" Think about how proud you feel for complimenting your friend.*

LESSON Z PLOT SITUATION:

Ask students to pretend that their new eraser is missing from their desk at school.

LESSON Z ROADBLOCK EXAMPLES:

- Accepting a compliment when you are not sure if the person giving the compliment is sincere

- Feeling embarrassed when people point out the good things you do

- Having the tendency to think negatively or pessimistically (e.g., not believing someone) when given a compliment

- Using appropriate words but inappropriate body talk when giving or receiving a compliment

- Being taught to be "humble" when complimented, rather than to acknowledge and confidently accept the compliment

Giving and Receiving Compliments

Name _____

Giving Compliments T-Chart

LOOKS LIKE... | SOUNDS LIKE...

using appropriate body talk

- looking at the person you compliment
- smiling
- giving a "thumbs up" or a pat on the back

a sincere tone of voice

•••••••••••••••••

saying
- "I like your haircut." (outside compliment)
- "You're a great listener!" (inside compliment)

Social Star

Name _____

Receiving Compliments T-Chart

LOOKS LIKE... | SOUNDS LIKE...

LOOKS LIKE...

using appropriate body talk

- looking at the person who complimented you
- smiling
- having a straight, confident posture

SOUNDS LIKE...

a happy tone of voice

•·•·•·•·•·•·•·•·•·•

a volume that can be heard

•·•·•·•·•·•·•·•·•·•

saying

- "Thank you."
- "Thanks."

© 1994 Thinking Publications — Duplication permitted for educational use only.

SHOW TIME

HOME
Pretend your mother made your favorite meal. Show how to give her a compliment about her cooking.

SCHOOL
Pretend you are at school. Your teacher gives you a compliment for sharing your colored pencils with another student. Show how to accept the compliment.

COMMUNITY
Pretend you are with your parents at their friends' home. Someone gives you a compliment about your new haircut. Show how to accept the compliment.

When You Receive a Compliment Say... *Thank You!*

Giving and Receiving Compliments

GIVE COMPLIMENTS

Invite Others to Feel GOOD!

© 1994 Thinking Publications • 249 • *Duplication permitted for educational use only.*

HOME-A-GRAM

Dear Family,

At school, we have been talking about the social skill called

GIVING AND RECEIVING COMPLIMENTS

I learned that *giving a compliment* means saying something sincerely nice about another person.

I learned that when I'm with others, I can ask myself, "What compliment can I give?"

I can feel proud when I give compliments because it invites people to feel good about themselves.

I learned that *receiving a compliment* means someone says something sincerely nice about me.

I learned that when I'm with others, I can ask myself, "Am I receiving a compliment?" If I am, I can be polite and confident by saying the words I have colored in below:

Thank You!

When I give or receive a compliment at home tonight, please sign my "Giving and Receiving Compliments" badge so I can return it to school and become a SOCIAL SUPER STAR this week.

From: _____

Building a Positive Reputation

Social Star

UNIT GOAL:

To demonstrate comprehension and use of strategies for building a positive reputation

EDUCATOR INFORMATION:

1. This unit teaches students what reputations are and how they are built. It lets students know that sometimes reputations are based on truth and sometimes they are not. Unfortunately for some students, reputations are established early in elementary grades and become more stable each year (Meichenbaum, 1991). Since reputations are based on the opinions of others, students are encouraged to choose actions that may lead to a positive reputation (being friendly, polite, loyal, organized) and to avoid actions that may lead to a negative reputation (lying, stealing). Students are reminded to treat all people with respect and to look for positive qualities in everyone. The feelings of students with negative reputations are discussed.

2. It is strongly recommended that the educator discourage teasing that can lead to negative reputations for students (e.g., "Hey, stinky," "You're so poor," "You're the ugliest creature on earth"). An activity called "Home Court" (described in the Related Activity section) helps provide a classroom atmosphere that is free from teasing.

3. The educator should consider the ways that different cultures or groups currently feel about what constitutes a positive reputation. For example, some students may be primarily concerned about their reputation within their gang. In some groups, being "good" in school may earn students poor reputations. The educator should exert sensitivity and care in generalizing rules about positive reputations into the children's home cultures.

RELATED ACTIVITIES:

1. Have students create a puppet show about a character who builds a positive reputation.

2. Have students compose lyrics about reputations to a familiar melody. An example follows:

   (Sung to the melody of "Yankee Doodle Dandy")
   As you work and as you play
   Beside your friends and neighbors,
   Words and actions that you choose
   Will build your reputation.

3. Discuss the term "stereotype." Talk about the problems that occur as a result of stereotyping various groups of people. (See the *Anti-Bias Curriculum* by Louise Derman-Sparks [1989] for a list of common stereotypes.) Read statements which include stereotypes for students to analyze (e.g., "All boys like football," "All girls want to be cheerleaders"). Adults from other cultures may be invited in to discuss their encounters with stereotypes.

4. Have students create a video commercial about the importance of building a positive reputation.

5. Use the "Home Court" advantage (La Meres, 1990) in your classroom. Ask students why a basketball team usually does better on its home court. Possible answers include: the players are familiar with the court, the fans are cheering and supporting the team. Explain that the fans really want the team to win. Tell students that you would like your classroom to be like a home court, where everyone supports each other and there are no put-downs. This may discourage the formation of undeserved negative reputations.

6. Have students visit a local employer to discuss the importance of reputations when getting a job.

It is important for educators to provide opportunities for students to work in groups so they can experience social skills in contexts where social communication is needed. Therefore, educators are encouraged to have students complete the Related Activities in small groups whenever possible. Educators trained in cooperative learning could incorporate the five elements (see page 33) into the group activity.

RELATED LITERATURE:

Wait for Me (1992) by Susan Shreve, Ill. by Diane de Groat, Tambourine Books. (Text) Winning the 5th grade race gives Molly a new status among her family and friends. (pages 93–95)

The Hotshot (1977) by Alfred Slote, Photographs by William LaCross, Franklin Watts. (Text) Paddy earns his reputation by being a good team player. (pages 67–78)

SOCIAL SKILLS ALL DAY LONG:

Look for opportunities to teach social skills throughout the day (incidental teaching). Four ways to reinforce appropriate social skills and an example of each follow:

Encouragement

Jolisa, you always do your best on your schoolwork. Doing your best on your schoolwork will help you build a positive reputation with your teachers.

Personal Example

I have the reputation of being an unorganized person. I am becoming more organized by making lists for myself, because I want to change that reputation.

Prompting

Before we go out for recess, let's discuss some things you can do to help yourself build a positive reputation.

Corrective Feedback (must be positive, private, specific, and nonthreatening)

Lee, just now you kicked Mike when you were angry. You could use words instead of kicking to tell people when you are angry. Say, "I am angry because...." This will help you build a more positive reputation.

Social Star

Lesson A

OBJECTIVES:

1. To state the meaning of *building a positive reputation* and tell why it's important
2. To listen to the self-talk associated with the skill

MATERIALS:

1. A brick for educator use
2. *Building a Positive Reputation* (See page 256; one copy per student and one transparency.)
3. *Thought Bubble* (See *Appendix O*; one for educator use.)

PREPARATORY SET:

While holding up the brick, ask students to think about how a brick building is built. Explain that the bricks are added one by one to make it sturdy. Tell students that in this unit they will learn how to build something called "a positive reputation." Explain to students that each positive choice they make will help them to build a positive reputation with others.

PLAN:

1. Distribute and display *Building a Positive Reputation*. Discuss the definition. Explain the skill step and the symbol next to it. Remind students that the symbol is there to help them visualize and remember the skill step. Refer to the body-talk symbol in the left-hand margin. Remind students that appropriate body talk is important in building a positive reputation. Discuss the reasons for using this social skill.

2. Model use of the skill step for building a positive reputation while thinking aloud. A scripted example follows:

Introduction

I am going to pretend to be someone your age. It is the first day of the school year. I have a new teacher and some new classmates. I will show what things I can do to help me build a positive reputation with others. I'll tell you the thoughts I am having. When I hold up this Thought Bubble, *you'll know the words that I'm saying are actually what I'm thinking.*

Actual Model

While holding up the *Thought Bubble* say, *OK. What can I do to build a positive reputation? I'll respect everyone. I won't tease or make fun of anyone.*

Put the *Thought Bubble* down and say, *Hi, how was your summer?* Hold the *Thought Bubble* up and say, *I'm doing a good job being friendly and it's helping me to build a positive reputation.*

3. Complete the bottom of *Building a Positive Reputation* by reading the stories about Mike and Victor. Ask students to discuss who they think is building a more positive reputation.

4. Pair students using the *Inside-Outside Circle* activity (see *Appendix P*). Ask student pairs to take turns telling each other the meaning of *building a positive reputation* and why it's important. Students could be reminded that the information they are to say is printed on *Building a Positive Reputation.*

   As an option to add structure to this activity (see *Appendix Q*), ask partners to come to an agreement about which person will be called "Alexander Graham Bell" and which person will be called "Thomas Edison." After students have made their decisions, ask "Alexander" to tell "Thomas" the definition of *building a positive reputation*. Next, ask "Thomas" to tell "Alexander" the definition. Ask students to use the same procedure to tell each other the reasons for building a positive reputation.

5. Ask partners to face each other and stand an arm's length away. Encourage students to use friendly and confident body talk. Ask partners to shake hands and in unison repeat the following statement after you: *I can choose what I say. I can choose how I act. My choices will affect how I get along with others.*

Social Star

Name _____

★ Building a Positive Reputation

**MEANING OF BUILDING
A POSITIVE REPUTATION:** Making responsible choices that invite others to have positive thoughts about you

SKILL STEP:

1. Ask myself: What can I do to build a positive reputation?

REASONS FOR USING THIS SKILL:
When you build a positive reputation, people may treat you better. It helps you feel proud of yourself.

DIRECTIONS: Listen to the stories below. Decide which boy may be building a more positive reputation.

Mike never makes fun of other students. He sticks up for students that others are teasing. He is usually in a happy mood and treats everyone with respect.

Victor sometimes teases other students. He says mean things to hurt their feelings. He is often in a crabby mood, and complains a lot.

© 1994 Thinking Publications   Duplication permitted for educational use only.

Building a Positive Reputation

Lesson B

OBJECTIVE:

To identify actions that help to build a positive reputation

MATERIALS:

1. *Building a Positive Reputation* classroom poster (See page 13.)

2. *Your Actions Speak Loudly* (See page 260; one per pair of students and one transparency.)

3. *Brainstorming Guide* (See Appendix AA; one per pair of students and one transparency.)

4. Large sheets of yellow butcher paper (One per student)

5. Dark crayons or markers (One per student)

6. Scissors (One per student)

7. Staplers and staples

8. Newspaper (To use as stuffing)

PREPARATORY SET:

Tell students that you will be naming some characters they may have heard about. Ask them to put their thumbs up if they think the character has built a positive reputation and their thumbs down if they think the character has built a negative reputation. Proceed by naming the following characters or others more familiar to the students: (from Cinderella) the stepmother, the fairy godmother, the stepsisters. Ask students to explain how they think each character has built a positive or a negative reputation.

PLAN:

1. Review the definition and skill step for *building a positive reputation* by referring the class to the *Building a Positive Reputation* classroom poster.

2. Pair students (see *Appendix P*). Distribute and display *Your Actions Speak Loudly*. Ask student pairs to read each situation and complete as directed. After students have completed the activity, call on student pairs to share their answers. Discuss why students chose their answers.

3. Share the expression, "Actions speak louder than words," with students and discuss its meaning.

Social Star

4. Distribute and display the *Brainstorming Guide*. Explain the rules for brainstorming. Write "positive reputation actions" on the blank line inside the brainstorming cloud. Have students work with their partners to brainstorm responsible choices they could make to build a positive reputation (e.g., be honest, help others, smile, get work done on time, give compliments). Call on pairs to share their ideas and write them on the transparency.

5. Distribute the yellow butcher paper. Tell students to fold their paper in half and then draw a large star on it. See the diagram below.

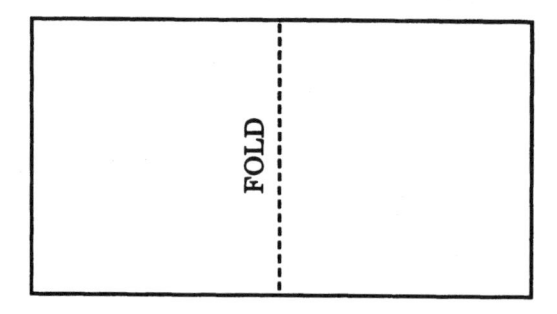

6. Distribute the dark crayons or markers. Ask students to write "Reputation Stars" on the inside of their stars. Next, ask students to write something a person can do to build a positive reputation on each point of their stars. They may choose from the list developed in step 4 or think of other examples. See the following diagram.

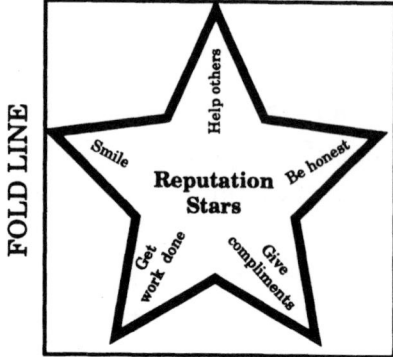

7. Distribute the scissors and staplers. Ask students to cut out their stars and staple the two pieces together, leaving an opening. See the following diagram.

258

8. Distribute the newspaper. Ask students to crumple the paper, use it to stuff their stars, and then staple the openings shut. Hang the stars from the ceiling for a very attractive display.

9. Ask student pairs to take turns telling each other the skill step for building a positive reputation. Follow the procedure described in step 4 of Lesson A. (As an option, ask students to decide who will be "Martha Washington" and who will be "Betsy Ross.") Next, ask students to work with their partners to think of a time when doing things to build a positive reputation is important. Tell students that one or more pairs will be called on to share their situation. Have one or more pairs share their situation.

10. Say with excitement to the class: *You are all social super, super, super stars! Remember, you have a responsibility to use your social skills and to invite other people to use good social skills too.*

Social Star

Names _____

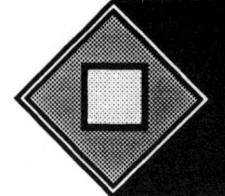

Your Actions Speak Loudly

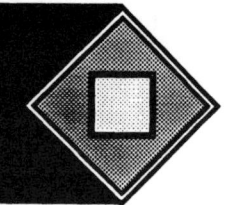

DIRECTIONS: Read each situation below. Write the reputation you think the person might be building.

1. Ann is often by herself. Kids ask her to play on the playground. She looks the other way.
   Ann's actions might build a reputation of being:

   _____

2. Victor is kind to others. He helps kids with their work. Sometimes there is a new student. He makes that student feel welcome.
   Victor's actions might build a reputation of being:

   _____

3. Maria tells mean jokes about other kids. She wants to hurt their feelings. Sometimes kids make mistakes. She laughs at them.
   Maria's actions might build a reputation of being:

   _____

4. Sometimes Mike borrows things. He gives them back on time. He gives them back in good condition. He never takes things without asking.
   Mike's actions might build a reputation of being:

   _____

5. Jolisa sees people doing little things wrong. She runs over to a parent or a teacher to tell on them.
   Jolisa's actions might build a reputation of being:

   _____

6. Lee has a hard time telling the truth. He makes up stories. He wants to get out of trouble with his friends and family.
   Lee's actions might build a reputation of being:

   _____

© 1994 Thinking Publications — Duplication permitted for educational use only.

Lesson C

Building a Positive Reputation

OBJECTIVES:

1. To tell the importance of treating others respectfully by looking beyond negative reputations for positive qualities

2. To brainstorm roadblocks a person may encounter when changing a negative reputation to a more positive one

MATERIALS:

1. *Social Star Club Meeting—Reputations* (See pages 264–268; enlarge, color, and laminate, if desired, one copy of the story for educator use; as an alternative, duplicate one copy per student and let students color the illustrations in their copies.)

2. *Checking Myself* (See *Appendix I*; one per student and one transparency.)

3. *Thought Bubble* (See *Appendix O*; one for educator use.)

PREPARATORY SET:

Write the word REPUTATION vertically where students can see it. Ask students to think of words or phrases about positive reputations for each of the letters in REPUTATION. An example follows:

Remembering to use polite manners

Eating politely

Picking up

Using a friendly voice tone

Treating others respectfully

Asking permission

Telling people their positive qualities

Inviting others to join in

Opening a door to help someone

Noticing when people need help

PLAN:

1. Read *Social Star Club Meeting—Reputations* to students. Stop to interact directly with students when a star appears in the story.

2. Distribute and display the discussion guideline sheet called *Checking Myself*. Ask students to complete the goal statement with the words "think about an answer to each question asked," or use another classroom discussion goal more

appropriate for your group (see pages 25–26). Tell students that you will be having a discussion about the Social Star Club story they just heard. During the discussion, it is important that each of them think about an answer to each question, even if they are not called on. Instruct them to circle a T-shirt star each time they think of an answer to a question. It's important to provide enough "wait time" before calling on a student to orally answer each question.

3. Model use of the *Checking Myself* sheet while thinking aloud. A scripted example follows:

Introduction

I am going to pretend to be one of you completing this sheet during the discussion we will be having. I will tell you the thoughts I'm having while I'm completing this sheet. When I hold up this Thought Bubble, *you'll know the words I'm saying are actually what I'm thinking.*

Actual Model

While holding up the *Thought Bubble* say, *OK, the teacher just asked what things I could do to help someone who sometimes lies and has built a negative reputation. I need to think about an answer. I could remind others to look for good things about that person. I'll circle a star on my paper because I just thought of an answer for that question.* Put the *Thought Bubble* down and circle a star on the transparency.

4. Proceed with the actual discussion by asking the following questions. During the discussion, periodically remind students to be thinking of answers to the questions and to mark their discussion guideline sheets.

   - What did Mr. Aaron ask the Social Star Club to help him with?
   - How did the Social Star Club decide to help Mr. Aaron's student?
   - Can you think of any other ways the Social Star Club could help Mr. Aaron's student?
   - What did the Social Star Club mean when they said we should look for the positive qualities in everyone, even someone who has a negative reputation?
   - At the end of the story, Lee asked if the boy really could change his reputation. Mr. Aaron said, "Yes, but he may run into some roadblocks." What do you think Mr. Aaron meant when he said that?
   - What roadblocks might the boy run into if he starts telling the truth to change his reputation? (Answers might include: It might be hard to break the habit of lying. Even if he starts telling the truth, people may continue to think of him as someone who lies.) Ask students to identify strategies he could use to "overcome" these roadblocks.

5. Process use of the sheet by asking the following questions or others more appropriate for your group:

    • Why is it important to think of answers to questions during a discussion?

    • What can you do if you're having a difficult time staying on task and thinking of answers to questions during a discussion?

6. Ask students to face another student and stand an arm's length away. Ask partners to use friendly and confident body talk. Ask partners to shake hands and in unison repeat the following statement after you: *Learning social skills is mighty fine. You can use your social skills all the time.*

Social Star

Social Star Club Meeting

Reputations

Building a Positive Reputation

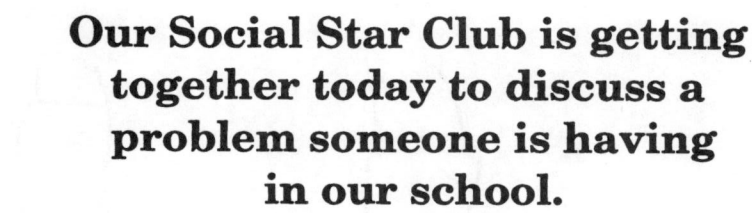

Hi, club members! Thank you for coming to this special club meeting! I am concerned about a boy in our school who has built a negative reputation. I'd like to get your ideas about how we might help him and other students like him.

Our Social Star Club is getting together today to discuss a problem someone is having in our school.

Mr. Aaron is going to speak to us about the problem. We'll need your ideas to help us too!

Well, he sometimes says things that are not true, either to try to get attention or to try to get out of trouble. The other kids know he's not telling the truth, and now he has the reputation of being someone who lies. I'm also concerned because the kids are doing and saying unkind things to him now.

Why are you worried about him? What reputation does he have?

Building a Positive Reputation

What can we do to help?

I think we need to let others know that it is important to be kind to everyone—even to kids who sometimes do things that we don't like. We need to remember that this guy is an important person and he has feelings too!

Let's put some posters up around school reminding kids to be kind to everyone. We can remind others to look beyond someone's negative reputation for positive things. Can you think of what we might say on the posters? ☆

Social Star

[Panel 8]

"What if this boy decides to change and start telling the truth? Do you think he can change his reputation?"

"That's a good question, Lee! I think he *can* change his reputation, but he may run into some roadblocks. Maybe we can talk about that at our next meeting."

[Panel 9]

"Let's hear it for the Social Star Club! By working together, you help to make our school a great place for everyone."

Hip, Hip, Hooray!

© 1994 Thinking Publications · *Duplication permitted for educational use only.*

Lessons X, Y, and Z

Building a Positive Reputation

Due to similarities in format, the final three lesson plans for each unit in *Social Star* are provided in *Appendix A*. Substitute the words "building a positive reputation" whenever a "____" appears in the lesson plans. Information specific to this unit follows.

LESSON X PREPARATORY SET:

Pair students. Give each pair a copy of *Tick-Tack-Toe* (see *Appendix BB*). Have each pair play *Tick-Tack-Toe* by telling an action that builds a positive reputation before marking X's or O's in their squares. Students may refer to the stuffed stars from Lesson B to get ideas for positive actions.

LESSON Y PREPARATORY SET:

Darken the room, if you prefer, and ask the students to visualize themselves correctly using this social skill by reading the following script:

Let's take a few moments to relax.... Make sure you are in a comfortable position.... Close your eyes if you feel like it.... On the count of three, take a very slow, deep breath. Remember to breathe in quietly through your nose. One ... two ... three.... Breathe in deeply.... Now breathe out slowly and quietly through your mouth. Let your entire body relax.... Now imagine yourself working hard at your new job raking leaves for the neighbor. You stick with the job until it's done. Think about how proud you feel for finishing the job and earning a positive reputation of being a hard worker with your neighbor.

LESSON Z PLOT SITUATION:

You and your brother or sister fight often. Your parents feel frustrated about the fighting and so do you.

LESSON Z ROADBLOCK EXAMPLES:

- Feeling frustrated because you made an irresponsible choice and everyone keeps talking about it

- Being friends with someone who has a negative reputation and others assume that your behaviors are the same as your friend's

Social Star

Name _____

Building a Positive Reputation T-Chart

LOOKS LIKE...

using appropriate body talk
- using friendly facial expressions
- giving eye contact to others
- using polite manners
- being helpful
- volunteering for a job
- being clean
- any other actions that bring a proud feeling inside and that others view positively

SOUNDS LIKE...

a respectful tone of voice

a volume that is right for the situation

saying
- "Mom, I'm building a positive reputation at school."
- "I don't think I should do that because it could lead to a negative reputation."
- "Sure, I'll help you."

SHOW TIME

HOME

Pretend your brother or sister has gotten into some trouble at school and comes to you for advice. Show what you could say to let your brother or sister know the importance of building a positive reputation.

SCHOOL

Pretend that a student in your class is having a difficult time building a positive reputation. Show what you could say to remind yourself to focus on the positive qualities of the person and treat the person with respect.

COMMUNITY

Pretend a new family moves into your neighborhood. Show what you could do and say to build a positive reputation with them.

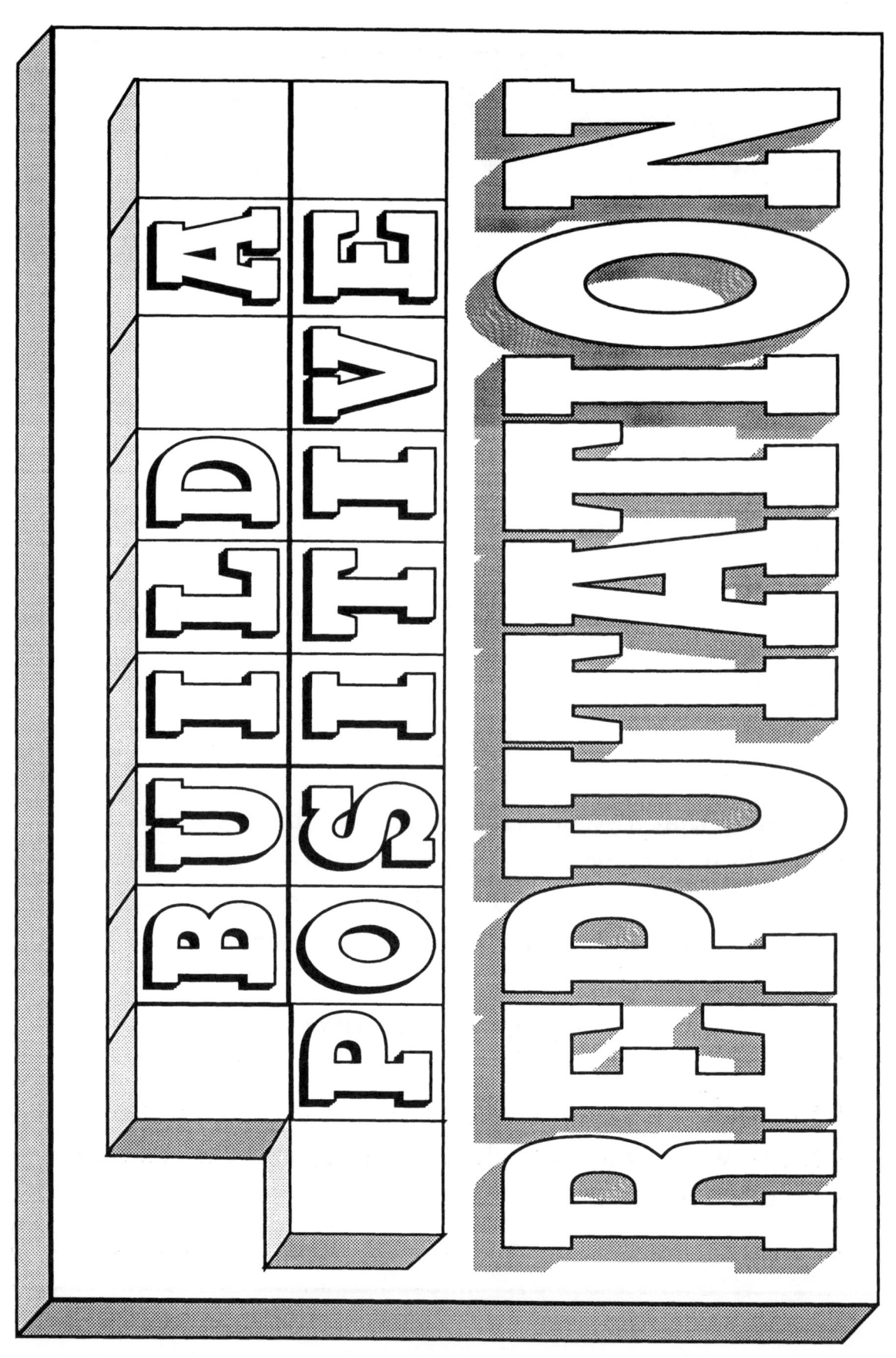

BUILD A POSITIVE REPUTATION

Building a Positive Reputation

HOME-A-GRAM
Social Star

Dear Family,

At school, we have been talking about the social skill called

BUILDING A POSITIVE REPUTATION

I learned that *building a positive reputation* means making responsible choices that invite other people to have positive thoughts about me.

I know that it is important to ask myself, "What can I do to build a positive reputation?"

I know when I make choices that I feel proud about inside, it may help me build a positive reputation and other people may treat me better.

Below, I have listed two people who have built positive reputations with me. I have written the reason(s) why I view them positively.

1. _____ has built a positive reputation with me because _____
_____

2. _____ has built a positive reputation with me because _____
_____

I'll show you what I know about building a positive reputation by discussing some of the actions I can choose to build a positive reputation for myself. After I do, please sign my "Building a Positive Reputation" badge so I can return it to school and become a SOCIAL SUPER STAR this week.

From: _____

© 1994 Thinking Publications — Duplication permitted for educational use only.

Dealing with Teasing

Social Star

UNIT GOAL:

To demonstrate comprehension and use of strategies for dealing with teasing, which is referred to as "being a teasebuster" in this unit

EDUCATOR INFORMATION:

1. This unit revolves around the theme "We're a teasebuster team! We're tease free and totally together!" This unit focuses on positive strategies students can use:

   - when they are tempted to tease others in a mean way
   - when they see others being teased in a mean way
   - when they are being teased in a mean way

2. This unit recognizes that in some contexts, teasing is used in an appropriate way to express affection. The unit's main focus, however, is on dealing with teasing that is negative or mean, and therefore not OK. The educator is reminded that when the term "teasing" is used within the unit, it refers to teasing that is inappropriate. The educator should exert sensitivity and care in generalizing rules about teasing into the children's home cultures.

3. Educators should set a class policy that does not permit teasing because of its negative effects. According to Madelaine Hunter (1992), "When you lose your dignity, you're incapable of learning anything. All of your brain power is used in restoring it."

RELATED ACTIVITIES:

1. Rewrite words to the theme song from the 1984 Columbia Pictures movie *Ghostbusters* to correspond with the teasebuster concept discussed within the unit. (See Lesson A.)

2. Have students plan how they could promote the "Tease Free and Totally Together" concept from this unit schoolwide (e.g., banners around school, daily announcements, a teasebuster awards ceremony).

3. Have students interview other teachers to determine the strategies those teachers use to discourage teasing in their classrooms.

4. Visit a local radio, newspaper, or television center to share information about the teasebuster concept and to invite coverage.

5. Invite adults from different cultures to talk about how their cultures' conventions for dealing with teasing compare with the concepts presented in this unit.

It is important for educators to provide opportunities for students to work in groups, so they can experience social skills in contexts where social communication is needed. Therefore, educators are encouraged to have students complete the Related Activities in small groups whenever possible. Educators trained in cooperative learning could incorporate the five components (see page 33) into the group activity.

RELATED LITERATURE:

The Hundred Dresses (1944) by Ealeanor Estes; Ill. by Louis Slobodkin; Harcourt, Brace, and World. (Text) Two examples of how Wanda responds to the teasing of Peggy and Maddy about her 100 dresses. (pages 10–19, 69–80)

Aldo Applesauce (1979) by Johanna Hurwitz, Ill. by John Wallner, William Morrow. (Text) Teasing about his name results when Aldo, at this new school, accidentally spills his applesauce. (pages 26–35)

SOCIAL SKILLS ALL DAY LONG:

Look for opportunities to teach social skills throughout the day (incidental teaching). Four ways to reinforce appropriate social skills and an example of each follow:

Encouragement

At lunch, I saw you step in and help another student who was being teased. That type of responsible behavior helps to make our classroom and school "tease free and totally together."

Personal Example

Last night, I ate dinner with my niece and nephew. When I heard them teasing each other in a mean way, I said, "This teasing is mean and that is not OK. I would like you to stop."

Prompting

While we are outside playing T-ball, why will it be important to make positive comments to people and not tease?

Corrective Feedback (must be positive, private, specific, and nonthreatening)

Ann, when Jolisa teased you, you gave her a put-down and teased her back. Instead, you could have used a teasebuster strategy. What teasebuster strategy might have worked?

Dealing with Teasing

Lesson A

OBJECTIVES:

1. To state the meaning of *being a teasebuster* and tell why it is important
2. To listen to the self-talk associated with correct use of the skill
3. To sign a contract for becoming a teasebuster team member

MATERIALS:

1. The theme song from the 1984 Columbia Pictures movie *Ghostbusters* (For students to hear during the Preparatory Set)
2. *Being a Teasebuster* (See page 280; one per student and one transparency.)
3. Megaphone (One homemade megaphone with the word "teasebuster" written on the side for educator use.)
4. *Teasebuster Team Contract* (See page 281; one per student and one transparency.)
5. *Thought Bubble* (See *Appendix O*; one for educator use.)
6. Banner (Create a teasebuster team banner that says, "We're a Teasebuster Team—Tease Free and Totally Together." The banner should be large enough so all students can sign their names on it.)

PREPARATORY SET:

Play the theme song from *Ghostbusters*. Ask if anyone knows what the Ghostbusters do. (Ghostbusters are characters from a movie and then from a cartoon. They worked together to bust or stop ghosts from doing mean things). Tell students that this unit is not about being a Ghostbuster, but it is about being a teasebuster. Ask students to guess what a teasebuster does (accept all guesses).

PLAN:

1. Ask a student(s) to look up the word "tease" in the dictionary and discuss its definition as a class. (Most dictionaries define *teasing* as irritating or annoying someone.) Discuss the difference between negative, mean teasing (teasing that hurts feelings) and affectionate teasing (teasing that doesn't hurt someone's feelings). Tell students this unit will look at positive strategies for dealing with mean teasing.

2. Tell students that mean teasing is a problem. When people get teased, many times they feel bad. They may not know positive ways to help themselves feel better, so they tease back or tease someone else. This leads to something called the "teasing cycle." To symbolize the teasing cycle, draw the following illustration where students can see it:

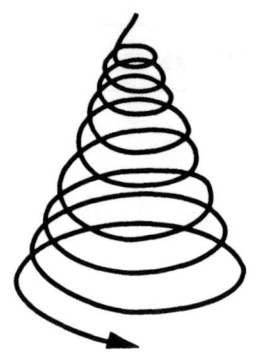

3. Distribute and display *Being a Teasebuster*. Discuss the definition for *being a teasebuster*. Explain the skill step for being a teasebuster and the symbol next to it. Remind students that the symbol is there to help them visualize and remember the skill step. (The entire symbol will make better sense to the students after completing Lesson E.) Discuss the reasons for being a teasebuster. Refer to the body-talk symbol in the left-hand margin. Remind students that appropriate body talk is important when being a teasebuster.

4. Read the story on the bottom half of *Being a Teasebuster* to the students. Discuss what things Maria did to be a teasebuster.

5. Write the BUST acronym vertically where all students can see it. Tell students that today they will be learning about the "B" part of the BUST skill-step symbol. Circle the "B" and tell students that "B" stands for "Be a teasebuster." (Write this phrase after the "B.")

6. Using an "emcee" voice, talk loudly through the megaphone while reading the following script:

Calling all kids and adults.... This is a teasebuster membership rally. Let it be known that the teasebusters will be working together to keep our class, our school, and our world tease free and totally together. Sign up today to become a member of the teasebuster team. We need each and every one of you to work together to make this a tease-free zone!

7. Distribute and display *Teasebuster Team Contract*. Read it aloud to the students. Continue talking through the megaphone in an "emcee" voice and say, "Come one, come all to sign up. Become a teasebuster today."

8. Model use of the "B" part of the skill step for being a teasebuster while thinking aloud. A scripted example follows:

Introduction

I am going to pretend to be a student in this class who is thinking about signing up to be a teasebuster. I will tell you the thoughts I'm having while I'm completing the sheet. When I hold up this Thought Bubble, *you'll know the words I'm saying are actually what I'm thinking.*

Actual Model

While holding up the *Thought Bubble* say, *OK, the teacher just invited me to become a member of the teasebuster team. Do I really want to do this? I don't like it when someone teases me, and I'll bet other people feel bad when they get teased too. I guess I do want to become a teasebuster so I can learn more about how to stop the teasing cycle in a positive way!* Put the *Thought Bubble* down and sign your name on the *Teasebuster Team Contract* transparency.

9. While students are signing their contracts, tape the teasebuster team banner on a wall where students can reach it. Tell students that if they have chosen to sign their contracts, they can come up and sign their names on the teasebuster team banner, which will remain hanging in the classroom or school. Tell students who are uncertain about signing their contracts that they are welcome to become a teasebuster team member any time they feel comfortable doing so.

10. Pair students (see *Appendix P*). Ask student pairs to take turns telling each other the meaning of *being a teasebuster* and why it's important to use the skill. Students should be reminded that the information they are to say is printed on *Being a Teasebuster*.

    As an option to add structure to this activity (see *Appendix Q*), ask partners to come to an agreement about which person will be called "Wolfgang Mozart" and which person will be called "Leonardo da Vinci." After students have made their decision, have "Wolfgang" tell "Leonardo" the definition of *being a teasebuster*. Next, ask "Leonardo" to tell "Wolfgang" the definition. Ask students to use the same procedure to tell each other the reasons for being a teasebuster.

11. Through the megaphone, say with excitement to the class: *I'm excited about learning ways to be a social star. I know that being a teasebuster is an important way to do that. I hope you're excited too!*

Social Star

Name _____

Being a Teasebuster

MEANING OF BEING A TEASEBUSTER: Knowing that mean teasing is not OK and using positive strategies to stop the teasing cycle

SKILL STEP:

1. Ask myself: What can I do to stop the teasing cycle?

REASONS FOR USING THIS SKILL:

When you choose a positive strategy to deal with teasing, you can feel proud inside and others will respect you.

DIRECTIONS: Listen to the story below. Tell what things Maria did to be a teasebuster.

> On the playground, some kids were teasing a younger boy. Maria felt bad when she saw him being teased. Then the other kids wanted Maria to tease the boy too. She did not want to. She found Victor and Ann and told them about the teasing. They decided to ask the kids to stop teasing and then started playing with the younger boy.

© 1994 Thinking Publications — *Duplication permitted for educational use only.*

Name _____

Teasebuster Team Contract

I choose to be a **T**easebuster.

I will work to keep our class **T**ease **F**ree and **T**otally **T**ogether.

I will help stop the teasing cycle!

Signed: _____

Social Star

Lesson B

OBJECTIVES:

1. To brainstorm examples of teasing

2. To identify the feelings associated with being teased

3. To understand that mean teasing is never OK

MATERIALS:

1. The theme song from the 1984 Columbia Pictures movie *Ghostbusters* (For students to hear during the Preparatory Set)

2. *Being a Teasebuster* classroom poster (See page 13.)

3. *Thinking Skills Web* (See *Appendix T*; one per pair of students and one transparency.)

4. *Checking Myself* (See *Appendix I*; one per student and one for educator use.)

5. *Thought Bubble* (See *Appendix O*; one for educator use.)

PREPARATORY SET:

Play the theme song from *Ghostbusters*. After the students listen to the song, chant the following questions to the beat of the original song:

- When teasing's going on in your neighborhood, who ya gonna be? (Cup your hand by your ear and have students shout, "Teasebusters!")

- When teasing's going on in our very own school, who ya gonna call? (Cup your hand by your ear and have students shout, "Teasebusters!")

- When teasing's going on in your very own home, who ya gonna be? (Cup your hand by your ear and have students shout, "Teasebusters!")

PLAN:

1. Review the definition and skill steps for *being a teasebuster* by referring the class to the *Being a Teasebuster* classroom poster.

2. Pair students using the *Line Up–Fold Up* activity (see *Appendix P*). Have students line up according to the order of their birthdays. Ask student pairs to take turns telling each other the skill step for being a teasebuster. Follow the procedure described in step 10 of Lesson A. (As an option, ask students to decide who will be "Paul Revere" and who will be "Ben Franklin.") Next, ask students to work with a partner to think of a situation when it would be important to be a teasebuster. Tell students that one or more pairs will be called on to share their situation. Have one or more pairs share their situation.

3. Distribute and display the *Thinking Skills Web*. Write "things kids get teased about" on the inside circle of the transparency. Tell students that you have noticed that kids get teased about their names. Write "their names" on one of the lines extending out from the web. Ask students to think of another thing kids get teased about and write the example on the transparency. Then ask students to work with their partners to brainstorm a list of other things kids get teased about and to write their ideas on the lines of the web. After student pairs have had time to complete the activity, ask for one or more pairs to share their answers and write them on the transparency.

4. Distribute and display the discussion guideline sheet called *Checking Myself*. Ask students to complete the goal statement with the words "use eye contact" or use another classroom discussion goal more appropriate for your group (see pages 25–26). Tell students that you will be having a discussion about the feelings that are involved when people tease one another. When a student is answering a question or making a comment during the discussion, it's important for everyone to give that student eye contact. Instruct them to circle a T-shirt star each time they give eye contact to a student who is speaking.

5. Model use of the *Checking Myself* sheet while thinking aloud. A scripted example follows:

   ### Introduction

   I am going to pretend to be one of you completing the sheet during the discussion we will be having. I will tell you the thoughts I'm having while I'm completing the sheet. When I hold up this Thought Bubble, *you'll know the words I'm saying are actually what I'm thinking.*

   ### Actual Model

   While holding up the *Thought Bubble* say, OK, *the teacher just called on Allison. I'd better give Allison eye contact so she knows I'm listening to her answer. I'll circle a T-shirt star on my sheet because I gave her eye contact.* Put the *Thought Bubble* down and circle a T-shirt star on the overhead transparency.

6. Proceed with the actual discussion by asking the questions that follow. During the discussion, periodically remind students to give eye contact to the person who is talking and to mark their discussion guideline sheets.

   - Why do you think kids might tease one another? (Answers might include: kids feel powerless, they are continuing the teasing cycle, they don't like themselves.)

   - What feelings do you have when someone teases you?

Social Star

- What feelings do you think others might have when they are being teased?
- Do you think that it is ever OK to tease someone in a mean way? Explain why or why not.
- Do you think it is possible to tease others in a friendly way to make them laugh or smile? Explain why or why not.

After the discussion, have students complete the bottom of *Checking Myself*.

7. Process the use of the sheet by asking the following question or another one more appropriate for your group:

   - Why do you think it's important to give eye contact to the person who is speaking during a discussion?

   Process further by asking the students who volunteered to speak during the discussion to share their answers to the following question:

   - You answered one of the questions during our discussion. How did you feel when the other students gave you eye contact while you were talking?

8. Write the BUST acronym vertically where all students can see it. Remind students that in Lesson A they learned the "B" stands for "Be a teasebuster." (Write this phrase after the "B.") Tell students that today's lesson helped them understand what the "U" stands for. Explain that the "U" stands for "Understand that mean teasing is never OK." (Write this phrase after the "U.")

9. Model use of the "U" part of the skill step for being a teasebuster while thinking aloud. A scripted example follows:

   ### Introduction

   I am going to pretend to be a student in this class. I see someone being teased. I will tell you the thoughts I am having. When I hold up this Thought Bubble, *you'll know the words I'm saying are actually what I'm thinking.*

   ### Actual Model

   While holding up the *Thought Bubble* say, *I see that some kids are teasing John. I am a teasebuster and I understand that it is never OK to tease someone in a mean way because it hurts others' feelings. I need to think of a way to stop the teasing.*

10. Remind students of the *Teambuster Team Contract* signed in Lesson A. Extend an invitation to sign the contract to any students who have previously chosen not to sign it. If after this lesson there are students who continue to choose not to sign, extend the invitation during the remaining lessons of this unit. Encourage those who have signed the contract to remember to use their teasebusting skills.

11. Say with excitement to the class: *It is very exciting to watch you practice your social skills! I would like to invite you to use your social skills outside of this room, wherever you go.*

Social Star

Lesson C

OBJECTIVE:

To identify positive strategies to use when someone else is being teased

MATERIALS:

1. Megaphone (Created in Lesson A)
2. *Oh No! They're Teasing Her!* (See page 289; one per student and one transparency.)
3. *Teasebuster Red Alert Signal* (See page 290; one per student, and one transparency.)
4. Red construction paper (One 8½ x 11" sheet per student)
5. Scissors and glue (One of each per student)
6. *Thought Bubble* (See *Appendix O*; one for educator use.)

PREPARATORY SET:

Talk seriously and loudly through the megaphone and read the following script:

> *Attention, all teasebuster team members! This is a teasebuster red alert. A report has just come in that teasing has been observed on our school grounds. This is a job for the teasebusters. Teasebusters report for duty please!*

PLAN:

1. Write the BUST acronym vertically where all students can see it. Remind students that they have already learned what the "B" and "U" stand for in the BUST skill step symbol. Remind them that:

   "B" stands for "Be a teasebuster." (Write this phrase after the "B.")

   "U" stands for "Understand that mean teasing is never OK." (Write this phrase after the "U.")

   Tell students that today they will learn the "S" part of the BUST skill-step symbol. Circle the "S" and tell students that "S" stands for: "Seek a strategy for teasebusting." (Write this phrase after the "S.")

2. Tell students they will be reading a story in which Lee sees some kids teasing Ann. Explain that after the story, they will be called on as teasebusters to decide what strategies Lee could use to stop the teasing.

3. Distribute and display *Oh No! They're Teasing Her!* Read the story aloud.

4. Discuss the story by asking the students the following questions:

- How could Lee tell that Ann was being teased?
- How do you think Ann was feeling?
- What were Lee's thoughts about the teasing?

5. Distribute and display *Teasebuster Red Alert Signal*. Explain that when there is a red alert, it means there is a serious situation that needs to be dealt with. Have students give several specific examples of red alert situations to which they may need to respond. Tell students that in the story *Oh No! They're Teasing Her!* Lee was in a red alert situation. He realized that Ann was being teased. Explain that even though the class has signed a contract to be a teasebuster team, there may still be times when teasing occurs. Tell students that when teasing does occur, they will all need to be on the alert to remember the strategies they can use to help stop the teasing.

6. On the transparency, fill in the statement "Strategies for being a teasebuster when _____ being teased" with the words "someone else is."

Direct students to write the same words on their *Teasebuster Red Alert Signal*.

7. Pair students (see *Appendix P*). Ask students to work with their partners to discuss answers to the following question:

   - When there is a situation like Lee was in, what positive strategies could a teasebuster use to help someone else who is being teased?

As students identify strategies, write them on the transparency and ask students to write them on their *Teasebuster Red Alert Signal*. Be sure that the ideas include the following three strategies:

- Don't join in the teasing.
- Get help to stop the teasing.
- Give support to the person being teased.

8. Discuss things students could do or say to stop themselves from joining in the teasing.

9. Discuss people students could go to for help. Be sure that the students identify that they can get help from other kids or from a variety of adults in their lives (e.g., parent, teacher, playground supervisor, day care provider).

10. Explain to students things they could do or say to support the person being teased. This should include what to say or do to the teasers (be certain that what is said to the teasers does not include teasing or mean statements). The students can also identify supportive things to say to the person being teased.

Social Star

11. Distribute the construction paper, scissors, and glue. Direct students to cut out their *Teasebuster Red Alert Signal* and glue it on the red construction paper. Collect the completed red alerts for use in Lesson D.

12. Model use of the "S" part of the being a teasebuster skill step while thinking aloud. A scripted example follows:

Introduction

I am going to pretend to be someone your age who sees another student getting teased. I will tell you the thoughts I'm having. When I hold up this Thought Bubble, *you'll know the words I'm saying are actually what I'm thinking.*

Actual Model

While holding up the *Thought Bubble* say, *I see my friend Beth getting teased. I'm a teasebuster and I know that mean teasing is not OK. Let's see. Is there a strategy for teasebusting that I can use to help? I can call to Beth to come over here so she gets away from the teasers.* Put the *Thought Bubble* down and call out, *Hey Beth! Come over here! Let's play.*

13. Say with excitement to the class: *Each of you is truly becoming a social super star!*

Dealing with Teasing

Name _____

Oh No! They're Teasing Her!

DIRECTIONS: Look at this story about Lee, Ann, and some kids from another class. Think of strategies Lee could use to be a teasebuster.

"Look at Ann's ugly shoes."

"Hey Ann. What garbage can did you dig those out of?"

"Hey, Lee, look at Ann's ugly shoes. We think they came out of somebody's trash!"

That teasing is mean. Ann feels terrible! I feel bad too. What can I do to be a teasebuster?

© 1994 Thinking Publications 289 *Duplication permitted for educational use only.*

Social Star

Name _____

TEASEBUSTER RED ALERT SIGNAL

DIRECTIONS: Write positive strategies a teasebuster can use. Write on the lines provided.

Teasebuster Red Alert Signal

_____
Name

Strategies for being a teasebuster when
_____
being teased

© 1994 Thinking Publications — Duplication permitted for educational use only.

Lesson D

OBJECTIVE:

To identify positive strategies to use when you are being teased

MATERIALS:

1. *Please Stop Teasing Me!* (See page 295; one per student and one transparency.)
2. *Teasebuster Red Alert Signal* (See page 290; one per student and one transparency.)
3. *Thought Bubble* (See Appendix O; one for educator use.)
4. *Teasebuster Red Alert Signal* (On red construction paper saved from Lesson C)
5. Scissors and glue (One per student)
6. *Teasebuster Report* (See page 296; one per student and one transparency.)

PREPARATORY SET:

Read the following story to the students:

> *Once there were three brothers. The oldest brother got teased at school, so he kept the teasing cycle going by teasing the middle brother. The middle brother kept the cycle going by teasing the younger brother. The little brother kept the teasing cycle going by teasing the kid next door.*

Ask students the following question:

- Do you think this teasing cycle is good or bad? Why?

Tell students they will be talking more about this story later in the lesson.

PLAN:

1. Write the BUST acronym vertically where all students can see it. Remind students that the "B" stands for "Be a Teasebuster," and the "U" stands for "Understand that mean teasing is never OK." Circle the "S." Remind students that in Lesson C they discussed that the "S" means "Seek a strategy for teasebusting." Tell students that in today's lesson they will learn how to use teasebuster strategies when they are being teased.

2. Distribute and display *Please Stop Teasing Me!* Read the story aloud.

3. Discuss the story by asking the students the following questions:

    - How could Victor tell that he was being teased?
    - What thoughts did Victor have about being teased by others?

4. Distribute and display *Teasebuster Red Alert Signal*.

5. On the transparency, complete the statement, "Strategies for being a teasebuster when ____ being teased" with the words "I am."

   Direct students to write the same on their *Teasebuster Red Alert Signal*.

6. Pair students (see *Appendix P*). Ask students to work with their partners to discuss answers to the following question:

   - When there is a situation like Victor was in, what positive strategies could a teasebuster use when getting teased?

   Call on several pairs to share their answers. As students identify strategies, write them on the transparency and ask students to write them on their *Teasebuster Red Alert Signal*. Be sure that the ideas include the following four strategies:

   - Don't tease back.
   - Ignore (remove yourself if possible).
   - Tell the teasers to stop (in a firm and confident way).
   - Get help to stop the teasing.

7. After the strategy of not teasing back has been identified, remind students of the story about the three brothers that they heard at the beginning of the lesson.

   Tell students that sometimes when people are being teased, they decide to tease back by saying or doing something mean or by finding someone else to tease. Explain that teasing back leads to a situation in which the teasing gets bigger and bigger and becomes a cycle that never really ends. Draw the cycle illustration, where students can see it as you did in Lesson A, to demonstrate this concept.

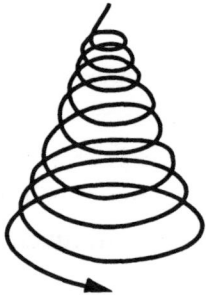

8. After the strategy of ignoring has been identified, help students understand what people should look like and sound like when they totally ignore (often students think they are ignoring, but they really aren't).

   Model use of the ignoring teasebuster strategy while thinking aloud. A scripted example follows:

Introduction

I am going to pretend to be a teasebuster who is getting teased. I will show the teasebuster strategy of ignoring and tell you the thoughts I'm having. When I hold up this Thought Bubble, *you'll know the words I'm saying are actually what I'm thinking.*

Actual Model

While holding up the *Thought Bubble* say, *This kid is teasing me about wearing glasses. I'm a teasebuster and I know that mean teasing is not OK. I hardly even know this kid. What teasebuster strategy can I use? I'm going to totally ignore him. He must be teasing me because he likes to see people get upset. If I ignore him, he won't get to see me upset. To totally ignore him, I won't look at him, I won't say anything to him, I won't look like I'm upset, and I'll walk away.* Put the *Thought Bubble* down and walk away.

9. After the strategies of telling the teaser to stop and getting help to stop the teasing have been identified, remind students of what they learned about these strategies in the last lesson.

10. Distribute completed *Teasebuster Red Alert Signals* from Lesson C, scissors, and glue. Direct students to cut out their new *Teasebuster Red Alert Signals* and glue them onto the other side of the *Teasebuster Red Alert Signals* completed in Lesson C. Tell students that they could keep the signals in their desks to refer to when they need help remembering strategies for being a teasebuster.

11. Tell students that in a few days they will be finishing this unit about being a teasebuster. Explain that you would like to keep hearing about how their teasebusting is going.

12. Distribute and display *Teasebuster Report*. Explain to students that you will be setting a stack of the reports in a specified spot in the classroom for them to use to report about how their teasebusting is going.

13. Ask students to pretend they are in the following situation:

    At lunch, several kids have been teasing a boy about the food he needs to eat for his special diet. You and the other kids at the table have not joined in the teasing and you have asked the kids to stop teasing the boy about his lunch. The teasing hasn't stopped. Today the boy started to cry when he was teased. You decided to ask an adult in the lunchroom for help.

14. Demonstrate how to fill out the top of the *Teasebuster Report* based on the information in the situation just described.

15. Explain that on the bottom of the report, students can either report how they resolved the teasing problem or that they need help with the problem.

16. Encourage students to attempt to solve teasing problems on their own. Tell them that they will feel more powerful when they resolve a situation themselves.

17. Tell students that if they were able to solve the problem using their teasebusting strategies, it is important for them to use self-talk to encourage themselves. Explain that in the next lesson they will be practicing self-talk to encourage themselves for appropriately dealing with teasing.

18. Tell students that there are times when they will need to get help with a teasing problem. They need to remember all of the people they can go to for help. Ask students to list people who can assist them with teasing. Be sure the students remember that they can get help from other students or from a variety of adults.

19. Describe the procedure that will be used once the *Teasebuster Reports* have been turned in to the teacher (e.g., "I will read them and respond to them as soon as I can." Respond to all students to avoid having anyone feeling left out and to encourage further reports. Some reports may need individual conferences).

20. Ask partners to face each other and stand an arm's length away. Encourage partners to use friendly and confident body talk. Ask partners to shake hands and in unison repeat the following statement after you: *I enjoy learning new social skills. Social skills make the world a happier place!*

Dealing with Teasing

Name _____

Please Stop Teasing Me!

DIRECTIONS: Listen to this story about Victor. He is being teased. Think of strategies Victor could use to be a teasebuster.

"Hey Victor, when are you going to learn how to catch a ball?"

"Victor couldn't catch a ball if he tried all day."

"Victor has two left hands!"

Those kids are teasing me and I don't like it! What teasebusting strategy can I use?

© 1994 Thinking Publications 295 *Duplication permitted for educational use only.*

Social Star

TEASEBUSTER REPORT

Who was being teased? _____

When? _____

Where? _____

Describe the teasing situation
(or draw a picture of it) in the box below:

[ ]

Did you solve the teasing problem? (Circle one)

YES   NO

If yes, describe how: Do you need help from an adult?

_____   _____ I need help

_____   _____ I do not need help.

_____   Who are some adults who can help you?

_____   _____

If you helped the teasebusting, use   _____
self-talk to encourage yourself.

Reported by: _____

© 1994 Thinking Publications   *Duplication permitted for educational use only.*

Lesson E

OBJECTIVE:

To identify the importance of using positive self-talk after successfully dealing with teasing

MATERIALS:

1. Megaphone (Created in Lesson A)

2. Telephone (One for educator use)

3. Large piece of paper and a marker

4. *Teasebuster Report* (See page 296; one transparency.)

5. *Dominoes* (See *Appendix U*; one set cut apart per pair of students, and one set of transparency dominoes.)

6. *BUST Cards* (See pages 300–301; one set cut apart per pair of students.)

7. A globe or a map of the earth (One for educator use)

PREPARATORY SET:

Write the BUST acronym where all students can see it. Using the megaphone, lead a class cheer by asking the following questions:

- What does the "B" stand for? (Cup your hand by your ear and have students shout, "Be a teasebuster!")

- What does the "U" stand for? (Cup your hand by your ear and have students shout, "Understand that mean teasing is never OK!")

- What does the "S" stand for? (Cup your hand by your ear and have students shout, "Seek a strategy for teasebusting!")

PLAN

1. Tell students that the "T" stands for "Tell yourself something positive about being a teasebuster." (Write this phrase after the "T.") Explain that it is important to give ourselves encouragement when we do a good job at being a teasebuster.

2. Say the following:

   I am expecting a call any moment from Trenton T. Teasebuster. Trenton is an old student of mine and, I might add, a founding member of the teasebusters. He sometimes calls to let me know how he is doing at teasebusting. He has been working on the "T" step of BUST and he promised to call me about it.

Social Star

3. Pretend you hear the phone ringing and say, "Oh! There's the phone now." Pick up the receiver and say:

Hi, Trenton! How is your teasebusting going?... Oh really? That's great!... What's that?... Oh, you want me to tell my students how important it is for them to tell themselves something positive when they perform their teasebusting duties. As a matter of fact, Trenton, that is exactly what we were talking about when you called. I was just telling my students that the "T" in BUST stands for: "Tell yourself something positive about being a teasebuster." Trenton, you've always got such good ideas. Could you give us an example of what you say to yourself after you use a teasebuster strategy?... Oh, so you say something like, "I did a great job handling that teasing. I sure feel powerful!" Thank you, Trenton. That's a great example!... Yes, I agree 100 percent! Using positive self-talk really does help us feel good about ourselves. Well, Trenton, I'd better get going. It has been fun talking with you. When we hang up, I'm going to ask my students what other things they can say to themselves about being a teasebuster. Goodbye, Trenton. Keep in touch.

Hang up the phone.

4. Ask students the following question:

- What other self-talk phrases can you say to compliment yourself for being a teasebuster?

As students respond, use a marker and write their answers on a large piece of paper to be posted in the room as a reminder to students about how they can positively reinforce themselves for being teasebusters (when they are being teased, or when someone else is being teased). Periodically ask students if they have thought of any new positive self-talk and record it on the posted paper.

5. Display *Teasebuster Report*. Remind students that in Lesson D they discussed how to complete the *Teasebuster Report* to let you know how their teasebusting is going. Remind students to fill out the report when they deal with teasing. Refer students to the bottom-left section of the report. Read the statement, "If you helped the teasebusting, use self-talk to encourage yourself." Explain to students that this statement is on the report to remind them to encourage themselves for using the social skill.

6. Tell students they will be playing a game called "BUST Dominoes."

7. Model specifically how to play *Dominoes* using an overhead and the transparency dominoes.

8. Pair students (see *Appendix P*). Distribute a set of *Dominoes* and *BUST Cards* to each pair. Tell students that before they make a move with the dominoes, they should pick up a *BUST Card*, read it aloud, and then tell the positive self-talk that could be used to encourage themselves for being teasebusters in the situation specified. Model an example of how to do this by actually drawing a card, reading it aloud, telling what positive self-talk could be used in the situation, and then making a move with the dominos.

9. Have students play the game. Remind them to refer to the posted paper from step 4 of this Plan for help with self-talk.

10. Show the globe or picture of the earth. Say, "When you are a teasebuster, you help make our classroom a better place. You help make our school a nicer place. You help to make our town (city) a friendlier place. You help make our state a better place, and you make our country a better place. Best of all, you help make the world a better place." (Return to the spiral effect described earlier in the unit, if you wish, by showing that the positive use of social skills can have the same spiral effect.)

11. Ask the class to brainstorm ways that they could get the teasebuster message out to students in other places (other classes, other schools, other cities). Have the class decide on and complete at least one activity they will do to spread the teasebuster message.

12. Say with excitement to the class: *I am different from you and you are different from me. That makes us each special. I like you because you're different and special!*

Social Star

BUST Cards

BUST
Other kids were calling a boy in gym class fat. You said, That teasing is mean. Please stop.

BUST
You ignored kids who were teasing you about your haircut. You calmly walked away.

BUST
Some neighbor kids were teasing your younger brother. He still has training wheels on his bike. He started to cry. You decided to get one of your parents.

BUST
You have ignored some kids. They have been teasing you for several days. You calmly said, "Please stop teasing me. I don't like being teased."

BUST
Some kids in your class teased the new girl about the color of her skin. You did not join in. They wanted you to tease her too.

BUST
Others teased you by saying, "You're a baby." You used self-talk. You told yourself that what they were saying shouldn't get you upset.

© 1994 Thinking Publications — Duplication permitted for educational use only.

BUST Cards

BUST — You noticed some kids poking a stick at a boy in your class. They poked him whenever the playground supervisor wasn't looking. You got help from the playground supervisor.

BUST — Some older kids followed you home from school. They called you names. You decided to ask an adult for help.

BUST — Some kids teased a student in your group about being slow. You said, "Stop teasing her. She's doing just fine."

BUST — Your older sister teased you last night. You thought about teasing back. You decided not to. Instead, you left the room.

BUST — An old man lives nearby. Your friends like to yell mean things at him. You say, "Why are you guys being so mean? Find something more positive to do."

BUST — You were at the park. Some kids grabbed a ball away from you. They wouldn't give it back. You told the kids they needed to give the ball back or you'd need to get help from your dad.

Lessons X, Y, and Z

Due to similarities in format, the final three lesson plans for each unit in *Social Star* are provided in *Appendix A*. Substitute the words "being a teasebuster" whenever a "_____" appears in the lesson plans. Information specific to this unit follows.

LESSON X PREPARATORY SET:

Tell the students that since they are now official members of the teasebuster team, they will be receiving their official membership cards. Have students brainstorm how they can use their cards as a reminder of their responsibility to end teasing. Pass out membership cards (see page 303).

LESSON Y PREPARATORY SET:

Darken the room, if you prefer, and ask the students to visualize themselves correctly using this social skill by reading the following script:

Let's take a few moments to relax.... Make sure you are in a comfortable position.... Close your eyes if you feel like it.... On the count of three, take a very slow, deep breath. Remember to breathe in quietly through your nose. One... two... three.... Breathe in deeply.... Now breathe out slowly and quietly through your mouth.... Let your entire body relax.... Now imagine that someone just called you a mean name. You say to yourself, "I'll be a teasebuster and ignore this teasing. I'll walk away and I won't tease back." Think about how proud you feel for not continuing the teasing cycle.

LESSON Z PLOT SITUATION:

Ask students to pretend one of their relatives teases them in a mean way about their weight.

LESSON Z ROADBLOCK EXAMPLES:

- Feeling really angry and upset when someone teases you

- Others begin teasing you when you step in to stop them from teasing someone else

- Feeling afraid to tell someone that you're being teased

TEASEBUSTER MEMBERSHIP CARDS

IS AN OFFICIAL MEMBER OF

The Teasebusters Team

...WORKING TO KEEP OUR WORLD TEASE FREE AND TOTALLY TOGETHER!

Member's Signature

Trenton T. Teasebuster
Founding Member

Classroom Teacher

IS AN OFFICIAL MEMBER OF

The Teasebusters Team

...WORKING TO KEEP OUR WORLD TEASE FREE AND TOTALLY TOGETHER!

Member's Signature

Trenton T. Teasebuster
Founding Member

Classroom Teacher

IS AN OFFICIAL MEMBER OF

The Teasebusters Team

...WORKING TO KEEP OUR WORLD TEASE FREE AND TOTALLY TOGETHER!

Member's Signature

Trenton T. Teasebuster
Founding Member

Classroom Teacher

IS AN OFFICIAL MEMBER OF

The Teasebusters Team

...WORKING TO KEEP OUR WORLD TEASE FREE AND TOTALLY TOGETHER!

Member's Signature

Trenton T. Teasebuster
Founding Member

Classroom Teacher

Social Star

Name _____

Being a Teasebuster T-Chart

LOOKS LIKE... | SOUNDS LIKE...

LOOKS LIKE...

using appropriate body talk

- looking at the person you are talking to
- using a friendly or serious facial expression (depending on the situation)
- using an assertive or friendly body posture (depending on the situation)

getting help from other teasebusters

ignoring, and walking away (when you are being teased)

SOUNDS LIKE...

nothing (if you are being teased and you want to ignore)

a serious or friendly tone of voice (depending on the situation)

saying

- "Why are you being mean? Find something more positive to do."
- "I don't tease people in a mean way."
- "Ben is getting teased. Let's go over and see what we can do to stop the teasing."
- "I don't like this teasing! I want you to stop!"
- "Mr./Mrs. Jones, Sue is getting teased and she is upset. I thought you should know."

© 1994 Thinking Publications — *Duplication permitted for educational use only.*

SHOW TIME

HOME

Pretend your older sister wants you to tease your younger brother in a mean way. Show what you could say to her to let her know you don't like mean teasing.

SCHOOL

Pretend a boy at school is teasing you at lunch. Show what you could say to yourself to help ignore the teasing.

COMMUNITY

Pretend that a group of kids always picks on a younger boy while waiting for the bus. Show what you could do or say to help stop the teasing.

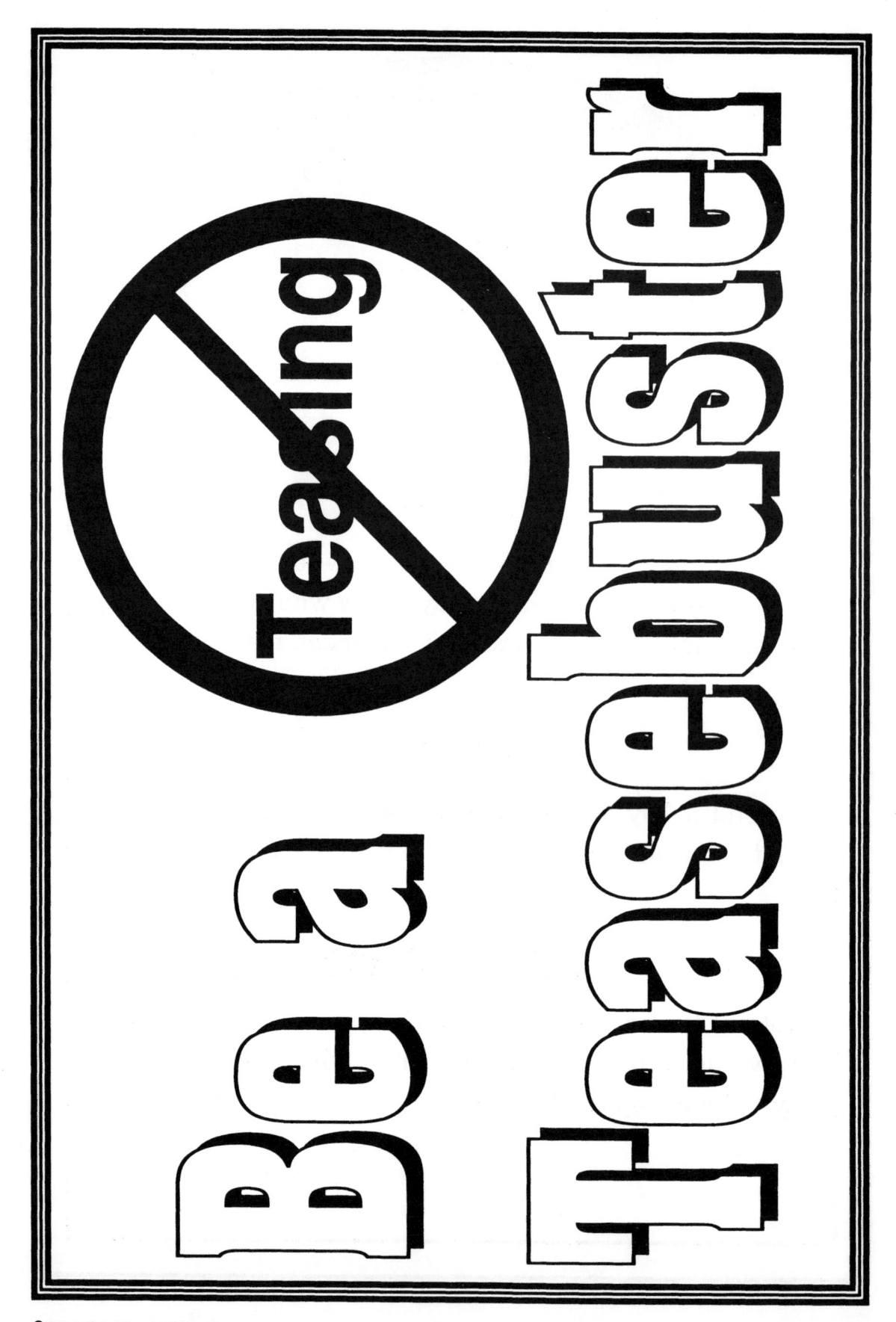

Be a Teasebuster

🚫 Teasing

HOME-A-GRAM

Dear Family,

At school, we have been talking about the social skill called

BEING A TEASEBUSTER

I learned that *mean teasing* means irritating or annoying someone.

I learned that *being a teasebuster* means knowing when teasing is not OK and using positive strategies to stop the teasing cycle.

To be a teasebuster, I know I should ask myself, "What can I do to stop the teasing cycle?"

When I choose a positive strategy to deal with teasing, I can feel proud inside and others will respect me.

I learned that one positive strategy I can use as a teasebuster is to use positive self-talk. I have written something positive I can say to myself the next time someone teases me:

_____

_____

_____

_____

I'll tell you about another positive strategy I can use to be a teasebuster. After I do, please sign my "Being a Teasebuster" badge so I can return it to school and become a SOCIAL SUPER STAR this week.

From: _____

Collaborative Skills

Social Star

The following five units in *Social Star: Peer Interaction Skills (Book 2)* deal with skills important when students are working in group situations at school. The units include the following:

- *Getting into a Group*
- *Giving Put-ups*
- *Participating*
- *Staying on Task*
- *Disagreeing Politely*

In many classrooms, students are asked to work collaboratively with others. The authors have identified the five skills listed as helpful in promoting successful group interaction.

Lesson A of each unit identifies and defines the social skill and provides skill steps and a symbol for each.

Lesson B of each unit provides an opportunity for students to closely examine what the specific social skill "looks like and sounds like" (i.e., a T-chart activity). The students then have the opportunity to practice the collaborative skill. Following each practice, students process their individual use of the skill.

The final lessons in each collaborative skill unit follow a slightly different format than the other units in *Social Star*. Lessons X and Y are eliminated, although elements from each are included in Lessons A and B. Lesson Z is included in each unit.

The authors recommend that the social skill called *getting into a group* be taught first. The remaining units may be taught in the order listed or in random order. Educators may need to periodically review units with students throughout the school year.

These units contain elements that will be familiar to those trained in cooperative learning (refer to pages 32–35). A list of additional cooperative learning resources is provided on page 40.

Getting into a Group

Social Star

UNIT GOAL:

To demonstrate comprehension and use of strategies for getting into a group appropriately

EDUCATOR INFORMATION:

1. Before teaching this unit, educators are encouraged to read the introductory section on teaching collaborative social skills found on page 309.

2. Several interpersonal skills affect the success of a collaborative effort, one of which is the ability to move into cooperative learning groups. Johnson, Johnson, and Johnson Holubec (1990) state, "Work time in groups is a valuable commodity and little time should be spent in rearranging furniture and moving into learning groups. Students may need to practice the procedure for getting into groups several times before they become efficient in doing so" (page 93).

3. This unit teaches students the importance of being able to appropriately get into a group during cooperative learning situations at school. It emphasizes that students show they are willing to work with whoever is in their group (e.g., by using positive body talk or by not complaining about who they are asked to work with). The unit stresses the importance of accepting all members of the group. It also teaches students how to move quickly and quietly into their groups.

RELATED ACTIVITIES:

1. Discuss the following with students:
   - situations outside of school when students might need to work in groups (e.g., Boy Scouts/Girl Scouts, 4-H, church youth groups, recreational groups).
   - groups that adults join (e.g., political groups, bowling leagues).

2. Create a play about the importance of getting into groups appropriately. Present the play to another group of students.

3. Have students write a message about getting into groups using a secret code (e.g., writing words backward, using symbols for letters).

4. Visit a local business. Have the employer explain why it is important for employees to be able to work in groups (and more specifically, to be able to get into groups quickly and be willing to work with whoever is in their group).

5. Invite adults from different cultures to talk about how their cultures' conventions for getting into groups compare with the components discussed in this unit.

It is important for educators to provide opportunities for students to work in groups, so they can experience social skills in contexts where social communication is needed. Therefore, educators are encouraged to have students complete the Related Activities in small groups whenever possible. Educators trained in cooperative learning could incorporate the five components (see page 33) into the group activity.

RELATED LITERATURE:

The Bathwater Gang (1990) by Jerry Spinelli; Ill. by Meredith Johnson; Little, Brown, and Co. (Text) An unusual captain forms a new group. (pages 55–59)

Chester (1980) by Mary Francis Shura; Ill. by Susan Swan; Doff, Mead, and Co. (Text) It takes more than one person to search for a lost goat. (pages 67–75)

SOCIAL SKILLS ALL DAY LONG:

Look for opportunities to teach social skills throughout the day (incidental teaching). Four ways to reinforce appropriate social skills and an example of each follow:

Encouragement

When these four people got into their group, they went straight to their group spot. More importantly, they had smiles on their faces when they were getting into their group. They showed they were willing to work with whoever was in their group.

Personal Example

Last night I went to a meeting. I was sitting by my good friend. The leader had us get up and move into different groups, so I couldn't sit by my friend. I felt disappointed, but I smiled and was friendly to my new group members. It turned out to be fun getting to know some other people.

Prompting

When I say "go," I'd like you to go directly to sit by your other group members. Also, remember to use body talk that says you're willing to work with everyone in your group.

Corrective Feedback (must be positive, private, specific, and nonthreatening)

Lee, just now when I asked you to go to your group, you made a face and said, "I'm not working with that slob." Remember, it's important to work cooperatively with all people. You could have had either a serious face or a smile. You could have kept your comment to yourself.

Lesson A

OBJECTIVES:

1. To state the meaning of *getting into a group* and tell why it is important
2. To listen to the self-talk associated with correct use of the skill

MATERIALS:

1. Clock, watch, or stopwatch
2. *Getting into a Group* (See page 317; one per student and one transparency.)
3. *Thought Bubble* (See *Appendix O*; one for educator use.)
4. *Checking Myself* (See *Appendix I*; one per student and one transparency.)
5. *Picture Puzzle* (See *Appendix P*; one per pair of students.)

PREPARATORY SET:

Use a strategy to get students into groups of three or four (e.g., have them number off). Let students know where each group should meet. Tell students that when you say "go," they should move quickly and quietly into their groups. As students move, keep track of the time it takes them to form their groups. When the groups are formed, tell them how much time it took. Write the time where everyone can see it. Explain to students that during this unit, they will be talking about how to get into a group. Tell them they'll have more opportunities to get into groups to see if they can beat today's time.

PLAN:

1. Distribute and display *Getting into a Group*. Discuss the definition for *getting into a group*. Explain the skill steps for getting into a group and the symbols next to them. Remind students that the symbols are there to help them visualize and remember the skill steps. Refer students to the body-talk symbol in the left-hand margin. Remind students that appropriate body talk is important when getting into a group. Discuss the reasons for getting into a group.

2. Model use of the skill steps for getting into a group while thinking aloud. A scripted example follows:

    Introduction

    I am going to pretend to be someone your age getting into a work group. I will show you how I appropriately get into a group and tell you the thoughts I'm having. When I hold up this Thought Bubble, *you'll know the words I'm saying are actually what I'm thinking.*

Social Star

Actual Model

While holding up the Thought Bubble *say,* The teacher just asked us to go to our group. OK, I know I can work with whoever is in my group. I need to go right away and not disturb others along the way. *Put the* Thought Bubble *down. Move quickly, quietly, and with positive body talk toward a group of students. Before proceeding with Step 3 ask,* What did my body talk look like when I moved into my group?

3. Read the story at the bottom of *Getting into a Group*.

4. Distribute and display the discussion guideline sheet called *Checking Myself*. Ask students to complete the goal statement with the words "use interested body talk," or use another classroom discussion goal more appropriate for your group (pages 25–26). Tell students that you will be having a discussion about the story they just heard. Encourage students to demonstrate body talk that shows they are interested in the discussion (e.g., sitting up, leaning slightly forward, nodding, giving eye contact). Tell students that during the discussion they should ask themselves if their body talk says, "I'm interested in this discussion." Instruct students to circle a T-shirt star each time they are using interested body talk and a new person begins to speak.

5. Model use of the *Checking Myself* sheet while thinking aloud. A scripted example follows:

Introduction

I am going to pretend to be one of you completing this sheet during the discussion we will be having. I will tell you the thoughts I'm having while I'm completing the sheet. When I hold up this Thought Bubble, *you'll know the words I'm saying are actually what I'm thinking.*

Actual Model

While holding up the Thought Bubble *say,* A different person just started talking. Am I using interested body talk? Yes, I am sitting up straight and giving her eye contact. I'll circle a star on the T-shirt. *Put the* Thought Bubble *down and circle a star on the transparency.*

During the discussion, periodically remind students to mark their discussion guideline sheets whenever they find themselves using body talk that shows they are interested.

6. Proceed with the discussion by asking these questions: (The story may need to be reread first.)

- What positive things did Mike and Maria do as they got into their group?

- How do you think Mike felt when he saw that Maria smiled?
- What thoughts do you think Maria had about the way Mike moved into their group?
- What did Ann do that caused Ms. Hess to ask her a second time to move into her group?
- What body talk did Ann use when she moved into her group?
- How might Maria and Mike have felt if they had noticed Ann's body talk and heard the words she said?
- Why do you think Ann rolled her eyes and took so long to get to her group?
- What negative things could happen because of the way Ann entered the group?
- What could Ann have done to be more positive, instead of rolling her eyes and saying, "I wanted to work with Jolisa"?
- What self-talk could Ann use to remind herself to move positively the next time she is asked to get into a group?
- What could Mike and Maria do to encourage Ann to get into a group more appropriately?

After the discussion, ask students to complete the bottom thought bubble statement on *Checking Myself*.

7. Process use of the sheet by asking the following question or another one more appropriate for your group:

- Why do you think it is important to use appropriate body talk during a discussion?

Process further by asking the students who volunteered to speak during the discussion to share their answers to the following questions:

- You shared one of your answers during the discussion. How could you tell if someone was using interested body talk when you were talking?
- How did you feel when others used interested body talk while you were speaking?

8. Pair students using the *Picture Puzzle* activity (see *Appendix P*).

9. Ask student pairs to take turns telling each other the meaning of *getting into a group* and why it's important to use the skill. Students could be reminded that the information they are to say is printed on *Getting into a Group*.

Social Star

As an option to add structure to this activity (see *Appendix Q*), ask partners to come to an agreement about which person will be called "Eli Whitney" and which person will be called "George Washington Carver." After students have made their decisions, ask "Eli" to tell "George" the definition of *getting into a group*. Next, ask "George" to tell "Eli" the definition. Ask students to use the same procedure to tell each other the reasons for using the skill.

10. Ask partners to face each other and stand an arm's length away. Encourage partners to use friendly and confident body talk. Ask partners to shake hands and in unison repeat the following statement after you: *You're a social star! You're a social super star! You can use great social skills every day!*

Getting into a Group

Name _____

★ Getting into a Group

MEANING OF GETTING INTO A GROUP:
Moving in a positive way to form a team to work with

SKILL STEPS:

1. Tell myself: I am willing to work with whoever is in my group

2. Go straight to my group (move quickly and quietly)

REASONS FOR USING THIS SKILL:
Knowing how to get into a group saves time and makes a positive impression on others. You invite others to feel good when you show that you are willing to work with them.

DIRECTIONS: Listen to the story below. Look at the pictures of Maria, Mike, and Ann while you listen. Decide who got into the group appropriately and who did not.

When Ms. Hess asked her students to get into their groups, Maria and Mike went right away. They moved without disturbing others. They smiled to show they were willing to work with whoever was in their group. Ann stopped to talk to other kids on her way. Ms. Hess needed to say, "Ann, remember to move quickly and quietly." When Ann saw who was in her group, she rolled her eyes and sat down. She said, "I wanted to work with Jolisa."

© 1994 Thinking Publications   317   Duplication permitted for educational use only.

Social Star

Lesson B

EDUCATOR INFORMATION:

During this lesson, students are asked to practice the social skill of *getting into a group* and then to work cooperatively to complete an activity. Johnson, Johnson, and Johnson Holubec (1990) describe five components necessary for cooperative learning. The five components are described on pages 33–35; review the information before teaching this lesson. A short description of how the five components have been incorporated into this lesson follows:

Positive Interdependence—Students feel they are linked together to complete the round robin activity in step 10 of this lesson. The goal of completing the round robin activity requires group members to work as a team.

Individual Accountability—Due to the nature of the round robin activity, students feel individually accountable for participating in the activity. The goal of completing the round robin activity requires each person to contribute.

Face-to-Face Interaction—Students are shown how to sit and face each other in step 4 of this Plan.

Social Skills—During this lesson, students are asked to practice the social skill of *getting into a group* appropriately. Ask students to use any other collaborative social skills that may have been previously taught.

Group Processing—Students are asked to process during step 13 of this Plan.

OBJECTIVES:

1. To demonstrate getting into a group in a positive way
2. To process use of the skill

MATERIALS:

1. *Getting into a Group* classroom poster (See page 13.)
2. *Getting into a Group T-Chart* (See page 322; one per student and one transparency.) or *Blank T-Chart* (See *Appendix L*; one per student and one transparency.)
3. Class roster (Used for grouping students; refer to step 7 of this Plan before teaching this lesson.)
4. Stopwatch (One for educator use)
5. *How Did I Do?* (See page 323; one per student and one transparency.)

PREPARATORY SET:

Darken the room, if you prefer, and ask students to visualize themselves correctly using this social skill by reading the following script:

Let's take a few moments to relax.... Make sure you are sitting in a comfortable position.... Close your eyes if you feel like it.... On the count of three, take a very slow, deep breath. Remember to breathe in quietly through your nose. One ... two ... three.... Now breathe out slowly and quietly through your mouth.... Let your entire body relax.... Pretend I ask you to work in a group with two other students. When you find out who will be in your group, one of the kids is not your favorite person. Imagine yourself thinking, "I can work with everyone in my group. I can do it!" Picture yourself smiling, walking straight to your group location, sitting down, and facing and giving eye contact to all members of your group. Think about how proud you feel because you know how to get into a group.

PLAN:

1. Review the definition and skill steps for *getting into a group* by referring the class to the *Getting into a Group* classroom poster.

2. Pair students (see *Appendix P*). Ask student pairs to take turns telling each other the skill steps for getting into a group. Follow the procedure described in step 9 of Lesson A. (As an option, ask students to decide who will be "Louis Pasteur" and who will be "Jonas Salk.") Next, ask students to work with a partner to think of a situation when it would be important to get into a group appropriately. Tell students that one or more pairs will be asked to share their situation. Have one or more pairs share their situation.

3. Distribute and display the *Getting into a Group T-Chart*. Tell students it is a chart showing what a person looks and sounds like when appropriately using the social skill of *getting into a group*. Review the information listed in the chart and encourage students to make additions. Send the completed T-chart home with students during Lesson Z. Although time-consuming, T-charts can be more used more effectively by having students create their own with your help and then compiling the information on a single T-chart for all to see. If you choose this option, use the *Blank T-Chart*.

4. Tell students you will be asking three of them to model getting into a group in front of the class. Explain that those doing the model should refer to the T-chart to help them remember what the skill looks like and sounds like.

   Draw the following picture to show how you want the three students to sit when they form their group:

Social Star

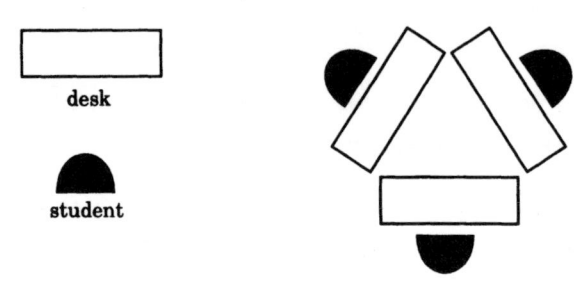

Those who are watching the model should observe carefully and be ready to provide feedback as to how the modelers do. Remind them that you will want to hear positive comments first.

5. Ask for three volunteers or choose three students to perform the model. Explain that when you say "go," they should come to the front of the class and form their group. Let students complete the model, **even if some aspects of the skill are not performed correctly.**

6. Allow the modelers to comment on what they did well. Ask students who observed to tell what the modelers did correctly, and then, if needed, tell ways the modelers could improve.

7. During the remainder of this lesson, students will be getting into three different groups of three. Before teaching this lesson, use a class roster to plan the groups students should form. Students should work with as many different people as they can.

8. Tell students that you will be asking them to get into groups of three so they can all practice the skill steps. Tell students not to move until you say "go." Then tell students what groups they will be in and where their groups should meet. Ask them to sit and face each other the same way the modelers did. (If necessary, remind students to move quickly and quietly without pushing or shoving.) Say "go," then time students and observe them as they get into groups.

9. Once students are in their groups, tell them how long it took and compare their time to the time recorded during Lesson A. Based on your observations, give feedback (see pages 20–21) to students relating to their use of the skill steps for getting into groups.

10. Describe the cooperative learning structure called "round robin" used by Kagan, (1992). During round robin, students take turns giving an oral response in their group. Tell the students that you would like them to do round robin and give the names of foods in alphabetical order. Ask them to decide who will go first and then proceed in a clockwise direction. Use one group to quickly model how this is done. Say, "For example, Mike could start and give the name of a food that starts with the letter A, Jolisa would then name a food that starts with the letter B, and so on. Continue going around until I tell you to stop. You will have

320

two minutes to see how many foods you can come up with. Any questions?... OK, start now." After two minutes, ask the groups to stop.

11. Repeat steps 8–10, asking students to form new groups of three. (During the two-minute round robin activity, ask students to name animals in alphabetical order.)

12. Repeat steps 8–10, asking students to form new groups of three. (During the two-minute round robin activity, ask students to list people's first names in alphabetical order.)

13. Ask students to move quickly and quietly back to their own seats when you say "go." Distribute and display *How Did I Do?* After students complete the page as directed, ask them to share their ideas about how the class did when forming their groups. Discuss other collaborative social skills used by the groups during the activity.

14. Say with excitement to the class: *You are very special. There is no one exactly like you in the entire world! Using social skills will help you get along with others so you can discover how they are special too!*

Social Star

Name _____

Getting into a Group T-Chart

LOOKS LIKE... | SOUNDS LIKE...

LOOKS LIKE...

using appropriate body talk

- giving eye contact to all group members
- having a friendly facial expression
- walking quickly to the group's location
- sitting near all group members
- walking safely to the group location

SOUNDS LIKE...

quiet footsteps

quiet voices (or no voices)

saying

- "Hi! It'll be fun working with you."
- "Our group will be great!"

a friendly and sincere tone of voice

desks, chairs, and tables sliding quietly

papers rustling

Getting into a Group

Name _____

How Did I Do?

DIRECTIONS: Think about when you got into your groups. Answer each of the questions below. Circle YES or NO.

★ When I got into my groups:

I moved quickly.	YES	NO
I moved quietly and didn't distract others.	YES	NO
I told myself, "I am willing to work with whoever is in my group."	YES	NO
My body talk showed that I was willing to work with whoever was in my group.	YES	NO

★ I feel proud because: _____

_____

_____.

★ Next time, I can do an even better job by: _____

_____

_____.

Social Star

Lesson Z

LESSON Z

In this unit, Lessons X and Y will not be used. Lesson Z will be used. The plan for this lesson can be found in *Appendix A*. Substitute the words "getting into a group" whenever a "____" appears in the lesson plan. Information specific to this unit follows. (Students should decorate their *Show Time* sign, page 325, for use during this lesson.)

LESSON Z PLOT SITUATION:

Ask students to pretend they are working in a group of three at school, and one of the group members is refusing to look at them, face them, or listen to their ideas.

LESSON Z ROADBLOCK EXAMPLES:

- Having to be in a group with someone who has been very unkind to you

- Preferring to work alone rather than in a group

- Being unsure of which group you are supposed to go to either because you were not listening or the teacher gave unclear directions

I CAN
GET INTO A GROUP

Social Star

HOME-A-GRAM

Dear Family,

At school, we have been talking about the social skill called

GETTING INTO A GROUP

I learned that *getting into a group* means moving in a positive way to form a team to work with.

I learned that I can tell myself that I'm willing to work with whoever is in my group, and then I can go straight to my group, moving quickly and quietly.

When I know how to get into a group, I can save time and make a positive impression on others. Also, I can invite others to feel good when I show that I am willing to work with them.

Below, I have drawn what my face could look like when I get into a group, to show that I am willing to work with whoever is in my group:

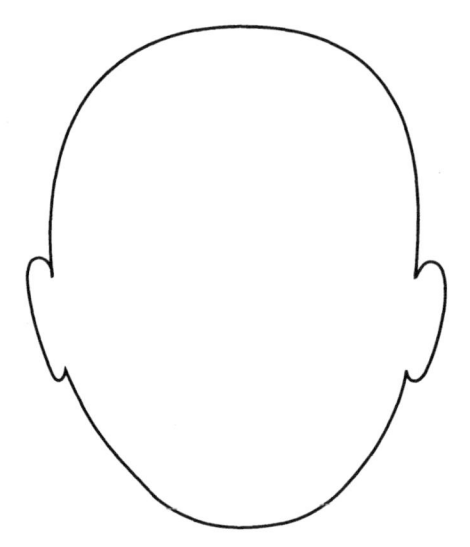

After I explain the attached T-chart to you (showing what a person can look like and sound like when getting into a group), please sign my "Getting into a Group" badge so I can return it to school and become a SOCIAL SUPER STAR this week.

From: _____

© 1994 Thinking Publications — *Duplication permitted for educational use only.*

Giving Put-ups

Social Star

UNIT GOAL:

To demonstrate comprehension and use of giving put-ups in a group

EDUCATOR INFORMATION:

Before teaching this unit, educators are encouraged to read the introductory section on teaching collaborative social skills found on page 309. This unit addresses the need for students to talk positively with one another when working in a group. The students are encouraged to give put-ups to one another and to avoid the use of put-downs. Curran (1990) identifies "happy talk" as one of the three standard social skills required for a comfortable, positive atmosphere in which cooperative learning can occur. Examples of giving a put-up include smiling at someone, giving a compliment, encouraging someone to share ideas or to try harder, and telling someone it's OK to make a mistake.

RELATED ACTIVITIES:

1. Discuss the following with students:

    - situations aside from working in a group at school when students may want to give put-ups (e.g., playing with others, working with family members).

    - situations when it's important for adults to give put-ups (e.g., teachers giving put-ups to students, giving put-ups to other workers on the job).

2. Have students create a story using an animal that typically has a "mean" reputation (e.g., wolf, snake, rat). Instruct students to give that animal a positive reputation by having the animal character give many put-ups to other characters in the story they create.

3. Have students decorate a shoe box. On index cards, write ways a person can give put-ups to other people. Tell students that when they are not feeling good about themselves and are tempted to put others down, they can go to the shoe box and pull out an idea to remind themselves of how to be positive with others.

4. Have the students make a classroom collage of pictures of smiles (and other forms of body language put-ups) cut from magazines.

5. Visit a local sports team during their practice time. Have students listen and record the put-ups they observe among team members.

6. Invite adults from different cultures to talk about how their cultures' conventions for giving put-ups compare with the components discussed in this unit.

It is important for educators to provide opportunities for students to work in groups so they can experience social skills in contexts where social communication is needed. Therefore, educators are encouraged to have students complete the Related Activities in small groups whenever possible. Educators trained in cooperative learning could incorporate the five components (see page 33) into the group activity.

RELATED LITERATURE:

Best Friends for Frances (1969) by Russell Hoban, Ill. by Lillian Hoban, Harper and Row. (Picture book) (pages 26–29)

The Fourth-Grade Wizards (1988) by Barthe DeClements, Viking Kestrel. (Text) "Hey, you're looking fine." (page 26)

Maniac Magee (1990) by Jerry Spinelli; Little, Brown, and Co. (Text) Maniac rejoices when Grayson learns to read. (pages 103–105)

SOCIAL SKILLS ALL DAY LONG:

Look for opportunities to teach social skills throughout the day (incidental teaching). Four ways to reinforce appropriate social skills and an example of each follow:

Encouragement

I've been listening to this group. I heard Maria say "Good job" to Mike and I heard Lee tell Victor, "I like your picture." I saw a lot of smiling going on. Great job with put-ups!

Personal Example

Last night at the parent-teacher meeting, I heard many positive comments. It really made the meeting fun. I left the meeting feeling wonderful.

Prompting

Jolisa, remember to give put-ups when you work with your group today. Keep reminding yourself about a reward you are trying to earn, or keep reminding yourself how powerful you'll feel when you give put-ups.

Corrective Feedback (must be positive, private, specific, and nonthreatening)

Ann, just now you gave Lee a put-down when you rolled your eyes and said, "That's dumb." You could have reminded yourself to say something positive or not to say anything at all. Giving put-ups can help your whole group get along better.

Lesson A

OBJECTIVES:

1. To state the meaning of *giving put-ups* and tell why it is important to give them

2. To listen to the self-talk associated with correct use of the skill

MATERIALS:

1. A helium balloon and a rock (For use during the Preparatory Set)

2. *Giving Put-ups* (See page 333; one per student and one transparency.)

3. *Thought Bubble* (See *Appendix O*; one for educator use.)

4. *Checking Myself* (See *Appendix I*; one per student and one transparency.)

PREPARATORY SET:

Display a helium balloon and a rock where everyone can see them. Say, "Pretend you just struck out during a softball game. When you walk back to the bench, one of your teammates crosses his arms, rolls his eyes, and says to you with a sarcastic tone, 'Way to go.'" Ask students to discuss whether the teammate's actions and words invite them to feel like a rock or a balloon. Next say, "Again, pretend you just struck out during a softball game, only this time when you walk back to the bench, one of your teammates turns toward you with a smile and says with a cheery voice, 'No problem, it happens to everyone!'" Ask students to discuss whether the teammate's actions and words invite them to feel like a rock or a balloon. Use this discussion as a means of introducing the skill of *giving put-ups*.

PLAN:

1. Distribute and display *Giving Put-ups*. Discuss the definition for *giving put-ups*. Explain the skill step and the symbol next to it. Remind students that the symbol is there to help them visualize and remember the skill step. Refer students to the body-talk symbol in the left-hand margin. Remind students that appropriate body talk is important when giving put-ups.

2. Model use of the skill step for giving put-ups while thinking aloud. A scripted example follows:

    Introduction

    I am going to pretend to be working in a group. I will show you how I give a put-up to someone in my group and tell you the thoughts I'm having. When I hold up this Thought Bubble, *you'll know the words I'm saying are actually what I'm thinking.*

Social Star

Actual Model

While holding up the *Thought Bubble* say, *Sally is really doing a nice job staying on task. Let's see, what put-up can I give her? Oh, I know!* Put the *Thought Bubble* down and say, *I'm glad you're in our group. You're really doing your part!*

3. Complete the bottom half of *Giving Put-ups* as directed.

4. Distribute and display the discussion guideline sheet called *Checking Myself*. Ask students to complete the thought bubble statement with the words, "listen to others" or use another classroom discussion goal more appropriate for your group (see pages 25–26). Tell students that you will be having a discussion about the story they just heard. When a student is answering a question or making a comment during the discussion, it's important for everyone to be polite by listening to that student. Tell students that they can show they are listening by giving eye contact, nodding their heads, asking relevant questions, or making relevant comments. Instruct them to circle a T-shirt star each time someone new talks and they are listening.

5. Model use of the *Checking Myself* sheet while thinking aloud. A scripted example follows:

Introduction

I am going to pretend to be one of you completing this sheet during the discussion we will be having. I will tell you the thoughts I'm having while completing this sheet. When I hold up this Thought Bubble, *you'll know the words that I am saying are actually what I'm thinking.*

Actual Model

While holding up the *Thought Bubble* say, *Emily is telling one of her answers. I'll be polite by looking at her when she's talking and smiling at her so she knows I'm listening. I'll circle a star on the T-shirt because I listened to Emily.* Put the *Thought Bubble* down and circle a star on the transparency.

During the discussion, periodically remind students to listen to the person talking and to mark their discussion guideline sheets.

6. Proceed with the discussion by asking the following questions: (The story may need to be reread first.)

- What did Victor do and say to give a put-up to Ann?

- How do you think Ann felt about Victor's put-up?

- Victor's put-up encouraged Ann to keep trying when she was having a difficult time. Tell about another time when it would be important to give a put-up to someone in your group.

- What did Jolisa do and say to give a put-down to Ann?

- How do you think Ann felt about Jolisa's put-down?

- What negative things could happen in the group because of Jolisa's put-down?

- Can someone give a put-down without saying any words? (Answers could include making a mean face or an inappropriate gesture.)

- Tell what you could do to avoid putting down someone in your group who is difficult to work with. (Answers could include giving encouragement, giving praise when the person does something positive, ignoring, not giving eye contact when behavior is inappropriate, etc.)

- What could you say or do if someone in your group gives a put-down to someone else?

7. After the discussion, have students complete the bottom thought bubble statement on *Checking Myself*.

8. Process use of the sheet by asking the following question or another one more appropriate for your group:

   - Why do you think it's important to listen to others while they are talking?

   Process further by asking the students who volunteered to speak during the discussion to share their answers to the following questions:

   - You shared one of your answers during the discussion. How could you tell which people were listening to you? How did you feel knowing others were listening?

9. Pair students using the *Line Up–Fold Up* activity (see *Appendix P*). Have students line up in alphabetical order using their last names.

10. Ask student pairs to take turns telling each other the meaning of *giving put-ups* and why it's important to use the skill. Students could be reminded that the information they are to say is printed on *Giving Put-ups*.

    As an option to add structure to this activity (see *Appendix Q*), ask partners to come to an agreement about which person will be called "Anne Sullivan" and which person will be called "Helen Keller." After students have made their decisions, ask "Anne" to tell "Helen" the definition of *giving put-ups*. Next, ask "Helen" to tell "Anne" the definition. Ask students to use the same procedure to tell each other the reasons for giving put-ups.

Social Star

11. Ask partners to face each other and stand an arm's length away. Encourage partners to use friendly and confident body talk. Ask partners to shake hands and in unison repeat the following statement after you: *I enjoyed working with you. You can use great social skills!*

Name _____

★ Giving Put-ups

MEANING OF GIVING PUT-UPS: Inviting all group members to feel positive

SKILL STEP:

1. Ask myself: How can I give put-ups to all my group members?

REASONS FOR USING THIS SKILL:
When you give put-ups, others will feel more comfortable about participating and the group will really be working together. Everyone's contributions can be recognized. You feel good inside knowing you give put-ups to everyone.

DIRECTIONS: Listen to the story below. Look at the pictures of Jolisa, Victor, and Ann while you listen.

Jolisa, Victor, and Ann were working in a group to create a story. Ann was having a difficult time completing her job. Victor smiled at her and said, "Keep going! You're almost there. You can do it!" Jolisa rolled her eyes, sighed, and said, "Ann is always so slow!"

© 1994 Thinking Publications — Duplication permitted for educational use only.

Social Star

Lesson B

EDUCATOR INFORMATION:

During this lesson, students are asked to practice the social skill of *giving put-ups* while working cooperatively to complete an activity. Johnson, Johnson, and Johnson Holubec (1990) describe five components necessary for cooperative learning. The five components are described on pages 33–35. The educator is encouraged to review the information before teaching this lesson. A short description of how the five components have been built into this lesson follows:

Positive Interdependence—Students feel they are linked together to complete the activity in step 14 of this Plan. The goal of beating the original score requires group members to work as a team.

Individual Accountability—Due to the nature of the counting activity, students feel individually accountable for participating in the activity. The goal of beating the score requires that each person contribute.

Face-to-Face Interaction—Students are shown how to stand and face each other in step 9 of this Plan.

Social Skills—During this lesson, students are asked to practice the social skill of *giving put-ups*. Ask students to use any other collaborative social skills that may have been previously taught.

Group Processing—Students are asked to process in step 17 of this Plan.

OBJECTIVES:

1. To demonstrate giving put-ups in a group
2. To process use of the skill

MATERIALS:

1. Class roster (Used for grouping students; refer to step 4 of this Plan before teaching this lesson.)

2. *Giving Put-ups* classroom poster (See page 13.)

3. *Giving Put-ups T-Chart* (See page 339; one per student and one transparency.) or *Blank T-Chart* (See *Appendix L*; one per student and one transparency.)

4. Counting activity materials (Refer to step 6 of this Plan. Select a counting activity before teaching this lesson.)

5. *Counting Activity Record* (See page 340; one per group and one transparency.)

6. Video camcorder, VCR player, monitor, and a blank video cassette tape

7. *101 Put-ups* (See page 341; one per student and one transparency.)

PREPARATORY SET:

Darken the room, if you prefer, and ask students to visualize themselves correctly using this social skill by reading the following script:

Let's take a few moments to relax.... Make sure you are sitting in a comfortable position.... Close your eyes if you feel like it.... On the count of three, take a very slow, deep breath. Remember to breathe in quietly through your nose. One . . . two . . . three.... Breathe in deeply.... Now breathe out slowly and quietly through your mouth. Let your entire body relax. Now imagine yourself sitting in your classroom working in a group with two other students. One of the students in your group thinks of a great idea. Picture yourself giving a put-up to this person. See yourself smiling and hear the words you say. Think about how good you feel because you know how to give put-ups. Tell yourself what a nice job you did!

PLAN:

1. Review the definition and skill step for *giving put-ups* by referring the class to the *Giving Put-ups* classroom poster.

2. Pair students (see *Appendix P*). Ask student pairs to take turns telling each other the skill step for giving put-ups. Follow the procedure described in step 10 of Lesson A. (As an option, ask students to decide who will be "Neil Armstrong" and who will be "John Glenn.") Next, ask students to work together to think of a time when it would be important to give a put-up. Tell students that one or more pairs will be called on to share their situation. Have one or more pairs share their situation.

3. Distribute and display the *Giving Put-ups T-Chart*. Tell students it is a chart showing what a person looks like and sounds like when giving put-ups. Review the information listed in the chart and encourage students to make additions. Although time-consuming, T-charts can be used more effectively by having students create their own with your help and then compiling the information on a single T-chart for all to see. If you choose this option, use the *Blank T-Chart*.

4. For the remainder of this lesson, students will be getting into groups of three or four to complete the counting game activity. Before teaching this lesson, use a class roster to plan the groups that students should form.

5. Tell students you will be asking all of them to form groups of three or four so they can do a fun counting game activity.

Social Star

6. A list of possible counting game activities follows. Before teaching this lesson, choose from the list or develop an activity more appropriate for your group of students. (Activities in which students do things one at a time were purposely chosen over activities in which everyone would be involved at the same time in order to give the observing students time to think of put-ups and to refer to the T-chart.)

   A. Ball Toss

   Materials: One ball per group

   Directions: Count how many times you can toss the ball from your right hand to your left hand without dropping it. Your hands must be at least one foot apart. Everyone in your group should have a turn. As soon as the ball is dropped, it goes to the next person to toss.

   B. Ball Dribble

   Materials: One bouncing ball per group

   Directions: Count how many times you can bounce the ball on the ground (dribble the ball). Do not catch the ball in between each bounce. Everyone in your group should have a turn. As soon as the ball rolls, it goes to the next person to dribble.

   C. Hoola Hoop Twist

   Materials: One Hoola Hoop per group

   Directions: Count how many times you can twist the Hoola Hoop around your waist. Do not touch the Hoola Hoop after you begin. Everyone in your group should have a turn. As soon as the Hoola Hoop touches the floor, it goes to the next person to twist.

   D. Jumping Rope Jump

   Materials: One individual-size jump rope per group

   Directions: Count how many times you can jump rope backwards or do "hot peppers." Everyone in your group should have a turn. As soon as you miss, pass the jump rope to the next person.

   E. Paddle Ball

   Materials: One paddle ball per group

   Directions: Count how many times you can hit the ball with the paddle. When you miss, pass the paddle ball to the next person.

   Distribute the counting game activity material to each group and give the directions for the activity. (Don't discuss giving put-ups at this time.) Ask groups to begin the activity, and keep going until everyone in the group has had a turn. Ask each group member to remember his or her score (by writing it down if necessary).

7. After each group has finished the activity, distribute and display the *Counting Activity Record* to each group. Have the students record their individual scores and then add them up to determine their group total. (*The Counting Activity Record* provides room for four names if some groups have four members.) Using the transparency, model how the students should write their results in the columns labeled "Names" and "Trial #1."

8. Tell students you will be asking one of the groups to model giving put-ups during the counting game activity for the rest of the class. Explain that those doing the model should refer to the T-chart to help them remember what the skill looks like and sounds like. Those who are watching the model should observe carefully and be ready to critique how the modelers do. Remind them that you will want to hear positive comments first.

9. Ask for one group to perform the model. Explain that when you say "go," they should come to the front of the class and form their group. Ask modelers to face each other during the activity and yet leave enough room for the person who is performing (e.g., dribbling the ball). Say "go" and allow time for the modelers to get situated.

10. Tell the modelers that while one person in the group is doing the activity, the others should give put-ups (e.g., complimenting a person who is doing really well, giving encouragement to help someone feel better about a low score, clapping, etc.).

11. Ask modelers to begin and continue the activity until you feel the model should end.

12. Allow the modelers to comment on what they did well. Ask students who observed to first tell what the modelers did correctly, and then, if needed, tell ways the modelers could improve.

13. Tell students you will be asking them to practice giving put-ups in their groups when they try to beat their first group total by doing the counting game activity again. If possible, explain that you will be videotaping each group, to record the put-ups you see or hear and that you will be showing the video to them later.

14. Have students do the counting game activity and videotape them. Tell students that when they finish, they should put their results on the *Counting Activity Record*. (If necessary, model how the students should write their results in the column labeled "Trial 2"). Depending on available time, share whether you want groups to do a third or fourth trial.

Social Star

15. After the activity is finished, rewind the videotape. Distribute and display *101 Put-ups* to each student. Tell students that when you were videotaping, you probably heard and saw at least "101 put-ups." Tell them they will be watching the video and writing down any four of the put-ups they see or hear on the tape (e.g., Tom said, "Nice job!" to Beatrice; Linda smiled at Kristen).

16. Show the video and give students time to finish the top section of *101 Put-ups*.

17. Ask students to complete the bottom section of *101 Put-ups* to evaluate their own use of put-ups.

18. Ask students to tell about some of the put-ups they observed. Discuss other collaborative social skills used by the groups during the activity.

19. Say with excitement to the class: *It is very exciting to watch you practice your social skills! I would like to invite you to use your social skills outside of this room wherever you go.*

Name _____

Giving Put-ups T-Chart

LOOKS LIKE...

using appropriate body talk

- looking at the person to whom you're giving a put-up
- using a friendly, sincere facial expression
- facing and leaning toward the person

using put-up body language with all group members

SOUNDS LIKE...

a friendly, sincere tone of voice

saying

- "Great job!"
- "Keep going, you can do it!"
- "That's a great idea!"
- "Don't worry about it. Everyone makes mistakes!"

Counting Activity Record

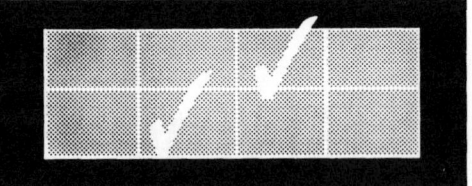

NAMES	TRIAL #1	TRIAL #2	TRIAL #3	TRIAL #4
GROUP TOTAL				

Giving Put-ups

Name _____

👍 101 Put-ups

DIRECTIONS: Watch the videotape. Write down four put-ups you saw or heard classmates giving.

1. _____
   _____

2. _____
   _____

3. _____
   _____

4. _____
   _____

⭐ ☆ ⭐ ☆ ⭐ ☆ ⭐ ☆ ⭐ ☆ ⭐ ☆ ⭐ ☆ ⭐

I saw myself giving a put-up.　　　　YES　　　　NO

If yes, the put-up I gave was: _____
_____

If no, what is a put-up that I could have given?
_____
_____
_____

© 1994 Thinking Publications　　　　*Duplication permitted for educational use only.*

Social Star

Lesson Z

In this unit, Lessons X and Y will not be used. Lesson Z will be used. The plan for this lesson can be found in *Appendix A*. Substitute the words "giving put-ups" whenever a "_____" appears in the lesson plan. Information specific to this unit follows. (Students should decorate their *Show Time* sign, page 343, for use during this lesson.)

LESSON Z PLOT SITUATION:

Ask students to pretend they are at a friend's house and they overhear their friend's parents put their friend down.

LESSON Z ROADBLOCK EXAMPLES:

- Working with someone who seems to be doing everything wrong
- Being in the habit of looking for the bad things people do and not the good things
- Giving a put-up to someone who has been mean to you
- Feeling your put-up might sound fake/insincere

I CAN Give Put-ups

Social Star

HOME-A-GRAM

Dear Family,

At school, we have been talking about the social skill called

GIVING PUT-UPS

I learned that *giving put-ups* means inviting all group members to feel positive.

I learned that put-ups can include giving someone a compliment for doing something well, encouraging someone who is having a hard time, and smiling.

When I work in a group and give put-ups, others will feel more comfortable about participating and the group will really be working together. Everyone's contributions will be noticed. I feel good inside when I give put-ups to everyone.

Below, I have drawn how my face might look and the words I might say when I give a put-up to someone.

When I give someone a put-up at home tonight, please sign my "Giving Put-ups" badge so I can return it to school tomorrow and become a SOCIAL SUPER STAR.

From: _____

© 1994 Thinking Publications — Duplication permitted for educational use only.

Participating

Social Star

UNIT GOAL:

To demonstrate comprehension and use of strategies for participating in a group

EDUCATOR INFORMATION:

1. Before teaching this unit, educators are encouraged to read the introductory section on teaching collaborative social skills found on page 309.

2. It is crucial that educators teach students how to participate successfully in groups. *Learning a Living: A Blueprint for America 2000*, a report issued by the Secretary's Commission on Achieving Necessary Skills (1992), describes the skills young people need to succeed in the world of work. It has identified "interpersonal skills" as one of five major competencies needed by students. The first skill in this category is "participates as member of a team—contributes to group effort." This unit teaches students the importance of participating and doing their part when they work in a group.

3. Educators may find that some students do not participate with other group members. Johnson, Johnson, and Holubec (1988) state that the major reason some students may not participate in cooperative learning groups is because they have had little experience with the concept of working together (i.e., "we sink or swim together"). Students have been encouraged by parents, teachers, and society to work individually and competitively, to hide knowledge from others, to want others to fail, and to care primarily about their own performance. This creates an atmosphere in which students are afraid of rejection and ridicule from classmates when working in a group (Johnson, Johnson, and Holubec, 1988).

4. A high status student (status based on race, social class, gender, reading ability, or attractiveness) is more likely to dominate a group discussion and is expected to make a greater contribution than a low status student (Cohen, 1986). The educator is referred to a book by Elizabeth Cohen (1986), titled *Designing Groupwork: Strategies for the Heterogeneous Classroom*. Cohen describes various ways to make a low status student the group expert when working in cooperative groups. She incorporates the concept of "multiple abilities" which teaches students that many different abilities are necessary for any given task and that not any one student will possess all abilities. Each student possesses some of these abilities.

RELATED ACTIVITIES:

1. Discuss the following with students:

- situations outside of school when it is important for everyone in a group to participate (e.g., on a swimming or track relay team, during a 4-H event).
- situations in which adults need to work cooperatively and participate in a group (e.g., collaborating with coworkers on a new computer project, sandbagging during a flood, etc.).

2. Have students visit with an area sports team or coach. Have the coach/players discuss the importance of all team players doing their part.

3. Have students earn and then make "cooperative treats" (e.g., if making a cooperative root beer float, one person would have the ice cream, one would have the root beer, one would have the cups, one would have the straws, and one would have the ice cream scoop). Do not allow students to eat until all treats are prepared. Other ideas for cooperative treats include tacos, subs, sundaes, and pizzas.

4. Invite adults from different cultures to talk about how their cultures' conventions for participating in a group compare with the concepts discussed in this unit.

It is important for educators to provide opportunities for students to work in groups so they can experience social skills in contexts where social communication is needed. Therefore, educators are encouraged to have students complete the Related Activities in small groups whenever possible. Educators trained in cooperative learning could incorporate the five components (see page 33) into the group activity.

RELATED LITERATURE:

Wait for Me (1992) by Susan Shreve, Ill. by Diane de Groat, Tambourine Books. (Text) Jack encourages Molly to practice running for the class race. (pages 57–62)

Ramona the Pest (1968) by Beverly Cleary, Ill. by Louis Darling, William Morrow. (Text) Show-and-tell time at school finds Ramona and Howie participating in an unusual way. (pages 46–51)

SOCIAL SKILLS ALL DAY LONG:

Look for opportunities to teach social skills throughout the day (incidental teaching). Four ways to reinforce appropriate social skills and an example of each follow:

Encouragement

I've been watching this group and noticed that each of the group members has been participating. Everyone has been leaning in slightly to listen to other group members, and I've seen each group member participating by sharing answers.

Personal Example

I'm on the "Positive Attitude" committee at our school. We met last night and we asked each group member to contact three parents to help at the ice cream social. I am really excited about making my parent contacts because I know that it's important for each person on the committee to participate and do his or her part.

Prompting

Soon you will be getting into your groups. Remember, it is important that each group member do his or her part so your group can complete the science experiment.

Corrective Feedback (must be positive, private, specific, and nonthreatening)

Maria, I watched your group complete the activity. I noticed that each time it was your turn to talk, you shrugged your shoulders and didn't give an answer. Next time you are in a group, you could use self-talk to remind yourself of the importance of participating and doing your part.

Social Star

Lesson A

OBJECTIVES:

1. To state the meaning of *participating* and tell why it is important
2. To listen to the self-talk associated with correct use of the skill

MATERIALS:

1. Inflated balloons (One per group)
2. *Participating* (See page 352; one per student and one transparency.)
3. *Thought Bubble* (See *Appendix O*; one for educator use.)
4. *Checking Myself* (See *Appendix I*; one per student and one transparency.)
5. *Go Together Cards* (See *Appendix P*; one per pair of students.)

PREPARATORY SET:

Ask students to stand together in groups of four or five. Give each group a balloon. Tell students that when you say "go," the members within each group should join hands and work together to see how long they can keep their balloon in the air. Have students brainstorm ways to hit their balloon (e.g., with their joined hands, with their heads, with their shoulders). Ask each group to count aloud to keep a tally of how many times members of the group have touched the balloon to keep it afloat. Announce that if students drop hands or the balloon touches the ground, then the group should begin counting over again. Say "go." After the activity is finished, ask the following questions:

- What happened while you were trying to keep the balloon in the air?
- Did everyone in your group join in and help keep the balloon in the air?
- What do you think would happen if one or more group members did not join in and do their share during the activity?

Use this activity as a means of introducing this unit.

PLAN:

1. Distribute and display *Participating*. Discuss the definition of *participating*. Explain the participating skill step and the symbol next to it. Remind students that the symbol is there to help them visualize and remember the skill step. Refer students to the body-talk symbol in the left-hand margin. Remind students that appropriate body talk is important when participating. Discuss the reasons for participating.

2. Model use of the participating skill step while thinking aloud. A scripted example follows:

Introduction

I am going to pretend to be someone your age participating in a group. I will show you how I participate and tell you the thoughts I'm having. When I hold up this Thought Bubble, *you'll know the words I'm saying are actually what I'm thinking.*

Actual Model

While holding up the *Thought Bubble* say, *Our group is working together to discuss and then write down what we learned about the ocean. How can I do my part? I can share the information that I remember.* Put the *Thought Bubble* down and say, *Oceans cover more than 70 percent of the earth.*

3. Read the story on the bottom half of *Participating*.

4. Distribute and display the discussion guideline sheet called *Checking Myself*. Ask students to complete the goal statement with the words "raise my hand," or use another classroom discussion goal more appropriate for your group (see pages 25–26). Tell students that you will be discussing the story they just heard and that it is important that everyone be willing to participate. Instruct them to circle a T-shirt star each time they raise their hands to share information (even if they don't get called on).

5. Model use of the *Checking Myself* sheet while thinking aloud. A scripted example follows:

Introduction

I am going to pretend to be one of you completing this sheet during the discussion we will be having. I will tell you the thoughts I am having while I'm completing the sheet. When I hold up this Thought Bubble, *you'll know the words I'm saying are actually what I'm thinking.*

Actual Model

While holding up the *Thought Bubble* say, *OK, the teacher is asking a question and I know the answer. I am going to raise my hand. She called on someone else, but I'll circle a T-shirt star because I raised my hand.* Put the *Thought Bubble* down and circle a T-shirt star on the transparency.

During the discussion, periodically remind students to raise their hands to verbally participate and mark their discussion guideline sheets.

Social Star

6. Proceed with the discussion by asking the following questions: (The story may need to be reread first.)

- How did Ann, Mike, and Victor participate while working in their group?

- How might Ann, Mike, or Victor feel about Maria not participating?

- What reasons might Maria have for not participating?

- How could Maria have participated?

- What could the others in the group do or say to encourage Maria to do her share? (Discuss the strategy of politely "giving a job away" to a nonparticipating group member.)

- Why is it important for everyone in a group to participate?

- Can someone be silent for a short period of time and still be participating? (Discuss the idea that someone who is being quiet may be participating by listening, thinking, or waiting for a turn to speak.)

- Pretend you're working in a group and someone tries to take over, do everything, or not let others participate. How would you feel? What could you do or say?

After the discussion, ask students to complete the bottom of *Checking Myself*.

7. Process the use of the sheet by asking the following questions or others more appropriate for your group:

- Why do you think it's important to raise your hand to share ideas and answers during a discussion?

- What was good about raising your hand even though you didn't get called on?

8. Pair students using *Go Together Cards* (see *Appendix P*).

9. Ask student pairs to take turns telling each other the meaning of *participating* and why it's important to use the skill. Students should be reminded that the information they are to say is printed on *Participating*.

As an option to add structure to this activity (see *Appendix Q*), ask partners to come to an agreement about which person will be called "Alice in Wonderland" and which person will be called "Robin Hood." After students have made their decisions, ask "Alice" to tell "Robin" the definition of *participating*. Next, ask "Robin" to tell "Alice" the definition. Ask students to use the same procedure to tell each other the reasons for participating.

10. Ask partners to face each other and stand an arm's length away. Encourage partners to use friendly and confident body talk. Ask partners to shake hands and in unison repeat the following statement after you: *It was nice working with you. You can use great social skills!*

Social Star

Name _____

★ Participating

MEANING OF PARTICIPATING: Doing your part in a group

SKILL STEP:

1. Ask myself: How can I do my part?

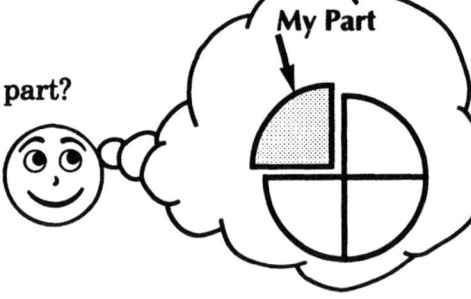

REASONS FOR USING THIS SKILL:

When you participate, you know you're doing your best and you feel proud. When you do your part to get a job done, others may like to work with you.

DIRECTIONS: Listen to the story below. Look at the pictures of Maria, Mike, Ann, and Victor while you listen. Decide which students are participating and which students are not.

Ann, Mike, Victor, and Maria were working in a group to write a story. Mike offered to write down the group's ideas. Ann and Victor agreed to draw the pictures. All three shared their ideas. Maria sat quietly and watched her group, but she didn't share her ideas or offer to do a job.

© 1994 Thinking Publications — Duplication permitted for educational use only.

Lesson B

EDUCATOR INFORMATION:

During this lesson, students are asked to practice the social skill of *participating* by working cooperatively to complete an activity. Johnson, Johnson, and Johnson Holubec (1990) describe five components necessary for cooperative learning. The five components are described on pages 33–35, and the educator is encouraged to review the information before teaching this lesson. A short description of how the five components have been built into this lesson follows:

Positive Interdependence—Students feel they are linked together to complete the hat-decorating activity described in this lesson. The goal of completing the hats requires materials to be shared.

Individual Accountability—Due to the nature of the hat-decorating activity, students feel individually accountable to complete their own hats. The goal of completing the hat-decorating activity requires each person to follow directions and participate by contributing assigned materials when asked.

Face-to-Face Interaction—Students are shown how to sit and face each other in step 6 of this Plan.

Social Skills—During this lesson, students are asked to practice the social skill of *participating* in a group. Ask students to use any other collaborative social skills that may have been previously taught.

Group Processing—Students are asked to process during step 15 of this Plan.

OBJECTIVES:

1. To demonstrate group participation
2. To process use of the skill

MATERIALS:

1. *Participating* classroom poster (See page 13.)
2. *Participating T-Chart* (See page 357; one per student and one transparency.) or *Blank T-Chart* (See *Appendix L*; one per student and one transparency.)
3. Class roster (Used for grouping students; refer to step 4 of this Plan before teaching this lesson.)
4. Hats to decorate (One per student, plus one extra; can be purchased from a paint or craft store, or handmade with paper, e.g., folding newspaper to make a sailor hat, rolling and taping construction paper to make a cone hat)

Social Star

5. Items to decorate hats (One set of decorating supplies—such as scissors, markers, construction paper, glue, tape, beads, glitter, noodles, sequins, straws—per group)

6. *I'm a Piece of the Pie* (See page 358; one per group.)

PREPARATORY SET:

Darken the room, if you prefer, and ask students to visualize themselves correctly using this social skill by reading the following script:

> *Let's take a few moments to relax.... Make sure you are sitting in a comfortable position.... Close your eyes if you feel like it.... On the count of three, take a very slow, deep breath. Remember to breathe in quietly through your nose. One ... two ... three.... Breathe in deeply.... Now breathe out slowly and quietly through your mouth.... Let your entire body relax.... Pretend you are in a group with three other students. Your group is having a discussion. You participate by sharing your ideas and you offer to write down your group's answers. You notice that one girl is not saying anything. You politely encourage her to share her ideas, and she does. Think about how proud you feel because you participated and because you encouraged someone else in your group to participate.*

PLAN:

1. Review the definition and skill step for *participating* by referring the class to the *Participating* classroom poster.

2. Pair students (see *Appendix P*). Ask student pairs to take turns telling each other the skill step for participating. Follow the procedure described in step 9 of Lesson A. (As an option, ask students to decide who will be "Robert E. Lee" and who will be "Ulysses S. Grant.") Next, ask students to think of ways they can show they are participating in a group. Tell students that one or more pairs will be asked to share their ideas. Have one or more pairs share their ideas.

3. Distribute and display the *Participating T-Chart*. Tell students it is a chart showing what a person looks and sounds like when appropriately using the social skill of *participating*. Review the information listed in the chart and encourage students to make additions. Although time-consuming, T-charts can be used more effectively by having students create their own with your help and then compiling the information on a single T-chart for all to see. If you choose this option, use the *Blank T-Chart*.

4. During the remainder of this lesson, students will be getting into groups of three or four to practice group participation. Before teaching this lesson, use a class roster to plan the groups that students should form.

5. Tell students you will be asking three (or four) of them to model group participation in front of the class. Explain that those doing the model should refer to the T-chart to help them remember what the skill looks like and sounds like. Those who are watching the model should observe carefully and be ready to provide feedback as to how the modelers do. Remind them that you will want to hear positive comments first and then the ways modelers could improve.

6. Choose one of your preplanned groups (from step 4) to perform the model. Explain that when you say "go," they should come to the front of the class and form their group. Draw the following picture to show how you want the students to sit when they form their group:

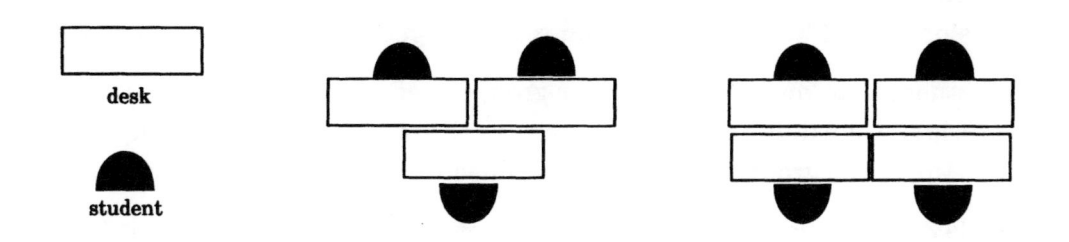

Say "go" and allow time for the modelers to get situated.

7. Tell the modelers they will be participating in their groups to decorate hats. Explain that each person in their group will be responsible for certain materials, and they will each have their own hat to keep when the activity is completed.

8. Ask the modelers to decide who will be Person 1, Person 2, and Person 3. Distribute specific materials to each person (e.g., Person 1 might have scissors, buttons, and glitter; Person 2 might have glue, beads, and noodles; and Person 3 might have construction paper, sequins, and feathers). Tell the modelers that each person can decide how his or her hat will be decorated, but when completed, each person should have used some of every type of material. Tell the modelers that the "trick" is that they can only touch the materials assigned to them.

9. Explain to the modelers that they will be given a short amount of time (specify an amount such as two minutes) to work together to start decorating Person 1's hat. Person 1 should name a material he or she would like used on his or her hat and specify where it should go (e.g., "I'd like a row of beads along the bottom edge of my hat, please"). Remind the modelers they can only touch their assigned materials and that they will need to ask politely if help from someone else is needed (e.g., "Could you please cut this strip of paper for me?" or "Could you put some glue right here so I can put the sequins on? Thanks!").

Social Star

10. At the end of the time period specified, ask the modelers to stop. Announce that they are finished modeling. Explain that if they were to continue, they would work together to decorate Person 2's hat, then Person 3's hat, back to Person 1's hat, and so on until the time available to work on hats has passed. Allow the modelers to comment on what they did well. Ask students who observed to first tell what the modelers did correctly, and then, if needed, tell ways the modelers could improve.

11. Tell students you will be asking all of them to get into groups to practice participating in a group. Explain that group members will decorate hats following the same procedure the modelers demonstrated. Tell students not to move until you say "go." Then tell students which groups they will be in and where their groups should meet. Ask them to sit and face each other the same way the modelers are. (The modelers should remain together as a group.) Say "go."

12. Tell students to number off in their groups. Call the 1's up and give them their materials. Continue with this process until everyone has their supplies. (The only supply the group who modeled will need is a new hat for Person 1.)

13. Display the *Participating T-Chart* and remind students to refer to it to remember what to look like and sound like while participating. Also, encourage students to use polite manners during the activity. Ask students to proceed with the activity. Remember to keep accurate time and tell students when to switch to the next person's hat.

14. When the total time available to work on hats has passed, ask students to stop working. Tell students that the hats are called "participating hats" and encourage them to think about the importance of participating in a group whenever they wear them. (Decide if you want students to take their hats home, or if you want them left in the classroom to be worn at times when participation is emphasized.)

15. Ask students to move quickly and quietly to return materials and then go back to their group location. Distribute and display *I'm a Piece of the Pie*. (The pie is divided into four sections to accommodate groups of three or four.) After students complete the page as directed, ask them to share their ideas about how it felt to participate in a group. Discuss other collaborative social skills groups used during the activity.

16. Say with excitement to the class: *Each of you is truly becoming a social super star!*

Name _____

Participating T-Chart

LOOKS LIKE... | SOUNDS LIKE...

LOOKS LIKE...

using appropriate body talk

- giving eye contact to all group members
- having a friendly facial expression
- sitting/standing close enough to other group members
- nodding in agreement

doing a job to help the group

- writing down an answer
- looking up information
- proofreading

politely giving a job to someone who is not participating

- handing the person what he/she should do
- pointing at what the person could do

SOUNDS LIKE...

a quiet volume

a friendly tone of voice

saying

- "I have an idea..."
- "I think we should..."
- "I'll be glad to..."

asking a question

- "What can I do to help?"

giving a job away by saying

- "Why don't you start on..?"
- "Would you want to..?"

Social Star

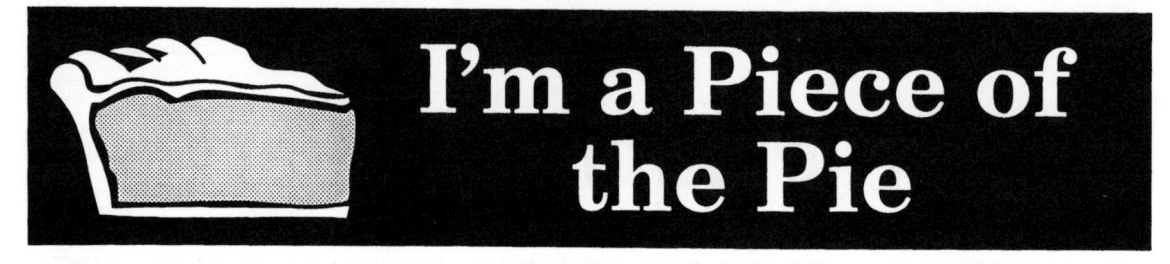

I'm a Piece of the Pie

DIRECTIONS: Think about how you participated in your group. When it is your turn, write your name in a piece of the pie. Write what you did to do your part in the group.

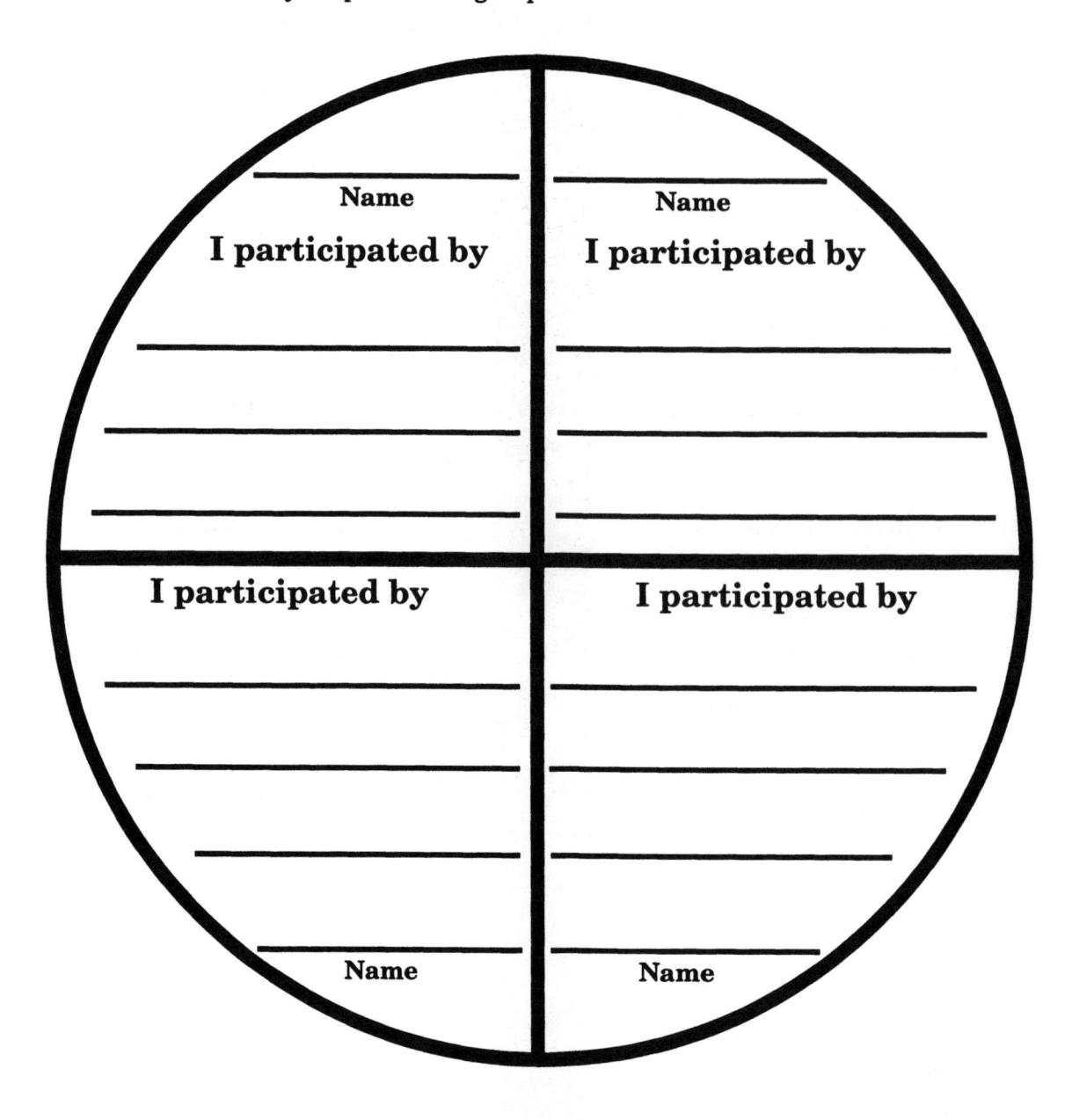

Name

I participated by

Name

I participated by

I participated by

Name

I participated by

Name

Lesson Z

In this unit, Lessons X and Y will not be used. Lesson Z will be used. The plan for this lesson can be found in *Appendix A*. Substitute the word "participating" whenever a "____" appears in the lesson plan. Information specific to this unit follows. (Students should decorate their *Show Time* sign, page 360, for use during this lesson.)

LESSON Z PLOT SITUATION:

Ask students to pretend that they are on a flag football team. One person keeps pulling everyone's flags off.

LESSON Z ROADBLOCK EXAMPLES:

- Working with someone who continues to not participate even after being encouraged by others to do so
- Being given a job that you really do not like or want to do
- Working with someone who takes over and does everyone else's job
- Participating in an activity that you do not understand
- Working with someone you don't get along with
- Being in a group when some group members treat another group member badly

Social Star

Participate
Do Your Part

YOUR PART

© 1994 Thinking Publications — 360 — *Duplication permitted for educational use only.*

HOME-A-GRAM

Social Star

Dear Family,

At school, we have been talking about the social skill called

PARTICIPATING

I learned that *participating* means doing my part in a group.

I learned that when I'm working in a group I can ask myself, "How can I do my part?" To participate, I can offer to do a job and share my ideas.

When I participate, I know I'm doing my best and I feel proud. When I do my part to get a job done, others may like to work with me.

Below I have drawn a picture that shows what I can do at home to participate and do my part for our family:

After I participate and do my part for our family, please sign my "Participating" badge so I can return it to school and become a SOCIAL SUPER STAR this week.

From: _____

© 1994 Thinking Publications — *Duplication permitted for educational use only.*

Staying on Task

Social Star

UNIT GOAL:

To demonstrate comprehension and use of strategies for staying on task in a group

EDUCATOR INFORMATION:

1. Before teaching this unit, educators are encouraged to read the introductory section on teaching collaborative social skills found on page 309.

2. This unit focuses on strategies that students can use to stay focused on a task (e.g., listening to other group members, maintaining eye contact with group members and group materials, staying seated with one's group). Students are taught to use self-talk and self-monitoring to stay on task.

3. Students working in cooperative groups can be encouraged to keep each other on task. In cooperative learning groups, students benefit from encouraging each other to achieve. This is in contrast to competitive situations in which children discourage other students' efforts to achieve (Johnson and Johnson, 1985). During this unit, students are taught specific encouraging comments they can make to others to help keep them on task.

4. This unit is a positive means of teaching students how to stay on task. Students with attention problems can benefit from learning to use self-talk to keep themselves on task. As always, educators must use a variety of positive interventions to foster growth in students who have a difficult time in the classroom.

RELATED ACTIVITIES:

1. Discuss the following with students:
   - other situations at school (academic and nonacademic) in which students might need to stay on task (e.g., playing in a baseball game, listening to directions).
   - situations when it's important for adults to stay on task at work and at home (e.g., finishing a project on time at work, listening to family members).

2. Have students set goals for how long they can stay on task at various activities (e.g., reading a book, running, sweeping the floor, writing a story), or have students graph how long they stay on task each day during the same activity.

3. Discuss how staying on task ("sticking with it" and practicing) can lead a person to excel in a certain area.

Study historic figures who stayed on task until achieving a desired result (e.g., Thomas Edison trying more than a thousand times before he invented the electric light bulb; Colonel Sanders being rejected more than a thousand times before someone agreed to finance his idea for a fried chicken restaurant chain).

4. Ask students to look through the *Guiness Book of World Records* and find examples of people who set records because of their ability to stay on task. Encourage students to set their own records.

5. Have students give examples of times they "stuck with it" to reach a goal or finish a task.

6. Have students visit a local agency in which the skill of *staying on task* is especially critical to meet a deadline or help a person (e.g., newspaper company, emergency medical treatment center, fast-food restaurant).

7. Have the class participate in a "Red Flag" activity (refer to page 30) in which the educator tells the students that sometime during the day the educator will purposely set up the students by creating a distraction to see how they will do at the social skill of *staying on task*.

8. Invite adults from other cultures to talk to the students about how their cultures' conventions for staying on task compare with the concepts presented within this unit.

It is important for educators to provide opportunities for students to work in groups so they can experience social skills in contexts where social communication is needed. Therefore, educators are encouraged to have students complete the Related Activities in small groups whenever possible. Educators trained in cooperative learning could incorporate the five components (see page 33) into the group activity.

RELATED LITERATURE:

The One in the Middle Is the Green Kangaroo (rev.) (1991) by Judy Blume, Ill. by Irene Trivas, Bradbury. (Picture book/text) Freddy's determination to be in the school play changes his self-confidence as well as his reputation.

A Chair for My Mother (1982) by Vera Williams, Greewillow. (Picture book) A girl, her mother, and grandmother save coins to replace the chair they lost in a fire.

Can Do, Jenny Archer (1991) by Ellen Conford; Ill. by Diane Palmisciano; Little, Brown and Co. (Text) A short book about Jenny's determination to win the school can-collecting contest. (pages 53–61)

SOCIAL SKILLS ALL DAY LONG:

Look for opportunities to teach social skills throughout the day (incidental teaching). Four ways to reinforce appropriate social skills and an example of each follow:

Encouragement

Jolisa, I noticed that you stayed in your seat today the entire time you were working in your group. How do you feel knowing you were on task and focused by staying in your seat?

Personal Example

I was at an important meeting last night that lasted a long time and I started to feel very tired. I kept using self-talk to remind myself to pay attention and stay on task.

Prompting

Today when you're working in your group, what are some nice ways you can remind other group members to be focused and stay on task?

Corrective Feedback (must be positive, private, specific, and nonthreatening)

Maria, during physical education, I noticed you didn't follow along with the rest of your group. You were watching other groups instead. What you could have done was to stay close to your group and do the same things they did, or ask for help if you didn't understand what to do.

Social Star

Lesson A

OBJECTIVES:

1. To state the meaning of *staying on task* and tell why it is important

2. To listen to the self-talk associated with correct use of the skill

MATERIALS:

1. *Staying on Task* (See page 370; one per student and one transparency.)

2. *Thought Bubble* (See *Appendix O*; one for educator use.)

3. *Checking Myself* (See *Appendix I*; one per student and one transparency.)

4. *Card Match* cards (See *Appendix P*.)

PREPARATORY SET:

Tell the following story. (Demonstrate the things Ollie does while telling the story, if you wish.)

> *I want to tell you about a girl named Off-task Ollie. Ollie has the hardest time paying attention to what is going on in class. When she is supposed to be working in a group, Ollie sometimes gets up and walks around to see what other groups are doing. When her group is talking about one thing, Ollie starts talking about something completely different. Even if she helps her group, she usually quits before the job is finished. If Ollie doesn't understand what is going on, she looks out the window and gives up. She loves to take things like pens apart and clutters her group's work area with all the pieces. School is difficult for Ollie.*

Ask students if they think Ollie can change if she wants to. (The story will be discussed in greater detail during step 6 of this Plan.) Use this story as a means of introducing the skill of *staying on task*.

PLAN:

1. Distribute and display *Staying on Task*. Discuss the definition for *staying on task*. Explain the skill step and the symbol next to it. (Define *self-talk* if necessary.) Remind students that the symbol is there to help them visualize and remember the skill step. Refer students to the body-talk symbol in the left-hand margin. Remind students that appropriate body talk is important to stay on task. Discuss the reasons for staying on task.

2. Model use of the skill step for staying on task while thinking aloud. A scripted example follows:

Introduction

I am going to pretend to be someone your age who is working with two or three other students in a group at school. I will show you how I stay on task and tell you the thoughts I'm having. When I hold up this Thought Bubble, *you'll know the words I'm saying are actually what I'm thinking.*

Actual Model

While holding up the *Thought Bubble* say, *We are supposed to be discussing the pages we just read. How can I stay on task? I'll look at the people in my group and think about what they are saying. I'll make a comment about what we read.* Put the *Thought Bubble* down and say, *I read that we can help save the air by planting trees. They help clean the air.*

3. Read the story on the bottom of *Staying on Task*.

4. Distribute and display the discussion guideline sheet called *Checking Myself*. Ask students to complete the goal statement with the words "think about an answer to each question asked," or use another classroom discussion goal more appropriate for your group (see pages 25–26). Tell students that you will be having a discussion about the story they just heard. Explain that after you ask each question, it's important for them to think about an answer, even if they are not called on. Instruct them to circle a star on their T-shirt each time they think about an answer to a question. It's important to remember to provide enough "wait time" before calling on a student to orally answer each question.

5. Model use of the *Checking Myself* sheet while thinking aloud. A scripted example follows:

Introduction

I am going to pretend to be one of you completing this sheet during the discussion we will be having. I will tell you the thoughts I'm having while I'm completing the sheet. When I hold up this Thought Bubble, *you'll know the words that I am saying are actually what I'm thinking.*

Actual Model

While holding up the *Thought Bubble* say, *OK, the teacher just asked, "What distraction could have gotten Mike off task?" I need to think of an answer. Listening to the other group could have gotten him off task. I'll raise my hand and circle a star on the T-shirt because I've thought of an answer.* Put the *Thought Bubble* down, raise your hand, and circle a star on the transparency.

During the discussion, periodically remind students to think of an answer to each question asked and to mark their discussion guideline sheets.

6. Proceed with the discussion by asking the following questions: (The story may need to be reread first.)

   - What distraction could have gotten Mike off task?

   (You may want to point to the skill-step symbol and share that if Mike had listened to the other group, his thoughts would have been off task.)

   - What distraction could have gotten Lee off task?

   (You may want to point to the skill-step symbol and share that if Lee had talked about his hamster, his words would have been off task.)

   - What distraction could have gotten Jolisa off task?

   (You may want to point to the skill-step symbol and share that if Jolisa had gotten up to sharpen her pencil, her actions would have been off task.)

   - What strategy did all three students use to keep themselves on task? (Self-talk)

   - What other distractions might these students have to deal with? (Examples include: being hungry, being angry, not understanding the experiment, wanting to comb their hair, wanting to look out the window at the rain.)

   - How are Jolisa, Mike, and Lee different from Off-task Ollie?

   - How would you feel if you were working with Off-task Ollie in a group?

   - Why do you think Off-task Ollie gets off task so often?

   - What could Off-task Ollie do to improve?

   - What could people working with Off-task Ollie do or say to encourage her to stay on task?

   After the discussion, have students complete the bottom thought bubble statement on *Checking Myself*.

7. Process use of the sheet by asking the following questions or others more appropriate for your group:

   - Why is it important to stay on task by thinking of answers to questions during a discussion?

   - Why is it sometimes hard to stay on task and think of answers?

8. Pair students using the *Card Match* activity (see *Appendix P*).

9. Ask student pairs to take turns telling each other the meaning of *staying on task* and why it's important to use the skill. Students could be reminded that the information they are to say is printed on *Staying on Task*.

   As an option to add structure to this activity (see *Appendix Q*), ask partners to come to an agreement about which person will be called "Harriet Tubman" and which person will be called "Frederick Douglass." After students have made their decision, ask "Harriet" to tell "Frederick" the definition of *staying on task*. Next, ask "Frederick" to tell "Harriet" the definition. Ask students to use the same procedure to tell each other the reasons for staying on task.

10. Ask partners to face each other and stand an arm's length away. Encourage partners to use friendly and confident body talk. Ask partners to shake hands and in unison repeat the following statement after you: *I can choose what I say. I can choose how I act. My choices will affect how I get along with others!*

Social Star

Name _____

Staying on Task

MEANING OF STAYING ON TASK: Giving your full attention to the group

SKILL STEP:

1. Ask myself: Am I on task?

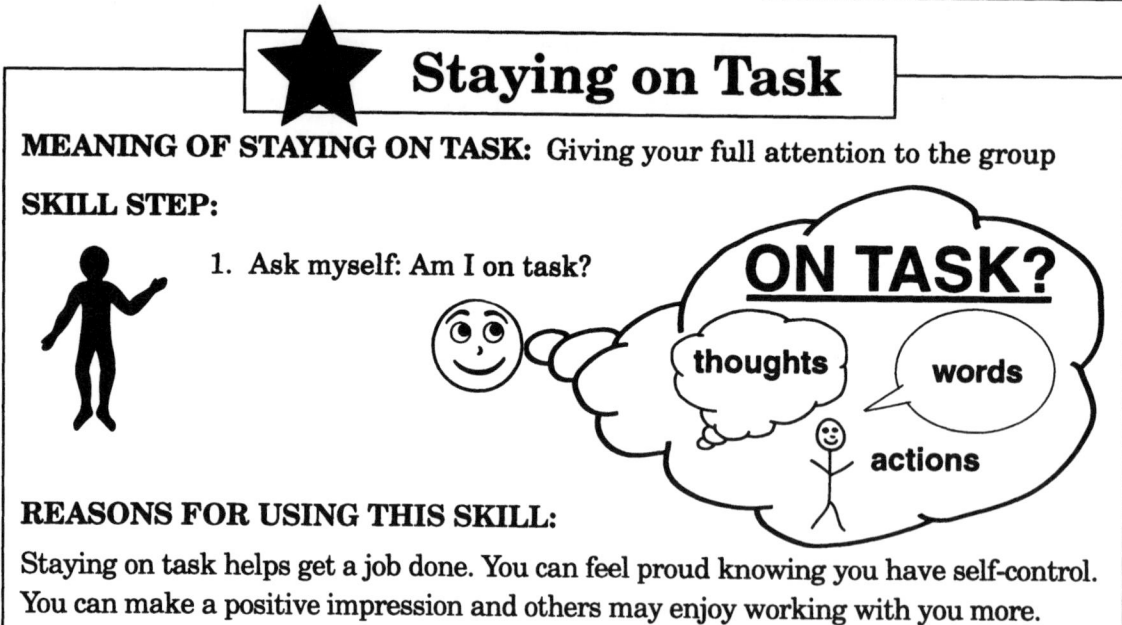

ON TASK?
thoughts   words   actions

REASONS FOR USING THIS SKILL:
Staying on task helps get a job done. You can feel proud knowing you have self-control. You can make a positive impression and others may enjoy working with you more.

DIRECTIONS: Listen to the story below. Look at the pictures of Mike, Lee, and Jolisa while you listen.

Mike, Lee, and Jolisa were working in a group to do a science experiment. Each person used self-talk to stay on task.

I can hear the other group. I won't think about what they are saying. I'll think about what my group is doing.

I want to tell them about my hamster, but I'll tell them later. Right now I need to help with this experiment.

I wish my pencil was sharper! I won't sharpen it now, because I want to stay on task for my group.

© 1994 Thinking Publications — Duplication permitted for educational use only.

Lesson B

EDUCATOR INFORMATION:

(Due to the length of this lesson, it may be divided into two parts, depending on the age and ability level of your students.)

During this lesson, students are asked to practice the social skill of *staying on task* in a group as they work cooperatively to complete an activity. Johnson, Johnson, and Johnson Holubec (1990) describe five components necessary for cooperative learning. The five components are described on pages 33–35; the educator should review the information before teaching this lesson. A short description of how the five components have been built into this lesson follows:

Positive Interdependence—Students feel they are linked together to complete the hidden picture activity in step 19 of this Plan. The goal of completing the hidden picture requires group members to work as a team.

Individual Accountability—Due to the nature of the hidden picture activity, students feel individually accountable for staying on task. The goal of completing the hidden picture requires each person to contribute.

Face-to-Face Interaction—Students are shown how to sit and face each other in step 11 of this Plan.

Social Skills—During this lesson, students are asked to practice the social skill of *staying on task* in a group. Ask students to use any other collaborative social skills that may have been previously taught.

Group Processing—Students are asked to process during step 21 of this Plan.

OBJECTIVES:

1. To demonstrate staying on task in a group
2. To process use of the skill

MATERIALS:

1. *Staying on Task* classroom poster (See page 13.)
2. *Who Did It?* (See page 377; one per pair and one transparency.)
3. A story (Four copies; see step 6 of this Plan. Choose something that students can read orally with ease.)
4. *Off-Task Slips* (See page 378; one set cut apart before class.)
5. *Staying on Task T-Chart* (See page 379; one per student and one transparency.) or *Blank T-Chart* (See *Appendix L*; one per student and one transparency.)

Social Star

6. *The Hidden Picture* (See page 380; one transparency and one per group of four students, plus one extra.)

7. Markers (One set per group of four students)

8. Class roster (Used for grouping students; refer to step 16 of this Plan before teaching this lesson.)

9. *Was I on Task?* (See page 381; one transparency and one per student.)

PREPARATORY SET:

Darken the room, if you prefer, and **ask students to visualize themselves correctly** using this social skill by reading the following script:

Let's take a few moments to relax.... Make sure you are sitting in a comfortable position.... Close your eyes if you feel like it.... On the count of three, take a very slow, deep breath. Remember to breathe in quietly through your nose. One . . . two . . . three.... Now breathe out slowly and quietly through your mouth. Let your entire body relax.... Pretend you are in a group with three other students. You are discussing some science ideas that are difficult for you to understand. You remind yourself to stay on task, so you ask for help to understand what's going on. Think about how proud you feel because you were on task in your group.

PLAN:

1. Review the definition and skill steps for *staying on task* by referring the class to the *Staying on Task* classroom poster.

2. Pair students (see *Appendix P*). Ask student pairs to take turns telling each other the skill step for staying on task. Follow the procedure described in step 9 of Lesson A. (As an option, ask students to decide who will be "Johann Sebastian Bach" and who will be "Ludwig van Beethoven.") Next, ask students to work with a partner to think of a situation in which it would be important to stay on task in a group. Tell students that one or more pairs will be asked to share their situation. Have one or more pairs share their situation.

3. Tell students that they will be playing a game called "Who Did It?" Explain that you will be asking four student volunteers to come to the front of the room. Explain that the volunteers will be given secret messages that tell them some off-task things to do while reading aloud in a group. Explain that the remaining students will need to be "detectives" and watch for how the volunteers get off task.

4. Ask for four volunteers (two sets of student pairs) to form a group at the front of the room.

5. Display and distribute *Who Did It?* to each pair of "detectives" (not to the volunteers). Explain that the "detectives" need to work with their partners to watch for each of the listed off-task behaviors. Read the off-task behaviors aloud. Explain that during the activity, when the "detectives" observe one of the listed off-task behaviors, they should write the name of the person who did the behavior in the magnifying glass next to the listed behavior. Say, "For example, if ____ stares out the window, write his name in the magnifying glass next to #2."

6. Tell the four volunteers they will be working as a group to read aloud a story. Distribute a story and two *Off-Task Slips* to each volunteer. Ask them not to share what is written on their slips.

7. Ask the volunteers to number off from one to four. Explain that Person 1 should begin by reading the first paragraph of the story, then Person 2 should read the second paragraph, etc. Explain that while one volunteer is reading, two of the remaining volunteers should take turns doing one of the off-task behaviors listed on their *Off-Task Slips*. Ask the volunteers to continue the activity until all the off-task behaviors have been demonstrated. Remind the "detectives" to mark the name of the person who is off task next to the behavior they observe.

8. Ask the volunteers to begin and allow time for student pairs to complete *Who Did It?* Ask student pairs to count how many off-task behaviors they were able to identify.

9. Distribute and display the *Staying on Task T-Chart*. Tell students it is a chart showing what a person looks and sounds like when appropriately using the social skill of *staying on task*. Review the information listed in the chart and encourage students to make additions. Although time-consuming, T-charts can be used more effectively by having students create their own with your help and then compiling the information on a single T-chart for all to see. If you choose this option, use the *Blank T-Chart*.

10. Tell students you will be asking for four new volunteers to model staying on task in front of the class. Explain that those doing the model should refer to the T-chart to help them remember what the skill looks like and sounds like. Those who are watching the model should observe carefully and be ready to give feedback to the modelers. Remind them that you will want to hear positive comments first.

11. Ask for four volunteers or choose four students to perform the model. Explain that when you say "go," they should come to the front of the class and form their group. Draw the following picture to show how you want the modelers to sit:

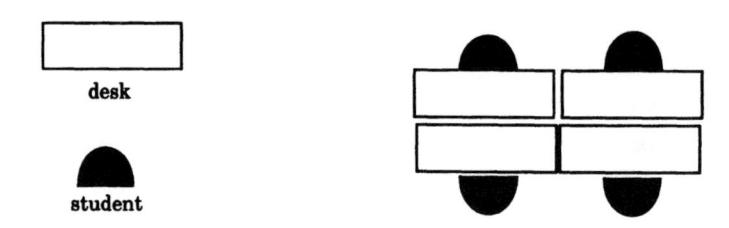

Say "go" and allow time for the modelers to get situated.

12. Ask the modelers to number off from 1 to 4. Tell the volunteers they will be modeling how to stay on task while working together to find a hidden picture.

13. Display *The Hidden Picture* and distribute one copy to the modeling group. Distribute one marker to each modeler. Explain that you will be giving directions for the modelers to take turns coloring in squares on the grid to complete a hidden picture. (The completed grid will form a "T.") Say, "If I ask Person 3 to color in B-6, then this is the square that Person 3 should color in." (Demonstrate how to find square B-6 and color it in on the transparency.) Tell the modelers they will need to stay on task, listen carefully, pass around *The Hidden Picture*, and follow directions precisely to find the hidden picture. Begin the model and give the following directions.

    Person 1, color in F-7.   Person 4, color in C-9.
    Person 3, color in C-5.   Person 2, color in C-6.
    Person 4, color in D-7.   Person 1, color in E-7.
    Person 2, color in C-7.   Person 3, color in C-8.

14. On *The Hidden Picture* transparency, show what the completed picture should look like, and compare it to the picture created by the modelers.

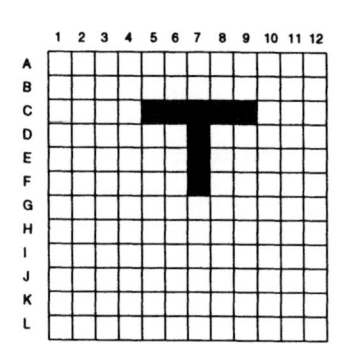

15. Allow the modelers to comment on what they did well. Ask students who observed to first tell what the modelers did correctly, and then, if needed, tell ways the modelers could improve.

16. During the remainder of this lesson, students will be working in groups of four (or three). Before teaching this lesson, use a class roster to plan the groups students should form.

17. Tell students you will be asking them to form groups of four so they can practice staying on task following the same procedure as the modelers. Tell students not to move until you say "go," and then tell students what groups they will be in and where their groups should meet. Ask them to sit and face each other the same way the modelers did. Say "go."

18. Ask students to number off from 1 to 4 in their groups. Distribute one copy of *The Hidden Picture* to each group.

19. Display the *Staying on Task T-Chart* and remind students to stay on task to help themselves and others in their group to follow directions and color in the correct squares to find the hidden picture. Proceed with the activity by giving the following directions:

Person 3, color in F-4.	Person 1, color in J-3.
Person 1, color in E-9.	Person 4, color in I-8.
Person 2, color in G-7.	Person 2, color in C-4.
Person 4, color in D-2.	Person 3, color in F-7.
Person 4, color in F-6.	Person 2, color in D-4.
Person 3, color in E-8.	Person 1, color in H-4.
Person 2, color in E-3.	Person 3, color in H-8.
Person 1, color in G-5.	Person 4, color in I-4.
Person 1, color in J-7.	Person 4, color in G-8.
Person 2, color in E-2.	Person 1, color in D-3.
Person 3, color in G-6.	Person 2, color in G-4.
Person 4, color in J-8.	Person 3, color in F-8.
Person 2, color in E-4.	Person 1, color in F-5.
Person 4, color in E-10.	Person 3, color in J-4.

20. On *The Hidden Picture* transparency, show what the completed picture should look like, and compare it to the pictures created by the students.

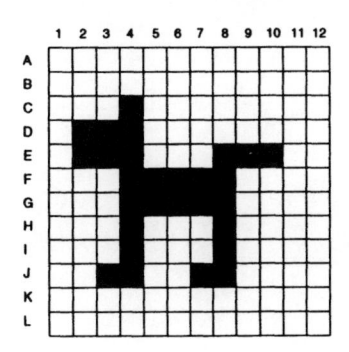

375

21. Ask students to move quickly and quietly back to their own seats when you say "go." Distribute and display *Was I on Task?* After students complete the page as directed, ask them to share their ideas about how they did at staying on task in a group. Discuss other collaborative social skills groups used during the activity. (Consider keeping completed copies of *Was I on Task?* so that the next time students are asked to work in groups, the copies can be used to remind students of the goals they set for staying on task.)

22. Say with excitement to the class: *I am different from you and you are different from me. That makes us each of us special. I like you because you're different and special!*

Staying on Task

Names _____

Who Did It?

DIRECTIONS: Read each off-task behavior listed below. Write the name of the person you observed off task. Write the name in the "spy glass" next to the behavior he or she did.

1. got up and walked around the room

2. stared out the window

3. went to sharpen a pencil

4. whispered to another person in the group

5. looked at other parts of the book

6. looked at other kids outside of the group

7. closed the book and laid head down

8. made a comment about something else

© 1994 Thinking Publications — Duplication permitted for educational use only.

OFF-TASK SLIPS

OFF-TASK	WALK AROUND THE ROOM. THEN COME BACK AND SIT WITH YOUR GROUP.
OFF-TASK	TURN AWAY FROM YOUR GROUP TO STARE OUT THE WINDOW. THEN GET BACK ON TASK.
OFF-TASK	SHARPEN A PENCIL. THEN COME BACK TO YOUR GROUP.
OFF-TASK	WHISPER TO ANOTHER PERSON IN YOUR GROUP. THEN GET BACK ON TASK.
OFF-TASK	LOOK AT OTHER PAGES OF THE BOOK. THEN TURN BACK TO THE RIGHT PAGE.
OFF-TASK	LOOK AT OTHER STUDENTS OUTSIDE YOUR GROUP. THEN GET BACK ON TASK.
OFF-TASK	CLOSE YOUR BOOK AND PUT YOUR HEAD DOWN. THEN SIT BACK UP AND GET ON TASK.
OFF-TASK	SAY ALOUD, "I WONDER WHAT WE'RE HAVING FOR LUNCH."

Name _____

Staying on Task T-Chart

LOOKS LIKE... | SOUNDS LIKE...

LOOKS LIKE...

using appropriate body talk

- looking at other group members or the task to be completed

- having a friendly facial expression

- body movements that show you are working (e.g., pencils moving, heads together)

SOUNDS LIKE...

an appropriate volume

•••••••••••••

a friendly tone of voice

•••••••••••••

statements or questions that are about the group's job

- "I think we should label the rivers first."
- "Are we supposed to draw the water cycle here?"

•••••••••••••

statements that keep the group on task

- "We're doing a great job staying on task."
- "Let's talk about that later. Right now we should be..."
- "Let's get back on task."
- "Come on, let's get this finished."

Social Star

Names _____
_____

The Hidden Picture

	1	2	3	4	5	6	7	8	9	10	11	12
A												
B												
C												
D												
E												
F												
G												
H												
I												
J												
K												
L												

© 1994 Thinking Publications

Duplication permitted for educational use only.

Staying on Task

Name _____

Was I on Task?

DIRECTIONS: Put an X in each box that tells what you did.

☐ I stayed in my seat.

☐ I listened to my group members.

☐ I looked at my group and not at other groups.

☐ I was thinking about what my group was doing.

☐ I used self-talk to remind myself to stay on task.

☐ I encouraged others to stay on task.

Next time, our group can do an even better job of staying on task by:
_____
_____
_____

Something new I learned about staying on task is:
_____
_____
_____

© 1994 Thinking Publications — Duplication permitted for educational use only.

Social Star

Lesson Z

In this unit, Lessons X and Y will not be used. Lesson Z will be used. The plan for this lesson can be found in *Appendix A*. Substitute the words "staying on task" whenever a "_____" appears in the lesson plan. Information specific to this unit follows. (Students should decorate their *Show Time* sign, page 383, for use during this lesson.)

LESSON Z PLOT SITUATION:

Ask students to pretend that their parents want them to have their rooms cleaned by a certain time, but they keep getting distracted by other things.

LESSON Z ROADBLOCK EXAMPLES:

- Hearing noisy distractions
- Being worried about something else
- Having other people in your group who are off task
- Not understanding what you are supposed to be doing
- Feeling that the task is boring
- Feeling tired or sick

STAY ON TASK

THOUGHTS · WORDS · ACTIONS

Social Star

HOME-A-GRAM

Dear Family,

At school, we have been talking about the social skill called:

STAYING ON TASK

I learned that *staying on task* means giving my full attention to the group.

I learned that when I'm working in a group, I can ask myself, "Am I on task?" I know that to stay on task I need to control my thoughts, words, and actions.

Staying on task helps get a job done. I can make a positive impression and others may enjoy working with me more. I can feel proud when I know I have self-control.

Below, I have written about something I can do at home to show you how I can stay on task:

_____
_____
_____
_____

After I complete the job I have written about, please sign my "Staying on Task" badge so I can return it to school and become a SOCIAL SUPER STAR this week.

From: _____

Disagreeing Politely

Social Star

UNIT GOAL:

To demonstrate comprehension and use of strategies to disagree politely when working in a group

EDUCATOR INFORMATION:

1. Before teaching this unit, educators are encouraged to read the introductory section on teaching collaborative social skills found on page 309.

2. When students work together in cooperative groups, controversy is likely to occur. Johnson and Johnson (1985) state that when controversy is managed constructively, it promotes curiosity about the correctness of one's ideas and an active search for more information, thus resulting in higher achievement and the retention of the material being learned. One of the most important skills "is to be able to disagree with each other's ideas while confirming each other's personal competence" (Johnson and Johnson, 1989, p.102).

3. For conflict to have value, students must possess the skills necessary to deal constructively with the conflict. It is helpful when (a) a cooperative environment for relationships is developed by the extensive use of cooperative learning, (b) the educator structures academic controversy, (c) students learn how to negotiate, (d) students learn how to mediate other students' conflicts, and (e) educators arbitrate only as a last resort (Johnson and Johnson, 1991).

4. This unit stresses that when working with others, disagreeing politely is important. Students learn to disagree with ideas or opinions without giving put-downs.

RELATED ACTIVITIES:

1. Discuss the following with students:

   - situations outside of school when students may disagree with others (e.g., when discussing which TV show to watch, when describing what happened in a situation, when telling that they don't like something).

   - determining when it may or may not be appropriate to disagree politely with adults/authorities.

2. Create a play about the importance of disagreeing politely. Visit another class to present the play.

3. Have students identify places in the world where there is strong disagreement between two groups of people that results in conflict or even war. If it is a "political" year, look for examples of conflict in the newspaper.

4. Discuss what happens when people are unable to reach an agreement. Introduce the skills of "mediation" and "agreeing to disagree" as means of peacefully coexisting. Apply these concepts to current conflict in the world.

5. Have students visit a "controversial" town board meeting to observe the appropriate (and inappropriate) manner in which people express their agreement/disagreement with various issues.

6. Invite adults from other cultures to talk to the students about how their cultures' conventions for disagreeing compare with the concepts presented within this unit.

It is important for educators to provide opportunities for students to work in groups so they can experience social skills in contexts where social communication is needed. Therefore, educators are encouraged to have students complete the Related Activities in small groups whenever possible. Educators trained in cooperative learning could incorporate the five components (see page 33) into the group activity.

RELATED LITERATURE:

The Robbers (1979) by Nina Bawden; Lothrop, Lee, and Shepard Books. (Text) Philip disagrees with his grandmother when she tries to convince him that a visit to his father and new stepmother will be a happy occasion. (pages 5–11)

Charlotte's Web (1952) by E.B. White, Ill. by Garth Williams, Harper. (Text) Fern's mother accuses her of inventing wild tales and Fern disagrees. (pages 105–107)

Ramona the Pest (1968) by Beverly Cleary, Ill. by Louis Darling, William Morrow. (Text) Mother and Ramona have different reasons for wearing boots to kindergarten. (pages 102–104)

SOCIAL SKILLS ALL DAY LONG:

Look for opportunities to teach social skills throughout the day (incidental teaching). Four ways to reinforce appropriate social skills and an example of each follow:

Encouragement

Lee, just now I heard you disagree with Ann politely. You said, "I disagree, Ann. I think that Wisconsin would be the nicest state to visit."

Personal Example

Last night, I was talking with my father-in-law. I used polite words and body talk when I disagreed with his ideas about how to build the downtown business center.

Prompting

In a few minutes, you will be getting into groups. Remember, it's important to disagree in a polite way. What words and body talk could you use to disagree without giving put-downs?

Corrective Feedback (must be positive, private, specific, and nonthreatening)

Maria, just now you gave Victor a put-down when you didn't agree with him. You could have disagreed in a polite way by saying, "Victor, I disagree. I think popcorn would be better for our treat."

Social Star

Lesson A

OBJECTIVES:

1. To state the meaning of *disagreeing politely* and tell why it is important
2. To listen to the self-talk associated with correct use of the skill

MATERIALS:

1. *Animal Cards* (See *Appendix P*.)
2. *Disagreeing Politely* (See page 392; one per student and one transparency.)
3. *Thought Bubble* (See *Appendix O*; one for educator use.)
4. *Checking Myself* (See *Appendix I*; one per student and one transparency.)

PREPARATORY SET:

Pair students using the *Animal Cards*. These same pairs will work together during step 9 of this Plan. Write the letters in the word "disagreeing" in scrambled order where all students can see them. Ask students to work with their partners to unscramble the word. Encourage students to use quiet voices, so the answer isn't given away. Periodically, give students a clue about what the word is. A list of possible clues follows:

- This word is in the name of the social skill we'll be talking about in this new unit.
- This word is something that might happen when you work with other people in a group.
- This word is something that happens when some people think differently than other people do.
- This word means the opposite of "agreeing."

If students are not able to unscramble the letters, tell them the word is "disagreeing" and use the activity as a means of introducing this unit.

PLAN:

1. Distribute and display *Disagreeing Politely*. Explain the skill step and the symbol next to it. Remind students that the symbol is there to help them visualize and remember the skill step. Refer to the body-talk symbol in the left-hand margin. Remind students that appropriate body talk is important when disagreeing politely.

2. Model use of the skill step for disagreeing politely while thinking aloud. A scripted example follows:

Introduction

I am going to pretend to be working in a group. I will show you how I disagree politely and tell you the thoughts I'm having. When I hold up this Thought Bubble, *you'll know the words I'm saying are actually what I'm thinking.*

Actual Model

While holding up the *Thought Bubble* say, *Jessica thinks that we should keep working on this problem until we come up with an answer. I don't agree. I think we're stuck and we're wasting time. How can I disagree with Jessica politely? I'll use a friendly face and voice tone.* Put the *Thought Bubble* down and say, *Jessica, I disagree. I think we're stuck on this one, I'm worried about having time for the rest of the problems. How about if we come back to this one if we have time?*

3. Read the story on the bottom half of *Disagreeing Politely*.

4. Distribute and display the discussion guideline sheet called *Checking Myself*. Ask students to complete the thought bubble statement with the words "listen to others" or use another classroom discussion goal more appropriate for your group (see pages 25–26). Tell students that you will be having a discussion about the story they just heard. When a student is answering a question or making a comment during the discussion, it's important for everyone to be polite by listening to that student. Tell students they can show they are listening by giving eye contact, nodding their heads, asking relevant questions, or making relevant comments. Instruct them to circle a T-shirt star each time they are listening when someone new talks.

5. Model use of the *Checking Myself* sheet while thinking aloud. A scripted example follows:

Introduction

I am going to pretend to be one of you completing this sheet during the discussion we will be having. I will tell you the thoughts I'm having while I'm completing the sheet. When I hold up this Thought Bubble, *you'll know the words that I am saying are actually what I'm thinking.*

Actual Model

While holding up the *Thought Bubble* say, *Paul is telling one of his answers. I'll be polite by looking at him when he's talking and I'll smile at him so he knows I'm listening. I'll circle a star on the T-shirt because I listened to Paul.* Put the *Thought Bubble* down and circle a star on the transparency.

Social Star

During the discussion, periodically remind students to listen to the people talking and to mark their discussion guideline sheets.

6. Proceed with the discussion by asking the following questions: (The story may need to be reread first.)

   - What positive things did Jolisa do to disagree with Victor?

   - How do you think Victor felt when Jolisa disagreed with him? Explain your answer.

   - What body talk did Lee use when he disagreed? What body talk might have been more polite?

   - What words did Lee use when he disagreed? What words might have been more polite?

   - How do you think Victor and Jolisa felt when they saw and heard how Lee disagreed?

   - What negative things could happen in their group because of the way Lee disagreed?

   - Why do you think Lee disagreed the way he did?

   - What could Victor and Jolisa do to encourage Lee to disagree more politely?

7. After the discussion, have students complete the bottom thought bubble statement on *Checking Myself*.

8. Process use of the sheet by asking the following question or another one more appropriate for your group:

   - Why do you think it's important to listen to others while they are talking?

   Process further by asking the students who volunteered to speak during the discussion to share their answers to the following questions:

   - You shared one of your answers during the discussion. How could you tell which people were listening to you? How did you feel to know others were listening?

9. Ask student pairs to take turns telling each other the meaning of *disagreeing politely* and why it's important to use the skill. Students could be reminded that the information they are to say is printed on *Disagreeing Politely*.

   As an option to add structure to this activity (see *Appendix Q*), ask partners to come to an agreement about which person will be called "Christopher Columbus" and which person will be called "Ferdinand Magellan." After the students have made their decision, ask "Ferdinand" to tell "Christopher" the definition. Next, ask "Christopher" to tell "Ferdinand" the definition. Ask students to use the same procedure to tell each other the reasons for disagreeing politely.

10. Ask partners to face each other and stand an arm's length away. Encourage partners to use friendly and confident body talk. Ask partners to shake hands and in unison repeat the following statement after you: *When I see you use your social skills today, I'll step right up and say, "Great social skills, partner!"*

Social Star

Name _____

Disagreeing Politely

MEANING OF DISAGREEING POLITELY: Telling someone you don't agree, without giving a put-down

SKILL STEP:

1. Ask myself: How can I disagree politely?

"I disagree because..."

REASONS FOR USING THIS SKILL:

When you use polite words and body talk to disagree, you can feel proud inside. You will get along better with other people.

DIRECTIONS: Listen to the story below. Look at the pictures of Victor, Lee, and Jolisa while you listen. Who disagreed politely and who did not?

Please choose a name for your group.

When Mrs. Marrera asked each group to come up with a group name...

Victor said, "I think we should call ourselves the Thoughtful Three." Using polite body talk, Jolisa said, "Or, how about if we call ourselves the Awesome Threesome? I think that would be a cool name!" Victor nodded and said, "Yeah! That would be good too!" Lee rolled his eyes, looked disgusted, and said, "The Thoughtful Three or the Awesome Threesome? Those both sound stupid! I can think of something better than that!"

© 1994 Thinking Publications   392   *Duplication permitted for educational use only.*

Disagreeing Politely

Lesson B

EDUCATOR INFORMATION:

During this lesson, students are asked to practice the social skill of disagreeing politely while working cooperatively to complete an activity. Johnson, Johnson, and Johnson Holubec (1990) describe five components necessary for cooperative learning. The five components are described on pages 33–35; the educator should review the information before teaching this lesson. A short description of how the five components have been built into this lesson follows:

Positive Interdependence—Students feel they are linked together to complete the activity in step 14 of this Plan. The goal of completing the activity requires each group to work as a team to use up their *Disagree Chips* and do their group cheer.

Individual Accountability—Due to the nature of the activity in step 14 of this Plan, students feel individually accountable for participating in the activity. The goal of completing the activity requires that each person contribute.

Face-to-Face Interaction—Students are shown how to sit and face each other in step 6 of this Plan.

Social Skills—During this lesson, students are asked to practice the social skill of *disagreeing politely*. Ask students to use any other collaborative social skills that may have been previously taught.

Group Processing—Students are asked to process during step 15 of this Plan.

OBJECTIVES:

1. To demonstrate disagreeing politely
2. To process use of the skill

MATERIALS:

1. *Disagreeing Politely* classroom poster (See page 13.)
2. *Disagreeing Politely T-Chart* (See page 397; one per student and one transparency.) or *Blank T-Chart* (See *Appendix L*; one per student and one transparency.)
3. *Disagree Chips* (See page 398; two chips per student, cut apart before class.)
4. Class roster (Used for grouping students; refer to step 11 of this Plan before teaching this lesson.)
5. *How We Did* (See page 399; one per student and one transparency.)

Social Star

PREPARATORY SET:

Darken the room, if you prefer, and ask students to visualize themselves correctly using this social skill by reading the following script:

Let's take a few moments to relax.... Make sure you are sitting in a comfortable position.... Close your eyes if you feel like it.... On the count of three, take a very slow, deep breath. Remember to breathe in through your nose. One ... two ... three.... Now breathe out slowly and quietly through your mouth.... Let your entire body relax.... Now imagine yourself sitting in your classroom working with two or three other students on a project. Pretend you disagree with one of your group members. Picture yourself using polite body talk by using a friendly facial expression. Hear yourself using polite words when you disagree. Think about how good you feel because you know how to disagree in a polite way. Tell yourself what a nice job you did!

PLAN:

1. Review the definition and skill step for *disagreeing politely* by referring the class to the *Disagreeing Politely* classroom poster.

2. Pair students (see *Appendix P*). Ask student pairs to take turns telling each other the skill step for disagreeing. Follow the procedure described in step 9 of Lesson A. (As an option, ask students to decide who will be "Florence Nightingale" and who will be "Marie Curie.") Next, ask students to work together to think of a time when it would be important to disagree politely. Tell students that one or more pairs will be called on to share their situation. Have one or more pairs share their situation.

3. Distribute and display the *Disagreeing Politely T-Chart*. Tell students it is a chart showing what a person looks like and sounds like when disagreeing politely. Review the information listed in the chart and encourage students to make additions. Although time-consuming, T-Charts can be used more effectively by having students create their own with your help and then compiling the information on a single T-Chart for all to see. If you choose this option, use the *Blank T-Chart*.

4. Write the following nine sentence starters where all students can see them:

    ### Sentence Starters 1–3

    - I think the best vegetable is...

    - I think the most delicious flavor of ice cream is...

    - I think the most awesome TV show is...

Sentence Starters 4–6

- I think the greatest book is...
- I think the best sport is...
- I think the nicest color is...

Sentence Starters 7–9

- I think the best pizza topping is...
- I think the tastiest fruit is...
- I think the most famous person is...

5. Tell students you will be asking three of them to model disagreeing in front of the class. Explain that those doing the model should refer to the T-Chart (from step 3 of this Plan) to help them remember what the skill looks like and sounds like. Those who are watching the model should observe carefully and be ready to provide feedback as to how the modelers do. Remind them that you will want to hear positive comments first.

6. Ask for three volunteers or choose three students to perform the model. Explain that when you say "go," they should come to the front of the class and form their group. Draw the following picture to show how you want the students to sit when they form their group:

[diagram: desk and student labels with seating arrangement]

Say "go" and allow time for the modelers to get situated.

7. Ask the modelers to number off (decide who will be Person 1, Person 2, and Person 3), and then give two *Disagree Chips* to each modeler to hold. Tell the modelers that they will take turns making statements and disagreeing in a polite way with each other. Each time they disagree politely, they can lay down one of their *Disagree Chips*.

8. Ask Person 1 to begin the model by reading and completing the first sentence starter ("I think that the best vegetable is..."). Remind Person 2 and Person 3 to pretend they disagree with the stated favorite vegetable, even if they really agree.

9. Ask Person 2 to politely disagree with Person 1 (e.g., "I disagree; I think ____ is the best vegetable") and then lay down a *Disagree Chip*. Ask Person 3 to disagree and then lay down a chip as well. Next, ask Person 2 to read and

Social Star

complete the second sentence starter. Person 1 and Person 3 should then take turns disagreeing and laying down a chip. Finally, ask Person 3 to read and complete the third sentence starter. Person 2 and Person 1 should then take turns disagreeing and laying down a chip. Tell the modelers that since all the chips have been laid down, they should stand up and celebrate by shouting, "Hurray for us!" Explain that the modelers are finished, although, if they were going to continue the activity, they would each pick up two chips, and use the same procedure for sentence starters 4–6 and again for sentence starters 7–9.

10. Allow the modelers to comment on what they did well. Ask students who observed to first tell what the modelers did correctly, and then, if needed, tell ways the modelers could improve.

11. During the remainder of this lesson, students will be forming groups of three to complete the sentence starters, following the same procedure as the modelers. Before teaching this lesson, use a class roster to plan the groups of three.

12. Tell students you will be asking all of them to form groups of three so they can practice polite disagreeing, following the same procedure as the modelers. Ask students not to move until you say "go." Tell students which group they will be in and where their group should meet. Ask them to sit and face each other the same way the modelers did. Say "go."

13. Ask students in each group to number off and distribute two *Disagree Chips* to each student.

14. Ask students to proceed with the activity. Display the *Disagreeing Politely T-Chart* and remind them to refer to it when making their statements of disagreement. Remind groups to stand up and cheer each time all the chips are laid down. (Groups should get as far as they can in the time available.)

15. Ask students to move quickly and quietly back to their own seats when you say "go." Distribute and display *How We Did*. Read the directions to the students and have them complete the page. After students complete the page, ask them to share their ideas about how it felt to disagree politely. Discuss other collaborative social skills used by the groups during the activity.

16. Say with excitement to the class: *It is very exciting to watch you practice your social skills! I would like to invite you to use your social skills outside of this room, wherever you go.*

Name _____

Disagreeing Politely T-Chart

LOOKS LIKE...

using appropriate body talk

- looking at the person you disagree with
- having a serious facial expression

SOUNDS LIKE...

a polite voice tone

an appropriate volume

saying

- "I disagree because..."
- "Or, how about if we..."
- "I have a different idea..."
- "Personally, I think..."
- "I'm not sure we should..."

Social Star

Disagree Chips

© 1994 Thinking Publications   398   *Duplication permitted for educational use only.*

Disagreeing Politely

Name _____

How We Did

DIRECTIONS: Write the names of all group members on the lines. Read each statement. Think about each group member. Circle whether you agree or disagree that each person did what the statements say. Add other social skills to #4 and #5 if your group was asked to use them.

	NAME _____	NAME _____	NAME _____
★1 Used polite body talk when disagreeing	Agree Disagree	Agree Disagree	Agree Disagree
★2 Used polite words when disagreeing	Agree Disagree	Agree Disagree	Agree Disagree
★3 Listened when others disagreed	Agree Disagree	Agree Disagree	Agree Disagree
★4	Agree Disagree	Agree Disagree	Agree Disagree
★5	Agree Disagree	Agree Disagree	Agree Disagree

© 1994 Thinking Publications   *Duplication permitted for educational use only.*

Lesson Z

In this unit, Lessons X and Y will not be used. Lesson Z will be used. The plan for this lesson can be found in Appendix A. Substitute the words "disagreeing politely" whenever a "____" appears in the lesson plan. Information specific to this unit follows. (Students should decorate their *Show Time* sign, page 401, for use during this lesson.)

LESSON Z PLOT SITUATION:

Ask students to pretend they are afraid because their parents want them to stay in the car while they go into a store. (The authors do not advocate leaving children alone in a car. Unfortunately, this situation occurs and thus the topic warrants discussion.)

LESSON Z ROADBLOCK EXAMPLES:

- Disagreeing with someone you know will become angry even if you disagree politely

- Feeling so strongly about your opinion that it is difficult for you to listen to anyone else

- Disagreeing when you are the only person who feels a particular way and the rest of the group feels differently

DISAGREE POLITELY

Without Giving a Pat-Down!

Social Star

HOME-A-GRAM

Dear Family,

At school, we have been talking about the social skill called

DISAGREEING POLITELY

I learned that *disagreeing politely* means telling someone I don't agree, without giving a put-down.

I learned that when I disagree, I can ask myself: How can I disagree politely?

When I use polite words and body talk to disagree, I can feel proud inside. Also, I will get along better with other people.

Below, I have written some words that I can use to start my sentences when I disagree with someone.

_____

_____

_____

_____

When I disagree with someone in a polite way at home tonight, please sign my "Disagreeing Politely" badge so I can return it to school tomorrow and become a SOCIAL SUPER STAR.

From: _____

© 1994 Thinking Publications — *Duplication permitted for educational use only.*

Appendix A

Lesson X

Social Star

OBJECTIVE:

To observe the appropriate use of _____ in a home, school, or community role play

MATERIALS:

1. _____ classroom poster (See page 13.)
2. _____ *T-Chart* (One per student and one transparency of page within the unit) or *Blank T-Chart* (See *Appendix L*; one per student and one transparency.)
3. _____ *Show Time* (One transparency of page found within the _____ unit)
4. *Thought Bubble* (See *Appendix O*; one for teacher and student use.)

PREPARATORY SET:

Follow the Preparatory Set described for Lesson X within the _____ unit.

PLAN:

1. Quickly review the definition and skill step(s) for _____ by referring to the _____ classroom poster.

2. Distribute and display the _____ *T-Chart*. Tell students it is a chart showing what a person looks and sounds like when appropriately using the social skill of _____ . Review the information listed in the chart and encourage students to make additions. Although time-consuming, T-Charts can be used more effectively by having students create their own with your help and then compiling the information on a single T-Chart for all to see. If you choose this option, use the *Blank T-Chart*.

3. Display _____ *Show Time*. Discuss each situation and explain that everyone will be role playing these situations during the _____ *Show Time* activity in the next lesson. Today will be a rehearsal for their _____ *Show Time*.

4. Model each situation and verbalize self-talk using the *Thought Bubble*. (Remind students that use of inappropriate body talk can sabotage any social skill.)

5. Choose a student to role play one of the situations twice (see pages 18–20). The first time, the student should verbalize self-talk using the *Thought Bubble*. The second time, the student should not verbalize self-talk.

6. Remind students that the next lesson will be _____ *Show Time*.

Appendix A (continued)

Lesson Y

Social Star

OBJECTIVE:

To demonstrate use of _____ in a home, school, or community situation

MATERIALS:

1. _____ *Show Time* (One transparency of page found within the _____ unit)
2. _____ *Show Time* sign (One or more per student; found in _____ unit immediately after _____ *Show Time*.)
3. Markers or crayons for each student

PREPARATORY SET:

Ask students to visualize by reading the script provided for Lesson Y within the _____ unit.

PLAN:

1. Display _____ *Show Time*. Review the home, school, and community situations which students will be role playing during today's _____ *Show Time* activity.

2. Distribute markers or crayons and a copy or copies of _____ *Show Time* sign to each student. Tell students that you will be calling on them to role play the _____ *Show Time* situations. While they are waiting their turns to role play, students should decorate their _____ *Show Time* signs so that they can be hung in predetermined locations throughout the school during Lesson Z. Encourage students to avoid interrupting so that you may observe the _____ *Show Time* role plays.

3. Students may be called to role play individually or in pairs. (For additional information on role playing, see pages 18–20.) If a pair is role playing, one person can be the observer while the other student role plays with the educator. The students should then switch roles. It is important to provide feedback to students. (For additional information on feedback, see pages 20–21.)

4. If time allows, ask students which past social skills they have used successfully. Have students identify how they feel when they use their social skills appropriately. Ask students which social skills they might like to improve.

5. Collect _____ *Show Time* signs to hang during Lesson Z.

Appendix A (continued)

Lesson Z

Social Star

OBJECTIVES:

1. To review and practice cognitive planning techniques
2. To identify and discuss _____ roadblocks
3. To prepare an activity to transfer use of _____ into the home

MATERIALS:

1. *Cognitive Planning Formula* chart (See page 12.)
2. *Secret Formula Pages* (See *Appendix N*; one of the two pages per student.)
3. *Self-Management Sheet* (See *Appendix H*; one of the 10 choices per student and one transparency.)
4. *Roadblock Sheet* (See *Appendix R*; one per student and one transparency.)
5. _____ *Home-A-Gram* (See page found in the _____ unit; one per student and one transparency.)
6. _____ badge (See *Appendix S*; one per student.)
7. *Social Super Stars* display (See page 13.)
8. Completed *Show Time* signs (Colored during Lesson Y)

PREPARATORY SET:

To foster internalization of the cognitive planning steps called STOP, PLOT, GO, SO, ask students to participate in a "Beat the Clock" activity (see pages 53–54).

PLAN:

1. Display the *Cognitive Planning Formula* chart and remind students that they can use the four steps to solve problems they may have in their lives. As an option to reinforce this concept, have students complete one of the two *Secret Formula Pages* by addressing a real-life problem they need to solve or just recently solved. (These pages do not need to be used in every Lesson Z but should be used occasionally. They may also be used at any time when a student is trying to solve a problem. This shows the usefulness of the STOP, PLOT, GO, SO strategy across all areas of daily living.)

Social Star

2. Review STOP with students by reminding them that STOP means stay calm and use self-control. Review what *self-control* means and why it's important. Ask students to practice one of the strategies for staying calm and using self-control by reading one of the six scripts on pages 48–49.

3. Review PLOT by reminding students that in whatever situations they find themselves, they should:

   - Decide exactly what the problem is
   - Brainstorm choices
   - Think about what might happen after each choice (consequences)
   - Pick a choice
   - Think about social skills needed

4. Have students practice the five steps to PLOT by asking them to pretend that.... (use the plot situation described for Lesson Z within the _____ unit). Students can work individually, with partners, in small groups, or as a whole class.

5. Review GO by reminding students that after they pick a choice, they need to actually go ahead with the plan by doing it.

6. Review SO by reminding students that after they use their choice, they should ask themselves "So, how did my plan work?" If the plan worked well, they could praise or reward themselves. If the plan did not work, they could think about why it didn't work or what they would do differently next time.

7. Bring the discussion back to the specific social skill of _____. Tell students it's important for them to check how they are doing at using _____ during and outside of class. Distribute the chosen *Self-Management Sheet* and give directions for its use. (See pages 24–25 for a general discussion of self-management strategies.)

8. Distribute and display the *Roadblock Sheet*. Tell students that it will sometimes be difficult to use _____ because of roadblocks. Explain that a roadblock is something that may get in the way of successful use of a social skill. Remind students not to become discouraged if use of their social skills does not always turn out right. Suggest to students that when a roadblock occurs, they may need to take a "detour" rather than give up. Make students aware that a roadblock situation is an opportunity for them to use the SO step of STOP, PLOT, GO, SO. They could ask themselves questions such as how they did, what might have gone wrong, and how the roadblock could be dealt with in a more positive way next time. Examples of _____ roadblocks are described in Lesson Z within each specific social skill unit. Give students the opportunity to think of additional roadblocks that may occur.

9. Distribute the ____ *Home-A-Gram* and a ____ badge to each student. Have students complete the *Home-A-Gram* as directed (see page 23).

10. Point to the *Social Super Stars* display. Remind students that their badges will be added to the display once they are brought back signed.

11. Distribute the completed ____ *Show Time* signs and ask students to hang them in the predetermined location(s).

Appendix B

Social Communication Skills Rating Scale

(Adult Form—Peer Interaction Skills)

Name of Student: _____ Grade: _____

Age: _____ Date rating scale completed: _____

Name of person completing rating scale: _____

Relationship with student (e.g., parent, case manager, regular education teacher):

_____

DIRECTIONS: Rate this student on how well he or she uses the following social skills. Circle:

    1—if the skill is **SELDOM** used correctly.

    2—if the skill is **SOMETIMES** used correctly.

    3—if the skill is **ALMOST ALWAYS** used correctly.

For example, a student who rarely plays with other students would be rated as follows:

    PLAYING COOPERATIVELY—Plays in a way that invites   ①   2   3
    everyone to have fun.

Please give examples or comments when appropriate (e.g., if you give a low rating for playing cooperatively, explain if the student plays alone, or doesn't share when playing, etc.).

RATING

SOCIAL COMMUNICATION SKILL	SELDOM	SOMETIMES	ALMOST ALWAYS
1. OPTIMISM—Words and actions indicate he/she has mostly positive thoughts. Comments:	1	2	3

© 1994 Thinking Publications   408   *Duplication permitted for educational use only.*

Appendix B: Social Communication Skills Rating Scale

RATING

SOCIAL COMMUNICATION SKILL	SELDOM	SOMETIMES	ALMOST ALWAYS
2. PLAYING COOPERATIVELY—Plays in a way that invites everyone to have fun. Comments:	1	2	3
3. RESPECTING DIFFERENCES—Understands that we are all unique and equally important. Comments:	1	2	3
4. BEING A FRIEND—Chooses word and actions that show someone he/she cares. Comments:	1	2	3
5. GIVING AND RECEIVING COMPLIMENTS—Says nice things to other people and says "Thank you" when someone says something nice about him/her. Comments:	1	2	3
6. BUILDING A POSITIVE REPUTATION—Makes responsible choices that invite others to have positive thoughts about him/her. Comments:	1	2	3

Social Star

RATING

SOCIAL COMMUNICATION SKILL	SELDOM	SOMETIMES	ALMOST ALWAYS
7. DEALING WITH TEASING—Knows that mean teasing is not OK and uses positive strategies to stop the teasing cycle. Comments:	1	2	3
8. GETTING INTO A GROUP—Shows a willingness to work with whoever is in the group and moves quickly and quietly. Comments:	1	2	3
9. GIVING PUT-UPS—Invites all members to feel positive when working in a group. Comments:	1	2	3
10. PARTICIPATING—Knows how to do his/her share when working in a group. Comments:	1	2	3
11. STAYING ON TASK—Gives her/his full attention when working in a group. Comments:	1	2	3
12. DISAGREEING POLITELY—Disagrees without giving put-downs. Comments:	1	2	3

Appendix C

Student Social Skill Summary Form

Social Star

STUDENT'S NAME:	Identified as a strength	Identified as problematic	Skill has been taught in class		
1. Optimism					
2. Playing Cooperatively					
3. Respecting Differences					
4. Being a Friend					
5. Giving and Receiving Compliments					
6. Building a Positive Reputation					
7. Dealing with Teasing					
8. Getting into a Group					
9. Giving Put-ups					
10. Participating					
11. Staying on Task					
12. Disagreeing Politely					

© 1994 Thinking Publications *Duplication permitted for educational use only.*

Appendix D

Class Summary Form

Social Star

Mark social skills identified as strengths with a "+" and those identified as problematic with a "–".

SOCIAL SKILLS:	STUDENTS' NAMES									
1. Optimism										
2. Playing Cooperatively										
3. Respecting Differences										
4. Being a Friend										
5. Giving and Receiving Compliments										
6. Building a Positive Reputation										
7. Dealing with Teasing										
8. Getting into a Group										
9. Giving Put-ups										
10. Participating										
11. Staying on Task										
12. Disagreeing Politely										

Appendix E

Socialville Buildings

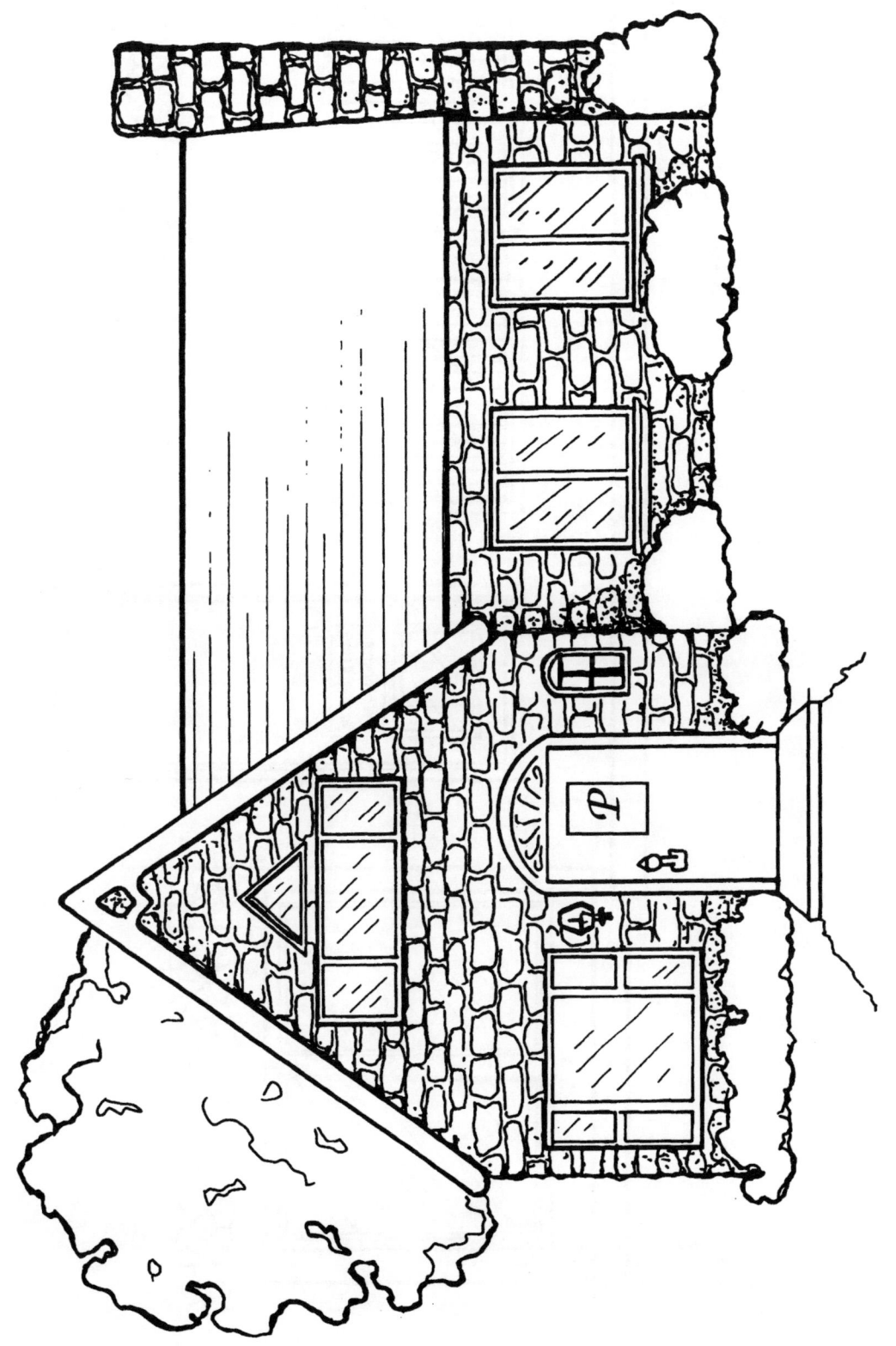

© 1994 Thinking Publications   413   *Duplication permitted for educational use only.*

Social Star

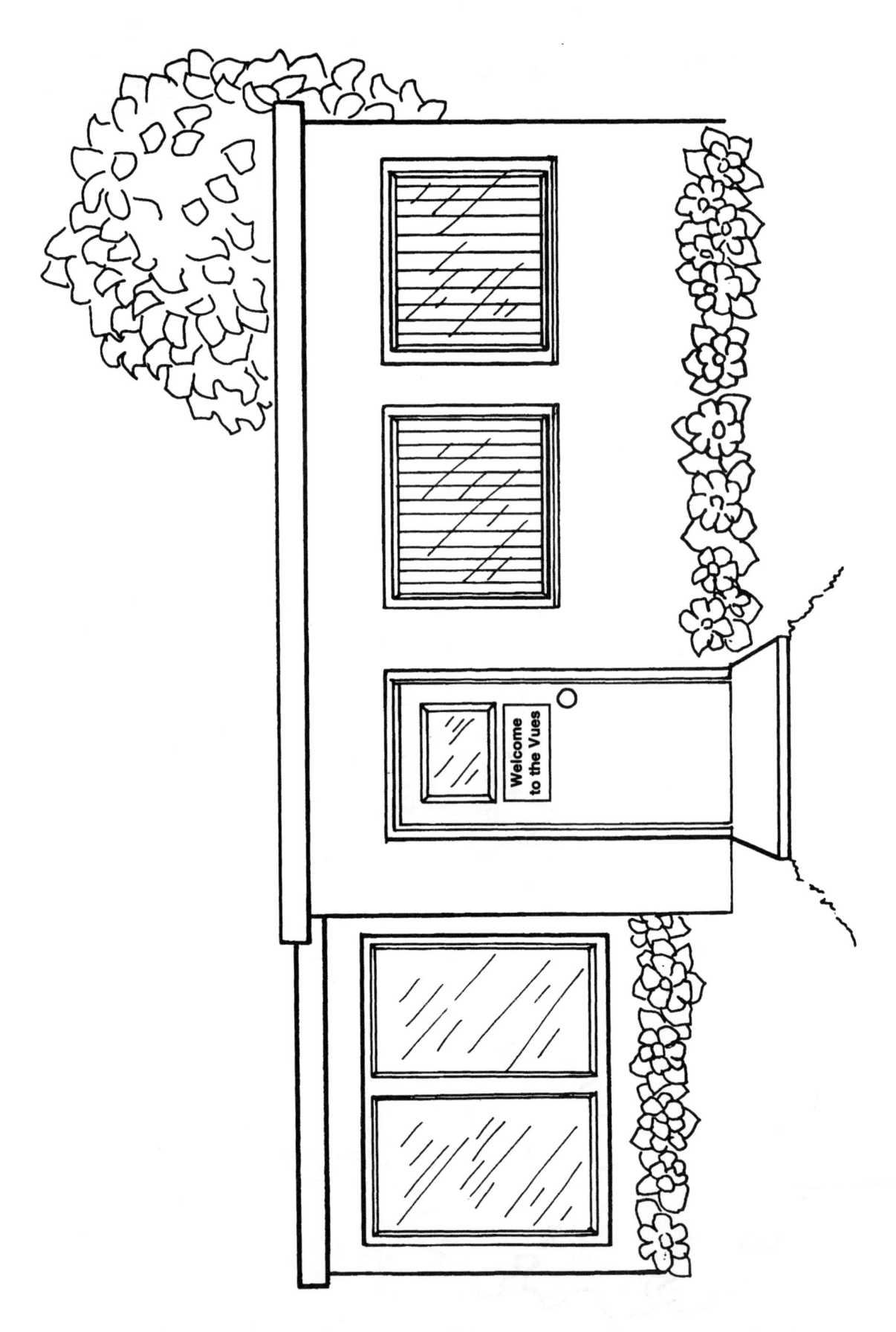

Welcome to the Vues

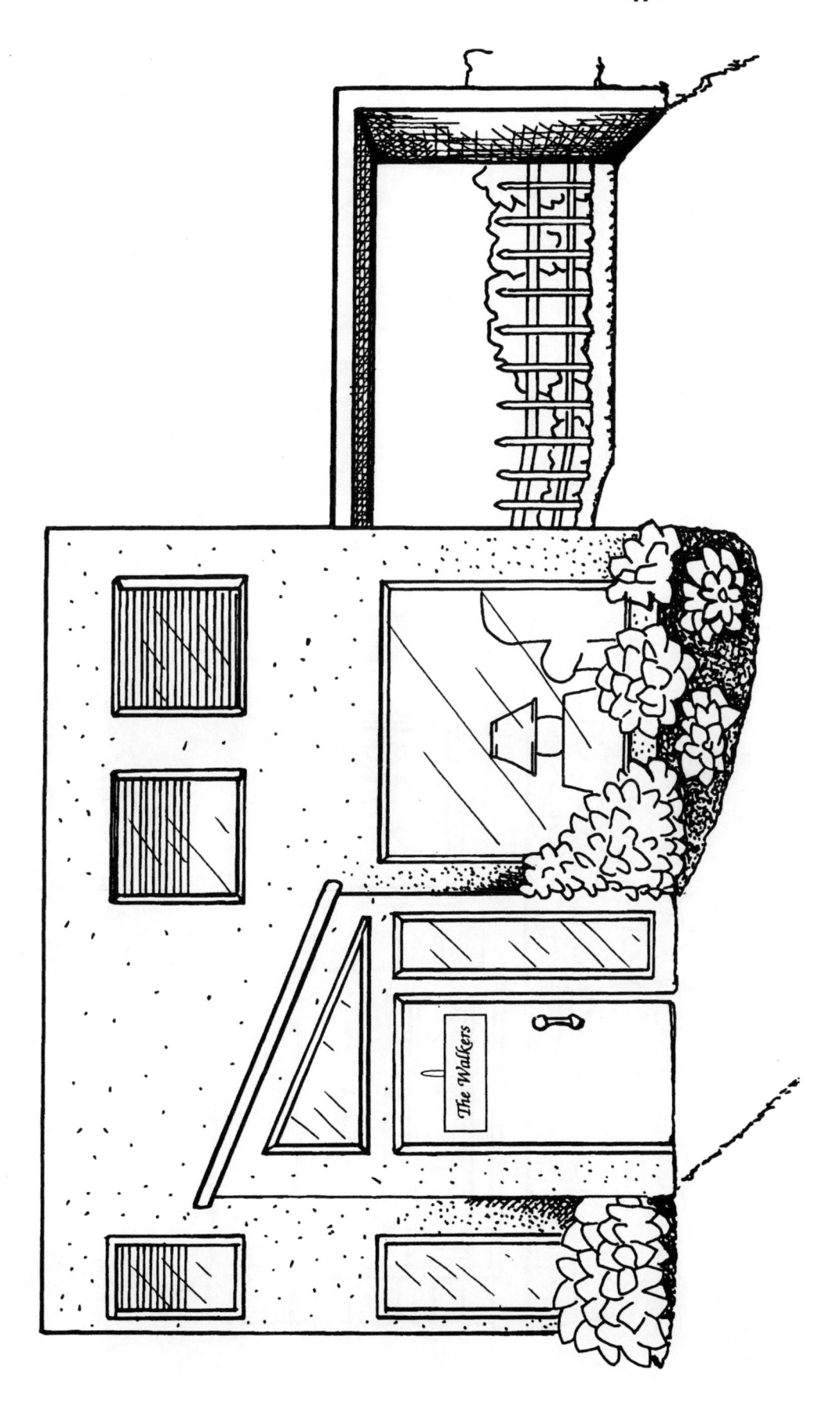

Appendix E: Socialville Buildings

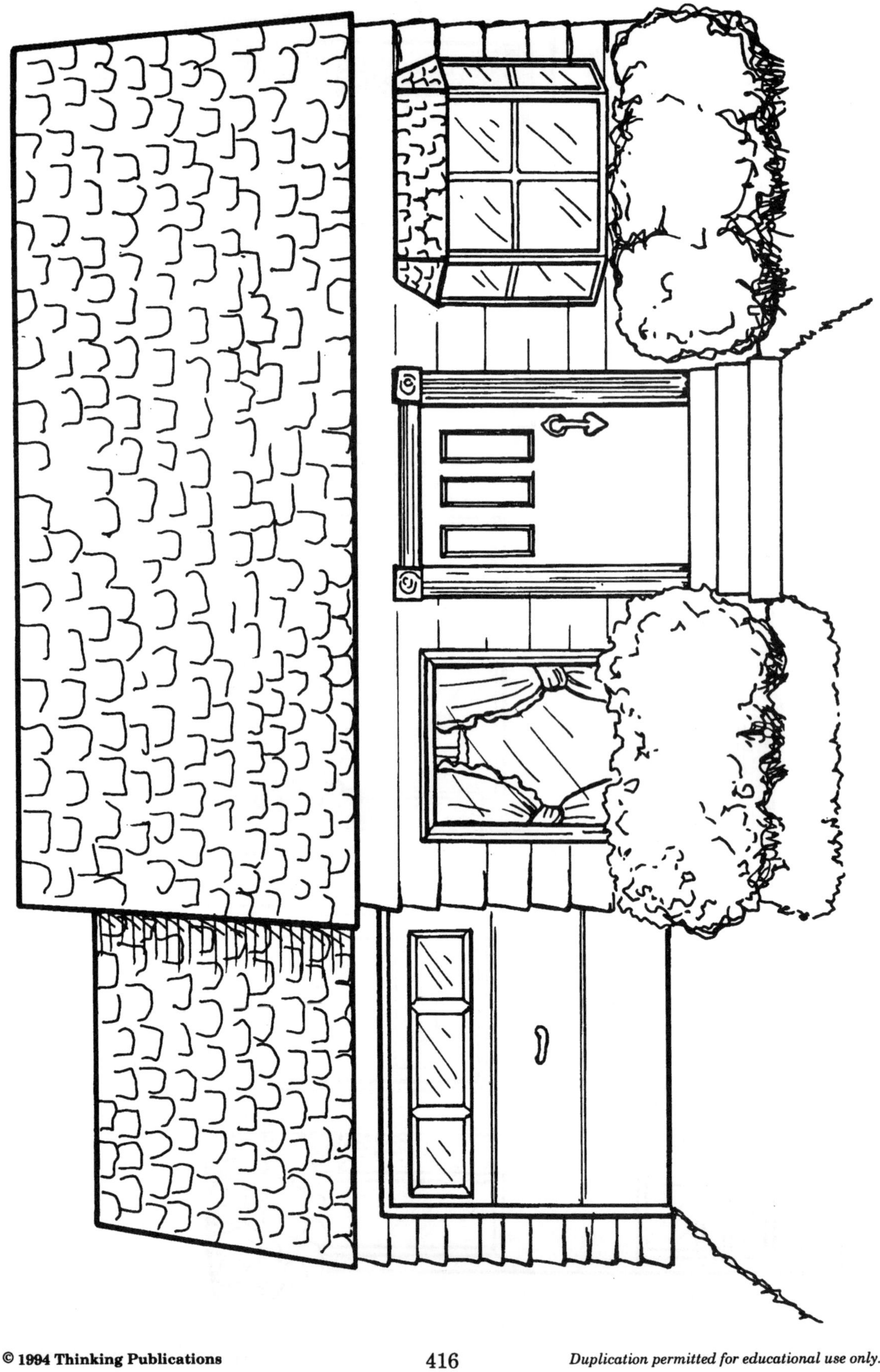

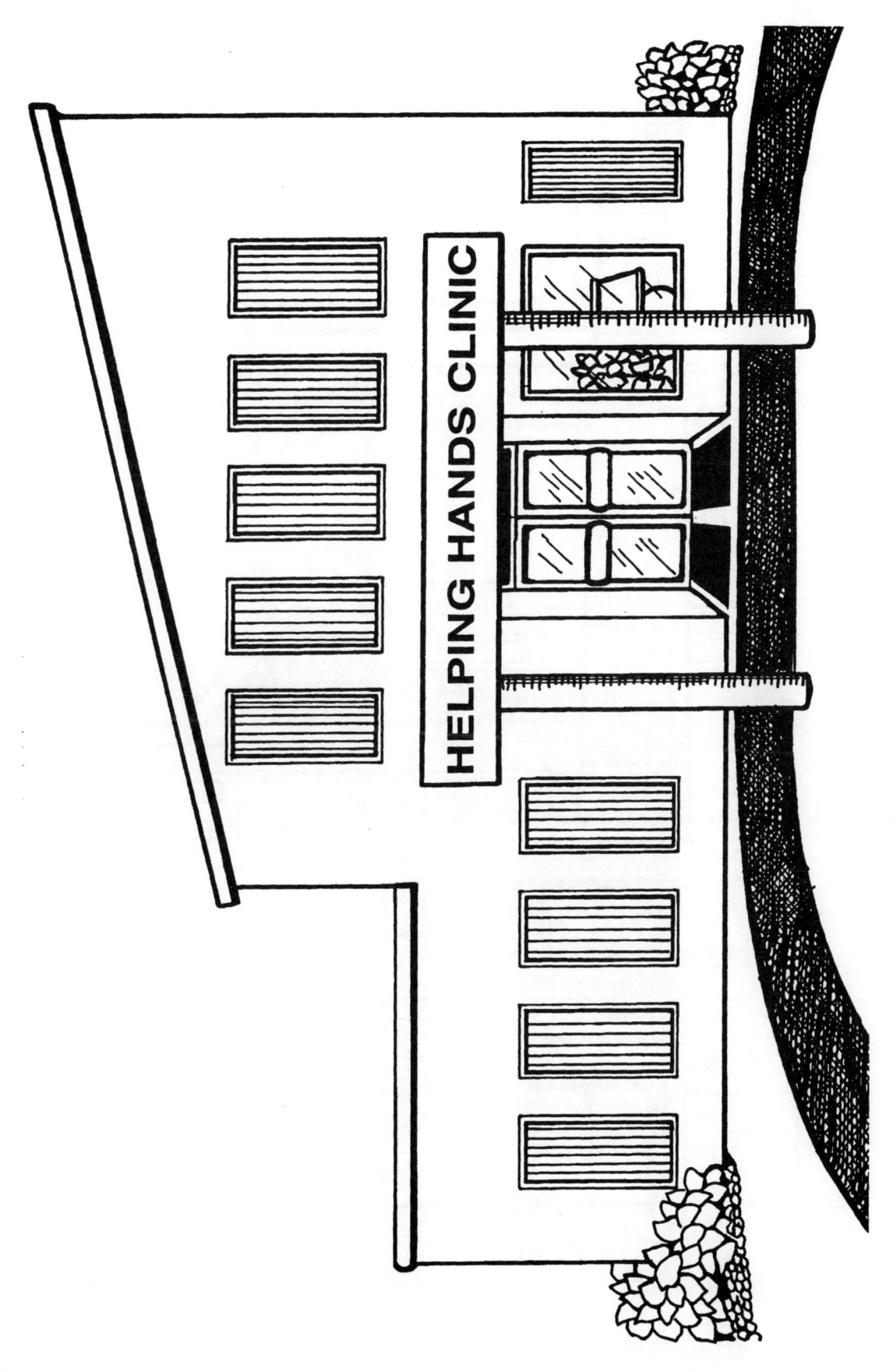

Appendix E: Socialville Buildings

HELPING HANDS CLINIC

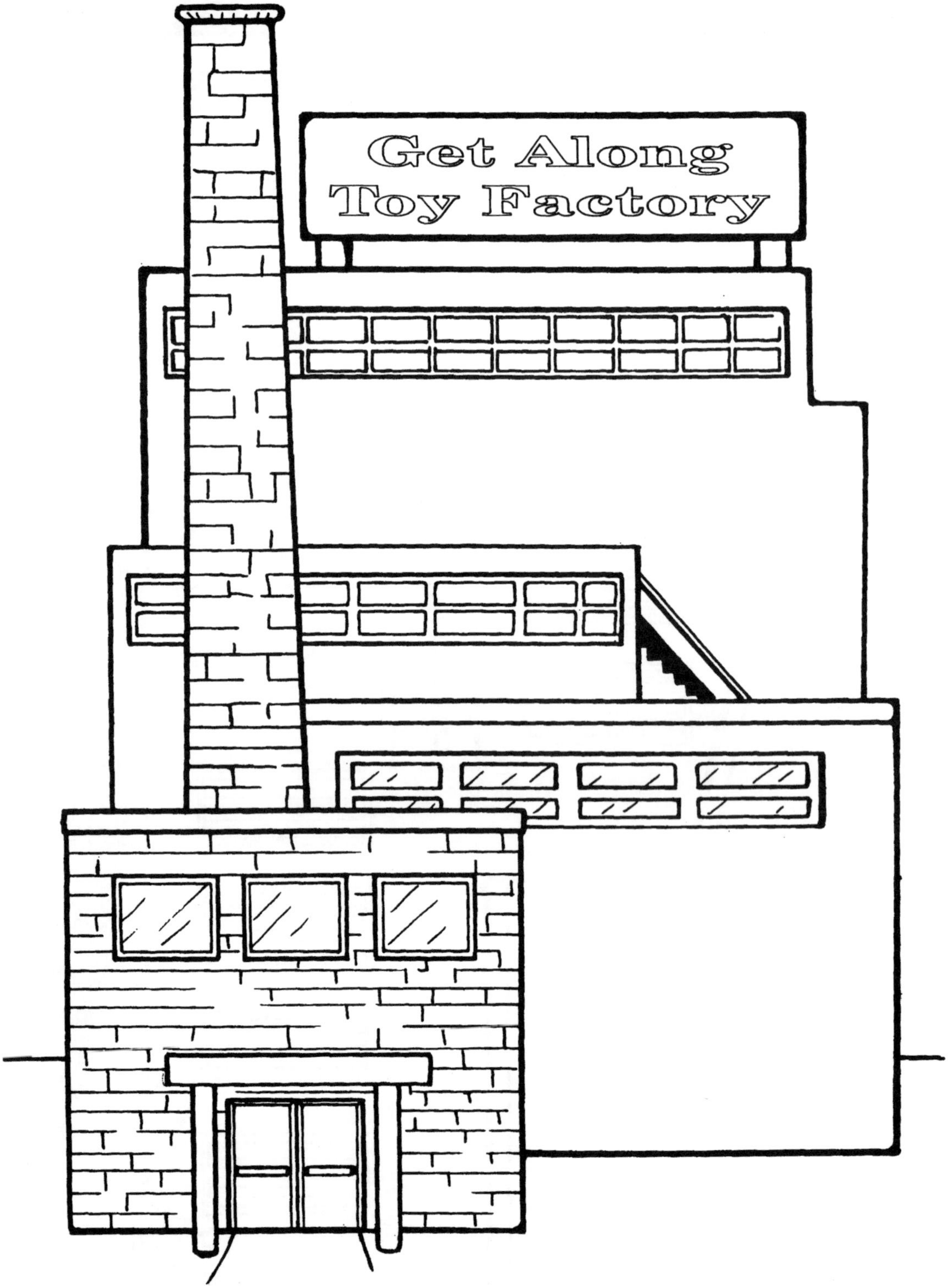
Get Along
Toy Factory

Appendix E: Socialville Buildings

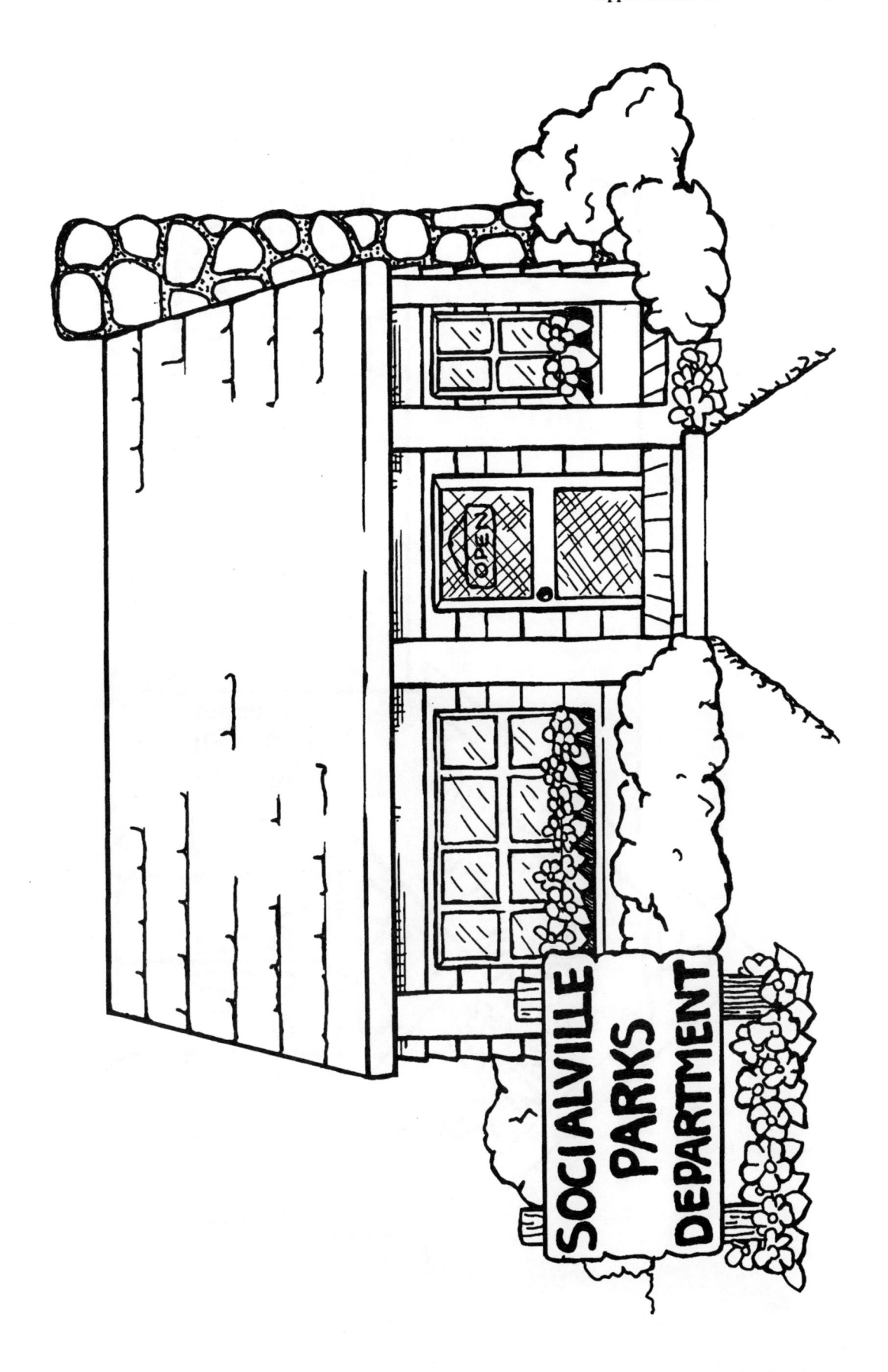

SOCIALVILLE PARKS DEPARTMENT

© 1994 Thinking Publications 419 *Duplication permitted for educationa*

Social Star

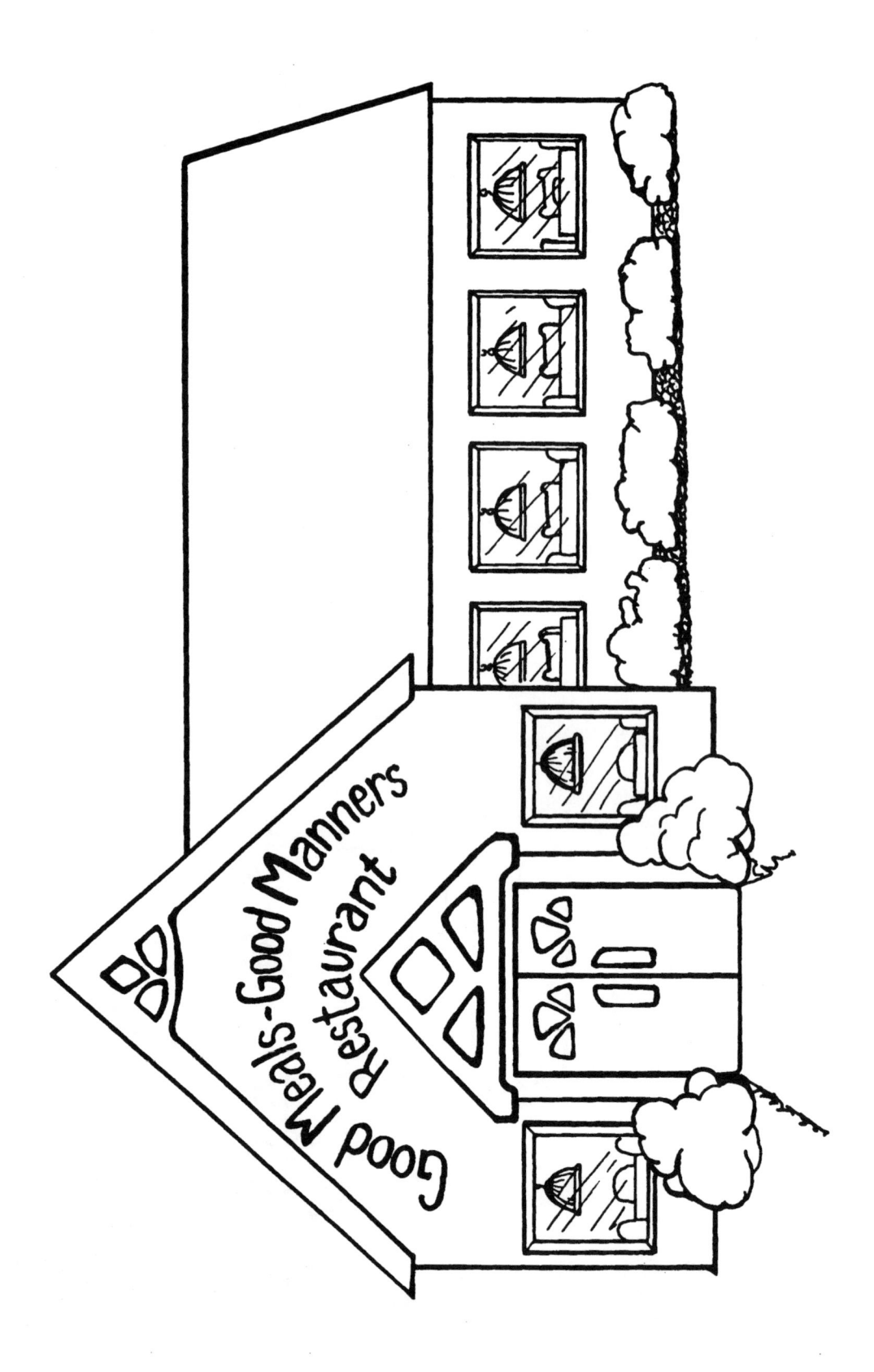

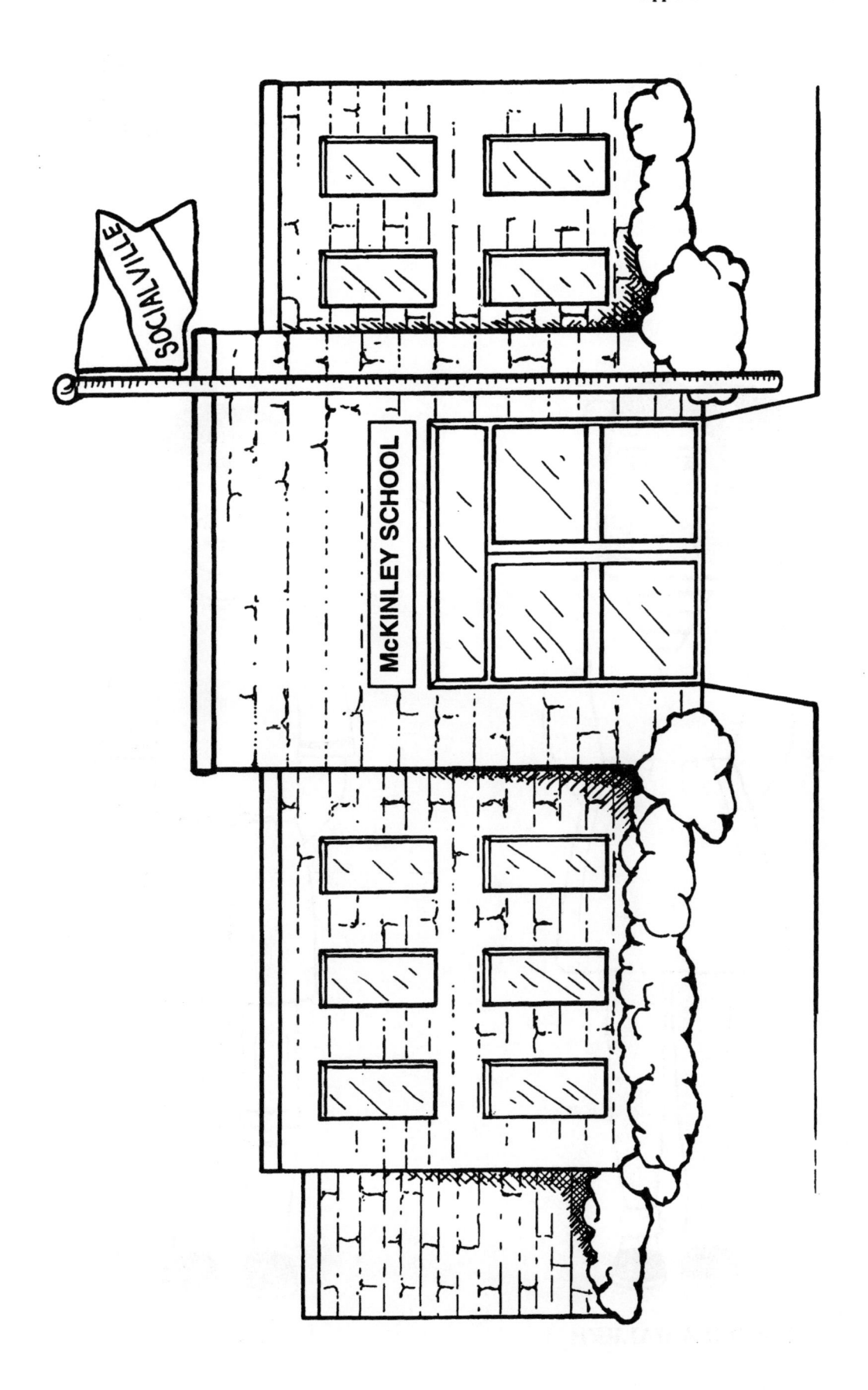

Appendix E: Socialville Buildings

Appendix F

Socialville Characters

Social Star

JOLISA WALKER

LEE VUE

© 1994 Thinking Publications *Duplication permitted for educational use only.*

Appendix F: Socialville Characters

JESSE WALKER

CORIN WALKER

Social Star

MIKA VUE   **HO VUE**

Appendix F: Socialville Characters

JOE JACKSON **MARY JACKSON**

© 1994 Thinking Publications   425   *Duplication permitted for educational use only.*

Social Star

ANN OLSON 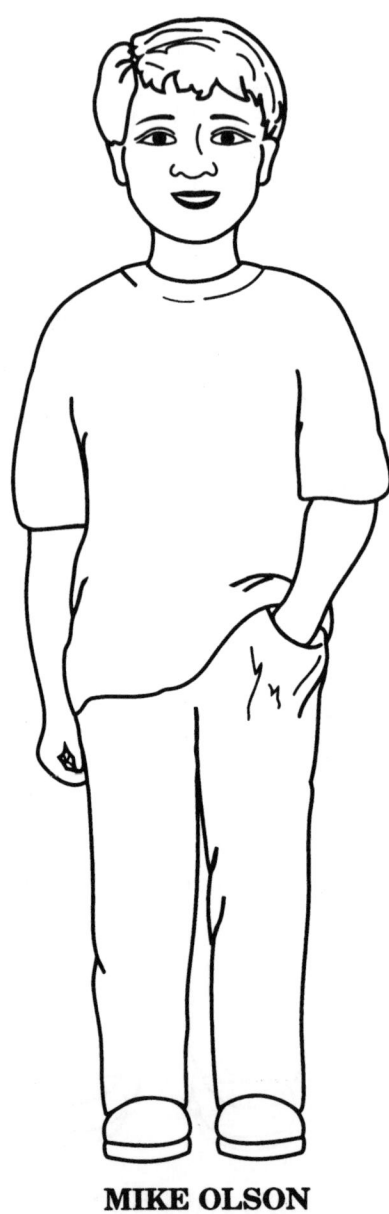　　　　　　　**MIKE OLSON**

© 1994 Thinking Publications　　　426　　　*Duplication permitted for educational use only.*

Appendix F: Socialville Characters

RICARDO PARRA

DR. JUANITA PARRA

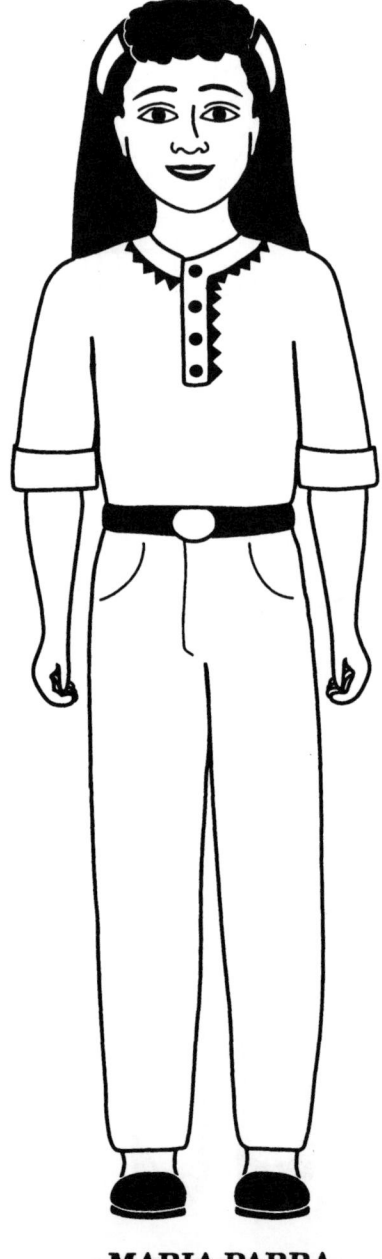

Social Star

MARIA PARRA  **VICTOR PARRA**

© 1994 Thinking Publications *Duplication permitted for educational use only.*

Appendix F: Socialville Characters

MRS. CORA MARRERO

MR. MARCUS AARON

© 1994 Thinking Publications *Duplication permitted for educational use only.*

Social Star

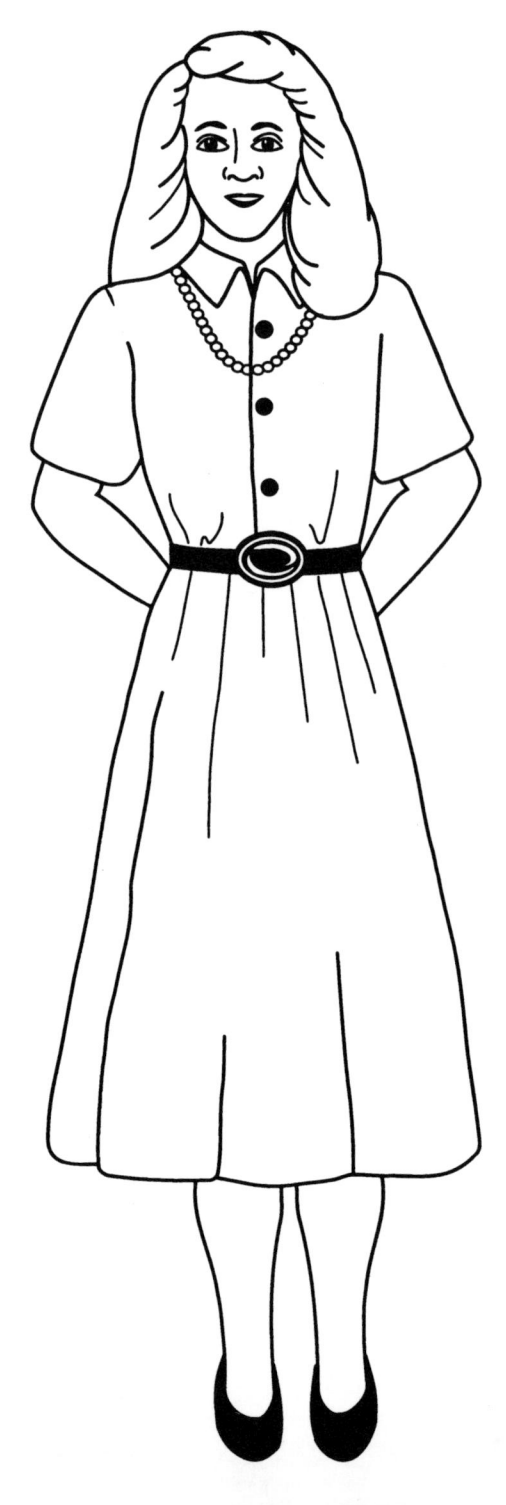

MS. PAULA HESS

© 1994 Thinking Publications　　　430　　　*Duplication permitted for educational use only.*

Appendix G

Parent Letter

Social Star

Dear

Your child will be participating in a social skills class. The purpose of the class is to teach children social skills which will help them get along better with others and to feel better about themselves. A list of social skills that will be taught during class is attached.

Each social skill taught is broken down into small steps with symbols to make them easier to learn. For example, the social skill of *playing cooperatively* has the following skill step and symbol:

1. Ask myself: How can I play cooperatively?

During class, your child will participate in a variety of activities that teach and provide practice for each social skill. In addition to these activities, it is critical that the skills be practiced in other settings including at home.

At the end of each social skill unit, your child will be bringing home a note called a *Home-A-Gram* and a *Social Super Star* badge. The *Home-A-Gram* will provide you with information about the skill. It will also describe an activity related to the skill for your child to complete at home with your participation and supervision. When the activity is successfully completed, please sign the *Social Super Star* badge and have your child return it to school. Returned badges will be displayed in the classroom.

I look forward to working together with you to expand your child's skills for getting along with others. If you would like further information about the class, please contact me any time. In addition, if you have any questions, concerns, or suggestions, I will be glad to discuss them with you.

Sincerely,

© 1994 Thinking Publications — Duplication permitted for educational use only.

Appendix H

Self-Management Sheets

Social Star

EDUCATOR DIRECTIONS: Fill in the name of a social skill and a description of the time during which it is to be evaluated (e.g., during science, during free time, during lunch) before making copies for student use.

DIRECTIONS: Rate yourself. Circle either "great," "OK," or "needs improvement." Write your comments if you want. Ask your teacher to rate you too.

SOCIAL SKILL	MY RATING	THE TEACHER'S RATING
_____ **EVALUATED DURING:** _____	GREAT OK NEEDS IMPROVEMENT Comments: _____ _____ _____ _____	GREAT OK NEEDS IMPROVEMENT Comments: _____ _____ _____ _____ _____ *Teacher's Signature*

© 1994 Thinking Publications — Duplication permitted for educational use only.

Appendix H: Self-Management Sheets

EDUCATOR DIRECTIONS: Fill in the name of a social skill and a description of the time during which it is to be evaluated (e.g., during a meal, while playing with friends) before making copies for student use. Send the self-management sheet home with the student. Attach any necessary information for the students' parent(s) concerning use of the sheet.

DIRECTIONS: Rate yourself. Circle either "great," "OK," or "needs improvement." Write your comments if you want. Ask a parent to rate you too.

SOCIAL SKILL	MY RATING	THE PARENT'S RATING
_____ **EVALUATED DURING:** _____ _____	GREAT OK NEEDS IMPROVEMENT Comments: _____ _____ _____ _____	GREAT OK NEEDS IMPROVEMENT Comments: _____ _____ _____ _____ _____ *Parent's Signature*

© 1994 Thinking Publications   433   *Duplication permitted for educational use only.*

Social Star

EDUCATOR DIRECTIONS: Before making student copies of either self-management sheet below, fill in where you want them to be turned in (e.g., on your desk, in a box, in your hand). Write the name of a specific social skill on the blank line or let the students write the name of any social skill they want to tell you about.

DIRECTIONS: Write your name below. Put this sheet _____ _____. As soon as possible, I'll come and ask you to tell me all about it.

Hey! I want to tell you about when I correctly used the social skill of:

_____

_____
NAME

DIRECTIONS: Write your name below. Put this sheet _____ _____. As soon as possible, I'll come and ask you to tell me all about it.

Just wait till you hear! I did a great job with:

_____

_____
NAME

© 1994 Thinking Publications · 434 · *Duplication permitted for educational use only.*

Appendix H: Self-Management Sheets

EDUCATOR DIRECTIONS: Fill in the name of a social skill and its skill step(s) on either self-management sheet below before making copies for student use.

DIRECTIONS: Draw a smile on one of the faces each time you use this social skill correctly. Then, IN YOUR MIND shout "Good Job!"

SOCIAL SKILL OF:
_____

SKILL STEP(S):
_____
_____
_____
_____

NAME

DIRECTIONS: Mark a Social Star each time you use this social skill correctly. Then, picture yourself jumping up and down cheering for yourself.

SOCIAL SKILL OF:
_____

SKILL STEP(S):
_____
_____
_____
_____

NAME

© 1994 Thinking Publications *Duplication permitted for educational use only.*

Social Star

EDUCATOR DIRECTIONS: Before copying either self-management sheet below for student use, fill in the name of a social skill, or let students write the name of any social skill they have previously learned about.

DIRECTIONS: Fill in the blanks.

Great Job!

I did a great job using the social skill of:

_____

When: _____

Who with: _____

I praised myself by: _____

_____

_____ _____

NAME

DIRECTIONS: Fill in the blanks.

I used the social skill of:

_____

When: _____

Who with: _____

So? How did I do? _____

_____

_____

Socialville

_____

NAME

© 1994 Thinking Publications   *Duplication permitted for educational use only.*

Appendix H: Self-Management Sheets

EDUCATOR DIRECTIONS: Fill in the name of a social skill and its skill step(s) on either self-management sheet below before making copies for student use.

DIRECTIONS: Each time you do a good job using this social skill, circle the next number below. (Start with 1.)

Social Skill: _____

Skill Step(s): _____

_____

_____

NAME

1 2 3 4 5 6 7 8 9 10 11 12

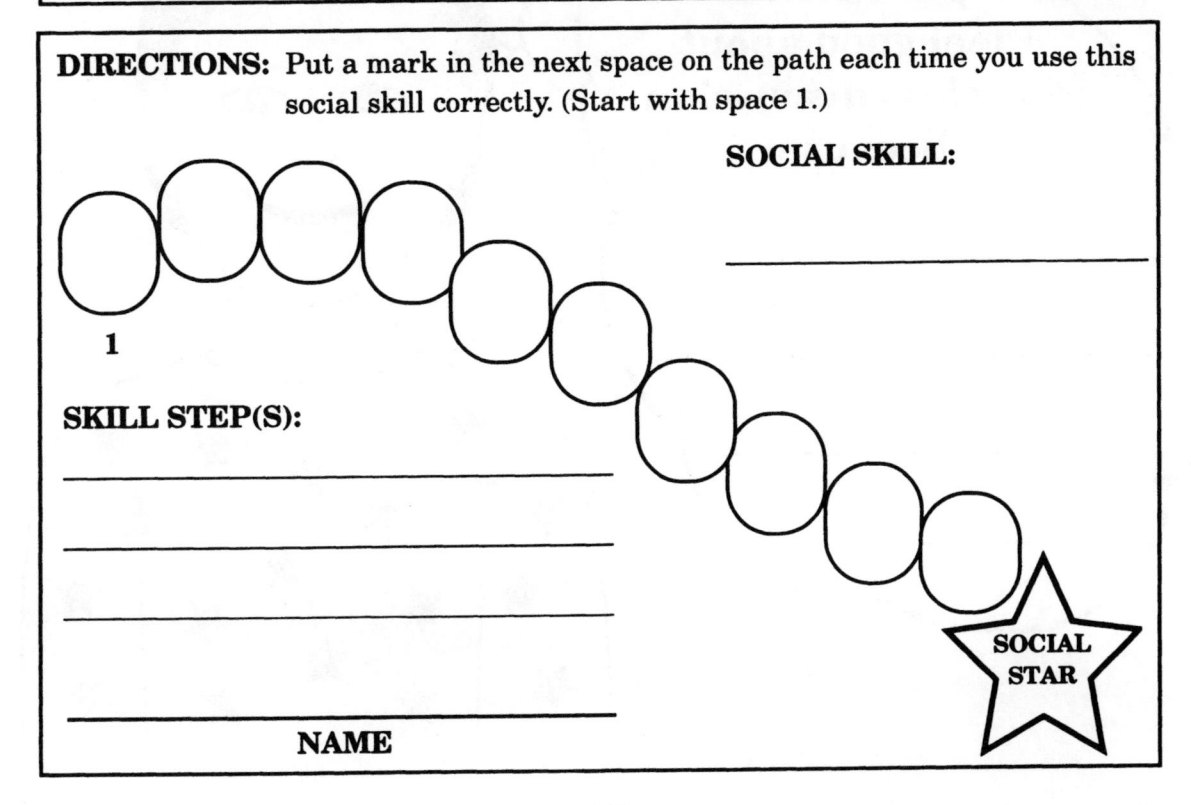

DIRECTIONS: Put a mark in the next space on the path each time you use this social skill correctly. (Start with space 1.)

SOCIAL SKILL:

_____

1

SKILL STEP(S):

_____

_____

_____

_____

NAME

SOCIAL STAR

© 1994 Thinking Publications   437   *Duplication permitted for educational use only.*

Appendix I

Checking Myself

Social Star

Name _____

During this class discussion I will:

_____
_____
_____
_____

I feel good about our class discussion because:

_____
_____
_____

© 1994 Thinking Publications — Duplication permitted for educational use only.

Appendix J

Social Gram

Social Star

SOCIAL GRAM

_____,

you did a great job using the social skill of

_____

when _____

_____

_____

_____

_____
Signature

© 1994 Thinking Publications *Duplication permitted for educational use only.*

Appendix K

Great Coupon Caper

Social Star

★ **COUPON** ★

NAME: _____

REASONS: _____

_____

_____

_____
Signature

★ **COUPON** ★

NAME: _____

REASONS: _____

_____

_____

_____
Signature

★ **COUPON** ★

NAME: _____

REASONS: _____

_____

_____

_____
Signature

★ **COUPON** ★

NAME: _____

REASONS: _____

_____

_____

_____
Signature

★ **COUPON** ★

NAME: _____

REASONS: _____

_____

_____

_____
Signature

★ **COUPON** ★

NAME: _____

REASONS: _____

_____

_____

_____
Signature

© 1994 Thinking Publications — *Duplication permitted for educational use only.*

Appendix L

Blank T-Chart

Social Star

Social Skill: _____

| LOOKS LIKE... | SOUNDS LIKE... |

Appendix M

Relaxation Scripts

Social Star

RELAXATION SCRIPT FOR YOUNG CHILDREN

MATERIALS:

One sponge (or piece of a sponge) for each child

PLAN:

Pass out a sponge to each child. Say the following to students in a slow, calm manner.

1. Look at the sponge you have in your hands. Take the sponge and scrunch it up tight like mine. (Show the scrunched up sponge.)
2. Now, let go of your sponge very slowly. See how the sponge opens back up.
3. Try it again. Squeeze your sponge tightly. Now let go slowly.
4. Now I'd like to collect your sponges. (Collect sponges.)
5. Pretend that you are a sponge. Scrunch up your body tightly. Hold it.
6. Let your body out slowly just like when you let go of the sponge.
7. Your body should feel relaxed.
8. Try it again. Scrunch up your body. Take a deep breath.
9. Now, slowly let your body relax. Feel how nice your body feels.
10. Sometimes when you get angry, your body tightens up. You can act like a sponge and relax your body. This will help you stay in control.

A good resource for other relaxation activities is *Lazy Dogs and Sleeping Frogs* (1988) by Darrel Lang and Bill Stinson, Coulee Press, LaCrosse, WI.

PROGRESSIVE RELAXATION SCRIPT FOR OLDER CHILDREN

MATERIALS:

None

PLAN:

The following script should be read in a slow, calm manner:

1. We are going to learn a way to relax our bodies. When we keep our bodies relaxed, it is easier to have self-control.
2. Sit in your chair with your feet flat on the floor. Let your arms hang loosely at your sides.

3. You may close your eyes if you wish.
4. Take a slow, deep breath. Breathe in, two, three and out, two, three. In, two, three and out, two, three.
5. Keep breathing deeply and slowly.
6. Make your hands into tight fists. Keep making tight fists. (Pause for a few seconds.)
7. Now slowly open your hands again. You are teaching your muscles how to relax.
8. Now tighten your arms and your hands. Keep them tight. (Pause for a few seconds.)
9. Slowly relax your hands and then your arms.
10. Keep breathing deeply and slowly.
11. Now tighten your feet. Keep them tight. (Pause for a few seconds.)
12. Slowly relax your feet.
13. Now tighten your feet and your legs. Keep them tight. (Pause for a few seconds.)
14. Slowly relax your feet and legs.
15. Let's move up your body to your neck and face.
16. Scrunch up your face real tight. Keep it scrunched. (Pause for a few seconds.)
17. Let the muscles in your face slowly relax.
18. Keep breathing deeply and slowly.
19. Let your head slowly tilt forward so that your chin almost touches your chest.
20. Now slowly bring your head back up.
21. Let your head slowly tilt backward.
22. Slowly bring your head back up.
23. Tilt your head slowly from shoulder to shoulder. (Pause a few seconds.)
24. Take a slow, deep breath. Breath in, two, three, and out, two, three.
25. Just sit quietly for a few seconds. Think about how relaxed your body feels. (Pause for five to ten seconds.)
26. You can use this way of relaxing whenever you want. Remember, people who are more relaxed have better self-control.

Appendix N

Secret Formula Pages

Social Star

Name _____

★ ★ SECRET FORMULA ★ ★

STOP

I can stay calm by:
_____
_____
_____
_____

PLOT

My problem is: _____
_____

Choices: Consequences:
1. _____ → _____
2. _____ → _____
3. _____ → _____

My choice: _____
_____

Social skills I need: _____
_____

GO

What I can say or do so I actually use my plan:
_____
_____
_____

SO

How did my plan work?
_____
_____
_____

© 1994 Thinking Publications   444   *Duplication permitted for educational use only.*

Appendix N: Secret Formula Pages

Name _____

★★★★ SECRET FORMULA ★★★★

STOP

I stayed calm by:
_____
_____
_____
_____

PLOT

My problem was: _____
_____

Choices: Consequences:
1. _____ → _____
2. _____ → _____
3. _____ → _____

My choice was: _____
_____

Social skills I needed: _____
_____

GO

What I said or did so I actually used my plan:
_____
_____
_____
_____

SO

How did my plan work?
_____
_____
_____
_____

© 1994 Thinking Publications — *Duplication permitted for educational use only.*

Appendix O

Thought Bubble

Social Star

Appendix P

Pairing Activities

Social Star

Pairing activities are fun activities for getting students into pairs. These activities increase the amount of socialization students do while learning new social skills. (Students cannot practice newly learned social skills if they are continually working by themselves.)

Each unit in *Social Star* includes several opportunities for students to work in pairs. Sometimes a specific pairing activity is suggested and other times the educator is asked to choose a pairing activity from the list that follows (or to develop a new one). Some of the pairing activities require prior preparation (e.g., copying, laminating, cutting). These materials are meant to be reused.

The pairing activities often require that students mingle and communicate with one another while forming pairs. Learning to work with several different people, despite personal preferences, is a critical skill. Before using pairing activities in the classroom, discuss with the students that the partner they work with may or may not be someone they were hoping for. Explain that they will be working with a variety of partners in class and that they need to cooperate and respect individual differences while working together. Students must learn to use body language that doesn't show disappointment. You may wish to demonstrate the body language (e.g., facial expression, voice tone, posture, proximity) students could use when they find their partners. It is helpful to demonstrate this in a humorous, exaggerated manner (e.g., use a huge smile, shake hands, say, "I'm so glad to be your partner").

SHOE MATCH

Have students remove one shoe and place it on a pile. Hold up two shoes from the pile. Have the owners retrieve their shoes and become partners.

ANIMAL SOUNDS

Before this is used, duplicate two copies of the *Animal Cards* (see page 450). Choose one pair of animal cards for every two students (e.g., two pigs, two cows). Distribute one animal card to each person. Have students walk around the room and make the animal sounds on their cards. When they find another student making the same animal sound, have them become partners. For a variation, have students close their eyes during this activity.

LINE UP–FOLD UP

Ask students to cooperatively form a line in a specific order (e.g., according to the months of their birthdays, the first letters of their first or last names, their heights). After telling students the chosen criteria for forming a line, have them interact and line up. Give minimal assistance. As a variation, instruct the students not to talk and thus to find alternative methods of communicating with one another. After the students have formed a line, have the line fold up. Have the two students at opposite ends become partners. Ask the students who are second from each end to become partners and so on towards the center of the line.

PICTURE PUZZLE

Before this activity is used, choose a variety of pictures. (These pictures can be drawn by students or cut from magazines.) Cut the pictures in half in "puzzle-piece" fashion. Choose one set of puzzle pieces for every two students. Give each student one puzzle piece. Have students find partners by locating other students whose puzzle pieces match theirs.

INSIDE-OUTSIDE CIRCLE

Ask half of the group to form a circle. Have the remaining students form an outside circle around the first circle. Tell the students to rotate in their circles in opposite directions until they are instructed to "stop." The inside circle should then face outward and the outside circle should face inward so that the students are looking at one another. Have the students be partners with the person each one is facing.

PICK-A-CARD ANY CARD

Write the name of each student on a separate card. Choose the top card, read the person's name, and ask that person to draw a card from the deck. Have the person named on the card chosen be the partner. Proceed in this manner until each student has a partner.

OPPOSITES MATCH

Before this activity is used, duplicate *Opposites Match—A* and *B* (see pages 451–452). Choose one pair of opposite cards for every two students (e.g., black/white, short/tall). Give one card to each student. Have each student find a partner by locating the person who has a card with a picture that is the opposite of the student's picture.

GO TOGETHER CARDS

Before this activity is used, duplicate *Go Together Cards—A* and *B* (see pages 453–454). Choose one pair of *Go Together Cards* for every two students (e.g., fishbowl/fish, beach/beach ball). Give one card to each student. Have students find their partner by locating the person who has a card that "goes together" with theirs. You may choose to make additional sets of matching cards related to concepts in the classroom. For example, matching states with state capitals, lowercase with uppercase letters, clock faces with numbered times, coins with numbered values, faces of famous men or women with descriptions of their accomplishments, song titles and composers.

NUMBERED STONES

Before this activity is used, gather one stone for each student. On each pair of rocks write the same number (e.g., two rocks would have the number one, two rocks would have the number two). Choose one pair of rocks for every two students and place the rocks in a bag. Ask each student to draw a rock from the bag. When all of the rocks are distributed, have the students find their partners by looking for the rock number that matches.

CARD MATCH

Using a deck of playing cards, choose one matching pair of cards for every two students (e.g., two fours, two kings). Give a card to each student. Have the students find their partners by locating the card number that matches.

Social Star

ANIMAL CARDS

BEES "Buzz-z-z-z"	BIRD "Tweet-tweet"	CAT "Meow"	COW "Mooo"
DOG "Woof-woof"	DONKEY "Hee-haw"	DUCK "Quack-quack"	FROG "Ribbit"
HORSE "Neigh"	LION "Roar"	OWL "Whoo"	PIG "Oink"
SHEEP "Baa"	SNAKE "S-s-s-s"	ROOSTER "Cock-a-doodle-do"	TURKEY "Gobble-gobble"

Duplication permitted for educational use only.
© 1994 Thinking Publications

Appendix P: Pairing Activities

OPPOSITES MATCH—A

NEAR	COLD	BOY	DOWN
OUT	SHORT	WHITE	NARROW
QUIET	SLOW	HARD	DECORATED
UNDER	SUMMER	SMOOTH	FULL

Social Star

OPPOSITES MATCH—B

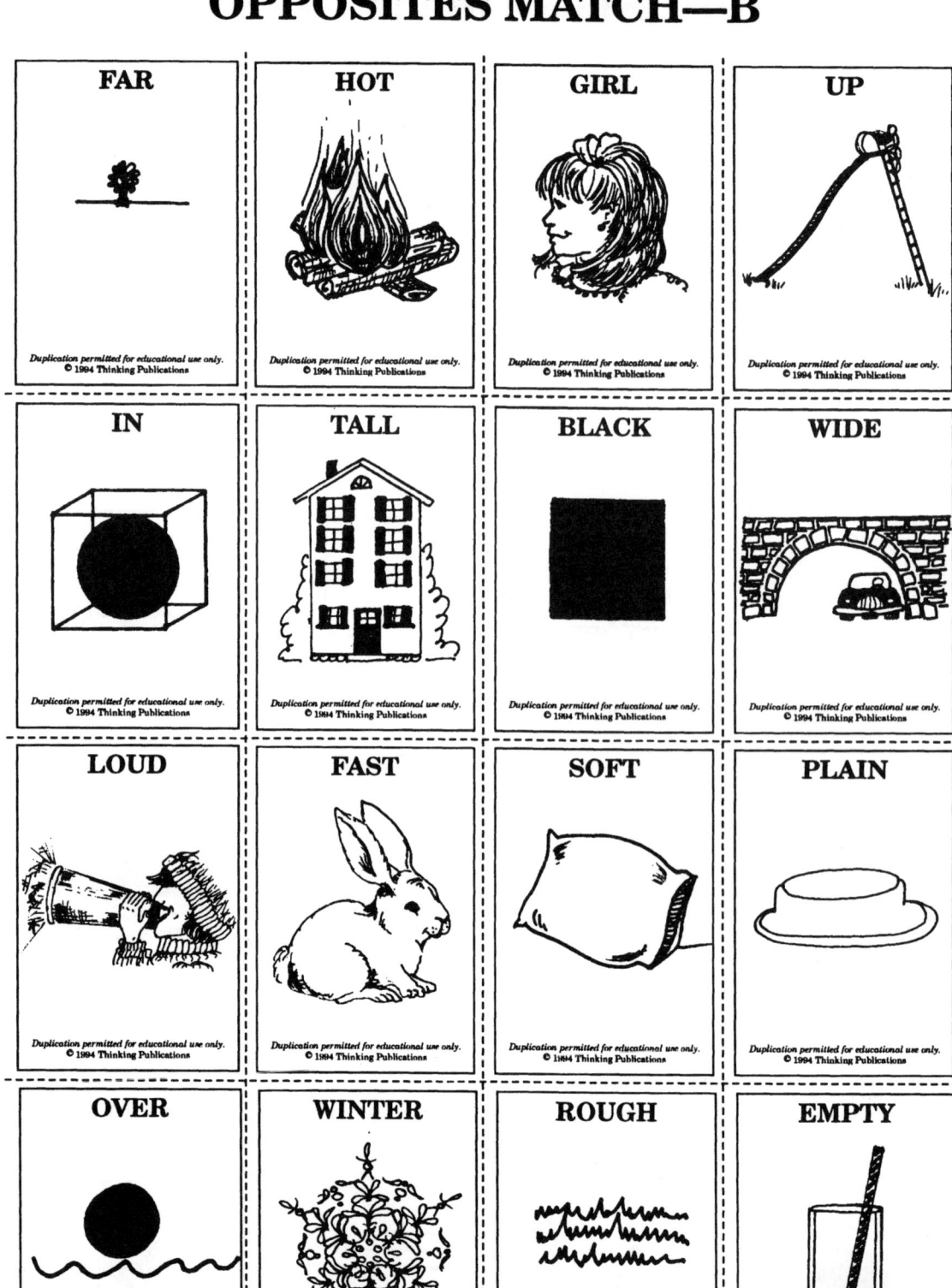

FAR	HOT	GIRL	UP
IN	TALL	BLACK	WIDE
LOUD	FAST	SOFT	PLAIN
OVER	WINTER	ROUGH	EMPTY

452

Appendix P: Pairing Activities

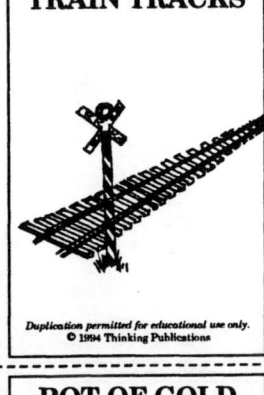

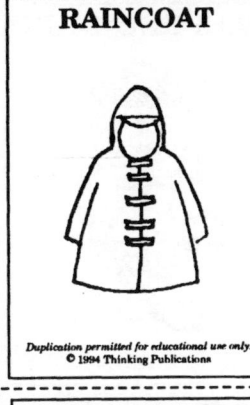

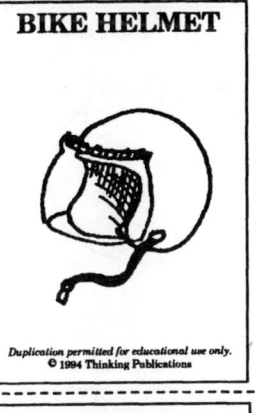

GO TOGETHER CARDS—A

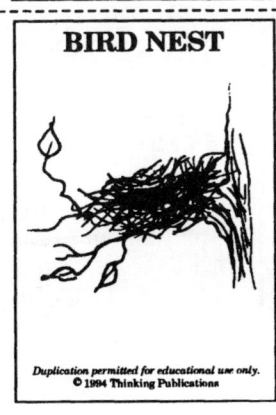

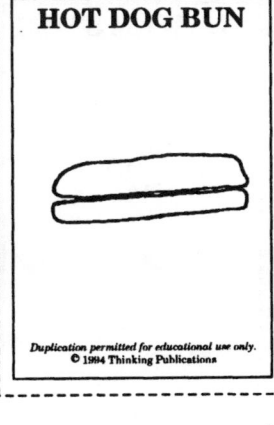

BABY BOTTLE	FISHBOWL	BASEBALL BAT	BEACH
HAMBURGER BUN	TOOTHPASTE	TRAIN TRACKS	ICE CREAM CONE
STAR	RAINCOAT	POT OF GOLD	BIKE HELMET
BIRD NEST	HOT DOG BUN	FLOWER PETAL	CHALK

453

Social Star

GO TOGETHER CARDS—B

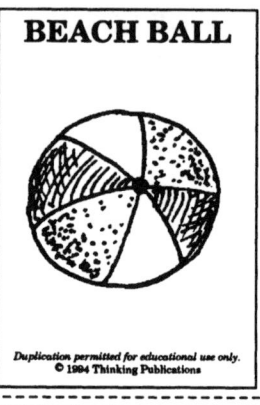

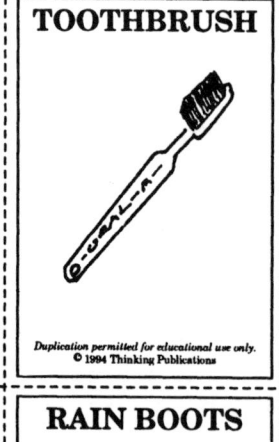

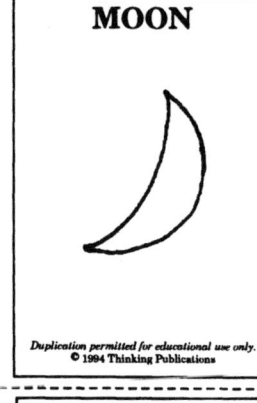

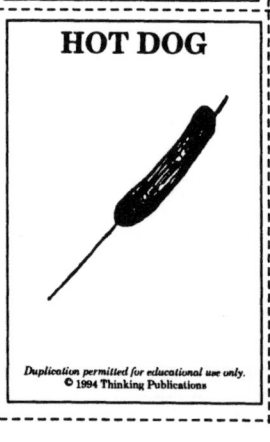

BABY	FISH	BASEBALL	BEACH BALL
HAMBURGER	TOOTHBRUSH	TRAIN	ICE CREAM
MOON	RAIN BOOTS	LEPRECHAUN	BIKE
BIRD	HOT DOG	FLOWER STEM	CHALKBOARD

Appendix Q

Drill and Practice

Social Star

Each *Social Star* unit contains at least two opportunities for students to work in pairs to tell each other the definition, skills step(s), and rationale for the social skill. As an option to provide more structure, to keep the activity moving in a timely fashion, and to make the activity more interesting and fun, students can be asked to assume new names during each drill and practice opportunity. The unit lesson plans provide the educator with the names of two notable people or story characters. After presenting students with those names, they are given an opportunity to use their social skills to decide who will take which name. Do not assign these names, but rather let the students decide. The names are also listed alphabetically below with a short comment about what each person or character is noted for. Most of the names are taken from *A First Dictionary of Cultural Literacy* (Hirsch, 1989), which includes information Americans should know. Dr. Hirsch defines the core knowledge that children need in order to understand American culture and to enhance their progress in school. The educator may wish to spend a short period of time giving information about the people or characters—not, however, to the extent that it would distract from the purpose of the activity (to drill and practice critical components of the social skill).

Aladdin—Character from *Arabian Nights* who rubbed a magic lamp, causing a genie to appear

Alcott, Louisa May—American author of the 1800s; wrote children's novels such as *Little Women* and *Little Men*

Ali Baba—Character from *Arabian Nights* who opened a cave by saying "Open, Sesame."

Alice in Wonderland—Character from Lewis Carroll's books *Alice's Adventures in Wonderland* and *Through the Looking-Glass*

Andersen, Hans Christian—Danish author of the 1800s; wrote *The Ugly Duckling, The Emperor's New Clothes,* and *The Princess and the Pea*

Antoinette, Marie—Queen of France; executed by revolutionaries

Armstrong, Neil—Astronaut; first person to walk on the moon

Bach, Johann Sebastian—German composer and organist

Barnum, P. T.—Showman of the 1800s; started the Barnum and Bailey Circus

Beethoven, Ludwig van—German composer; grew deaf midway through his career

Bell, Alexander Graham—Invented the telephone

Boone, Daniel—Pioneer who explored and settled Kentucky

Carver, George Washington—Improved farming methods in the south and discovered many uses for peanuts

Columbus, Christopher—Italian explorer who "discovered" America in 1492

Crockett, Davy—Frontier settler, politician, and folk hero of the early 1800s; known for his shooting abilities; died defending the Alamo

Curie, Marie (Madame)—Won Nobel prize; pioneered work with radioactivity

da Vinci, Leonardo—Italian artist who painted "The Last Supper" and the "Mona Lisa"

Disney, Walt—First to make full-length animated cartoons; created Mickey Mouse and Donald Duck (Disneyland, Walt Disney World, and Epcot are based on his ideas)

Douglass, Frederick—Abolitionist who escaped from slavery; wrote and spoke about slavery

Edison, Thomas—Invented the light bulb and phonograph

Finn, Huckleberry—Character from *The Adventures of Huckleberry Finn* written by Mark Twain; escaped from a cruel father and traveled down the Mississippi River

Frank, Anne—Dutch-Jewish girl who spent two years in hiding from Nazis; kept a diary

Franklin, Benjamin—A founding father of the U.S.; printer, author, scientist, and inventor (proved that lightning is electricity)

Geronimo—Apache chieftain; one of the last to fight against whites

Glenn, John—First American astronaut to orbit the earth

Grant, Ulysses S.—Union army general; later became U.S. president

Henry, John—Character in a popular folk song; strong black man with a hammer who tried to build more railroad track than a machine

Robin Hood—Legendary English outlaw who stole from the rich and gave to the poor

Captain Hook—Character from the story *Peter Pan*; an evil pirate whose hand was bitten off by a crocodile and was replaced by a hook

Jones, Casey—Character in a popular folk song; railroad engineer who died in a crash

Keller, Helen—American author; blind and deaf; learned sign language, overcame handicaps, graduated from college

Kennedy, John F.—36th U.S. president; first Catholic and youngest president; encouraged space program; assassinated

King, Martin Luther, Jr.—Clergyman who led the civil rights movement; promoted nonviolent means to overcome segregation and racial prejudice; assassinated

Lee, Robert E.—Confederate army general

Lincoln, Abraham—16th U.S. president (during the Civil War); abolished slavery

Magellan, Ferdinand—Portuguese explorer; first to sail around the world in the 1500s

Mozart, Wolfgang—Austrian musician; began composing at age five

Nightingale, Florence—Famous army nurse of 1800s

Odysseus—Character in Greek mythology who fought in the Trojan War in the *Odyssey*

Pandora—Character in Greek mythology who opened a box given to her by Zeus

Pasteur, Louis—French scientist who developed a vaccine to prevent rabies and proved that many diseases are caused by bacteria; the process of pasteurization is named after him

Picasso, Pablo—Famous Spanish contemporary painter

Pocahontas—Daughter of Indian chief; prevented her father from killing John Smith

Poseidon—Character in Greek mythology; god of the sea

Rembrandt—Famous Dutch painter

Revere, Paul—Revolutionary War patriot who took the midnight ride to warn colonists that the British were coming

Robinson, Jackie—First black man to play major league baseball

Ross, Betsy—Made the first American flag

Ruth, Babe—Baseball player for the New York Yankees; first great home run hitter

Salk, Jonas—Microbiologist who developed the first vaccine effective against polio

Sawyer, Tom—Character from *The Adventures of Tom Sawyer* written by Mark Twain; loved adventure (tricked friends into painting a fence)

Sitting Bull—Sioux chief who led warriors at the Battle of the Little Big Horn (Custer's Last Stand)

Smith, Captain John—English soldier; settled Jamestown, Virginia in the 1600s

Sullivan, Anne—Helen Keller's teacher

Tubman, Harriet—Slave who escaped and helped others escape through the underground railroad

Twain, Mark—Pen name of Samuel Langhorne Clemens, American author of the 1800s; wrote *The Adventures of Tom Sawyer* and *The Adventures of Huckleberry Finn*

Washington, George—First U.S. president; leader during the Revolutionary War

Washington, Martha—First "First Lady"

Whitney, Eli—Invented the cotton gin, which made it easier to get seeds out of cotton

Wright, Orville and Wilbur—Invented the airplane in the early 1900s

Zeus—Character in Greek mythology; ruler of the gods

Appendix R

Roadblock Sheet

Social Star

Social Skill

Alternative Route

ROADBLOCKS

1.
2.
3.
4.

© 1994 Thinking Publications — Duplication permitted for educational use only.

Appendix S

Social Super Star Badges

Social Star

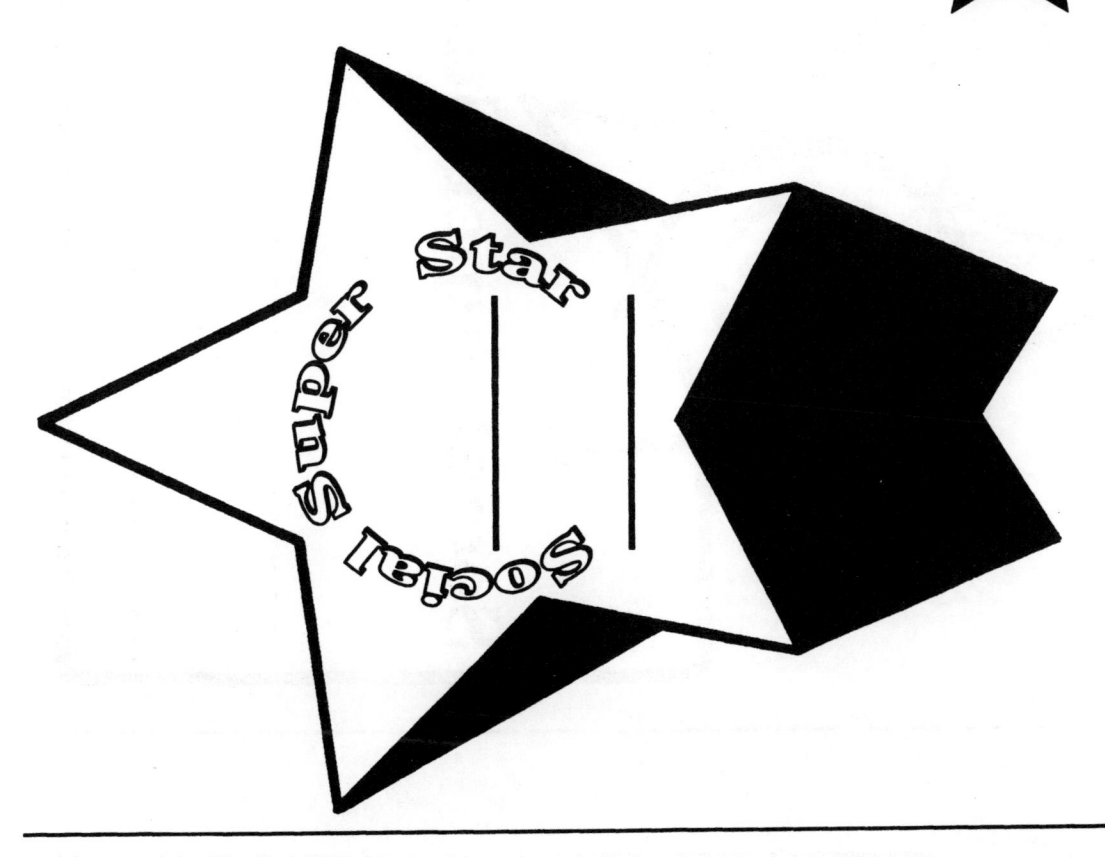

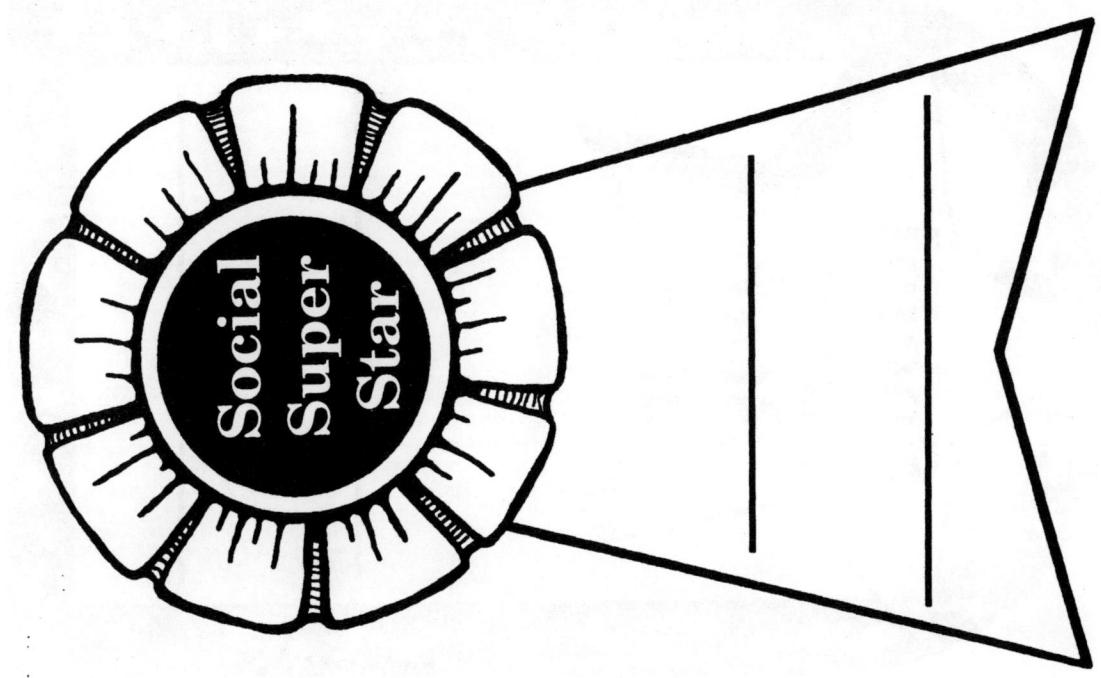

Social Super Star

Social Super Star

© 1994 Thinking Publications 459 *Duplication permitted for educational use only.*

Social Star

Social Super Star

Social Super Star

© 1994 Thinking Publications 460 *Duplication permitted for educational use only.*

Appendix T

Thinking Skills Web

Social Star

Names _____

Appendix U

Dominoes

Social Star

© 1994 Thinking Publications — 462 — *Duplication permitted for educational use only.*

Appendix U: Dominoes

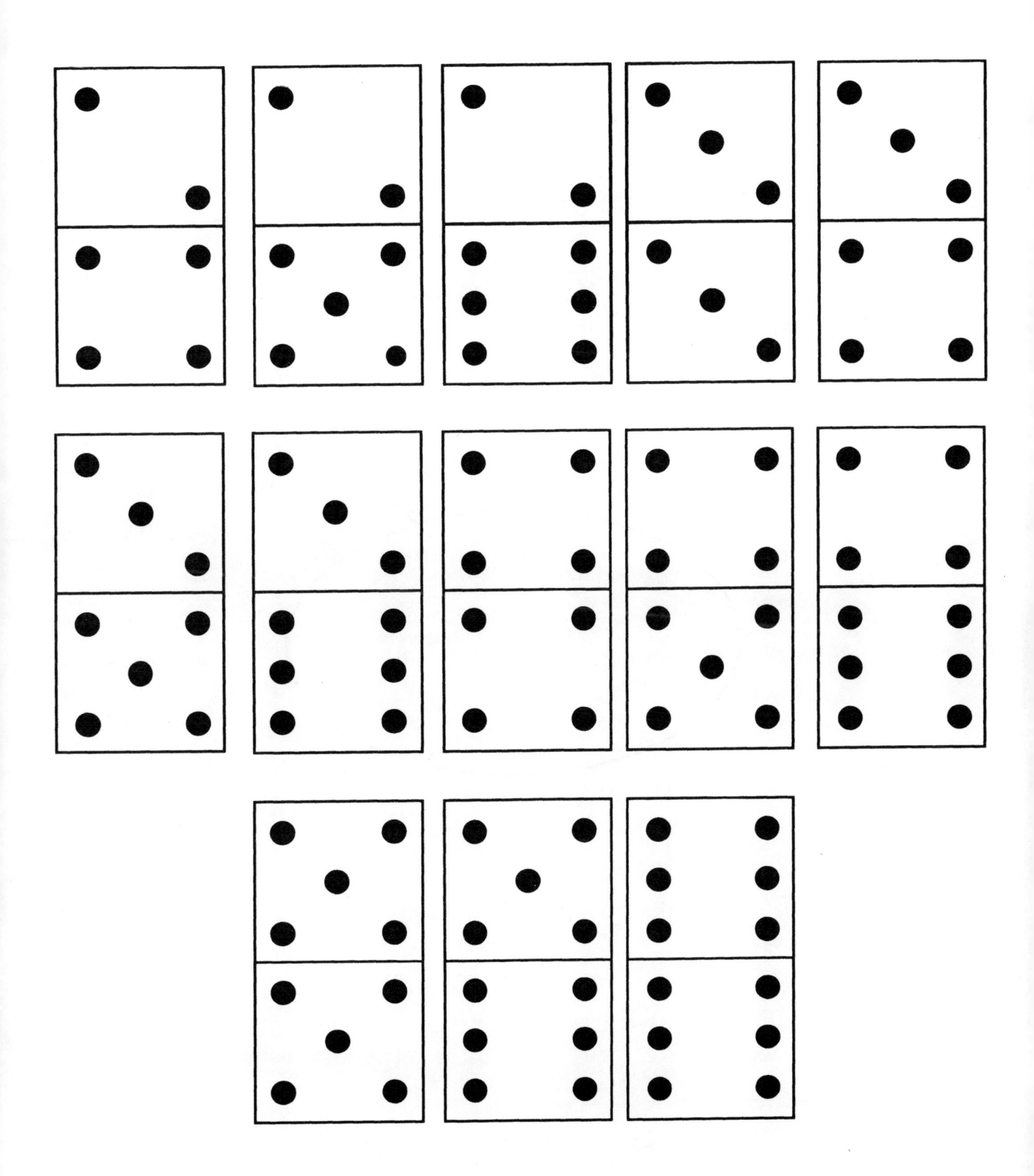

Appendix V

Mind Map

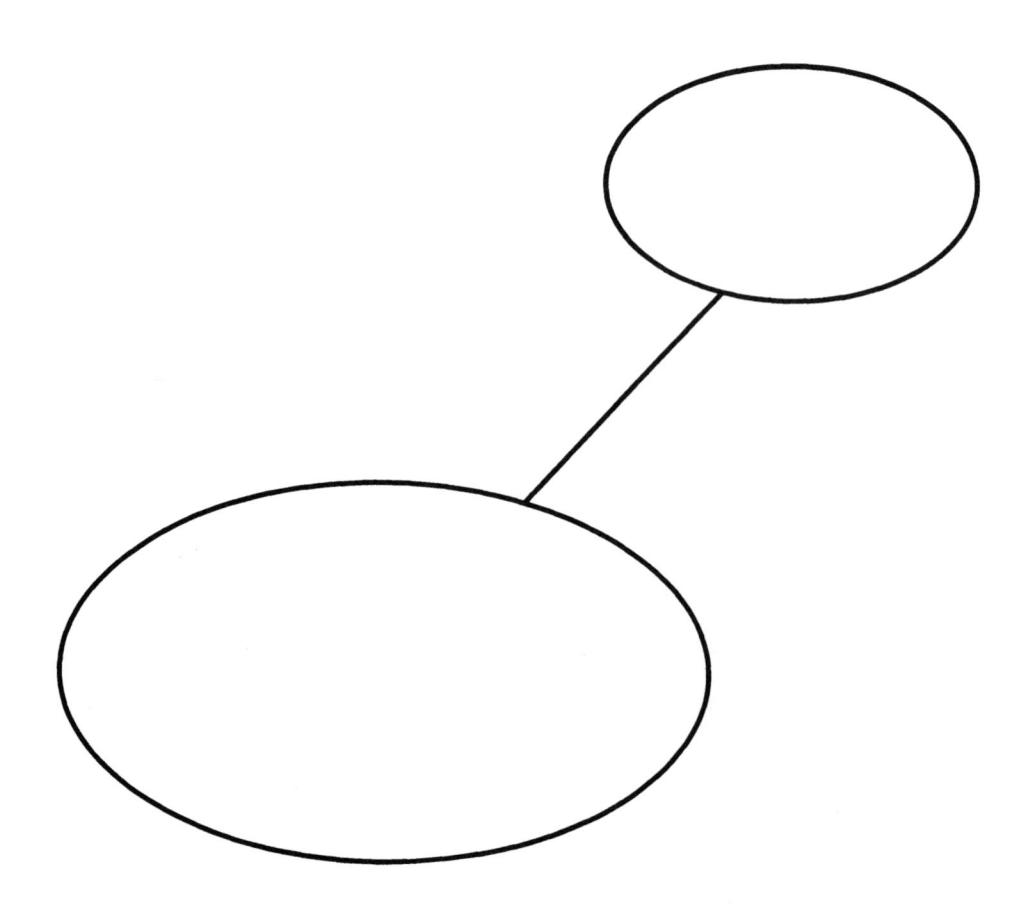

Appendix W

Venn Diagram

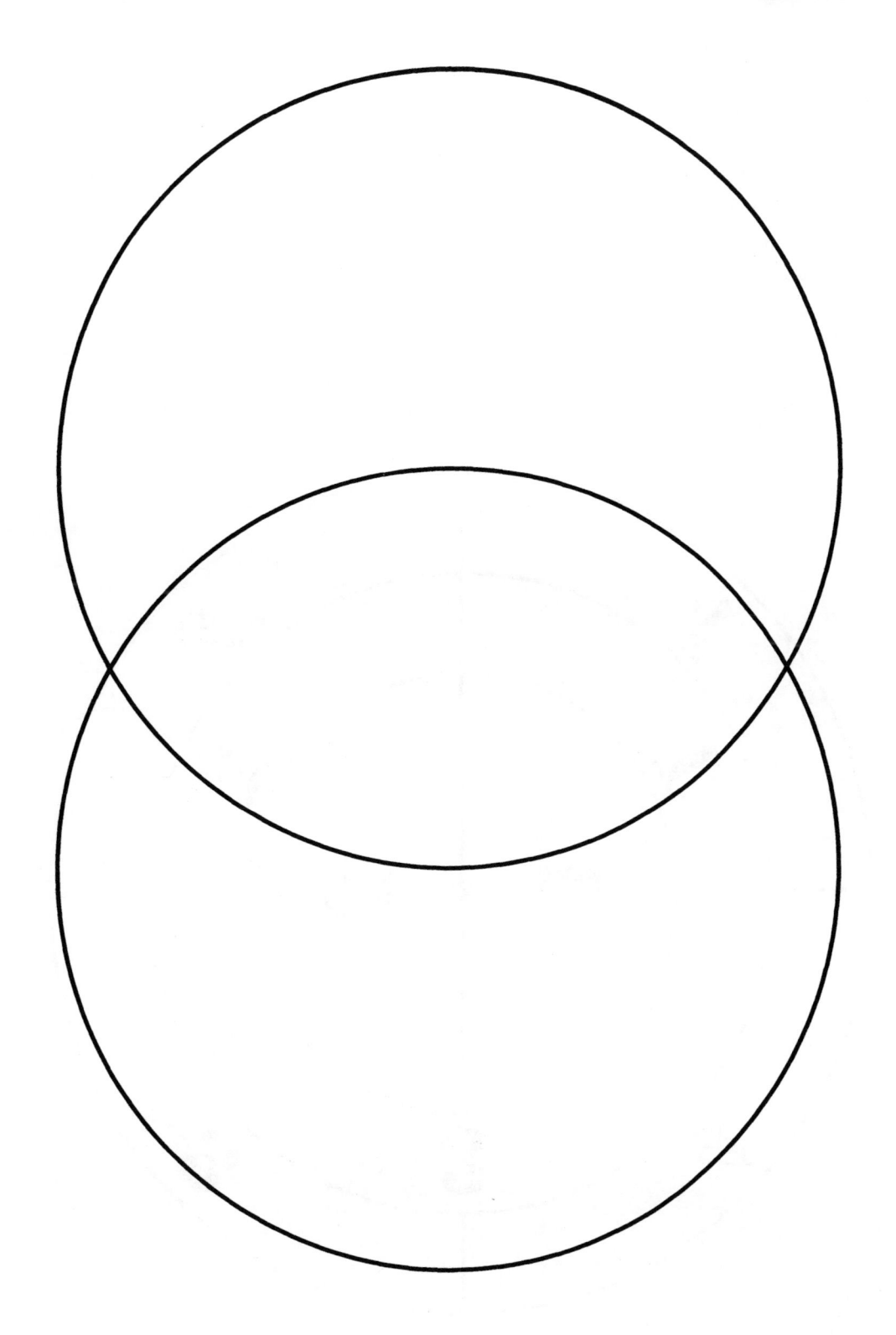

Social Star

Appendix X

| Numbered Heads Together Spinner | Social Star |

EDUCATOR DIRECTIONS:

Make a transparency of the illustration below. Insert a spinner into the center of the illustration on the transparency. (Spinners are available at most learning stores, or you can develop your own using an arrow and a brass fastener.) When you are at the point in the *Numbered Heads Together* structure that you need to ask students with a certain number to raise their hands, display the transparency and spin the spinner so students watch to see which number is chosen. This adds a new element of fun to the group structure. If students are in groups of two, use the inner circle, with groups of three, use the middle concentric circle, and with groups of four, use the outer concentric circle. A ready-made *Numbered Heads Transparency Spinner* can be purchased from Spencer Kagen, San Juan Capistrano, CA, 1-800-Wee-Coop.

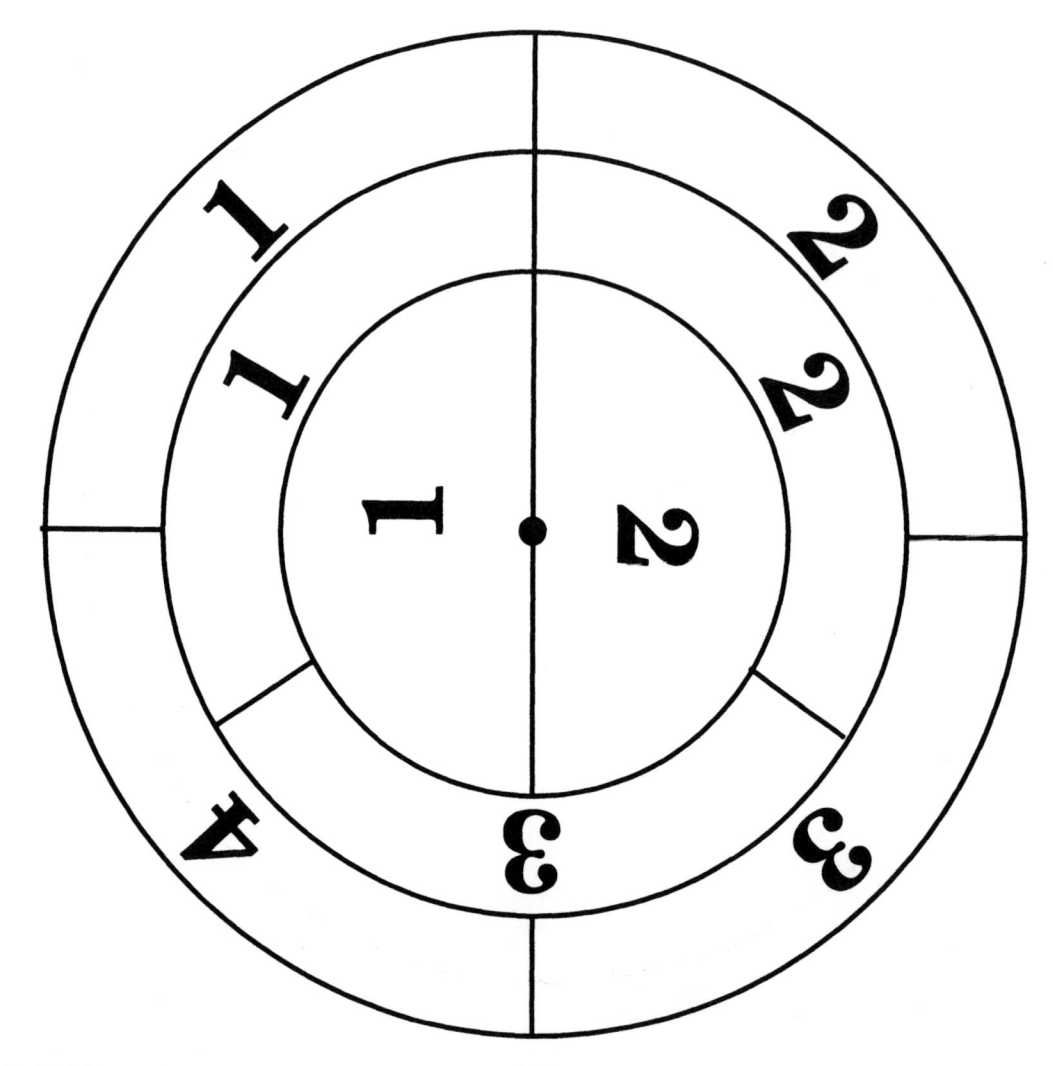

© 1994 Thinking Publications

Duplication permitted for educational use only.

Appendix Y

My Contract	Social Star

★ ★ My Contract ★ ★

I, _____,

agree to use the social skill of _____

when I'm _____.

Put a "+" or "-" in the box to show if your goal was met.

MON ____   **TUE** ____   **WED** ____   **THU** ____   **FRI** ____
    date   date   date   date   date

☐   ☐   ☐   ☐   ☐

If I do this _____,
                                Criteria

I will earn _____.
                                Reward

Signed _____
                            Student

_____
                          Teacher/Administrator

Appendix Z

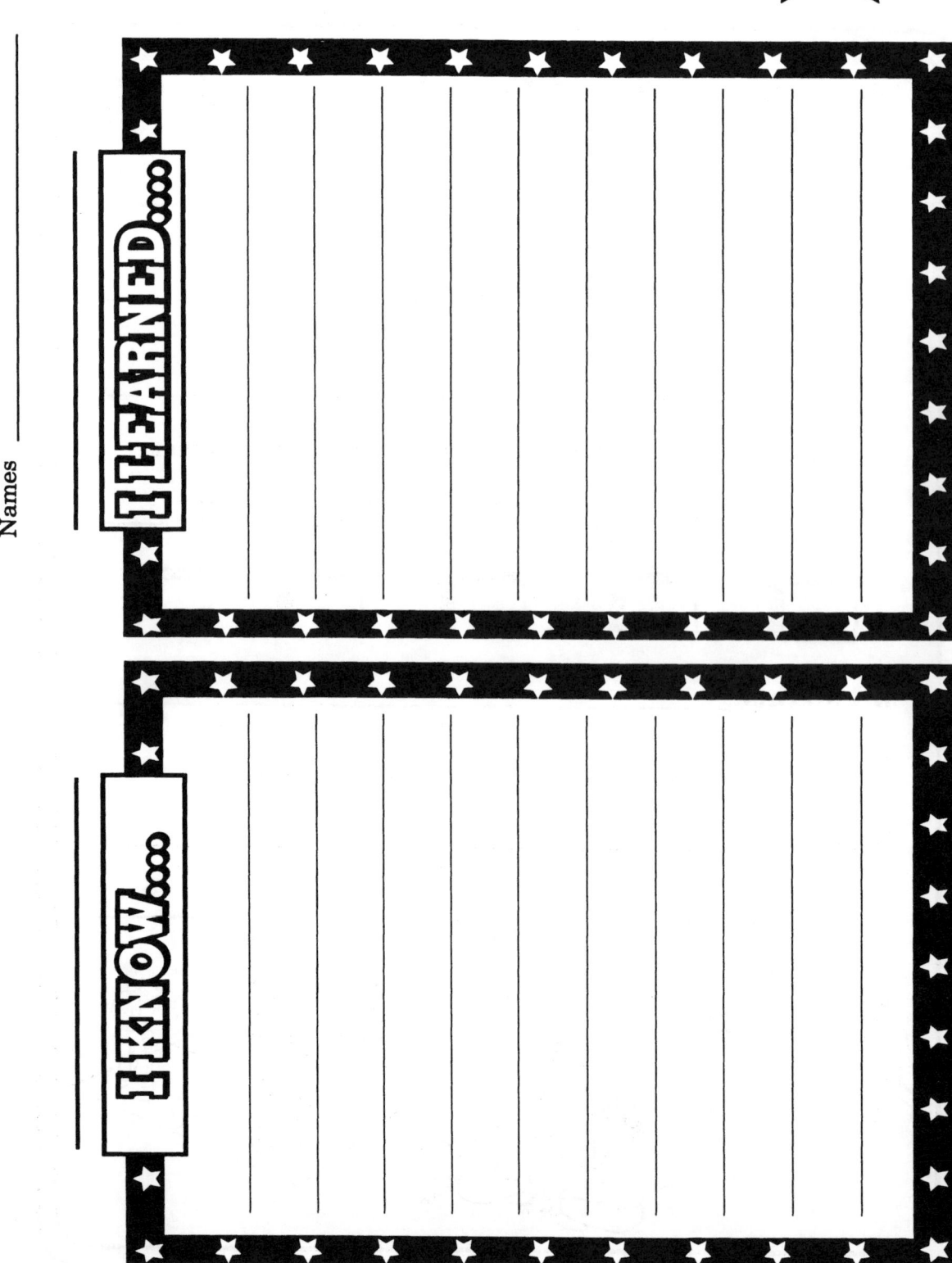

I Know....

Social Star

I LEARNED...

I KNOW...

Names _____

Appendix AA

Brainstorming Guide

★ Social Star

Names _____

BRAINSTORMING:

_____

1. Offer as many ideas as possible. Accept all ideas.
2. Everyone should participate.
3. Do not "put down" any ideas.

1. _____

2. _____

3. _____

4. _____

5. _____

6. _____

7. _____

8. _____

© 1994 Thinking Publications   469   *Duplication permitted for educational use only.*

Appendix BB

Tick-Tack-Toe

Social Star

Names _____

TICK-TACK-TOE

More Social Skills for

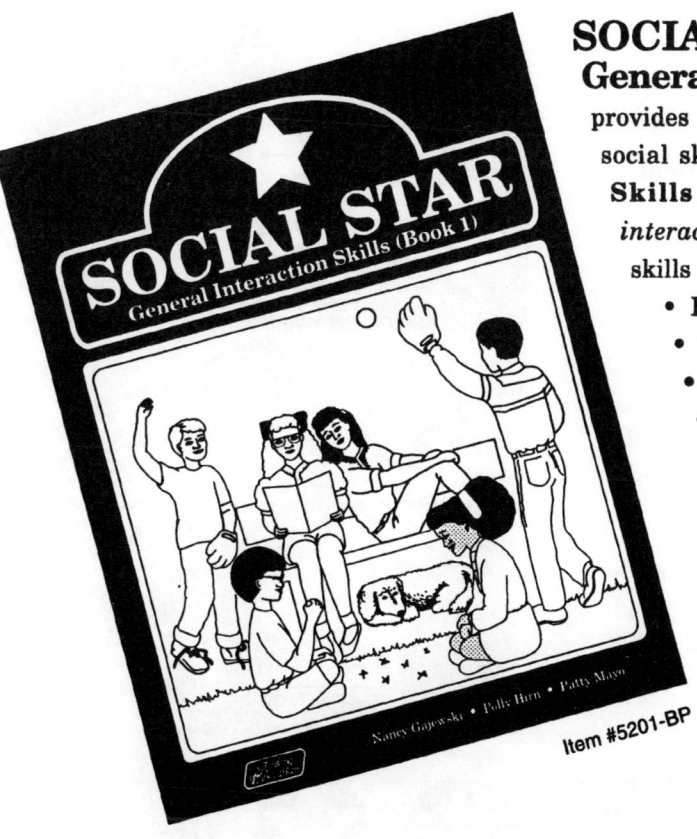

SOCIAL STAR:
General Interaction Skills (Book 1)

provides the same interactive format for teaching social skills as **Social Star: Peer Interaction Skills (Book 2)** and focuses on 15 *general interaction* skills for instruction. The following skills are presented:

- Eye Contact
- Volume
- Tone of Voice
- Facial Expression
- Posture
- Personal Space
- Hygiene
- Body Talk
- Manners
- Listening Basics
- Staying on Topic/Switching Topics
- Conversations
- Interrupting
- Right Time and Place
- Being Formal or Casual

Item #5201-BP

Reinforce Elementary Social Skills—Boldly and Brightly!

Social Star Posters

Social Star Classroom Posters can be constant reminders of the skill steps students need to use. Each colorful poster has skill steps for a social skill boldly printed. Posters measure 17½ x 22½ inches and are available in sets corresponding to the skills in **Social Star (Book 1)** and **(Book 2)**.

(Book 1) 15 posters	Item #5301-BP
(Book 2) 12 posters	Item #5304-BP

Our **Cognitive Planning Formula Chart** provides a quick reminder for your students to think "Stop, Plot, Go, So" as they discover how useful this cognitive strategy is in their daily lives. The multi-colored chart measures 24 x 36 inches and is printed on heavy stock.

Item #5302-BP

Have a special place to display **Social Super Star** badges to help your students feel proud! The **Social Super Stars Badge Display** measures 17½ x 22½ inches and is just the focal point you need to culminate each **Social Star** unit.

Item #5303-BP

Elementary Students!

Compliment Your Students!

Use brightly colored **Reinforcement Certificates**, **Stickers**, and **Note Pads** to send special compliments to your social super star students!

Social Skill Reinforcement Certificates include 30—8 x 5 inch certificates per pad. Choose from one of four designs:

Social Super Star (Book 1 skills)	Item #6020-BP
Blastoff! (Book 2 skills)	Item #6021-BP
Terrific Social Skills	Item #6023-BP
Excellent Social Skills!	Item #6024-BP

Colorful **Social Star Stickers** will be proudly worn by your students. Each pack of 150 stickers corresponds to **Social Star (Book 1)** or **(Book 2)** social skills. Social Star Stickers include 15—1⅝ inch stickers per sheet; 10 sheets per set.

Social Star Stickers

Set 1 **(Book 1** Skills)	Item #6001-BP
Set 2 **(Book 2** skills)	Item #6002-BP

Social Skill Note Pads can deliver special messages to parents or students on two different note pad designs. Note pads are 5½ x 4¼ inches.

Social Skill Note Pads   Item #6010-BP
(Includes two pads; each of a different design.)

For more information or to receive a catalog, call **1-800-225-GROW**.

THINKING PUBLICATIONS
A Division of McKinley Companies, Inc.

424 Galloway Street
Eau Claire, WI 54703
(715) 832-2488
FAX (715) 832-9082